Praise from Early Readers

As is clear from the start, William Eaton has not so much studied Wittgenstein as interiorized him, and with all the intimacy that implies. As language games were anything but games for Wittgenstein, so the witty, at times even chatty, progress of *And now, I think, we can say* is full-on serious. The genuine questions are raised and reflected upon and the life of a mental traveller all but surrounds us as we read.

— Sven Birkerts, author of *Art and Attention in the Internet Age*

A remarkably creative, contrapuntal text. Interweaving personal experience, imagined dialogue, passages from Wittgenstein, and passages from Wittgenstein's biographers, with (on occasion provocatively idiosyncratic and psychoanalytically speculative) interpretations of Wittgenstein's writings, remarks, letters and diaries, and with engagingly wide-ranging references and asides, William Eaton uncovers a good deal about the subtleties that determine the meaning of what we say and write. Creative writing, intricate biographical assemblies, and scholarly reflections intertwine here to show that words—anything but abstract blunt instruments—are always the words of a person, always the voice of a sensibility.

— Garry L. Hagberg, author of *Describing Ourselves: Wittgenstein and Autobiographical Consciousness*, and *Living in Words: Literature, Autobiographical Language, and the Composition of Selfhood*

If our responses to Wittgenstein, as to our language itself, can become all too settled—like well-worn paths across a landscape we've largely ceased to see—*And Now, I Think, We Can Say* appears as an unexpected visitor who wrests us from our familiar ways and reveals the mysteries and (sometimes frightful) wonders of our home.

Taking the form of a conversation between a pair of old friends about a single section of Wittgenstein's *Philosophical Investigations*—a conversation overheard, transcribed, and extensively commented upon by an exceptionally erudite humanities professor—*And Now* combines close textual exegesis with an insistent contextualization often missing in philosophy—contextualization within the circle of ordinary human cares and concerns, within the historical period of Wittgenstein's life, and within the dynamics of the Wittgenstein family and Ludwig's own psychology and sexuality.

The result is a powerfully unsettling reading of Wittgenstein that is less focused on the comforting stability of the ordinary than on highlighting the ambiguous, the exceptional, and the wayward voices of the *Investigations* and that calls on us to consider how much of our philosophical loquaciousness is designed to distract from what we will not say—that we remain, ineliminably and essentially, strangers to our language, our world, others, and ourselves.

— Steven G. Affeldt, Associate McDevitt Chair in Religious Philosophy, Le Moyne College

Eaton's book takes Wittgenstein's words and looks past their facing surfaces and to the vast, ramiculated network of lines that tie those words to Wittgenstein's life, to our lives, and to life. The book reminds us that words want more life and more-than-life. As Wittgenstein once wrote, how words are understood is not told by words alone. Eaton's Cubist reading of Wittgenstein reveals the startling hosts of points of view in Wittgenstein's texts and the resolute depths at which Wittgenstein investigates the interrelationships between points of view and the possibility of meaning.

— Kelly Dean Jolley, Goodwin-Philpott Professor, Auburn University, author of *The Concept 'Horse' Paradox and Wittgensteinian Conceptual Investigations,* as well as *Stony Lonesome* (a book of poetry). Editor of (and contributor to) *Ludwig Wittgenstein: Key Concepts.*

AND NOW, I THINK, WE CAN SAY

*A conversation about Wittgenstein
and the comforts of our life in language*

By William Eaton

And Now, I Think, We Can Say:
*A conversation about Wittgenstein
and the comforts of our life in language*

Copyright © William Eaton Warner, 2011

with very slight corrections made in 2020

All Rights Reserved

Published by Serving House Books

Copenhagen, Denmark and South Orange, NJ

www.servinghousebooks.com

ISBN: 978-1-947175-39-6

Library of Congress Control Number: 2020944549

No part of this book may be used or reproduced in any manner whatsoever without the prior written permission of the copyright holder except for brief quotations in critical articles or reviews.

Member of The Independent Book Publishers Association

First Serving House Books Edition 2021

Cover Design: Isabel Bortagaray

Author Photograph: Ayako Shido

Serving House Books Logo: Barry Lereng Wilmont

As *And Now* was developing, two related articles were published:

"On Pointing" in *Agni* 75, 2012

"Strangers in a Strange Land: Wittgenstein, Flies, Us Too," *Philosophy and Literature* 41: 2, 2017

These journals and their editors are thanked for their support!

This book is dedicated to my long-time friend, fellow writer, correspondent and publisher, Walter Cummins! Without him . . . And I speak not only for myself. So many writers who have had the good fortune to get to know Walter have themselves said, Without him . . . Without his engagement and encouragement, without his astute editorial comments, without his unflagging friendship . . .

Many, many thanks, Walter!

Contents

Introduction (Professor Thorn) 11

Main Text

1 Abel and Marsalina's conversation begins ("Someone coming into a strange country" 21

Professor Thorn's First Interpolation (Wittgenstein biography) 47

2 Abel and Maralina continue *(Manchmal richtig, manchmal falsch*: sometimes right, sometimes wrong) 73

Second Interpolation (Language learning and the miracle of faith) 97

3 Abel and Marsalina (Augustine describes the learning of human language) 107

4 Abel and Marsalina (So, als käme das Kind in ein fremdes Land: as if the child came into a strange country) 127

5 Abel and Marsalina (Und verstehe die Sprache des Landes nicht: and did not understand the language of the country) 138

Third Interpolation (the molten core of Ludwig Wittgenstein and his *Investigations*?) 149

6 Abel and Marsalina (As if the child already had a language) 190

7 Abel and Marsalina (Als könne das Kind schon denken: as if the child could already think) 201

8 Abel and Maralina (And "think" would here mean something like "talk to itself") 212

Appendices

Appendix A: Pointing, The Exception, Gaps and Scaffolding   215

Appendix B: Explanations and reflections regarding Plotinus, Augustine and Wittgenstein   245

Appendix C: Decontextualizing . . . Hume . . . The Good . . . Marx . . . Moore . . . Freud   283

Backmatter

Acknowledgments   311

End Notes   317

Works Cited   323

Texts of Augustine's *Confessions* I:8 and Wittgenstein's *Philosophical Investigations* §32   343

About the Author   347

Wittgenstein's redemptive work is not directed in the first instance toward philosophical difficulties themselves, but toward uncovering and treating the multiple and diverse human fantasies, cravings, dissatisfactions and the like which lie behind the first steps into philosophical confusion, emptiness, fixation, insistence and the like.

— Steven Affeldt, "Captivating Pictures and Liberating Language"

Such writing has its risks: not merely the familiar ones of inconsistency, unclarity, empirical falsehood, unwarranted generalization, but also of personal confusion, with its attendant dishonesties, and of the tyranny which subjects the world to one's personal problems. The assessment of such failures will exact criticism at which we are unpracticed.

— Stanley Cavell, "The Availability of Wittgenstein's Later Philosophy"

What is true is: In the culture depicted in the *Investigations* we are all teachers and all students—talkers, hearers, overhearers, hearsayers, believers, explainers; we learn and teach incessantly, indiscriminately; for we are all elders and all children, wanting a hearing, for our injustices, for our justices.

— Stanley Cavell, "Declining Decline"

Introduction

A FEW YEARS AGO *I made a trip to New York to speak with the young man who oversees money that my relatives and I have inherited from an apparently single-minded, clever, likely not very nice man and his dutiful son. The fortune was amassed centuries ago now, and there have been many relatives born since, so my share is not large, but as the only direct male descendant, as the grandson of the son, I have assumed a certain responsibility to keep an eye on how our "wealth manager" is doing his work. And the fact is, too: that I have developed an affection for this man, for the enthusiasm with which he gathers information about financial trends, companies he is interested in; the enthusiasm with which he plots his strategies, tells me about ways he has invested our money—gold! VIPERS!—that would seem to have been particularly astute, or lucky, another might say. And never news of any investments that have not worked out so well, or not so well at all.*

    Such stuff—the little details of my and my family's life—do not have much to do with the subjects of the dialogue between a librarian and a government official that I will shortly reproduce—a dialogue that might be said to take off like a firework from a section of Ludwig Wittgenstein's Philosophical Investigations. *Except—one connection at least—Wittgenstein was also wealthy, though vastly more wealthy than me. When his father died in 1913, Ludwig became one of the wealthiest men in Europe. The story is told that when he was about 20, an engineering student in Manchester, England, he wanted to go to the beach at Blackpool, but there was no suitable train, and so he proposed to a fellow student that they hire a special train, a private train, just for the two of them to go to the beach.**

---

* Monk, *Ludwig Wittgenstein*, 34. Before Karl Wittgenstein, Ludwig's father, died, he moved the family's investments abroad, out of Austria, to the United States above all. Thus, in the aftermath of the First World War, when Austria, Germany and other parts of Europe were in the throes of economic crisis, Ludwig's relative wealth became much greater still. By this point, however, himself in the throes of a severe personal crisis, Ludwig gave his share to his siblings. Although he insisted the money not be held in trust for him, one gets the sense that Ludwig always had plenty to meet his needs. Edmonds and Eidinow report (86) that in her memoirs, Ludwig's sister Hermine records the agonies Ludwig [the youngest of the family]

Ludwig's father, Karl, was the Andrew Carnegie of Central Europe. In 1913, the announcement of Karl's death in the Economist *stated:* "[T]he Austrian iron and steel trade owes its rapid growth and development solely to him." *I have read, too, the following, which I take to be inaccurate at best, ignoring the less genteel qualities and activities necessary for "succeeding" in business.*

> He [Karl Wittgenstein] had an extraordinary capacity for utilizing his technological knowledge to transform failing factories into booming and productive enterprises. No small part of his success sprang from his fantastic capacity for work—day and night, and days upon end, without rest. By 1895, he was an undisputed master of the technique which came to be known as the "rationalization of industry".

A Viennese contemporary said in praise of Karl, "Er war win Mann von Eisen und Stahl" (*He was a man of iron and steel*), *which led the great Viennese satirist Karl Kraus to reply,* "Er war ein Man von Eisen, und stahl. (*He was a man of iron, and stole*.) *From a 1900* Economist *article: Herr Wittgenstein will "soon have the power of fixing iron prices in Hungary also, as he fixes them in Austria."**

In his book about the Wittgenstein family, Alexander Waugh writes:

> In his business dealings Karl was an opportunist whose great fortune was accumulated as much by the successful outcomes [of] the risks he took as by his hard work and lively intuition. He made promises, unsure as to how he could ever fulfill them, he agreed to buy companies and shares with money he did not possess, and he offered for sale stocks that had already been promised to other clients. In the end he trusted to his wits to extricate himself from the problems he created.

At the end of his career Karl liked to hear himself described as a

---

went through with the despairing notary to assure himself that he had put his fortune irretrievably out of reach. However, she also records that an essential part of his outlook was "his completely free and relaxed acceptance of the fact that he was ready to let his brother and sisters help him in any future situation."

* Gottlieb, "A Nervous Splendor."

"self-made man," but the term was only partially accurate.... Karl tended to overlook the fact that he had married a lady of considerable fortune, without whose bountiful trust fund he might never have succeeded in making the first leap from business employee to capitalist owner.

Regarding the size of the Wittgenstein fortune, it has been estimated at 200 million kronen, an extremely large sum at the beginning of the twentieth century. Karl Wittgenstein was, Waugh writes, "stupendously rich".

To some extent *I am here just loafing to invite the soul (or just loafing).*[*] But I am also one of a small but perhaps increasing minority who believe philosophical works should be considered in their social and psychological contexts. (See my anti-decontextualizing remarks in Appendix 2.) And thus I will now quote comments made by Wittgenstein's leading biographer, Ray Monk. After noting that, as of 1990, approximately 6,000 articles and books had been written about Wittgenstein and work, Monk observes that

> interest in Wittgenstein . . . suffers from an unfortunate polarity between those who study his work in isolation from his life and those who find his life fascinating but his work unintelligible.

Monk gives his biography a goal which the present work shares: to make clear "how this work came from this man, to show—what many who read Wittgenstein's work instinctively feel—the unity of his philosophy concerns with his emotional and spiritual life."

For his own part, Wittgenstein, in one of the many notes which were published after his death, stated that his philosophy was the product of his

---

[*] As regards Wittgenstein and loafing—or, rather, lolling—see O.K. Bouwsma's review of Wittgenstein's "Blue Book" (179):

> This author spends seventy and more pages lolling. He does not, of course, say that he is lolling, which seems anyway obviously enough, since he does it so strenuously, . . . In any case it does strike some readers that this book is the work of a strangely articulate and irresponsible author.

This is a particularly rich comment since many of Wittgenstein's contemporaries would have laughed at the idea that Ludwig, his father's son, ever lolled or loafed. In the memoirs and biographies one reads again and again that Wittgenstein had no hobbies or diversions, other than occasionally taking in a concert or going on a long walk with a friend, a walk that would be spent discussing Wittgenstein's philosophical ideas.

circumstances. "*I believe that my originality (if that is the right word) is an originality that belongs to the soil, not the seed. (Perhaps I have no seed of my own.)*"

So let us now, with such things in mind, return to the minerals in the Viennese soil that were Karl Wittgenstein and Karl Kraus. One way to understand Wittgenstein's work, I propose, is—perhaps not as an attempt to redeem his father's good name—yet certainly, fundamentally, as an attempt to live up to the ideals Kraus set for the talented, nouveau riche, Viennese youth of his time. It has been said that for Kraus the distinguishing characteristic of all that is moral and artistic was integrity, and thus similarly, Wittgenstein's work was less an endless struggle to find a way to talk about ethics than itself an ethical deed.* Monk writes that Wittgenstein "*was arguing for a morality based on integrity, on being true to oneself, one's impulses—a morality that comes from inside one's self rather than one imposed from outside by rules, principles and duties.*"

We may hear echoes of Socrates, Augustine, Montaigne, Descartes, Emerson—of so many philosophers down through the ages. Virtue begins in the attempt to be true to oneself, to know oneself and, we can say, in the attempt to speak and write truly.† "*Do not go out. Go in to yourself. Truth dwells in the inner man.*"‡

But for Wittgenstein the matter was not, let's say, so simple, because he also perceived (if at times dimly) that the inner self was in dialogue with other

---

* Allan Janik and Stephen Toulmin, *Wittgenstein's Vienna*, 24, 81, 169.

† "*L'être véritable est le commencement d'une grande vertu*": Montaigne, 427, citing Pindar.

It will help set the tone for the pages to come if I put this idea in post-Freudian perspective. Prior to Freud, under the powerful influence of Cartesian dogma, it was imagined (indeed many still imagine) that an individual human being has direct, and at least potentially infallible, access, via introspection, to the contents of his or her own mind. But Freud's model "places unintelligibility at the heart of mental processes," as Hugh Haughton phrases it (ix-x). "In fact, in an astounding transformation of the Cartesian project, [Freud] made self-unintelligibility the paradoxical cornerstone of psychic theory."

Wittgenstein was very taken with, at times fixated on, his Viennese contemporary's writings and ideas about how suffering people might be cured or helped. At one point he described himself as a "disciple" or "follower" of Freud (Monk, 438), and he came to think of his own approach to philosophy as a kind of "therapy."

(See the segment in Appendix C on Freud.)

‡ Augustine, *De vera religione*; as quoted in Miller, 219.

people, and that this dialogue, to include our self-expressions, depended on, was born of, a social construct: language. Herewith the first of many examples, the present one from a translation of a letter Wittgenstein wrote many years later to the wife of one of his professors—a couple with whom he had stayed as a student:

> [N]ow that I set about writing to you, I am faced with the choice of writing something not quite natural for me just in order to answer you; in order, as it were, to give you some sort of answer, or else of writing what I think but what will possibly be quite unintelligible to you. I think it is better that I should write in the way that is natural to me and so make understanding *possible* for you, even if difficult, rather than writing something that sounds halfway plausible but that can in no circumstances be understood, because it is not true.

Tortured—even the syntax of this English translation is tortured— but, from where I sit, the feeling is achingly beautiful.

All this is also to begin to again say something I have had occasion to say before: Philosophers can often appear to be wrapped up in ideas, imprisoned in ideas, but philosophy is nonetheless a psychological and social response: the best way certain people (philosophers) have found to respond to their circumstances, their longings and their fears—and to speak to other people about them. The dancer leaps and bends on a stage, the programmer writes code, teachers like me try to help others do better than we have been able to, a philosopher writes philosophy.*

Back to my narrative, *to the story of how I came upon the dialogue that makes up the bulk of this book. I was in New York and strolled from my hotel down to the financial district. Missy, the wealth manager's assistant, took my sandwich order, and Max, the manager, and I had lunch as we poured over the various charts he had prepared and as an electronic stock ticker streamed along the bottom of a large television screen on the wall above our heads. After an hour or two I had reached my limit. On my way out, I stopped at Missy's desk and asked how her half-brother was getting on. He was training to compete in*

---

* Wittgenstein "says that people who like philosophy will pursue it, and others won't, and there is an end of it. *His* strongest impulse is philosophy." Letter from Bertrand Russell to Ottoline Morrell, March 3, 1912; as quoted in Monk, 45.

the Winter Olympics in one of these new sports that seem to combine incredible acrobatic skill, an enthusiasm for risking one's neck, and a willingness to have one's spinning, life-endangered body serve as a billboard for a host of sports equipment and clothing companies. As a result, Max remarked as he walked me to the elevator, "At 19 the boy is making more money than you and me combined."

But the elevator still came, and Max and I clasped hands and arms and smiled, and I descended and began my walk back uptown. Awaiting in my hotel room were papers to grade and an article to proofread—tasks that I enjoy, in fact. But I was in a mood to enjoy a day off, to feel free. This was, as I said, a few years ago, when people were just beginning to embrace apps and e-books, and New York and many another American city still featured large bookstores. As I approached Union Square I remembered the very large Barnes & Noble there and its impressive collection of contemporary philosophy books, its cafe with a particular coffee cake that I liked. I decided to make a pit stop.

I had an idea at that time that I might develop a course on Wittgenstein, or a course that took advantage of Wittgenstein's approach in the second of the two books he had published: the Investigations. It was a vague idea which has yet to come to fruition, but it led me that afternoon in New York to pluck from the bookstore shelves a few of the many rich commentaries on Wittgenstein's later work. I took these books to the cafe area and sat down to read.

I began with Saul Kripke's Wittgenstein on Rules and Private Language, and I remember being quite pleased by the opening pages. For example, I now find on page 5: "[T]o attempt to present Wittgenstein's argument precisely is to some extent to falsify it". A nice hour or two of reading seemed in the offing.

As I was reading, however, I began to be distracted by a conversation which was taking place very near me—right next to me, in fact, though on the other side of one of the wooden partitions that used to divide the cafe into somewhat tranquil corners for reading or chatting. The partitions were not that *high*, but high enough so that I could not see my neighbors—the people engaged in this distracting, but hardly unwelcome conversation. There was a man's voice and a woman's voice, and it did not take me long to realize that they were talking about the Investigations. I decided to put down Kripke and have a listen. Soon enough I was jotting down intriguing bits on the back of my copy of Max's portfolio reviews and risk-reward matrices. And then I found myself scribbling as fast as I could, trying to preserve the whole conversation, detour by wise-crack by death-defying spin.

I wonder if I shouldn't pause to reflect on the ethics of this, of copying and then reproducing two strangers' conversation, and without asking their permission. Let us suppose—and how farfetched could this really be? Imagine the present text, including the words you are at this very moment reading, becoming a Kindle bestseller, or required reading in introductory philosophy classes. I receive a letter from a lawyer representing one or both of the conversants, Abel and Marsalina. People are outraged or want a cut, or both.

Wittgenstein could have had some fun with the Familienähnlichkeit *("family resemblance") between the cut that makes you bleed and the cut that gives you money, and the figure you may cut subsequently in your expensive clothes.* Perhaps all I have to say about the ethics of my actions is this: Should*

---

* Regarding *Familienähnlichkeit*, a fundamental concept in the *Investigations*, in §77 Wittgenstein proposes that some words (e.g., "good") "have a family of meanings". The demonstration and conclusion are given in §66 and §67:

> §66: Consider for example the proceedings of what we call "games". I mean board-games, card-games, ball-games, Olympic games, and so on. What is common to all of them?—Don't say: "There *must* be something common, or they would not be called 'games'"— but *look and see* whether there is anything common to all.—For if you look at them you will not see something that is common to *all*, but similarities, relationships, and a whole series of them at that. To repeat: don't think, but look!—Look for example at board-games, with their multifarious relationships. Now pass to card-games; here you find many correspondences with the first group, but many common features drop out, and others appear. When we pass next to ball-games, much that is common is retained, but much is lost.—Are they all 'amusing'? Compare chess with noughts and crosses [tick-tack-toe]. Or is there always winning and losing, or competition between players? Think of patience. In ball games there is winning and losing; but when a child throws his ball at the wall and catches it again, this feature has disappeared. . . . And we can go through the many, many other groups of games in the same way; can see how similarities crop up and disappear.
>
> And the result of this examination is: we see a complicated network of similarities overlapping and criss-crossing: sometimes overall similarities, sometimes similarities of detail.
>
> §67: **I can think of no better expression to characterize these similarities than "family resemblances"**; for the various resemblances between members of a family: build, features, colour of eyes, gait, temperament, etc., etc. overlap and criss-

such a letter ever arrive from a lawyer for Abel or Marsalina, I will forward it to my lawyer, asking her to try to reach a quick and amicable settlement. (Kierkegaard makes the larger point: "The desire to observe comes only when there is an emptiness in the place of emotion".)

It may, however, come to seem to some readers that a rather more serious ethical question is raised by the present text, as well as by some of the biographies, memoirs and collections of Wittgenstein's notes which are prominent sources for this text. The question is whether a dead man should be entitled to some degree—to what degree?—of privacy, whether some of the things he said or wrote during his lifetime should be allowed to die with him? This is a yet more complex question as regards Wittgenstein, for one because, after his death, a coterie of former students simultaneously tried to suppress discussion of his personal life—of his homosexuality—while also publishing volume after volume of philosophical notes that he himself had not quite wanted to publish, along with publishing their memories of him. And this question of privacy is more complex when the deceased is a writer like Wittgenstein who was deliberately trying to write down—in Wittgenstein's case, at times in a simple code—quite intimate details of his life and his thoughts. Indeed, in addition to his own diary-keeping and note-taking, Wittgenstein engaged many other people—students, colleagues, his professors—in copying down things he said. One of the goals and major activities of Wittgenstein's life was to try to get down on paper most everything he thought.

The critic Perry Meisel once described Wittgenstein as a melancholy narcissist, and readers may well come to feel that these two words put the matter too gently or politely.* For the moment I will simply observe that, as

---

cross in the same way.—And I shall say: 'games' form a family. [Boldface added.]

* Meisel, "Young Wittgenstein," with "melancholy narcissism" being the words actually used.

A tip of the iceberg, from three diary entries of David Pinsent, Wittgenstein's closest friend—or closest acquaintance, should we say?—during his first years as a student at Cambridge University. Wittgenstein paid for Pinsent and him to take a trip, first-class, to Iceland. In the course of the trip, Pinsent wrote in his diary, "I don't think he dislikes me!" And shortly after he returned, he wrote that this had been "the most glorious holiday I have ever spent!" A week later, Pinsent records, Wittgenstein remarked to Pinsent that he thought they had enjoyed the trip

with many writers, myself not excepted, in Wittgenstein's compulsive writing, in his compulsive record-keeping, may be found a narcissist's fascination with the products of his mind, a fascination not unlike many children's, and adults', fascination with other products of their bodies. But a part of Wittgenstein also believed that there were at least some things in his notes, in his thoughts, revelations, investigations that could be of value, possibly of great value, to people like you, dear readers, and me.

So where is this ethical question? you may be asking. That is, what would be unethical in quoting from and commenting on some—or any?—of Wittgenstein's notes? I will leave each reader to answer this question for herself or himself, and perhaps readers will find themselves answering the question differently at different moments in their reading of the present text. For my own part, clearly ethical concerns have not stopped me from putting together what I have put together. But there have been moments when I have felt a little queasy, perhaps not unlike a high-school student given a frog to dissect, or a medical student with a cadaver. Wittgenstein did in a sense split himself open for all to see, and feeling that there was nothing more fascinating than himself, Ludwig Josef Johann Wittgenstein, split open, but in his lifetime he insisted on holding the scalpel himself. It's a different matter when it's somebody else who's doing the dissecting.

All this said, it is time or past time for the transcript of my Barnes & Noble cafe scribbles. I have slightly edited them and fleshed them out in a few places in order to fill in blanks, particularly at the beginning of the conversation, before I had devoted myself fully to note-taking. In addition, slowly, over years, as if I were not one college professor, but a little overheated room of Talmudic scholars, I have, via footnotes, endnotes, appendices and a bibliography, provided references to the works quoted, along with explanations or commentary where such have seemed useful or possibly intriguing.* I will also enter the main body of the text with "stage directions," let's call them, and on several occasions in a much larger way.

As regards ethics, readers may come to decide that my greater crime lies in my not shutting up, in my horning in on Abel and Marsalina's conversation,

---

"as much as it is possible for two people to do who are nothing to each other". (Monk, 59, 61; quoting Pinsent diary entries of September 19, September 29 and October 5, 1912.)

* The numbered endnotes provide bibliographic information only. I have used footnotes, indicated with symbols, when I have a comment to make or additional material to quote.

in my using their conversation, their relationship, to say what I have to say—as it were to no one. Lacking anyone besides my students, and my young niece and nephew, to listen. But—I want to object—what about all the transcribing, all the typing, all the citation-tracking-down I've done? Haven't I earned a right to say a few things, or more than a few? It sounds a bit hollow—or looks that way, digitized on my computer screen.

I note, with a smile, a portion of a letter from the young Wittgenstein to C.K. Ogden, who took change of the English translation of Wittgenstein's first book, the Tractatus Logico-Philosophicus:

> As to the shortness of the book I am *awfully sorry for it; but what can I do*? If you were to squeeze me like a lemon you could get nothing more out of me. To let you print the *Ergänzungen* [the supplements] would be no remedy. It would be just as if you had gone to a joiner and ordered a table, and he had made the table too short and now would sell you the shavings and sawdust and other rubbish along with the table to make up for its shortness. (Rather than print the *Ergänzungen* to make the book fatter leave a dozen white sheets for the reader to swear into when he has purchased the book and can't understand it.) [The emphasis here in italics is Wittgenstein's.]

In the present case, some readers may come to feel that they are indeed being offered the shavings and sawdust—and without the dozen sheets to swear into. Nonetheless, quixotically, I remain hopeful that my footnotes and intertextual interventions add stability and polish to the table—the wonderful, many-leaved table—that is Abel and Marsalina's dialogue. And I promise not to be offended by any readers who choose to just read Abel and Marsalina's words. Not only that one afternoon, but for several years now, they have been saying many things to me. I must thank Abel and Marsalina for that.

— R. Thorn, Summer 2011

(1)

Someone coming into a strange country*

Marsalina: *Abel*, my dear friend, what's all this scribbling in the margins, all these different colored arrows and X-ing out?

Abel: Wittgenstein. I am trying to figure out section 32 of Ludwig Wittgenstein's *Philosophical Investigations*.

Marsalina: Perhaps you should try section 33, or section 1.

Abel: Yes, section 1. I can see now that this was the Garden of Eden, complete with five red apples and one forked-tongue philosopher.† But you

---

* The opening words of Elizabeth Anscombe's standard translation of section 32 of Ludwig Wittgenstein's *Philosophische Untersuchungen* (*Philosophical Investigations*). The text is divided into two parts, the first being presumably more polished, and the second consisting of notes for which the right shape and context (or garbage can) had yet to be found. For the "revised fourth edition," new editors divided the work in two, with the first part being called *Philosophische Untersuchungen* (*Philosophical Investigations*), and the second being presented as a separate work (though included in the same volume): *Philosophie der Psychologie—Ein Fragment* (*Philosophy of Psychology—A Fragment*).

Throughout the present text, references to Part I will be preceded by the word "section" or by the symbol §. References to Part II will be preceded by "Part II", a segment number in Roman numerals and a page number, with an "e" for English. These page numbers will be from Ludwig Wittgenstein, *Philosophische Untersuchungen / Philosophical Investigations: The German Text, with a Revised English Translation*, third edition, translated by G.E.M. Anscombe (Blackwell, 2001). I have made one alteration to Anscombe's spelling: "Shew" and "shewed" have become "show" and "showed."

Note also that Wittgenstein used quotation marks and dashes to dialogue within his text—as if, with a friend or just in his own mind, he were tossing an idea back and forth. Bouwsma (185) suggests that the voice, or voices, of Wittgenstein's notes "is frequently like a man groping in the dark."

† The fourth and final paragraph of §1 of the *Investigations*:

> Now think of the following use of language: I send someone shopping. I give him a slip marked "five red apples". He takes the slip to the shopkeeper, who opens the drawer marked "apples"; then he looks up the word "red" in a table and finds a colour sample opposite; then he says the series of cardinal

know what's funny, or pitiful? *There was a pause, as for a response, and I have imagined Marsalina shaking her head. No, she didn't know what was funny or pitiful.* I picked section 32 because it seemed the simplest.

Marsalina, laughing: I see. Maybe I can help. How long is it?

Abel: 102 words in German, 108 in English.

Marsalina: I'll start with the English. Give me the words.

Abel: And with such self-assurance did Magellan and 236 sailors set out to go east by going west. With none but Magellan possessing a map, and that one quite wrong. What matter! Three years later 18 people had made it back to Spain, Magellan not among them—killed in an unnecessary battle, and most of his crew dead of starvation. And it had become a little easier for Western Europeans to rape, exploit, subjugate other parts of the globe, infecting tens of millions of unsuspecting foreigners with one or another deadly disease, leaving ragged and destitute the few surviving members of great civilizations, civilizations that, but for a larger gene pool and closer contact with pigs, might be sharing their wonders with us today.*

> numbers—I assume that he knows them by heart—up to the word "five" and for each number he takes an apple of the same colour as the sample out of the drawer.—It is in this and similar ways that one operates with words.—"But how does he know where and how he is to look up the word 'red' and what he is to do with the word 'five'?—Well, I assume that he *acts* as I have described. Explanations come to an end somewhere.—But what is the meaning of the word "five"?—No such thing was in question here, only how the word "five" is used.

Or rather, I would add, how the word "five" was used in this particular language game of Wittgenstein's invention.

* Abel is touching on current theories that over the course of the fifteenth through the seventeenth centuries, more than 90 percent of the human population of the Americas was wiped out by European diseases against which these people had no defenses. According to these theories, one of the problems was that these Americans were all descended from a very small group. Their gene pool was limited, and thus their immune systems had limited abilities to recognize pathogens and combat them. Another of the "problems" was that the Americans had no domesticated animals—no pigs, cows, horses, chickens, goats, sheep, oxen . . . Thus they missed out on the plagues, the small pox and other diseases that came from close contact with diseased animals. And thus, we might say, rather than being a race of plague-survivors, relatively well defended against future onslaughts, the Americans were vulnerable in the extreme. And not just internally. They also did

Marsalina: Abel, I have an appointment at 4:30 to get my nails done.

Abel: So let's have our words and be quickly be done with them. Words like nails—to drive home points or scratch out eyes. Words like Oedipus's nails, punishing us for our desire to see, to understand.

Marsalina: Abel, you're losing me.

Abel: Ah, you must be one of those who say that words have little or nothing to do with nails. Words, you would say, are used to communicate with other people. But don't words also separate us from other people, and from what we would understand, and from how we would be understood?

Marsalina: Abel, please.

Abel: OK, OK, you want *the* words, Wittgenstein's words. I'll give you the first paragraph. There are only two. *Abel then recited the standard English translation of the first paragraph of section 32*:

> Someone coming into a strange country will sometimes learn the language of the inhabitants from ostensive definitions that they give him; and he will often have to *guess* the meaning of these definitions; and will guess sometimes right, sometimes wrong.*

Marsalina: Again.

Abel again recited.

Marsalina: Well, the first thing I would like to figure out is what the hell "ostensive" definitions are.†

---

not have social customs—isolating the sick, as opposed to gathering around their bedsides—and the psychology—the ability or willingness to endure the disfiguration of small pox, for example. Apparently there was a high rate of suicide among those who became infected.

More on this subject may be found in Mann, *1491: New Revelations of the Americas Before Columbus.*

* The full text of section 32 in German and English is reproduced on the very last page of the present document. *Note*: Here and with other quotations, italics are as used by the quoted author or translator. (And if you should encounter a quotation and wonder who it's from and do not wish to be bothered turning to the endnotes—it's from Wittgenstein.) The § symbol is used to refer to sections in Wittgenstein's texts. If no short title is given, the text is the *Investigations*.

† Latin: *ostendere*; English: to show.

Abel: Pointing, either with a physical gesture or with language. "When I point my finger at the moon, don't mistake my finger for the moon." But surely another person can't have THIS pain!"* Or, more prosaically, imagine that like Wittgenstein's stranger—or like Wittgenstein in one of his stranger moods—you have for the moment set aside feelings and other messy aspects of life, you are just interested in language, in learning new words, or in another, foreign way of being—perhaps a better way of being? You point at something with your finger and you ask what it is.

There was another pause here, and I have imagined that Abel had in fact grabbed Marsalina's forearm and was pointing it, pointing her hand, toward something—toward a paper cup.

Abel, resuming: And I say—enunciating very clearly, you hope, since you are just learning my foreign language—"coffee cup." And so you learn the word, or the name, "coffee cup." It's really quite simple.†

Marsalina, laughing: Yes, quite simple, and it's also quite clear that *you* don't think it is this simple.

---

* The first quotation is of a Zen aphorism. The second is from Wittgenstein, *Investigations*, §253.

† Here at the beginning of his conversation with Marsalina, Abel is seeking above all to get across the idea that our "life in language," as Wittgensteinians say, is rather more complicated than most of us realize—or than any of us realize most of the time. Allow me to contribute to this work, or entertainment.

First, I wonder if Abel, in making his "It's really quite simple" comment, did not have in a corner of his mind a discussion, in sections 47-60 of the *Investigations*, regarding what Wittgenstein refers to as "composite" and "simple" nouns. If you say, "Would you please bring me my broom," you are in a certain sense referring to the stick and the brush, but this is also not at all what you are saying. You have in mind not pieces but a composite: the broom. It is with the whole that you will be able to sweep. If you say to someone, "Would you please bring me my coffee," you are hoping s/he will bring the cup as well.

Secondly, I note an observation Wittgenstein made during the period leading up to the assembling of the *Investigations*:

> Augustine, in describing his learning of language, says that he was taught to speak by learning the names of things. It is clear that whoever says this has in mind the way in which a child learns such words as "man," "sugar," "table," etc. He does not primarily think of such words as "today," "not," "but," "perhaps."

Blue and Brown Books, 77.

Abel: Well, there is the question of whether it's a "tall" or a "small" coffee, or to what extent "tall" now means "small," and "gourmet"—nothing at all?*

But let's stick with just the coffee cup for the moment. You may come to decide that right there there's enough torment for one afternoon. It is, for example, somewhat peculiar to English that we have taken the word for what was once a piece of pottery or metal—a cup—and also for a quantity of a liquid or solid—a cup—and put this word, or words, to use to refer to a paper container of varying dimensions. If you go to Starbucks in the Dominican Republic, how would you ask for a "cup of coffee," or what would you call a "coffee cup"?

Marsalina: *Taza. Una taza de café.*

Abel: No. I'm not talking about a "cup of coffee," I'm talking about a "coffee cup."

Marsalina: *Una taza* then. A cup.

Abel: Good. But in fact the matter is more complicated than this, because—while as an American it was perfectly appropriate for me to point at that paper object and say not *taza*/cup, but "coffee cup"—in fact, that is the right word if and only if, or more or less if and only if, there is coffee in the container or there has been or might be coffee in the container. Otherwise this very same object may be a cup, but not a coffee cup.

But—*mea cupa*—this is not what I was heading out to say! What I meant to ask was: How did you know when I pointed at the coffee cup that I was referring to the container rather than to what was inside? How did you know that I wasn't referring to what, in my language, we call "white"; that is, perhaps I was trying to teach you my language's word for "white," which happens to be "coffeecup"?†

---

* Abel at moments brought to mind one of Shakespeare's fools. Here he was riffing both on the Starbucks company's nomenclature, by which a small cup of coffee is called a "tall" and a medium a "grande," and also on a habit of many New York "delis" (the many little grocery stores that dot the city). Along with offering a wide variety of chips, sugary drinks, fat-and-carbohydrate-laden dishes and chemically preserved salads, these stores like to attach the word "gourmet" to their names or signs.

† Abel is here inspired by section 33 of the *Investigations*:

Suppose, however, someone were to object: "It is not true that

As Wittgenstein puts it, "[A]n ostensive definition can be variously interpreted in *every* case." Or, to take this one more step: "This was our paradox: no course of action could be determined by a rule, because every course of action can be made out to accord with the rule."* We may take this, ulti-

> you must already be master of a language in order to understand an ostensive definition: all you need—of course!—is to know or guess what the person giving the explanation is pointing to. That is, whether for example to the shape of the object, or to its colour, or to its number [e.g., *one* coffee cup], and so on."—And what does 'pointing to the shape', 'pointing to the colour' consist in? Point to a piece of paper.—And now point to its shape—now to its colour—now to its number (that sounds queer).—How did you do it?—You will say you that 'meant' a different thing each time you pointed.—And if I ask how that is done, you will say you concentrated your attention on the colour, the shape, etc. But I ask again, how is *that* done?

N.B.: While it does not seem known whether or not Wittgenstein read Augustine's dialogue *De Magistro*, one cannot help but be struck by the Wittgensteinian (or Augustinian) highlighting of the shortcomings of ostensive definitions in this dialogue (ostensibly of Augustine with his son):

> *Augustine*: Supposing I had no idea of the meaning of the word 'walking,' and I were to ask you when you were walking what 'walking' means, how would you teach me?
>
> *Adeodatus*: I should walk a little more quickly. The change in speed would give notice that I was replying to your question, and I should still be doing what I was asked to demonstrate.
>
> *Augustine*: But you know there is a difference between walking and hastening. He who walks does not necessarily hasten and he who hastens does not necessarily walk. We speak of hastening in writing, reading and very many other things. Consequently, if, after my query, you did what you had been doing, only a little more quickly, I should conclude that walking was the same thing as hastening, for the acceleration was the new feature of your behaviour. So I should be misled.

Adeodatus goes on to say that you are no better off trying to teach someone what "walking" means by starting to walk than by speeding up one's walking; for your pupil might take you to mean not walking but walking a certain distance.

Text here is from Burnyeat, 12, using a revision of John H.S. Burleigh's translation of *De Magistro* (iii, 6), from *Augustine: Earlier Writings* (Library of Christian Classics Vol. VI, 1953).

* *Investigations*, §201. The latter observation could well be seen as moving the dis-

mately, as a question about ethics, about what to do at any given moment. How can I know what I should do since, among other things, no matter what I do, it is possible to show that I am following the rules, doing what I should? I believe, by the way, that your husband makes a very good living thanks to this very dynamic. No matter how much money his Wall Street clients steal, or how they steal it, he is able to show the courts that what they have done accords with the rules.

Marsalina, laughing: One good thing about having an alpha male for a husband is you don't have to waste time defending him against all the rubber darts that omega males lob at his feet.

Abel: And thank God for inventing money in order to distract alpha males. Otherwise we intellectuals would spend even more time than we do in onanistic pursuits. But let me see if I can't get us back to whatever it was we were discussing before you so rudely interrupted me.

Marsalina: To tell you the truth, I still haven't figured out what we are talking about—beyond that you're jealous of my husband and that some-

---

cussion away from language games and toward ethics, and lawyering and politics. How should we behave, as a polity or as individuals? I would also note that one of the richest propositions of the philosophy of science is the Duhem-Quine thesis: Any empirical evidence can always be accommodated to any theory by adjusting the underlying assumptions. See, for example, the epicycles, deferents and epitrochoids that Ptolemy devised in order to explain the apparent motion of the Moon, Sun and planets. Or the egg-shaped orbits, spherical shells and driving force of the Sun of Kepler's model. Or, if one were in a contentious mood, one might list the underlying assumptions necessary for the Darwinian and Creationist explanations of *homo sapiens*' appearance on the Earth.

See Wittgenstein's *Remarks on the Foundations of Mathematics*, Part II, §74, 98e:

> The danger here, I believe, is one of giving a justification of our procedure when there is no such thing as a justification and we ought simply to have said: *that's how we do it.*
>
> When somebody makes an experiment repeatedly "always with the same result", has he at the same time made an experiment which tells him *what* he will call "the same result," i.e. how he uses the word "the same"?

And see also this from Wittgenstein's posthumously published *Lectures on the Foundations of Mathematics* (226): "That which at first seemed out of the question, if you surround it by the right kind of intermediate cases, becomes the most natural thing possible." We shall get to the Holocaust soon enough.

times it can take a little work to figure out what other people—like Abel Dan—

Abel: I'll never forget the time you asked me if I would bring some of your problems to my therapist and report back on his responses.

Marsalina: I know you'll never forget it, but I have no idea why you're bringing it up now, except to make fun of me and put me down. I don't see what was hard to figure out in that exchange. We had different ideas of psychotherapy, end of story.

Abel: It's also the case that there are all sorts of risks involved in speaking—in who you speak to, and in what you say, and particularly if you try to speak from the heart, or close to it. We might want to say that all this is exemplified by our fears of speaking to psychotherapists, and of being caught speaking to them.

Marsalina: And some of these fears are very well grounded, and not least for those of us working in government. May I remind you that I am not a unionized librarian. I am "exempt," as in "exempt from civil-service protections." Something gets in the paper—she goes to a psychotherapist! she doesn't have both oars in the water, her tray table's not in the upright and locked position! Next thing you know I'm not only looking for a new job, I'm looking for a new line of work—in Antarctica.

Abel: Fair point and let me apologize for bringing the matter up again, and apologize in advance for the next time I bring it up. *He laughed.*

Marsalina, with a dry, sarcastic tone: At least you know how to keep yourself amused. But please tell me what, in any case, all this has to do with Wittgenstein and ostensive coffee cups?

Abel, seeming a bit frustrated, frustrated with himself: Well, maybe not that much, except in the general sense that, in this way and that, we have been exploring some of the many complexities of human communication, of language—and of relations between human beings, I would like to add. Among the things that have occurred to me as we've been talking is that this could be one of the basic "take-aways," let's call it, of section 32. Wittgenstein is suggesting—suggesting yet again, and not for the last time—that language—the uses of language and the meanings that may be found in our words—all this is simply much more complicated than we realize—or than his colleagues, intellectuals in and around Cambridge University in the middle of the twentieth century, realized.*

Marsalina: OK. That's a start at least! But I find myself wanting to object: How complicated is all this really? Sometimes I think life—my life—would be more interesting if human beings weren't so damned transparent!

Abel, reviving and reciting, and with pride in his voice, as for being able to recite this passage from the Investigations:

> We also say of some people that they are transparent to us. It is, however, important as regards this observation that one human being can be a complete enigma to another. We learn this when we come into a strange country with entirely strange traditions; and, what is even more, even given a mastery of the country's language. We do not *understand* the people. (And not because of not knowing what they are saying to themselves.)

Marsalina, more slowly: OK. Why don't "we"—why doesn't he, Ludwig—understand them? Or why do strangers have difficulties? Maybe that's what you need to figure out.

Abel: No wait! I knew it was going to be helpful trying to talk this all out with you. The mess—*I imagine he tapped his head; he was referring to the mess inside his head, in his thinking*—the mess is starting to get sorted into little *Smuler* at least.†

Marsalina: Glad to hear it.

---

* Wittgenstein, born in Vienna in 1889, first showed up in Cambridge to 1911 to study with Bertrand Russell. After serving in the Austrian army during the First World War and working for six years as a schoolteacher in rural Austria, in 1929 he returned to Cambridge, becoming a lecturer and then a professor of philosophy. From then until his death in 1951 he made Cambridge a sort of home base, as an orbiting space station may be considered a sort of home base.

Part I of the *Investigations* was complete by 1945; Part II abandoned, one might say, in 1949. The whole, at Wittgenstein's request, was published after his death, in 1953, with Elizabeth Anscombe and Rush Rhees doing the editing, and Anscombe providing the translation into English.

† *Smuler*—bits, scraps, crumbs, trifles—a Danish word, used by Kierkegaard in the title of his *Philosophiske Smuler* (*Philosophical Crumbs*, or *Philosophical Fragments*, it has been translated). I have read that Kierkegaard may have used *Smuler* in his title because of a Danish saying, *Smulerne es også Brød* (The crumbs are also bread). From Kierkegaard, *Repetition* and *Philosophical Crumbs,* note on page 181.

Abel: Here's the thing. It has to do with that word "ostensive," you might say, with another way of looking at it.

Marsalina: How's that?

Abel: The word's a distraction, basically. A false scent. Or like some superficial characteristic of another person that blocks us from seeing what they're really like "inside," as we say.*

Marsalina: Explain.

Abel: You read this sentence.

> Someone coming into a strange country will sometimes learn the language of the inhabitants from ostensive definitions that they give him; and he will often have to *guess* the meaning of these definitions; and will guess sometimes right, sometimes wrong.

It's that word "ostensive" that catches your eye, trips you up. It's like cleavage—or cleavage for a male—it catches my eye and holds my gaze even though I'm not a "breast man."

Marsalina, laughing: No, you're a book man.

Abel: You're right about that. I see a woman reading, and I'm craning my neck to get a peak—not at her underwear, but at the title. *I imagined him*

---

* *Cf*., Wittgenstein's discussion of "aspects" (*Aspekte*) in *Investigations*, Part II, xi, and Affeldt's commentary, "On the Difficulty of Seeing Aspects". Briefly here, from Affeldt: "We might say that the individual sees or hears what is before her, yet failing to recognize it *as* what it is, misses the aspect that is most important." And:

> The emergence of philosophical emptiness, that rupture of attention and its redirection toward a nothing that seems to be a something, is motivated. It is a manifestation of the recurrent human drive to repudiate the ordinary. So, blocking our appreciation of the most important aspects of things is not merely an unfortunate consequence of philosophical emptiness; it is its purpose.

What Abel means as regards §32 is that Wittgenstein's getting us to focus on this idea of "ostensiveness" may block our appreciation of the extent to which his subject is alienation and loneliness, misunderstanding and being misunderstood: our foreignness, one to another. *Cf.*, §123: *Ein philosophisches Problem hat die Form: "Ich kenne mich nicht aus."* A philosophical problem has the form: "I don't know my way about".

shaking his head. Ridiculous. Talk about "an impulse inhibited in its aim"!*

But to get back to Wittgenstein, what you're helping me realize—be conscious of—is that in a certain sense the most important words in this first sentence and in the whole section are the ones you and I so blithely skipped over—until you reminded me of that other passage about someone coming into a strange country.

Of course, in some sense we have no grounds for privileging one reading over another—for deciding the superficial is unimportant, it's what's "inside" that counts. But if we say that it's the inside, the deeper that interests us the most, then it seems to me that we have to say—we have to see—that this whole section of the *Investigations* is really about the experience of a stranger coming in to a strange country. Or let me put this another way: This section of Wittgenstein's *Investigations* offers us an opportunity—a great opportunity—to reflect on this experience, of being a stranger come to a strange country. And an opportunity to realize that we have all been that stranger.†

Marsalina: Explain please.

Abel: I might say the same thing to you.

Marsalina: Come again?

---

* Freud, *Civilization and Its Discontents*, 30: "The love of beauty seems a perfect example of an impulse inhibited in its aim. 'Beauty' and 'attraction' are originally attributes of the sexual object."

† I am sure there are many—philosophers, Wittgenstein scholars, first-time readers of this section of the *Investigations*—who would say that Abel's reading here is somewhere between just plain wrong and nuts. It is also the case that it is because of this reading—because of its power, or of the power Abel gives it—that I have now spent some years transcribing and annotating Abel and Marsalina's conversation. To encourage readers to pause and appreciate the paradigm shift, if you will, that is going on here—or the other view of the optical illusion or dilemma to which Abel is calling our attention—I am going to reprise one of the epigraphs, from Steven Affeldt:

> Wittgenstein's redemptive work is not directed in the first instance toward philosophical difficulties themselves, but toward uncovering and treating the multiple and diverse human fantasies, cravings, dissatisfactions and the like which lie behind the first steps into philosophical confusion, emptiness, fixation, insistence and the like.

Abel: Well, if I remember what you once told me, when you were in fifth grade you were all of a sudden airlifted by the CIA from the *pampas* of the Dominican Republic to—*

Marsalina, laughing: There are no "pampas" in the Dominican, only "Pampers," but don't let me stop you from telling me the story of my life.

Abel: All I want to say is that there you were, 10 years old or so, *in ein fremdes Land kommt*—all alone in a fifth-grade classroom in Queens, New York, and trying to learn English words and grammar as fast as you possi-

---

* The word "pampas," of course, is a word associated with Argentina and Uruguay. I suppose Abel was just trying to suggest the distance Marsalina had travelled: not only from the Dominican Republic to New York, but from the countryside to a big city.

As for the role of the CIA, this is a little harder to nail down. In 1961 the long-standing dictator of the Dominican Republic, Rafael Leónidas Trujillo Molina, was assassinated, and the CIA has long been implicated in this assassination. The sense I get is that Marsalina's father was a large landholder in the Dominican Republic, and so we might think that he was in some sort of alliance with the Trujillo regime, which for more than thirty years had its fingers in most every pie in the country. And so—fearful of a civil war or eager to achieve rather more complete "regime change," as US leaders have come to call such things—could it be that the CIA arranged to remove Marsalina's family from the country, and to New York, around the time of the assassination? Or perhaps . . . ?

As with many "developing countries," the Dominican Republic has had a sort of dual government. There have been nationals in charge of some aspects of the economy and security forces, while "Westerners," through their in-country advisers and out-of-country sources of funding and special trade agreements, have controlled other aspects of the economy and security operations. (See, for example, Pons, 294-95, 365-66 and 396-403.) As a member of the elite of such a country, Marsalina's father would have had contacts not only with "his" government officials, but also with officials of this shadow, and large-shadow-casting, government. My speculation here is that perhaps Marsalina's father asked these foreign officials—and perhaps not really knowing or caring whether they were on the CIA, USAID, Shell Oil, Nestlé, Gulf & Western, or National City Bank of New York payroll—to help him get his family out of the country at this troubled time.

In any case, it would seem that Marsalina began her life as a stranger in a strange country as a fifth-grade, non-English-speaking student in a school in Queens, New York, and likely this was in 1961, which would make her about 50 at the time of this Barnes & Noble conversation with Abel. As for Abel, he seems a little younger than Marsalina, and a little younger than 50, but this is just more conjecture on my part.

bly could. You might say—

Marsalina: You might say that in that one year I learned once and for all the vicious things that people—American government officials, priests in the Dominican, little middle-class American white girls confronted with a newcomer with nappy hair, brown skin and an African butt— What don't people do with language! Or rather, perhaps I should say, is there anything we won't do, won't dare do, with language?

Abel, softly: Wittgenstein might have liked that phrase: What people don't do with language. Perhaps he would have turned it, too, into a question, and proposed an answer to it. *Nichts, Intet, Нич*—[*]

Marsalina: Keep guessing, Sherlock, you might come up with the English word.

Abel: I am supposing, Wisenheimer, that Wittgenstein would have answered something like "Nothing." Everything we do we do with language. And what we might do without language is beyond our understanding. Our understanding is the product of our language—misshapen by the ages and ever-evolving from one misshape to another. And our understanding is imprisoned within that misshape, within the friendly or unfriendly confines of our language, and by the experiences of the world our language has offered us, framed for us.

Marsalina: And so, struggling to get back to our task, or maybe it's just my task, why don't "we"—we strangers come into foreign countries and pointing—

Abel: *Gib mir das!*

Marsalina, translating instinctively: Give me this. You— You know, I have to say that my experience is we're all strangers, no matter where we come from.[†] There are certainly times my husband feels like the strangest stranger I have ever known, and even my daughters . . .

Abel: Yes! Very good, Marchita. Now it seems to me we're coming into the

---

[*] Abel has given a version of the English "nothing" here in the other three languages Wittgenstein worked with in his adult life: German, Norwegian and Russian (ничего).

[†] See John 1:10 regarding Jesus, sent by God to bear witness to the Light: "He was in the world, and the world was made by him, and the world knew him not." This is from the King James version. Augustine quotes this passage in Latin in the *Confessions* VII:9: "*quia in hoc mundo erat, et mundus per eum factus est, et mundus eum non cognovit.*"

country that Wittgenstein, in his hot-cold heart of hearts, wanted us to come into—and to come into *with* him. We can—most of the time we *do*—feel that we know what the people around us, the people closest to us are saying. People seem "transparent to us." But then, at other times—when it most matters, it often seems—we feel like *in ein Fremdes Land kommt*. We don't know what the hell the people around us, closest to us, are talking about. We are living in the same rent-controlled apartment our parents rented before we were born. We speak the language we seem to have known all our lives—our mother tongue—and yet at times we feel there is nobody who can understand us, nobody to understand us, not even our mothers. Or we hear others speaking, we see them getting all excited—about some movie or political cause or new electronic product, it could be; or about some supposed outrage at the place where we work—and we just cannot find what there is to get so excited about. We can't empathize. And it may seem not only a matter of one human being being an enigma to another; we may feel as if it is us—or I feel it must be me—who is the enigma. Everyone understands except me.* The only thing I have left is my *Beherrschung*, my—

Marsalina: Your what?

Abel: *Beherrschung*—the German word that was translated as "mastery" in the Wittgenstein passage I quoted about people not always being transparent. I believe that in many contexts the English equivalent would be "control" or "self-control." So as regards our relations with other people, with

---

* *Cf.* Cavell, "Availability" (67):

> But if the question means: "How do I know at all that others speak as I do?" then the answer is, I do not. I may find out that the most common concept is not used by us in the same way. And one of Wittgenstein's questions is: What would it be like to find this out?"

Abel is taking this one step further: What does it *feel* like at those moments, however temporary, when you find this out? See Philip Roth's *American Pastoral*, which may be thought of as an extended exploration of this question. From 147:

> There was so much emotion in him, so much uncertainty, so much inclination and counterinclination, he was bursting so with impulse and counterimpulse that he could no longer tell which of them had drawn the line that he would not pass over. <u>All his thinking seemed to be taking place in a foreign language</u>, . . . (My underscoring.)

our families, I guess what I want to say is that sometimes—not all the time, but sometimes—it can feel that the only thing we have, the only thing we have to hold on to is this *Beherrschung*, this self-control, for whatever it may be worth.

Marsalina: That sounds right to me. I think you've described a lot of my life right there.

Abel: But—now the pendulum swings back the other way, or the thesis and antithesis try to find their synthesis. If, on the one hand, in this section and in his book, Wittgenstein is talking about some of the deepest feelings we human beings have—and he is certainly talking about alone-ness, his own alone-ness included—he is also talking about these feelings in quite specific, even limited contexts. In section 32 this comes down to challenges involved in learning the language of a strange country, which is also to say the challenge of learning any language at all.

Marsalina: You're focusing, Abel!*

Abel: So then focusing, or trying to focus, one of my questions regarding foreigners and language learning is: Was one of the things Wittgenstein was getting at—at least in the passage about the times when we are left with nothing but our self-control, when we don't understand—I think he was describing a very common situation of "strangers," of foreign-language learners.† You can master the tools of a language, you can master the vo-

---

* Perhaps this is the place to quote one of G.E. Moore's recollections of Wittgenstein's lectures:

> He concluded by a long discussion which he introduced by saying "I have always wanted to say something about the grammar of ethical expressions, or, e.g. of the word 'God'." But in fact he said very little about the grammar of such words as "God", and very little also about that of ethical expressions. What he did deal with at length was not Ethics but Aesthetics, . . . His discussion of Aesthetics, however, was mingled in a curious way with criticism of assumptions which he said were constantly made by Frazer in the *Golden Bough* and also with criticism of Freud. ("Wittgenstein's Lectures in 1930-33," 312.)

† This could also be a discussion *not* of foreigners, of others, but of "me," of us—of our moments of sanity and madness, of how mad we feel when it seems we have nothing left but the last threads of our self-control, when it seems the community of language can do nothing for us, or when it seems that there is no one else alive willing and able to take part in the community that we thought, that we were taught we were going to find through language, through speaking and listening.

cabulary, phonetics, grammar, and yet be lost when you try to bring this

---

One of the more frightening experiences of my life occurred the week I was graduating from college. (Was it the last thing college had to teach me? or the sign that, like the wind-blown wanderers of *The Wizard of Oz*, trying to find their way back to Kansas, I was not in college anymore?) I went into a little post office near the University of California at Berkeley campus to get a *postcard* stamp, but instead asked for a *postage* stamp. What kind of postage stamp? the clerk asked. A postage stamp, I repeated, more than once, getting quite upset as the clerk continued to not understand me, as he continued to act more and more as if there must be something wrong *with me*, as indeed there was.

Standing there in that sun-drenched little post office, demanding a postage stamp. I wonder now, to whom did I want to send a card? My parents had not come to my graduation, had not even proposed attending. Could I have written them? to tell them what, we might say, did not concern them: that I was all right?—that I, graduated by myself, was on my own?

It was only much later—years later—that I could realize that all that was standing there in that post office was my skinny body. My mind was at the edge of a cliff, or in that empty, electric box that high anxiety creates. At the time the idea commanding my conscious mind was that there was something deeply wrong—*not with me*, nor with my parents or the world at large—but with this postal clerk and with all the other people waiting, with increasing impatience, beginning to murmur, behind me in line. I began to sweat and looked around me at the strange faces. All of a sudden, it seemed, I had become a stranger in my little, beloved college town, the place in whose libraries and classrooms, gardens and cafes, protests and debates, I had been as happy as I ever had been or ever would be.

In §433, Wittgenstein writes (in discussing the use of arm movements to emphasize an order one is trying to give): "How does he know what use he is to make of the signs I give him, whatever they are?" And then, §504, from the clerk's perspective, we might say: "But if you say, 'How am I to know what he means, when I see nothing but the signs he gives?' then I say: 'How is *he* to know what he means when he has nothing but the signs either?'"

There are those moments when the signs go dead, or when their deadness is revealed—when they seem useless or no use can be made of them. You cannot be understood or understand. You are, as we say, lost to the world. (In a worst-case scenario—in medical dramas on television—there's just that one flat line next to your bed.)

But this was, of course, not my situation there in the post office. My sign ("postage stamp"), though inscrutable to the clerk, was not dead. My sign, my "postage stamp," spoke, and it has spoken over many decades, to one person—to me—telling me a whole story about anxiety, about being pushed out into the world all by myself. Or so it can feel to most all of us at various times.

"mastery" into a conversation, say, or to a newspaper. Pointing and learning names, rightly or wrongly, is far from enough.

I would also like to point out that, in the non-transparent passage, Wittgenstein italicized a form of the verb *vershtehen*. The translator renders this as "understand"—"We do not *understand*" these strange, other people. And I have been using this word, but I don't think it's right. It's not visceral enough. It doesn't bring home the feeling, the feeling of being on the outside looking in. In fact, my *Oxford-Duden* tells me *vershtehen*, the verb, the infinitive, might also be translated as "to make out."* We—

Marsalina: In other words, the reason he couldn't understand what anyone was saying was because some girl had her tongue in his mouth.

Abel, as if annoyed that Marsalina was not taking the discussion seriously enough: No, Marsalina. Not that kind of making out. *Ich konnte ihn bei dem Lärm nicht vershtehen*: I couldn't make out what he was saying because of the noise. Retranslating the verb has helped me understand better what Wittgenstein is saying, or describing, in this passage, and, if you will, as regards life in general. The feeling of being a stranger, a single human being, in this strange land of human social interaction. And all we have are our fingers, if you will, our pointing, our names. And at times it seems that no one can figure out what we're pointing at, or why we're pointing, or they don't have the same names for things that we do.

> Poor chap, he always loved larking
> And now he's dead
> It must have been too cold for him his heart gave way,
> They said.
>
> Oh, no no no, it was too cold always
> (Still the dead one lay moaning)
> I was much too far out all my life
> And not waving but drowning.†

On Friday nights, you know, I see the college girls in my neighborhood all dolled up, heading out to the bars to meet their friends, meet boys. And these days one of the styles is very short skirts. And I can't help

---

* I.e., *The Oxford-Duden German Dictionary*; German-English/English-German.

† The last two stanzas of Stevie Smith's "Not Waving but Drowning"—my wife's favorite poem. Events came to confirm that she knew all too well what Smith was writing about.

thinking that what I'm looking at—this ostensive thing—is, let's say, a tremendous shortening of the distance between the outside world, the air, the bar, the boy's hand, and the prize—the opening of the vagina, if I may be so crude.

Marsalina: Maybe you're not such a book man after all.

Abel: I told you, I'm just inhibited, disconnected. But my point is: If I told my description to a group of boys, they'd laugh and nod their heads. And if I told my description to a group of girls, not only would they think I was a nut, a pervert, they would think that I misunderstood entirely what it means to get dressed up on a Friday night, to try to look your best.

In any case, you can see that I find the social and psychological issues Wittgenstein touches on so fascinating, I keep wandering from the more purely linguistic ones. But I think I can pull the two threads together. In social situations—at times when you are a native speaker, and at times when you are trying to learn a new language—you could just be starting a new job, taking up yoga or scuba diving— At times in a group, one can feel lost. You can't quite "make out" what is being said. Or, as Wittgenstein put it: *Wir können uns nicht in sie finden.*[*] We can't find ourselves into the

---

[*] It is worth keeping in mind that during his years at Cambridge Wittgenstein was in an odd linguistic situation, all be this situation not uncommon for human beings. An émigré or exile, he was losing touch with his native language, and not keeping up with its ongoing evolution, and in his discussions and his writing he was mixing this archaic knowledge of Viennese German with his growing knowledge of English. And I have some question as to the extent to which he ever really mastered English, or wanted to. (Like many émigrés who remain emotionally connected to their country of origin, and who may, like Wittgenstein, regularly return home, Wittgenstein may have been anxious not to be or to feel too well assimilated in his country of refuge.) Clearly he did a lot of speaking in English, and one comes across postcards and so forth that seem perfectly well written, and in a colloquial style, but one also comes across other remarks. For example, after first meeting Wittgenstein, Russell remarked that he spoke very little English. This was after Wittgenstein had been studying in England for three years. Moore remarks that Wittgenstein seemed often to use the words "proposition" and "sentence" as if they meant the same thing (perhaps because the German word "*Satz*" might be properly used for either of these English words). And Monk (434) quotes from the diary of an adolescent whose home was visited by Wittgenstein in 1942: "Wink [as the boy called him] is awful strange—not a very good English speaker, keeps on saying 'I mean' and 'its "tolerable"' meaning intolerable." Here, we might say, are grounds for getting bewitched by language, and for bewitching others when

other people—into the group, the conversation.

Marsalina: Under the skirt.

Abel: Under the skirt, into the tent. Of course for true foreigners, if I can call some people that, there are special problems—for example, distinguishing sounds when they are coming from several different directions and when they are pronounced by people with whose accents, intonations

---

you speak to them.

In any case, during his many years at Cambridge Wittgenstein had English-mother-tongue students and fellow professors record his ruminations in English, and after his death these and others of his notes in German and translated into English were assembled and published as various books, e.g., *On Certainty, Culture and Value, Remarks on the Foundations of Mathematics, Preliminary Studies for the "Philosophical Investigations", generally known as The Blue and Brown Books.* (Books that Wittgenstein can be said to have contributed to, without authoring.) Presumably, when ruminating in English he was sometimes using his own quick (or subconscious) translations of German phrases and at times using phrases directly from English. When writing the final text of the *Investigations* in German, he was, presumably, often translating the notes in English back into German and sometimes writing directly in in the pre-First-World-War German of his Viennese childhood.

Thus we come to the oddity that is *Wir können uns nicht in sie finden*. I wrote a translator of German literature about this phrase and Elizabeth Anscombe's translation: "We cannot find our feet with them" (i.e., with the foreigners, or other humans, we hear speaking around us). My acquaintance's response:

> Wittgenstein's used an utterly unfamiliar German locution here, and Anscombe's translation is so creative, if you will, that I assume that Anscombe just threw up her hands and asked Ludwig himself what to do, and he just off-handedly said, "We cannot find our feet with them." And she took that and ran with it.

My acquaintance proposed as a possibility "We cannot find our way into them." Or, "We cannot identify with them." She liked Abel's ideas, particularly "We cannot empathize with them," writing:

> In German the standard way "to empathize with someone" is *"sich in jemanden einfühlen"* (literally: to feel oneself into someone), so that this notion of finding/feeling oneself/one's way into another is already familiar in the language.

Russell in letter to Morrell, October 18, 1911; as quoted in Monk, *Ludwig Wittgenstein*, 38-39. Moore, "Wittgenstein's Lectures in 1930-33", 262 and 268.

and particular rhetoric one may not be familiar. But Wittgenstein is more interested in the problem we all share: context. Insofar as we are not familiar with the local traditions, with the local *Lebensform* (the local form of life)—with the in-jokes, references, taboos of the group—we will be lost. "If a lion could talk we could not understand him."*

Marsalina: That's more or less what Lauren and Rosie and I say about "daddy"—about Jerry—sometimes. How does it go—"If a lion—"

Abel: "If a lion could talk we could not understand him."

Speaking of spouses—*Abel laughed*—the other night Sarah read something to me from a literary biography. Two "English" writers, two writers living in England—Joseph Conrad from Poland, and Ford Maddox Ford, whose father was German—went to a music hall where there was a comedian. And everybody was laughing and enjoying themselves except them. The humor of foreigners is one of the hardest things to *vershtehen*.

---

* *Investigations*, Part II, xi, 190e. We might add here that if, or when, fifth-grade, middle-class American girls could talk, the Spanish-speaking daughter of a Dominican *hacendado* could not understand them.

There is considerable debate in the philosophical literature regarding what Wittgenstein meant by *Lebensform*. (So much debate that I will come back to this issue in another footnote, many pages further on.) Some, myself included, think Wittgenstein is referring to what is also called "culture," so that the form of life in twenty-first century New England is different from that prevailing in this region in pre-colonial times. Others would have *Lebensform* refer to something closer to human nature, physiology included. See Kenny, 2 (citing, *inter alia*, *Investigations*, §185): ". . . a point often made by Wittgenstein, that the setting up of linguistic conventions presupposes a uniformity among human beings in their natural, pre-conventional, reactions to such things as pointing fingers." (My underscoring.) And Stroud, 518: We do not decide to accept or reject [our *Lebensformen*] at all, any more than we decide to be human beings as opposed to trees. To ask whether our human practices or forms of life themselves are "correct" or "justified" is to ask whether we are "correct" or "justified" in being the sorts of things we are.

Thus, on my end of the spectrum, our words and behaviors make sense in a particular cultural context (e.g., in Nazi Germany) and may not in other contexts, particularly in rather different cultures. At the other extreme there is something enduring in our *Lebensformen* that lends permanence to our meanings as well. And one might imagine a philosopher proposing—as sociobiologists, independently of Wittgenstein, certainly have—that we *can* speak of the correctness of and justification for various human practices by evaluating the extent to which they are rooted in our "being the sorts of the things we are."

At some point apparently, Conrad turned to Ford and said, "Doesn't one in spite of everything feel a stranger in this beastly country?"*

From one perspective this seems to me a leitmotif, or *the* leitmotif of the *Investigations*. Wittgenstein was speaking as best as he, with his particular psychological make-up and social position, could about what it feels like to be an alien. About what if feels like to be a girl or boy come new into a fifth-grade classroom.

In his own case, Ludwig—or Luki, as he was called—was first educated at home, at the "Palais Wittgenstein" as it was called, an immense mansion with half a dozen grand pianos, thirty servants—you can imagine. But when he was 13, Luki's father allowed him to go to a school: the

---

* Jeffrey Meyers. *Joseph Conrad*, 180. In the novel *The World As I Found It* (163), Bruce Duffy imagines the young Wittgenstein's first meeting with Wittgenstein's fellow Cambridge University philosophy student, David Pinsent, the first real friend (or almost friend) of Ludwig's life. The story offers a wonderful illustration of the life of a stranger in a stranger land, of the challenges of foreign sounds and intonations—and of making friends—and of some of Wittgenstein's ideas about learning names from ostensive definitions.

The fictionalized Pinsent is looking at a bird in a tree and Wittgenstein approaches and asks, "Tell me, please, what kind is this?"

The young student, deaf in one ear, misunderstands the question and answers, "Pinsent."

"I asked you what is this bird," Wittgenstein comes to say, "and you said it was a pinsent?" (An ostensive definition can be variously interpreted in every case.)

"*I'm* Pinsent," the boy says, rolling his eyes. "That's a mistle thrush. Just in early for the spring, you know. A harbinger."

I now pick up Duffy's narration (and punctuation and italicization):

> But—Wittgenstein was twisted up again—a thrush, it is a harbinger?
>
> No, a *thrrr-ush* is a *thrrr-ush*. Rolling the R's, the intonation harsh and British. [Pinsent] continued, A *harbinger* is one thing that signals the approach of another. The *thrrrush* presages the approach of spring.
>
> Stung, Wittgenstein said almost sorrowfully, It is for me a new word. Wittgenstein closed his eyes as if he were fixing these words like photographic exposures into his memory.

But, we might say, Ludwig was misunderstanding completely. It wasn't so much a new word as the possibility of a whole new experience: friendship.

Kaiserlich und königlich Staatsoberrealschule, a stronghold of German nationalism. (Among the other pupils: Adolf Hitler.) Apparently, when Ludwig was first sent to this school, he spoke an unusually pure form of High German, dressed elegantly, was sensitive and unsocial—you can imagine.

Marsalina: He was lucky to come out of there alive!

Abel: Perhaps he didn't. Or perhaps he didn't come out of his family or Vienna or the First World War alive.* The only thing that remained for him to cling to—like a piece of wood in a raging sea—was language. Or the idea that meaning—the meaning of suffering—the same question that plagued Augustine—must be findable in language and through language, for all he himself couldn't find it.

I have a picture of a boy all alone, making sand castles at the edge of the sea, his carefully crenelated towers and elaborate tunnels periodically washed away by the waves. He does not wish to look up and not see his parents, or see other children and adults staring at him. So he just keeps building.

Marsalina: You don't make our Luki sound like a very happy boy.

Abel, shaking his head, I imagine: No, although from what I've read he *was* happy in his sand-castle years—the baby of his family and so forth. It was when he began to think, and to perceive what was going on around him, and likely with a sharper eye, taking more in than most people do . . .

My sense is that Ludwig, feeling lost in the world beyond his palace—and coming to feel like he was suffocating any time he returned home . . . My sense is that he defended himself, his ego, by trying—by exerting extraordinary *Beherrschung*, self-control—to stay focused on the inverse of his problem, on language, to include the language of feelings, *rather than*

---

* Monk, 169:

> Like many war veterans before and since, Wittgenstein found it almost insuperably difficult to adjust to peace-time conditions. He had been a soldier for five years, and the experience had left an indelible stamp upon his personality. He continued to wear his uniform for many years after the war, as though it had become a part of his identity, an essential part, without which he would be lost. It was also perhaps a symbol of his feeling—which persisted for the rest of his life—that he belonged to a past age. For it was the uniform of a force that no longer existed. Austria-Hungary was no more, . . .

on feelings. Again and again in his writings—in his remarks, to others or to the air, that the others wrote down for him—Ludwig proposed that he understood better than everyone else. The problem was that everyone else was so confused. The only reason he felt so alone was that everyone around him misunderstood.

    Let me give you another line from the *Investigations*: "When philosophers use a word . . . and try to grasp the *essence* of the thing, one must always ask oneself: is the word ever actually used in this way in the language-game which is its original home?"* "*Wird denn dieses Wort in der Sprache, in der es seine Heimat hat, je tatsächlich so gebraucht?*" That's the German. "Would this word—in the language where it makes its home—ever really be used in this way?" That's one of my re-translations. Or, further retranslating *Heimat*—home town—as "Vienna". "Would this word ever really be used this way in Vienna?" "Was the word actually used in this way in Vienna when I was a boy?"† In Vienna before the empire collapsed?

---

* *Investigations*, §116. This might also be a question about the etymology, the original home of a word. I remember my nephew once, 8 years old, being disturbed to find in an old book a word spelled differently than he had been taught to spell it. How was it originally spelled? he was anxious to know. Not only would this information allow him to establish the right way to spell the word, but also, more importantly, it would reassure him that there was a right way.

Intriguingly, Wittgenstein, for his part, at least during his school years, was a bad speller, and he himself believed that this had a profound effect on his character. (McGuinness, *Wittgenstein: A Life*, 51.) *Cf.*, *Investigations*, §167: "Think of the uneasiness we feel when the spelling of a word is changed."

† There are of course many aspects of Wittgenstein's work that, even with Abel and Marsalina's great help, I have not been able to comprehend, however imperfectly, and many other aspects to which I remain blind, aspects I do not even realize merit comprehending. One section I have been stopping at is §212: "*Wenn jemand, den ich fürchte, mir den Befehl gibt, die Reihe fortzusetzen, so werde ich schleunig, mir völliger Sicherheit, handeln, und das Fehlen der Gründe stört mich nicht.*" When someone whom I am afraid of orders me to continue the series [e.g., a series of numbers], I act quickly, with perfect certainty, and the lack of reasons does not trouble me.

OK, but here is an "I," a person who, to put it mildly, was inordinately troubled by lacks of reasons. Here was a person who, when told there was no rhinoceros in a Cambridge University classroom, was not convinced there was any reason to believe—or, we might say, to not believe—this assertion. (The only thing that really exists, Wittgenstein was contending, are assertions.) So, in light of §212, where does the problem lie? Does it lie in the fact that any reason may be shown

before my brothers died? before my father died? before the Nazis arrived and wiped out the Jews and turned a cosmopolitan, multi-ethnic capital of European high culture into a racist, provincial backwater?[*]

Did you know (by the way) that before the First World War, Hitler—unemployed and basically unemployable, or employable only as *der Führer*—Hitler was kept alive by a Jewish charity for the homeless and by Viennese Jews who bought his pictures.

Marsalina: "Why are you angry with me? I never did anything for you."

Abel: Very good, *mayn yiddishe meydele*![†] And could we say that Wittgen-

---

to be insufficient, any assertion may be contradicted by another? Or does it lie in an absence or breakdown of authority? Does it lie in the collapse of "the empire," either in a political or cultural or familial sense? That is, in the collapse of the *kaiserlich und königlich Monarchie*—of the Austro-Hungarian empire—or in a loss of faith in an older way of viewing and doing things (*cf.*, the work of Wittgenstein's Vienna contemporaries Freud, Schönberg, Loos, Klimt, Schiele). Or does it lie in the loss of respect for authority occasioned by the murderous incompetence on all sides that was the First World War, or in Ludwig and his remaining siblings' increasing loss of respect for their father as one after another of the older brothers committed suicide?

The line about the only thing that exists are assertions is a recasting of a line in a letter from Russell to Morrell: Wittgenstein "was refusing to admit the existence of anything except asserted propositions." Monk, 40; quoting a letter of November 7, 1911. In a November 2, 1911 letter Russell wrote: "My German engineer [Wittgenstein], I think, is a fool. He thinks nothing empirical is knowable—I asked him to admit there was not a rhinoceros in the room, but he wouldn't." (McGuinness, *Wittgenstein: A Life*, 89.)

[*] Edmonds and Eidinow's *Wittgenstein's Poker* offers (93-141) an excellent, if unhappy account of the dashed hopes of assimilationist Jews in Vienna, and this is also a story of the destruction of the soul of what was once the most cosmopolitan city in Europe (as well as being a cautionary tale for those of us the world over who are, in one sense or another, assimilationists). On page 99 Edmonds and Eidinow quote (in translation, I assume) a ditty from 1850s Vienna. Later pages of the present work will show how misleading these words proved to be.

> The Christian, the Turk, the heathen and Jew
> Has dwelt here in ages old and new
> Harmoniously and without strife,
> For everyone's entitled to his own life.

See also, page 102's quotation of historian Peter Pulzer: "If any city in the world can claim to be the cradle of modern political anti-Semitism it is Vienna."

[†] My little Yiddish girl. Apparently, the saying about "Why are you angry?" is of

stein, like many an academic, has gotten pretty far away from home base when—instead of writing directly, passionately about the perversity of human nature, our strange admixture of charity and cruelty—he comes up with carefully crafted statements such as: "A philosophical problem has the form: 'I don't know my way about'." Or could we say, and with an eye on our section 32, could we say, "There was a time I *did* know my way about, when I lived in my palace, when I was still a little child, before the CIA came and the priests refused to give me communion and the children of my father's farmworkers threw rocks at my school bus—before I began to glimpse what language was all about. When I still thought it was just about "ostensive definitions," about pointing at things you wanted like so many pastries, and getting the things you wanted and being happy with them and their names. When I thought I could still use words to express my desires; before, like Augustine, I found myself, with the help of language, "launched deeper into the stormy intercourse of human life"?* It would seem that it is with the help of language that we are all exiled from the innocence of childhood.

Marsalina, with some sharpness: You'll excuse me for ignoring your obsession with other people's childhoods and trying to get back to the sentence we are supposed to be working on—trying to learn a foreign language, guess what people in a strange country mean, our stranger in a strange land, Ludwig Wittgenstein, not—

Yiddish or Jewish origin.

* Abel is quoting from an English translation of a sentence in Book I, Chapter 8 of Augustine's *Confessions*. As shall be seen later on in this piece, at the very beginning of the *Investigations*, and in section 32, Wittgenstein used a few sentences from this chapter to propel his reflections and arguments. The concluding sentence of the chapter, which includes this quoted phrase, Wittgenstein did *not* use.

As for the priests and the school bus, presumably these are references to things Marsalina had told Abel about the last days of her childhood in the Dominican Republic, before she was whisked away to the safety of a middle-class life in Queens. I have the sense that under Trujillo all aspects of life in the Dominican Republic—from who owned property and had police support, to the role of the Catholic Church, to the game of baseball—were politicized. People and institutions thrived insofar as they served the dictator's tastes and interests, helping him stay in power above all. So I can imagine that when it was becoming apparent that Trujillo had lost his strongest power base—the support of the US government . . . I imagine a feeling of anarchy and of release from bondage sweeping over the country, touching, *inter alia*, peasants and priests.

I presume she was going to say, "not Marsalina Marte," but Abel interrupted: Gershom.

Marsalina: Ai-yi-yi.

Abel: You're running out of patience with me, I know. And I know it's going to *seem like* I'm losing my way again—but "stranger in a strange land," you're quoting the Bible, *Exodus*. Perhaps without knowing it.

Marsalina, still with that edge in her voice: I saw the movie. Peter Sellers wasn't it?

Abel: George Bush. In any case, that's where that beautiful expression—stranger in a strange land—comes from. And this is why I've started calling Wittgenstein's stranger Gershom, as Moses called his son, according to *Exodus*. Gershom, "sojourner there."*

"And she bare him a son, and he called his name Gershom, for he said, I have been a stranger in a strange land." Sometimes it brings tears to my eyes just to read those words: "I have been a stranger in a strange land." It makes me think of my family, my wife and daughter. Just like you were saying before, about how we're all strangers.

And so, I suppose we might have to recognize, that—oddly, paradoxically—what we may share above all is our isolation, or this feeling of aloneness. We may be united in our being strangers to one another—islands connected by the bridges and boats of language.

> Suppose everyone does say about himself that he knows what pain is only from his own pain.—Not that people really say that, or are even prepared to say it. But *if everybody said it . . .* †

---

* This is the standard translation of Moses' son's Hebrew name. *N.B.*: In the story, Moses called his son Gershom *not* because of his son's status, but because he himself, Moses, had been a stranger in a strange land. This may have made Gershom, like a lot of sons and daughters before him and since, a bit of a stranger in his own name.

† Fragment of §295, interrupted. Perhaps this is the place to note an anecdote Alexander Waugh retails, without a source, in his book about the Wittgenstein family (116). It proposes that Karl Wittgenstein, Ludwig's father, had a habit of picking his young sons up by their ears. If they kept quiet he shouted "*Hochgeboren!*" (well bred!), but if they cried or squealed in pain he yelled "*Nichtgeboren!*" (lower class—literally, "not born").

First Interpolation

THERE WAS A BREAK IN THE CONVERSATION, *a silence, a not knowing what to say next. I found myself reminded of a famous line from Emerson's "Self-Reliance": "To believe your own thought, to believe that what is true for you in your private heart is true for all men,—that is genius." There is a sense in which both our cries of pain and our reports of our ideas, make, first and foremost, this claim of universality: "This can't just be me!" who hurts or has been wronged like this, or who has these thoughts. We might call these cries and statements a reaching for community. And community is created because, even if the specific contents of our cries and statements are misconstrued, our claim of community, our desire for community, resonates.*

I would like to take further advantage of this break to offer some thoughts about Wittgenstein's personal exile: about why he came to spend the greater part of his adult life in a foreign country, teaching and even at times ruminating in a foreign language. This will also lead me to discuss Wittgenstein's supposed last words—"Tell them I've had a wonderful life!"— and his character, and to make some comparisons with Pyrrhonian skepticism and with Oedipus's plight.

To begin, following Abel's lead, I would compare Ludwig's situation with Moses and Gershom's. The latter two were members of an enslaved tribe who (the legend would have it) after a long, incredible journey were able to find a land where they could, if only temporarily, enjoy some measure of peace, prosperity, freedom and dignity. Ludwig was born into the lap of luxury and culture, in a mansion in one of the world's capitals, a mansion that was frequented by some of the greatest composers, painters, writers and architects of the twentieth century. One of Klimt's most famous paintings was the bridal portrait of Wittgenstein's sister Margarete. Brahms and Mahler regularly gave concerts in one or another of the Wittgenstein family's music rooms. Richard Strauss came to play duets with one of Ludwig's brothers.

It was the end of an era, of the Austro-Hungarian empire, but it was hardly the end of the steel business, and if the center of Central European power had become not Vienna, but Berlin, . . . A rich young man could always move there, as indeed Ludwig's brother Rudi tried to do. Why did Ludwig instead move to a non-German-speaking country, a country where, no matter how long he lived there, he would never quite understand or be understood? Where he would feel yet more alienated than he would have in Berlin?

One possible answer is that, however chastely he may have lived for much of his life, Ludwig was a homosexual, a homosexual in a time when, to understate the case, it was hardly easy to be a homosexual.* (It was better

---

* *N.B.*: The more traditional rendering, which time has been wearing away, is that Ludwig was asexual. Perhaps the following two quotations give the best summary of the situation:

"Most people would think that I have had not relationships with women, but I have." (A statement of Wittgenstein's remembered by a friend, Rowland Hutt, as recalled to Ray Monk; as quoted in Monk, 369.)

"In the course of our conversations Russell would often exclaim: 'Logic's hell!'— And this *perfectly* expresses the feeling we had when we were thinking about the problems of logic; that is to say, their immense difficulty, their hard and *slippery* texture." (Wittgenstein notebook entry from 1937, with Wittgenstein's emphases; as quoted in Edmonds and Eidinow, 53.)

The following quotation is from Monk, 376, quoting from one of Wittgenstein's coded manuscripts held at Trinity College, Cambridge. The item is dated September 22, 1937 and concerns a visit of Francis Skinner, who beginning in the early 1930s became Wittgenstein's constant companion and collaborator. Skinner had come to visit Wittgenstein at the latter's country house in Norway. Again, I am quoting Monk quoting Wittgenstein:

> After Francis had arrived at the house, Wittgenstein was "sensual, susceptible, indecent" with him: "Lay with him two or three times. Always at first with the feeling that there was nothing wrong in it, *then* with shame." . . . Whether this was the only occasion on which he and Francis were sexually intimate, we do not know. It is certainly the only occasion mentioned in his [Wittgenstein's] coded remarks.

In the Appendix to his biography, Monk considers in some detail the question of Wittgenstein's homosexuality. He relies particularly on the "coded notebooks", which were written in a simple code (a=z, b=y, c=x, etc.). Quoting Monk again (585-86):

> What the coded remarks reveal is the extraordinary extent to which Wittgenstein's love life and his sexual life went on only in his imagination. This is most striking in the case of Keith Kirk (for whom Wittgenstein formed a brief obsession that he regarded as "unfaithful" to his love for Francis Skinner, . . .),

to be misunderstood, to be lost to empathy, than to be understood to be a homosexual?)

It is said that his brother Hans was also a homosexual. Hans—who was also a musical genius trying to get away from his father's demand that he go into the family steel business—exiled himself to the United States. It is commonly reported, and it came to be believed by the Wittgenstein family, that Hans committed suicide, disappearing from a boat in Chesapeake Bay, or perhaps in Venezuela.* A year after Hans's disappearance, Rudi, aged 22, walked into a bar in Berlin, asked the pianist to play a particular popular song—"Verlassen, verlassen, verlassen bin ich" (Forsaken, forsaken, forsaken am I)—drank some mixture of milk, mineral water and potassium cyanide, and died in agony.† He sent several farewell letters, one of which referred to his "doubts about my perverted disposition." It was reported at the time that Rudi had sought advice from the Scientific Humanitarian Committee, an organization that was campaigning against a section of the German Criminal Code which, until 1969, forbade die widernatürliche Unzucht (*unnatural sex acts*).‡ *He may have become identifiable as the subject of a published case study about homosexuality. After Rudi's death, Karl Wittgenstein—Rudi,*

---

but it is also evident in almost all of Wittgenstein's intimate relationships. Wittgenstein's perception of a relationship would often bear no relation at all to the perception of it held by the other person. If I had not met Keith Kirk, I would have been almost certain, from what I had read in the coded remarks, that he and Wittgenstein had had some kind of "affair". Having met Kirk, I am certain that whatever affair there was existed only in Wittgenstein's mind.

What is missing from this picture, though not from Monk's biography, is the fact that this was not a one-way street. There were also men who fell in love with Wittgenstein, and there were other homosexually oriented men, such as John Maynard Keynes, who may have been able to warm to Wittgenstein, despite his difficult personality, because they recognized that Wittgenstein shared their sexual orientation and at least some of the delights, struggle and alienation that went with it.

* Waugh, 27, proposes: "Hans may, of course, have lived a full life abroad and in secret from his family in Vienna, but the most likely scenario is that he did indeed commit suicide somewhere outside Austria."

† Waugh, 21-22. The song was composed by Thomas Koschat. Ironically, the "I" of the song feels forsaken because no *girl* loves him, his girl is dead and buried.

‡ A yearbook of the Committee stated: "Our influence did not reach far enough to turn him [Rudi] away from the fate of self-destruction." (Monk, 12.)

Hans and Ludwig's father—forbade the family from ever mentioning Rudi's name in his presence again.

> A note made by Ludwig in 1937:
>
> *Neimand kann mit Wahrheit von sich selbst sagen, daß er Dreck ist.* Denn wenn ich es sage, so kann es in einem Sinne wahr sein, aber ich kann nicht selbst von dieser Wahrheit durchdrungen sein: sonst müß te ich wahnsinnig werden, oder mich ändern.
>
> *Nobody can truthfully say of himself that he is filth.* Because if I do say it, though it can be true in a sense, this is not a truth by which I myself can be penetrated: otherwise I should either have to go mad or change myself.*

From paragraph 5.631 of the *Tractatus*, the book of Wittgenstein's youth:

> If I wrote a book called *The World As I Found It*, I should have to include a report on my body, and should have to say which parts were subordinate to my will, and which were not, etc., this being a method of isolating the subject, or rather of showing that in an important sense there is no subject; for it alone could *not* be mentioned in that book.

ANOTHER POSSIBLE ANSWER *as to why Ludwig ran away from home, as it were, is that the Wittgensteins were Jewish, or somewhat Jewish. Of Wittgenstein's four grandparents, one had no Jewish ancestry; the other three came from Jewish families but converted to Christianity in order to fit in—to avoid discrimination and murder.*†

In 1939, a few days before the invasion of Poland, Hitler granted

---

* From a note Wittgenstein made in 1937, later published in *Culture and Value*, 32, 32e. Italics as in the original. *Cf.*, Augustine, *Confessions* III:1, here as translated by Pine-Coffin: "I went to Carthage, where I found myself in the midst of a hissing cauldron of lust. . . . So I muddied the stream of friendship with the filth of lewdness and clouded its clear waters with hell's black river of lust."

† Ludwig was baptized in the Catholic Church. This, however, was largely a formality—for all the formality may have given Ludwig a confused sense of his own identity, or affiliations. I would here cite a bit from my own past. My own mater-

Mischlinge *(half-breed) status to the Wittgenstein children, on the pretext that their paternal grandfather had been the bastard son of a German prince.*[*] *Nobody believed this tale, but "the arrangement enabled the German*

---

nal grandparents emigrated to New York, one from Austria-Hungary and the other from what is now, I believe, Latvia. They didn't want to be Jews any more, nor Protestants or Catholics. They wanted to be Americans! They believed in America! Life, liberty and the pursuit of happiness. A man working his way up from son of an unwearying pushcart peddler on the Lower East Side to become a doctor and send his daughter to Smith and into the arms of old WASP money. In this spirit my grandparents and my mother and her brother celebrated Christmas—Christmas in the sense of a tree with decorations and lights and lots of consumer goods underneath. But since my grandfather was a doctor in a Jewish community, they had to do their celebrating with the curtains closed, to avoid offending clients or potential clients. (And you were saying something about alienation?)

Of course, the details here are quite different from Ludwig's experience growing up immensely rich in turn-of-the-twentieth-century Vienna. But there is a sense in which the experience of assimilationist Jews is much the same everywhere, as it is for assimilationists of other persuasions as well, to include homosexuals trying to pass as "straight." There is the fitting in and the not fitting in and the fear of being found out, the moments of exclusion. An acquaintance of mine—whose father, a Sephardic Jew from Turkey, managed to survive the Second World War in hiding in France—once proposed to me that the message in assimilationist Jewish families is: "Don't forget to forget."

But, of course, this is a message well known in many families, of all origins and nationalities. Don't forget to forget your father's infidelities or your mother's drug addiction or the time your uncle made you hold his penis or any number of things. I am hardly a specialist in this area—or in any area?—but I have wondered if there isn't a sense in which many families are simultaneously held together and split into isolated units by the secrets they share and feel under orders not to share either with anyone outside the family or even with anyone within in it. Which is also to say that often the family members are not conscious of the secret or secrets they are, with such effort and suffering, preserving.

I have strayed here a long ways from the Palais Wittgenstein on what was then the Alleegasse in Vienna. But I hope that I have conveyed something of the way in which Ludwig emerged from his family, and without considering himself Jewish. After the *Anschluss* (the annexation of Austria by Nazi Germany), when he found himself negotiating with the Nazis for his sisters' lives, he must have come closer to recognizing other aspects of the Jewish and assimilationist experience.

For a review of the Wittgenstein's negotiations with the Nazis, see either Edmonds and Eidinow's *Wittgenstein's Poker*, 93-141, or Waugh, 201-71.

* The following year the Wittgensteins' status was further improved by a German

Reichsbank to claim all the gold and much of the foreign currency and stocks held in Switzerland by a Wittgenstein trust". And it enabled Hermine and Helene Wittgenstein, the two of Ludwig's sisters who wished to stay in Vienna, to continue living there in relative peace and security while so many others were being carted by the train load to mass execution sites and concentration camps.†*

---

government proclamation that "racial classification under the Reich Citizenship Law [a.k.a., the Nuremberg Laws] presents no further difficulties." Even the regulations regarding half-breeds were no longer applicable to the Wittgensteins. (Monk, 400.)

* Gottlieb, "A Nervous Splendor," in the course of summarizing Waugh, 201-71.

† Of the 75,000 Jews who remained in Vienna in 1939, less than a thousand seem to have survived the war. The majority were eventually taken east and murdered in the death camp of Belzec, or in the Lodz ghetto, or at mass execution sites near Minsk, Riga and Kovno. See Misak, "The Jewish Community of Vienna." Misak also writes: "Despite the myriad of books about the Holocaust now available, relatively little has been published on the fate of the Jews of Austria. . . . What is better documented, however, is Austrian involvement in the SS and public support for Nazi policy."

Norman Bentwich, a British eyewitness to the *Anschluss*, wrote:

> Nobody was spared the savagery, the persecution, and the despair with which one of the most cultured Jewish communities in the world, and the third largest in Europe, was stricken. Vast queues gathered outside the consulates of possible host countries. They stretched for miles and were subject to constant attack. (Quoted in Edmonds and Eidinow, 122.)

See also Snyder, 381-82:

> Under German rule, the concentration camps and the death factories operated under different principles. A sentence to the concentration camp Belsen was one thing, a transport to the death factory Bełżec something else. The first meant hunger and labor, but also the likelihood of survival; the second meant immediate and certain death by asphyxiation. This, ironically, is why people remember Belsen and forget Bełżec. . . .
>
> The image of the German concentration camps as the worst element of National Socialism is an illusion, a dark mirage over an unknown desert. In the early months of 1945, as the German state collapsed, the chiefly non-Jewish prisoners in the SS concentration camp system were dying in large numbers. . . . Some of the starving victims were captured on film by the

(*As regards the price of this not being killed or forced to leave one's home, the weight of the Wittgenstein gold taken by the Nazis has been reported as 1.7 tonnes. This would be almost 4,000 pounds of gold, which, if sold by the troy ounce, would fetch about $60 million in 2011—i.e., $30 million per sister. Note, however, that more than just gold—and illusions—was taken from the Wittgensteins by the Nazis.*)

All this, however, was many years after Ludwig had found his rooms at the top of a tower in Whewell's Court, across from the great gate of Trinity College, Cambridge. Perhaps on a more general and perhaps subconscious level Ludwig recognized that there was something unhealthy and dangerous, something necrotic about twentieth-century Vienna. While soon enough I will again turn our attention to personal suicide, which became an obsession in early twentieth Vienna, I would here note as well the suicidal combination of lack of military preparedness and misguided strategy of the Austro-Hungarian political leadership and high command. The 1914 invasion of Serbia, which was unable to take any territory, involved a force of 450,000 men, 227,000 of whom were killed. During the 1916 Russian "Brusilov Offensive," the Austro-Hungarian army lost more than 1 million men, 400,000 of whom were taken prisoner, and the army was unable to mount a successful attack from that point onward.

As for personal suicide, three of Ludwig's four brothers committed suicide, as did an aunt and a cousin, as did the man Ludwig's sister Margarete married, as did this man's father, one of his aunts and possibly an uncle as well.* When he was a teenager, Ludwig wanted to study with the physicist Ludwig Boltzmann, a professor at the University of Vienna. Before Ludwig could begin his studies, however, Boltzmann hanged himself in his hotel

---

British and Americans. These images led Europeans and Americans toward erroneous conclusions about the German system. The concentration camps did kill hundreds of thousands of people at the end of the war, but they were not (in contrast to the death facilities) designed for mass killing. . . . Jews who were sent to concentration camps were among the Jews who survived . . . . The German policy to kill all the Jews of Europe was implemented not in the concentration camps but over pits, in gas vans, and at death facilities at Chelmno, Belzec, Sobibor, Treblinka, Majdanek and Auschwitz.

* *N.B.*: These latter were not Austrians, however. Margarete married an American, from the Upper East Side of New York. (Waugh, 19, 35, 215.)

bedroom while holidaying with his family in a seaside resort. (A boy might come to fear that everything, everyone he touched, or reached out to, must turn to dust—or be consumed by self-hatred.) The conductor of the orchestra at Ludwig's brother Paul's Vienna debut threw himself from a fourth-story, hotel window one Christmas Eve.* Not long after the Grand Duke of Mecklenburg pinned a Military Cross on Paul's chest, the Duke, lovelorn, went for a walk in the woods with his dog and shot himself in the head.†

In 1914, Wittgenstein gave Ludwig von Ficker, a writer and editor, some money to distribute to "Austrian artists who are without means."‡ Among the writers and artists Ludwig gave money to, one was a poet with

---

* Waugh, 5. For his part, very early in the war, Paul was wounded and captured at the Russian front. The wounding resulted in Paul, a concert pianist, losing one of his arms. A man of extraordinary determination and fortitude, he went on to have a very successful career as a one-armed concert pianist. It is commonly said that while he and Ludwig were both still living, Paul was much the more famous of the two brothers.

See also this note Ludwig made on October 28, 1914:

> I keep having to think of poor Paul who has so suddenly lost his career! How terrible. What philosophy is needed to get over it! If only this can be achieved in any other way than suicide!! [Waugh, 76.]

† Waugh, 109. Discussing how early twentieth century Vienna was "a city that considered suicide an art," Ross (41, 54) recounts that the Viennese expressionist painter Richard Gerstl, cuckolded by his wife [and I think he also ran off with Schönberg's wife], first burnt his paintings and then hung himself naked in front of a full-length mirror. With rather more effect, Otto Weininger, 23 years old, shot himself in the house where Beethoven had died, and thereby was able to make a bestseller of his previously scorned dissertation: *Geschlecht und Charakter* (Gender and Character, also often translated Sex and Character).

A later footnote will discuss some of Weininger arguments. Some had a great influence on Wittgenstein and some were used by Nazi propagandists. One may get an idea of Weininger—and of a corner of the hothouse in which Wittgenstein sprouted—from the following quotes from others of Weininger's writings. "I do not think that I could ever be wrong for any considerable length of time." "There are three possibilities for me—the gallows, suicide, or a future so brilliant that I don't dare to think of it." (Waugh, 27-28.)

‡ The decision of who was to get the money was left to Ficker, who was editor of the literary journal *Der Brenner* (The Burner). Among the recipients, Rainer Maria Rilke received a substantial sum, and Georg Trakl and Adolf Loos smaller amounts. See Monk, 106-10.

pharmacological training: Georg Trakl. Coincidentally, Trakl, too, served as a soldier on the Eastern front, but he was not made of the same strong stuff as Ludwig. After one battle he ended up in a psychiatric hospital in Krakow, from where, a story goes, he wrote to Wittgenstein, asking him to come visit. By the time Ludwig arrived, however, Trakl had been dead three days. He used his pharmacological training to prepare himself a mortal potion.

The Viennese satirist Karl Kraus had a nightmare vision of Vienna, the seedbed for Hitler and murderous anti-Semitism, as a "proving ground for world destruction." Switching perspectives and borrowing from a description of Ludwig's brother Kurt, we might say that many Viennese carried "the germ of disgust for life" within themselves. Or was it, more simply, that death—committing suicide—came to seem the best alternative? Kurt died at the Italian front at the end of the First World War, possibly intentionally shooting himself to avoid either having to desert the men under his command, or to lead them in a pointless, suicidal charge, or to be himself taken prisoner. Not long after meeting the young Ludwig, Bertrand Russell noted, "his health seems to me very precarious—he gives one the feeling of a person whose life is very insecure." Indeed!

For his own part, Ludwig told his closest friend, David Pinsent, that in 1912, when Russell assured him that he had a talent for philosophy, it had ended nine years of loneliness and wanting to die.* In 1917 Wittgestein—

---

* Monk, 41, 50. Monk places great emphasis on this moment when Russell, after reading a paper Wittgenstein wrote for him, assured Wittgenstein of his talent. One way the story is told is that the student, Ludwig, asked the great teacher, Russell, if he should return to his aeronautical studies or become a philosopher. Russell told him to write something on some philosophical subject. After reading only one sentence of the resulting text, Russell said: "No you must not become an aeronaut."

This sounds like an exchange many a student might have had with a revered teacher, but Monk underscores the greater intensity Ludwig brought to the exchange, as to most all his exchanges. Monk connects this moment with Russell with Wittgenstein's adolescent reading of Otto Weininger's *Geschlecht und Charakter* (Gender and Character), which Monk suggests was the book that most influenced Wittgenstein's life and thinking.

As an adult, Wittgenstein told Moore that the book's greatness lay "in that with which we disagree. It is [Weininger's] enormous mistake that is great." Be that as it may, the book has come to be best known for its proto-Nazi argument, and for the

showing what was to be a life-long interest in ethics and, perhaps, in escaping suicide—wrote in one of his wartime notebooks: "If suicide is allowed, then everything is allowed. If anything is not allowed, then suicide is not allowed."

In August 1918 Ludwig's favorite uncle died. In October he learned that a publishing company had decided not to publish his book, the Tractatus, *and his brother Kurt killed himself. He received a letter from Pinsent's mother saying that Pinsent had been killed in a plane crash. In November, Ludwig, a soldier in the Austrian army, was taken prisoner.* The following August, physically and mentally spent, he returned to his family in Vienna in August. He apparently talked incessantly about suicide, terrifying his sisters and Paul, his sole remaining brother. He decided to do two things: to get rid of his fortune and to become an elementary school teacher, a job for which he proved extraor-*

---

use of this argument by the Nazis in some of their propaganda. The (all-too-well-known) argument: Europe suffered from racial, sexual and ethical degeneration (whose root cause was the rampant sexuality of Woman). Jewishness and homosexuality were both symptoms of a feminized society. Only a masculine Genius could redeem the world. (*N.B.*: Weininger, like Wittgenstein, was a homosexual who had Jewish ancestors.)
Monk (23) writes:

> Unlike Woman, Man, according to Weininger, has a choice: he can, and must, choose between the masculine and the feminine, between consciousness and unconsciousness, will and impulse, love and sexuality. It is every man's ethical duty to choose the first of each of these pairs, and the extent to which he is able to do this is the extent to which he approximates to the very highest type of man: the genius.

In a less well-known part of the book, however, Weininger also argues that one must be a genius and live for one's genius, or not live at all—i.e., commit suicide. *Ergo*: If in Bertrand Russell's opinion Ludwig had no real genius, it would be clear that Ludwig, and certainly no more than the deceased Weininger himself, had no business going on living.

Summary of main argument from Ross, *The Rest is Noise*, 41. Wittgenstein-Russell exchange in Waugh, 48. Wittgenstein to Moore, August 23, 1931, as quoted in Waugh, 46.

* After volunteering for the army, Wittgenstein first served on a ship and then in an artillery workshop. In March 1916, he was posted to a fighting unit on the front line of the Russian front, and his unit was involved in some of the heaviest fighting. In January 1917, he was sent as a member of a howitzer regiment to the Russian front. In 1918 he was promoted to *Leutnant* and sent to northern Italy as part of an artillery regiment. Monk, 138-41, 153-54.

dinarily ill suited.

I quote from Monk's account of the close of Wittgenstein's schoolteaching career, and while noting that this was before corporal punishment of school children was outlawed:

> Joseph Haidbauer was an eleven-year-old pupil of Wittgenstein's whose father had died and whose mother worked as a live-in maid for a local farmer named Piribauer. Haidbauer was a pale, sickly child who was to die of leukemia at the age of fourteen. He was not the rebellious type, but possibly rather slow and reticent in giving answers in class. One day, Wittgenstein's impatience got the better of him, and he struck Haidbauer two or three times on the head, causing the boy to collapse. On the question of whether Wittgenstein struck the boy with undue force—whether he ill-treated the child—a fellow pupil, August Riegler, has (with dubious logic) commented: "It cannot be said that Wittgenstein ill-treated the child. If Haidbauer's punishment was ill-treatment, then 80 per cent of Wittgenstein's punishments were ill-treatments." On seeing the boy collapse, Wittgenstein panicked. He sent his class home, carried the boy to the headmaster's room to await attention from the local doctor . . . and then hurriedly left the school.
>
> On his way out he had the misfortune to run into Herr Piribauer, who, it seems, had been sent for by one of the children. Piribauer is remembered in the village as a quarrelsome man who harboured a deep-seated grudge against Wittgenstein. His own daughter, Hermine, had often been on the wrong side of Wittgenstein's temper, and had once been hit so hard that she bled behind the ears. Piribauer recalls that when he met Wittgenstein in the corridor, he had worked himself up into a fierce rage. "I called him all the names under the sun. I told him he wasn't a teacher, he was an animal trainer!"

Mr. Piribauer went to the police, and there was a trial in the case of Joseph Haidbauer. Monk recounts that the trial was "a great humiliation" for Wittgenstein, "the more so because, in defending himself against charges of brutality, he had felt the need to lie about the extent of corporal punishment he had administered in the classroom. The sense of moral failure this left him with haunted him for over a decade."

During the winter of 1936-37, Wittgenstein decided to formally confess his sins to a number of his colleagues, and his classroom behavior and subsequent lying about it figured prominently in this confession. During this same period he returned to the village and went door to door, in order to apologize in person to the children who, ten years earlier, he had physically hurt. Monk reports that Wittgenstein visited at least four of the children, and possibly more. Some responded generously, one saying that Wittgenstein had no need to apologize, he had learnt well from Wittgenstein's teaching. "But at the home of Mr. Piribauer he received a less generous response. There he made his apologies to Piribauer's daughter Hermine . . . To Wittgenstein's plea for pardon, the girl responded only with a disdainful, 'Ja, ja.'"

AND SO THEN, *skipping over 33 years of extraordinary philosophical reflection, we come to April 29, 1951, when Wittgenstein, just turned 62, was dying of prostate and bone marrow cancer in England.* His doctor and the doctor's wife had taken him into their home, and Wittgenstein's last speech act, it is said, was this statement to Mrs. Bevan, the doctor's wife: "Tell them I've had a wonderful life!" A student and friend of Wittgenstein's, Norman Malcolm, has proposed that "them" meant Wittgenstein's friends.

Was Wittgenstein's ability and desire to make this statement owing in no small part to his ability to exile himself from Vienna and his family, to embrace the life of a sojourner, however trying, sad and insufficient it may have been?* *Was running away from Austria and disappearing into philosophical problems Ludwig's salvation? His only hope?*† He was apparently

---

* Wittgenstein "was in the habit of retreating to cold and desolate parts of Europe—to the west of Ireland, to Iceland or to Norway," Edmonds and Eidinow write (196), going on to quote from Pinsent's diary: Wittgenstein "swears he can never do his best except in exile."

† As with many of those who run away, for Ludwig once was hardly enough. From England and his adopted father figures Bertrand Russell and G.E. Moore, he ran to rural Norway, building himself a home on a fjord, learning Norwegian. Later he began studying Russian with an eye to emigrating to that country. It could be said that this is one of the disadvantages of being rich: Running away, physically at least, is so easy. It is also the case that those who run away from home

fond of recalling an observation of the German physicist Heinrich Hertz which suggested that seemingly intractable problems might be made to disappear if we simply changed the way we spoke about them.*

We might say that, unlike his older brothers, and perhaps learning from their tragic examples, Ludwig indeed managed to find not the right way to live, but a way to live. The Österreichisch-Ungarische Monarchie *crumbled. German and Japanese imperialist ambitions, and power struggles in Russia and China, among other countries, unleashed a reign of terror such as the world had never known. Scientists realized that their formulas gave them the power, not to turn lead into gold, but to annihilate a whole city over breakfast. Although, even now, in 2011, the news has hardly gotten past the US border guards, or into the capitalist media, or into our apologists' minds, nonetheless the fact remains: In the twentieth century, the Enlightenment dream—that through reason human beings could control their fate—came to show, and all too vividly, its nightmare side. As the great Viennese writer Stefan Zweig observed in his final work, written as the Nazis were overrunning Europe, the very elements of the Renaissance and of humanism that human beings had thought were going to be their salvation, our salvation—these elements had become a deadly poison.*† *They are a deadly poison, their other virtues and wonders notwithstanding.*

Overwhelmed (and Jewish), Zweig, accompanied by his young second

---

or try to turn their backs or minds on their families tend to remain, on a psychological level, more tied down and more set in their families' ways than those who are able to stay closer and more aware. We might say of Ludwig and of so many others of us: We run because there is no running away.

* Quoting Monk (26):

> In *Principles of Mechanics* Hertz addresses the problem of how to understand the mysterious concept of "force" as it is used in Newtonian physics. Hertz proposes that, instead of giving a direct answer to the question: "What is force?", the problem should be dealt with by restating Newtonian physics without using "force" as a basic concept. "When these painful contradictions are removed," he writes, "the question as to the nature of force will not have been answered; but our minds, no longer vexed, will cease to ask illegitimate questions."

† My gloss of an extract from *Europäisches Erbe*, Zweig's last book. I do not believe the book has been translated into English, but the title might be rendered "European Heritage."

wife, took refuge in Brazil. There, in 1942, they together committed suicide. But Ludwig, in the midst of all this, was able to make a wonderful life.

Bertrand Russell once remarked that Wittgenstein was the only man he had ever met "with a real bias for philosophical scepticism; he is glad when it is proved that something can't be known." Did Ludwig understand that the only way for him to survive in the circumstances in which he found himself, and perhaps the best way for many people to survive, was to run away not only physically, but also intellectually, calling the certainties with which he had been raised into question? We cannot know what is really happening, and we cannot know if it really matters. But we may find diversion in looking at how we talk about what seems to be happening.

Cf., Sextus Empiricus's second century A.D. Outlines of Scepticism:

> When we investigate whether things are such as they appear, we grant that they appear, and what we investigate is not what is apparent but what is said about what is apparent—and this is different from investigating what is apparent itself. For example, it appears to us that honey sweetens (we concede this inasmuch as we are sweetened in a perceptual way); but whether . . . it is actually sweet is something we investigate—and this is not what is apparent but something said about what is apparent.*

Similarly, for example, instead of investigating the Holocaust, we could examine what is said about the Holocaust, the language that is used. Or instead of investigating the range of experiences and emotions of a stranger coming into a strange country, we could examine how he might learn the local language—from ostensive definitions, for example.

In academic works, one reads such things as "Wittgenstein's private language arguments undermine classical foundationalism. It is replaced . . . by socialized epistemology."† Or, in Wittgenstein one reads:

---

* Sextus Empiricus, *Outlines of Scepticism*, 8. Long before Wittgenstein, the Pyrrhonists proposed that there were large questions—how we acquire language among them—that could not be answered, only ignored.

† Robert L. Arrignton and Hans-Johann Glock's "Editors' Introduction" to *Wittgenstein and Quine*. The text that I have found to give the best *feel* for what Wittgenstein is trying to describe, the best sense of the depth at which Wittgenstein is working, is some comments made by the artist Robert Irwin to the writer Lawrence Weschler, recorded in the latter's book about the former: *Seeing is Forgetting*

But I did not get my picture of the world by satisfying

the Name of the Thing One Sees.. Wittgenstein might well have appreciated that Irwin is here talking not about spoken language, but about pictures, real pictures, we might call them (or visual language). From 107-08:

> Take a painting by Barnett Newman on display at a museum, one of those where he's made a line down the center, hard on one edge and soft on the other, across a large field of, say, red. If as a young artist you were to take that seriously as a purely aesthetic experience [i.e., devoid of social context]—how that line coursed through that space, what its relationship to the physical world was—then, given what I'm adding to it, it would be very difficult to understand how they could hang that painting on those two rods coming down from the ceiling: How were you supposed to separate the line in the painting from the rods on the wall?
>
> Well, of course, you do it on a scale of values. . . . In other words, the line in the center has some kind of compounded meaning which gives it the emphasis to be focused on. Whereas the rod on the wall, of course, is very meaningless. So therefore you can, in a sense, just not see it; in other words, you can just dilate it right out of your visual range. So what we're really talking about in this whole process is not anything to do with the painting itself, but rather something to do with this thing of value, that which makes an object exist in the world with the ability to isolate itself. . . .
>
> But now, when you have a construct like that, that's how you go through the world. In other words, you don't just do it when you're looking at painting. We're talking about a mental construct to which the whole civilization has deeply committed itself. And what it says, simply, is that as I walk through the world, I bring into focus certain things which are meaningful, and others are by degrees less in focus, dependent upon their meaningfulness in terms of what I'm doing, to the point where there are certain things that are totally out of focus and invisible. We organize our minds in terms of this hierarchical value structure, based on certain ideas about meaning and purpose and function.

And from 129:

> [I]n our ordinary lives we move through the world with a strong expectation-fit ratio which we use as much to block out information as to gather it in—and for good reason, most of the time; we block out information which is not critical to our

myself of its correctness; nor do I have it because I am satisfied with its correctness. No: it is the inherited background against which I distinguish between true and false.

Examples from Wittgenstein's Remarks on the Foundations of Mathematics *I, §5, and from the* Investigations *§381):*

> How should we get into conflict with truth if our footrules were made of very soft rubber instead of wood and steel?—"Well, we shouldn't get to know the correct measurement of the table."—You mean: we should not get, or could not be sure of getting, *that* measurement which we get with our rigid rulers.
>
> *Wie erkenne ich, daß diese Farbe Rot ist?—Eine Antwort wäre:* "*Ich habe Deutsch gelernt*". (How do I know that this colour is red?—It would be an answer to say: "I have learnt English".)

Or, another example: Some people may at one point in history have wished to say that "shower" means "gas chamber," or that "gas chamber" means "shower." Well, . . . The meaning of a word is its use.[*] *And nothing more, we might add. We cannot know if I am Jewish or homosexual or Germanic, or if these words really mean anything. But we certainly know ways in which these words are used!*

Sextus Empiricus proposed:

> Scepticism is an ability to set out oppositions among things which appear . . . , an ability by which, because of the equipollence in the opposed objects and accounts, we come first to suspension of judgment and afterwards to tranquillity.

---

activity. Otherwise we might well become immobilized. But after a while, you know, you do that repeatedly, day after day after day, and the world begins to take on a uniform look.

[*] A key concept in Wittgenstein's later work. See *Investigations*, §43: "For a *large* class of cases—though not for all—in which we employ the word 'meaning' it can be defined thus: the meaning of a word is its use in the language." An example given in *On Certainty*, §476: "Children do not learn that books exist, that armchairs exist, etc., etc.,—they learn to fetch books, sit in armchairs, etc., etc."

But we can see in the shower example that there are, if you will, limits to this approach, to its apparent social usefulness and psychological effectiveness.

I note that Wittgenstein's phrase on his death bed was not "I've had a wonderful life." Nor, of course, can we say with any certainty that he had a wonderful life or did not—for all the Investigations is one of the most wonderful pieces of writing Western civilization has produced. I must say that in working on this text—in working my way through the various memoirs and biographies of Wittgenstein—I have felt increasingly that Ludwig had quite a hard life. Not economically, of course, but even the extraordinary luxury in which he grew up seems to have added to his alienation from other people. Take just these bits, however: part Jewish amid rising, murderous anti-Semitism; homosexual long before gay liberation; forever imprisoned in the empty if fastidiously furnished palace of solipsism; three of his four older brothers dying, killing themselves, while he was still young; a prisoner of war and a front-line soldier on the losing side—or were they all losing sides in the slaughterhouse that was the First World War?*

What the possibly apocryphal report of Wittgenstein's last words tell us is that he wanted "them"—be they his friends or perhaps his family members, living and dead; or some less definable group of others that he had long felt were opposing or misunderstanding him?— He wanted them to be told he had had a wonderful life.

I cannot help but be reminded of the last words of Plato's Socrates as reported in the Phaedo (*that is, as imagined by Plato for the text of that dialogue*). Socrates had drunk the hemlock. Phaedo tells us—so many of us, down through the ages—that the executioner, the man who had given Socrates the poison, pressed Socrates's foot hard and asked him if he could feel, and Socrates said no, and then Socrates's leg, and so upwards and upwards, showing the men gathered around the death bed that Socrates was getting cold and stiff. He was leaving behind not only his friends and those who would learn from

---

* Apparently some psychiatrists have argued that Ludwig also exhibited several features of high-functioning autism and/or suffered from a schizoid personality. My sense is that these challenges are not ignored in the present text, for all neither Abel nor I use this psychiatric terminology. Wikipedia cites German psychiatrist Sula Wolff as regards the schizoid personality, and, as regards autism, cites: Michael Fitzgerald, "Did Ludwig Wittgenstein have Asperger's syndrome?", *European Child & Adolescent Psychiatry* 9, No. 1, 61–65; and the chapter on Wittgenstein in Fitzgerald's *Autism and Creativity: Is There a Link Between Autism in Men and Exceptional Ability?* (Routledge, 2004).

or be entertained by him, he was also leaving his wife and two young sons. He had been sentenced to death by his fellow Athenians through some combination of his own refusal to compromise or bargain and their need to find a scapegoat for their fatuous political decisions and military failures.

> He was beginning to grow cold about the groin when he uncovered his face, for he had covered himself up, and said (they were his last words)—he said: "Crito, I owe a cock to Asclepius; will you remember to pay the debt?"

Traditionally, in ancient Greece, sick people who slept in one of Asclepius's temples would sacrifice a cock to him, hoping for a cure. Socrates's implication was that he, too, needed to sacrifice a cock, hoping—against hope?—that the hemlock or the death it was bringing would prove to be a cure for the ills of life.

"*Tell them I've had a wonderful life!*" Wittgenstein said.

WE CAN ACHIEVE A LITTLE MORE PERSPECTIVE *on this quotation by turning now to comments on Wittgenstein's personality. I have to say that the more I read in his biography, the more unpleasant I find him. To the point where I have stopped reading about him for fear of losing all interest in his philosophical ruminations. That said, I will begin with some of the more positive material I have collected. In particular, I found these two descriptions very helpful:*

- A graduate student reported Wittgenstein at a philosophy seminar wrestling

  visibly with his ideas, holding his head in his hands, occasionally throwing out staccato remarks, as though each word were as painful as plucking thorns, and muttering, "God am I stupid today" or shouting "Damn my bloody soul! . . . Help me someone!"[32]

- The Vienna Circle, "logical positivist" philosopher Rudolf Carnap has written:

  His [Wittgenstein's] point of view and his attitude toward people and problems, even theoretical problems, were much more similar to those of a creative artist than to those of a scientist; one might almost say, similar to those of a religious prophet or seer. When he started to formu-

late his view on some specific philosophical problem, we
often felt the internal struggle that occurred in him at
that very moment, a struggle by which he tried to pene-
trate from darkness to light under an intense and painful
strain, which was even visible on his most expressive face.
When finally, sometimes after a prolonged arduous effort, his answer came forth, his statement stood before us
like a newly created piece of art or a divine revelation.[33]

One acquaintance compared Wittgenstein to such Dostoevsky characters as Aloysha and Prince Myshkin—"a picture of stirring loneliness at first glance."[34] Another acquaintance, the English High Court judge Sir John Vinelot, said Wittgenstein was "incandescent with intellectual passion."

He was a difficult man because his honesty and directness
were uncomfortable to most ordinary people. . . . Very
withdrawn, a huge great forehead, very penetrating eyes,
but above all, when he concentrated standing up talking
to somebody . . . he had so many anxiety lines on his
forehead that they made a checkerboard. I've never seen a
human face like it in my life before.[35]

Continuing with the positive, I note that Wittgenstein could be generous and empathetic, in word and deed.

I know there is a sick man lying here? Nonsense! I am
sitting at his bedside, looking attentively into his face.—
So I don't know then that there is a sick man lying here?
Neither the question nor the assertion has sense.[36]

During the Second World War he left Cambridge University to work as a hospital orderly and laboratory assistant, inter alia, devising an apparatus for recording pulse pressure.[37]

He could also be rude, insensitive, domineering and phenomenally self-absorbed, ever the very-rich boy who expected everyone around him to cater to his needs, control their moods while indulging his, listen to him talk on and on about himself and his problems.* For all he extolled discussion, there is a sense in which he was lost to it because he could not quite understand that

---

* One observer of Wittgenstein at Cambridge refers to "his usual grotesquely arrogant, self-opinionated, rude and boorish manner." (Peter Gray-Lucas, as quoted in Edmonds and Eidinow, 17.)

it involved at least two people. Carnap writes that Wittgenstein "tolerated no critical examination by others, once the insight had been gained by an act of inspiration".[38] *G.E. Moore in his diary complained that "discussion" with Wittgenstein meant Wittgenstein talking and Moore listening.* Monk writes that dialogue with Wittgenstein was possible only if one shared his convictions (something that may be true of most of us?).*[39] *A Cambridge University student magazine of the period lampooned Wittgenstein for telling everybody off for misusing language while he himself was doing all the talking.*[40] *Russell once described his mentee as "the most perfect example I have known of genius as traditionally conceived: passionate, profound, intense and dominating."*[41] *He said no one could be more destitute than Ludwig "of the false politeness that interferes with truth".† Borrowing a phrase from Russell—"cold steel in the hand of passion"—the British philosopher and biographer Ray Monk notes Wittgenstein's combination of "a rigorously logical mind and an impulsive and obsessional nature"*[42] *Malcolm has described Wittgenstein as having "ruthless integrity." "Of the things that came to his attention in the normal passage of events, hardly any gave him pleasure and many produced in him an emotion that was not far from grief."*[43] *And, "Wittgenstein once told me that he had given away his fortune, when a young man, so that he would not have any friends on account of it, but now he feared that he had friends for the sake of the philosophy they could get out of him."*[44]

The problem with exile, as with travel, is that your self comes with you? Contrary to what Wittgenstein thought, the seed is more powerful than the soil? Or is it rather that for humans—though not for plants—the particular being once developed from a particular combination of "seed" and "soil," develops little further, even if transplanted?

---

* Monk, 102. In *Wittgenstein's Poker*, 37, Edmonds and Eidinow describe how Wittgenstein so dominated discussion at the Cambridge Moral Sciences Club, an influential discussion group for philosophy dons and students, that special meetings were organized in order to give people besides Wittgenstein a chance to speak. Finally, in the face of complaints, Wittgenstein had to stop attending entirely.

† Monk, 44; quoting letter from Russell to Morrell, March 10, 1912. Monk and others have described how Wittgenstein was a virtuoso whistler, capable of whistling whole movements of symphonies. However—as regards false politeness that interferes with truth?—during the Second World War, when Wittgenstein was a hospital employee, he would apparently stop and correct his fellow employees when he heard them whistling something incorrectly. (Monk, 443.)

*So mußt du sein, dir kannst du nicht entfliehen.
Und keine Zeit und keine Macht zerstückelt
Geprägte Form, die lebend sich entwickelt.*

So it must be, there is no escaping.
No time there is, no power, can decompose
The minted form that lives and living grows.*

It has been written that Wittgenstein took out his intense self-loathing on everyone he met.† He was known to get angry when any of his students wanted to pursue philosophy. He convinced Francis Skinner, his close friend/lover, to go to work as a mechanic in a factory, rather than pursue a promising career in mathematics.

> He would never be happy in academic life," he [Wittgenstein] decided, and Francis, as always, accepted his decision. It was not, however, the view of Francis's family, nor that of many of his friends. . . . [Francis's] mother particularly came to dislike deeply the influence that Wittgenstein was exerting on her son. She reacted with greater consternation . . . to the idea that Francis should abandon his potentially brilliant academic career. His sister . . . was equally incredulous. "Why?" she

---

* Goethe, "DAIMON," from "Urworte Orphisch," *Selected Poems*, 230. The first line I have translated myself. The couplet is in Christopher Middleton's translation in the volume here cited, 231. I have appreciated Middleton's rhythm and rhyme. It is worth noting that Goethe's chosen verb *zerstückeln* is used to refer to decomposition not in the sense of rotting, but in the sense of breaking up into small pieces, as in the dismembering of a corpse. *Geprägte*—the special character or aura—*sich entwickelt*—develops itself, as, if you will, a girl's special genes and hormones develop themselves, develop her *Form*, into its particular womanly shape.

† Richard Rorty, "The Education of John Dewey." Rorty continues: "The moral perfectionism that many found seductive made [Wittgenstein] unable to cherish those whom he fascinated."

Monk, 4, puts this more gently and in a wider context:

> It is as though his life was an ongoing battle with his own nature. In so far as he achieved anything, it was usually with the sense of its being in spite of his nature. The ultimate achievement, in this sense, would be the complete overcoming of himself—a transformation that would make philosophy itself unnecessary.

demanded. "Why?"*

Wittgenstein's student become friend Norman Malcolm concluded:

> When I think of [Ludwig's] profound pessimism, the intensity of his mental and moral suffering, the relentless way in which he drove his intellect, his need for love together with the harshness that repelled love, I am inclined to believe that his life was fiercely unhappy. Yet at the end he himself exclaimed that it had been 'wonderful'! To me this seems a mysterious and strangely moving utterance.[45]

B<small>EFORE RETURNING TO</small> A<small>BEL AND</small> M<small>ARSELINA'S CONVERSATION</small>, *I would like to say one more thing about Ludwig and his family, and, I'm afraid, about a personal experience that I myself have only begun to get in touch with after more than six decades of life. I would begin (not ignoring personal experiences) by noting something that, oddly, seems to have gone largely overlooked by Freud and many another in their interpretations of Sophocles' "Oedipus Rex". Before Oedipus succeeded, if by accident, in killing his father, his father, with his mother's complicity, tried quite intentionally to kill him. To kill his son when his son was an entirely defenseless infant, and this because the father was afraid that if his son were allowed to reach adulthood, to come to his full power, he would kill him, the father. (Of course in "real life," this killing often takes a figurative form: a son may overshadow his father or surpass him. Or, alternatively, the father may "win," keeping his son, or daughter, in his shadow, hamstringing him or her so that s/he never makes full use of his or her talents, never flourishes as s/he might.)*

What I am suggesting is that this is a way to understand Karl Wittgenstein's attitude toward his children—the boys and the girls, but the boys in particular. I came to this realization while musing on three questions. One: Why did a supposedly domineering father allow one of his daughter's—Ludwig's sister Margarete—to marry a bankrupt and psychologically unstable American fortune hunter? Why did the family, with all its resources and connections in the United States, never inquire into this man's background, and find out that he was travelling in Europe under an assumed name and had no money? Two: Why was Karl, the father, unable to support the musical interests and

---

* Monk, 359-60.

genius of his first-born son, Hans? Karl himself was a talented violinist and a tremendous lover of music and supporter of musicians, Brahms and Mahler included. Three: *Why did the Wittgenstein family, and with a good deal of enthusiasm* voire *compulsion, send all three of its remaining sons to the front lines—indeed to the nightmare that was the Russian front—during the First World War?* In fact, according to Edmonds and Eidinow, Ludwig "used his family's social connections not to avoid combat but instead to obtain a posting to the front, when an operation at seventeen for a double hernia would have allowed him to remain far from the sound of gunfire."*

I suppose the answer to this third question is more social than psychological, insofar as we recognize that as assimilationist Jews, the Wittgensteins were anxious to show their patriotism and, through their war service, to secure their place in Austrian society.† Likely we are here dealing

---

* Edmonds and Eidinow, 89-90. Traditionally, the sons of the wealthy—however patriotic and eager they may be to serve their countries and to get into the thick of the fighting—traditionally their parents find ways to get their children posts that keep them at least at a little remove from the bullets and shells. And I have read that in Austria at the time of the First World War, "writers and artists in the old imperial army were still accorded privileged status. If at all possible, they were not sent to the front but given tasks in safe institutions such as the Army Museum or the War Press Office." On this basis Egon Schiele was given a makeshift studio at an officers' POW camp, and then transferred to the army supply commissary, where his superior officer assigned him to draw the food supplies. (Fischer, 41.)

† In better times, Austrian Jews used to say, mockingly, of a fellow Jew who gave up his God to try to get ahead or save his skin: *Das hat ihm auch nicht viel genützt*—it didn't do him much good either. This from Edmonds and Eidinow, 126-27:

> [T]he Wittgensteins' first attempt to escape the clutches of the Nuremberg Laws took the form of Hermine [one of Paul and Ludwig's sisters] producing a list of Paul's and Ludwig's First World War medals—evidence of the family's courageous attachment to Austria. This category of reclassification was dealt with in Berlin, by the Interior Ministry, and the Reich Chancellery, and Hermine and Paul took the medals to "high places" there. But by 1938 the Führer was rebuking those who were forwarding such petitions: "I get buckets and buckets of such applications for exemption, buckets and buckets, *meine Parteigenossen* [my fellow party members]! Obviously you know of more decent Jews than there are Jews in the whole of the German Reich. That's a scandal! I won't tolerate it."

with what psychologists call an overdetermined event, with insufficient self-protectiveness and assimilationist anxiety combining to send three sons to the front (one to commit suicide, one to have an arm shot off, and the third, Ludwig, to work on the Tractatus Logico-Philosophicus *in a prisoner of war camp*).

Nonetheless, taking my three questions all together, and with the Oedipus legend in mind, I have come to feel that the Wittgenstein children, for all they were raised in a palace, were insufficiently protected—and not entirely unlike the infant Oedipus, exposed to bears and eagles and wolves on a mountain side. And, as with Oedipus, it seems that the lack of protection in the Wittgensteins' case was closely linked to an ostensibly powerful father's fear of being surpassed by his children and to a self-effacing, obedient wife's complicity.*

From this perspective, what seems to me most wonderful, and impressive, about Ludwig's life is how he was able to escape his toxic father, to escape Vienna and business and even music and the brutal effects of the war to some extent, and to try to live his own life. And rather than feeling the need to "kill" his own father, to triumph over him in some way, Ludwig found that he could live by, and with, simply keeping his distance. Of course his own life became a commentary on this past and this escape. But are we hoping for more? Are we—am I?—ready to accept that this degree of autonomy may constitute a wondrous, if not wonderful, life?

Ever since my wife died *I have gone weekly—and not weakly—to a psychotherapist.* At first, like most beginning patients, I assume, I was looking for a cure, or for relief at least. (For my wife not to have died? For all my regrets and regretting to have died with her?) Then there was a stage when, under the influence of Ian Craib's extraordinary book, The Importance of Disappointment, I thought the purpose of my therapy must be "learning how to suffer"; learning to accept the suffering, conflict, ruptures of life; to become aware of authentically bad, and good, aspects of relationships and of the self, of my self; to recognize my limits, our limits; to feel the disappointment and the hopes that can be found in "therapy."† But for some time now I have gone to

---

* Knowing himself willing to risk everything just to come out on top, Karl imagined that others, his sons in particular, must be willing to do the same thing?

† "Learning how to suffer" are the concluding words of Craib's book (194). The

therapy, above all, for the pleasure of the 45 minutes. To have this time, away from so many other things, to try and get in touch with what I am feeling and thinking, with what is going on with myself and with the people I am closest to and in the larger world around us.

It seems to me that what we are involved in here—we Ludwig, Abel, Marsalina and me, in the little boat that is this book; and also, perhaps, "we" in a larger sense—is what Wittgenstein in the Investigations *referred to as the rotation of our examination* "aber um unser eigentliches Bedürfnis als Angelpunkt," *about the fixed point of our real need.*[*] *Before I started working on this book, I, for some reason, thought that—for all the point in the center— mortality, consciousness, the challenges involved in being a social animal—was fixed, the rotation itself was not continual. That is, one might—I might, with the help of my therapist perhaps—rotate from a point (a)—not so good—to a point (b): better. And this even, somehow, if neither I, nor my therapist,*

---

rest of the sentence was adapted from Craib, 177-78. More, from the concluding pages (189 and 193):

> Psychotherapy . . . can enable the formation of relationships based less on the illusion of common identity than on the reality of individual separation, difference and dependence. But this achievement means recognition of the real internal pain of fragmentation, of internal conflicts and of our manifold limitations. . . .
>
> One way of putting all this is that the central value of psychoanalysis is difficulty. If I put a hand in the fire and it is burnt, I will not do it again in a hurry; psychotherapy says, in one sense, put your hand in the fire and keep it there. Psychological development depends on "staying" in the fire, to the point where we begin to understand the pain and find that it is bearable, and that it might even be used in some way. This is a process which perhaps in other ages might simply have been called "life", and it certainly has to do with being, not with doing. Perhaps one way of characterising psychotherapy is as a process of learning to be, when neither the process nor the being itself is necessarily a comfortable experience. They are experiences that are not encouraged by the modern forms of life, where the emphasis is always on doing, or on being only in the limited sense in which it is equated with immediate satisfaction.

* *Investigations*, §108: "Man könnte sagen: Die Betrachtung muß gedreht werden, aber um unser eigentliches Bedürfnis als Angelpunkt." One might say: the axis of our examination must be rotated, but about the fixed point of our real need.

nor anyone else could say what was necessarily good or better.* But it has now occurred to me that rotation may well be a continuous, uninterrupted or interruptible process.

  A rotating restaurant comes to mind for some reason, and then a faint picture of such a restaurant in Las Vegas. I wonder if my wife and I did not once, when we went to visit the Mojave, have dinner in such a place. From this perspective, rotating involves seeing above all (and "looking," to use Wittgenstein's idea). Certainly there is something soothing, even restful, in being up so high and able to look down on the world; to see the world spreading beneath your window in what appears to be a rather logical, well-organized fashion—the grid of the streets, the desert and mountains in the background. With the help of a glass of good French wine, one may feel that one is indeed on top of the world. For all one is just in an overly air-conditioned, rotating tower, and asked, before leaving, to settle the bill.

---

* See Craib (an Englishman), 189:

> It would be hard for the Chancellor of the Exchequer to say that he or she had only a limited understanding of the economy; that there were no policies that could be guaranteed to overcome the recession and no good reasons for preferring one policy over another; that cycles of recession and expansion were normal and so on. Yet the analytic psychotherapist must say something like this to prospective patients.

(2)

Manchmal richtig, manchmal falsch

Meanwhile, back in the Barnes & Noble cafe, Abel's talk about Gershom and so forth had led Marsalina herself to ask about Jewishness.

Marsalina, sounding a bit perplexed: So what you're saying, Abel, is that this whole thing about being a stranger trying to learn a foreign language and guessing right or wrong, it has something to do with being Jewish?

Abel laughed. Maybe I could write one of those books about how a text—the *Investigations* in this case—is in fact written in a kind of code; it's a Kabbalistic text. Under the guise of talking about language and philosophy Wittgenstein was actually writing about what it meant to be Jewish in Europe in the twentieth century.

Or maybe I'm underestimating myself or Wittgenstein. It's not just the twentieth century. It's the whole endless Diaspora. It's not just one stranger coming into one country; it's the thousands upon thousands of us, over too many centuries, coming into too many countries. From *das Gelobte Land* to Russia, from Russia to the Lower East Side, from the Lower East Side to Great Neck, from Great Neck to West Hollywood, and from West Hollywood to a kibbutz and never-ending war with the Palestinians. "Thou shalt be a dispersion in all kingdoms of the Earth."*

And of course the Jews are hardly the only people to have wandered, or to have been enslaved and murdered by the thousands, the millions. What

---

* Translation of "*Ese diaspora en pasais basileias tes ges,*" a phrase in the *Septuagint*, the long-revered Greek translation of the Hebrew Bible. The translation was begun in the third century before the birth of Jesus, and this is said to be the first written mention of a diaspora created as a result of exile. (Since the present work is greatly interested in the challenges of translating from one language or mind to another, I note that, according to legend (and the Talmud, *Tractate Megillah 9*), the *Septuagint* was created after King Ptolemy II of Egypt gathered 72 elders and placed them in 72 separate chambers without revealing to them why they had been summoned. The King entered each person's room and said: "Write for me the Torah of Moshe, your teacher." God then put it in the heart of each to translate identically as all the others did.)

Das Gelobte Land: the Promised Land.

about the West African diaspora—the people sold into slavery to work in the gold mines and sugar mills and on the cotton plantations of the new and improved world? What about the Latin American diaspora, the people—the progeny of the former slaves and of the indigenous people not killed by Western diseases and guns and slave labor, now driven off their land by the *Machtergreifung* of the United Fruit Company?* Or what about the landless nobility of Portugal and Spain who got the whole thing started in the first place? Fernão de Magalhães (Magellan), Francisco Pizarro, Hernando Cortes. Talk about a stranger coming into a foreign country and having to guess what foreigners' signs meant and what his signs meant to them! Talk about guessing right an extraordinary amount of the time, and saving his skin and enslaving a whole nation thereby! Here, Hernando Cortes, is human greatness personified—extraordinary cleverness and audacity and desperate optimism, and not knowing what the hell you are in fact doing!

And this is just to remain on the political level, on the level of whole peoples, when perhaps it is the individual experience—our own personal experience—that concerns us, and interests us, the most.

I heard paper rustling, Abel apparently searching for a piece of paper from which he then read the following words, as translated from Kierkegaard:

> Most men live in relation to their own self as if they were constantly out, never at home. . . . Spiritually and religiously understood, perdition consists in journeying into a foreign land, in being "out."†

---

* *Machtergreifung*: power grab, seizure of power; the word is used in the context of Hitler and the Nazi party's coming to power in Germany in 1933. *Note*: As a result of various financial transactions and name changes the United Fruit Company eventually became part of the United Brands Company, and is now part of Chiquita Brands International.

† Soren Kierkegaard, *The Book on Adler, or A Cycle of Ethico-Religious Essays* (title also translated *The Religious Confusion of the Present Age*), as quoted in Cavell, "Declining Decline," 39.

See also the opening lines of Nietzsche's *Zur Genealogie der Moral* (*The Genealogy of Morals*), here as translated by Francis Golffing:

> We knowers are unknown to ourselves, and for a good reason: how can we ever hope to find what we have never looked for? . . . Rather, as a man divinely abstracted and self-absorbed

Marsalina: Abel, *cálmate*.

Abel: I'm sorry. And, by the way, I don't think the *Investigations* is about Cortes, or about the Diaspora or the Holocaust, or even about being Jewish—or not that much. I do think that, in addition to Gershomitude, it's about language and philosophy, and on another level it is about the most fundamental problems of ethics, of knowing what we should do, how to live, of distinguishing right and wrong—of guessing right and wrong, if you will. "How is it to be decided what is the right step to take at any particular stage?" "[H]ow can a rule show me what I have to do at *this* point?"*

It's a beautiful day—here's one of the little, or not so little, conundrums I wrestle with. I go out of my apartment building, I'm on the top of the steps there, and I realize—or I feel—that it's a beautiful day. Typically, with me, this means there's a lot of sun, or perhaps a crispness in the air, or a mildness, a slight humidity. In any case, at such moments I feel that I should do something different from what I usually do. I should alter a little the pattern of my life, or of my day, in response to the beauty of the day. Is it a matter of enjoying this beauty—which would mean staying outside a little longer? going for a walk during my lunch break? Or is it more a matter of honoring or appreciating this beauty, and perhaps beauty more generally? And, I may ask myself, why have I decided that this day, or days like this, are beautiful, and others are not? And then I get in the elevator at work, going up to my floor, and I say to someone—a

---

> into whose ears the bell has just drummed the twelve strokes of noon will suddenly awake with a start and ask himself what hour has actually struck, we sometimes rub our ears after the event and ask ourselves, astonished and at a loss, "What have we really experienced?"—or rather, "Who are we, really?"

* *Investigations*, §186 and §198. A bit more of §198 (which may, *inter alia*, cause some footnote readers to recall the Duhem-Quine thesis mentioned in an earlier footnote):

> "But how can a rule show me what I have to do at *this* point? Whatever I do is, on some interpretation, in accord with the rule."—That is not what we ought to say, but rather: any interpretation still hangs in the air along with what it interprets, and cannot give it any support. . . .
>
> "Then can whatever I do be brought into accord with the rule?"

student, professor, security guard, fellow librarian, "What a beautiful day!" or something like that. And *unerbittlich* (inexorably), someone in that elevator remarks that it's too hot or too cold. To me there's a whole lot of Wittgenstein, and a whole lot of human life, in this experience.

Marsalina: I'm sorry, Abel, I'm having a little trouble following you.

Abel: *I'm* sorry, it's my fault. I was heading off again. What I wanted to say some ways back there—what I had it in my mind to say—was that, re-reading the *Investigations* this fall as part of this New School course I'm taking, one thing that strikes me is the book's obsessive quality. The text can be divided up into sections, as my professor is doing. There is some talk about "language-games" and then arguments about the "family resemblances" of words, or of our uses of them. There is the discussion of rule following and of "private language"—what would this mean?—and of pain and pain-behavior, and of seeing and mental states. But still, there we are, more than 200 pages into Wittgenstein's text and back to "when we come into a strange country with entirely strange traditions"—the line I already quoted to you. And while I don't wish to be reductive or repetitive, I can't help noting that this is simply a direct statement of Wittgenstein's particular predicament—to have come into a strange country and to have gotten in touch with the strangeness of human existence as a result.

> Suppose you came as an explorer into an unknown country with a language quite strange to you. In what circumstances would you say that the people there gave orders, understood them . . . ?
>
> Let us imagine that the people in that country carried on the usual human activities and in the course of them employed, apparently, an articulate language. If we watch their behaviour we find it intelligible, it seems "logical". But when we try to learn their language we find it impossible to do so. For there is no regular connection between what they say, the sounds they make, and their actions; . . .*

---

* *Investigations*, §206, second paragraph, and §207. The first paragraph of §206 shows Wittgenstein, again, grasping at ethics—or for order, for boundaries, I will propose at a later point in this text.

> Following a rule is analogous to obeying an order. We are

You know, I don't think I ever told you this—it must have been during that time we weren't speaking—but—

Marsalina: What time was that?

Abel: Oh, I don't know, 1995 to 2005? After Sarah moved into my apartment, and while you—or both you and me—were getting over the fact that my book went unreviewed and I was never going to amount to anything more fantastic than a research librarian.[*]

Marsalina: I don't know what you're talking about.

Abel, sadly: No. But, in any case, what I was going to say was that once, during this time, I did ten sessions of Gestalt therapy in part to try to learn, from the inside as it were, what it was all about—what Gestalt therapy was all about, in any case.

A core idea of Gestalt therapy, in my still limited understanding of it, is that if a therapist holds a patient at his or her "stuck point," change may well occur, because it is when—it is *only* when—we are in pain that we seek for solutions and are willing to take the risks necessary to truly change. And you can well imagine that at the end of the ten sessions (at $135 a pop) the therapist wanted me to continue. And he was right that we hadn't really gotten much of anywhere as yet. But I had to get away from him and his sadistic little laugh and smile. It was torture. The fly trapped in the fly bottle.[†] Every time I thought I saw a light, a tunnel through which I

---

trained to do so; we react to an order in a particular way. But what if one person reacts in one way and another in another to the order and the training? Which one is right?

[*] Googling, I discovered further that Abel had written a book on *The Emotional Life of Large Animals*, a book I have now read and with pleasure. The part that has stuck in my mind are the pages on the cruelty of our keeping social animals in solitary or semi-solitary confinement in our zoos. Readers can imagine the mixture of erudition and feeling that Abel was able to bring to this subject. But apparently, for whatever reason—he didn't know the right people? he got in a fight with his editor? he was leery of selling himself and his book?—these pages and the others on the emotional life of large animals have gone largely unread.

[†] *Investigations*, §309: "What is your aim in philosophy?—To show the fly the way out of the fly-bottle." In §133 Wittgenstein writes: "The real discovery is the one that makes me capable of stopping doing philosophy when I want to." The various memoirs of Wittgenstein give the strong impression that he never made that discovery. Few were the waking moments when he was not at work on the philosophical problems that he posed for himself.

might escape from my predicament and my feelings at that time, and from the larger challenges of my life and of life in general—every time there seemed to be a little hope—the therapist would remind me of my feelings and of the predicament or predicaments, and I'd be stuck again, with all the attendant feelings of despondency and desperation, and of stuckness above all!

In Wittgenstein's case—as with many obsessive people? or as with many people in general?—it's as if he's holding *himself* at his stuck point. Two hundred pages in he's still on square 1, as it were—square 1 of his predicament and square 1 of philosophy:*

> It is possible to imagine a case in which I *could* find out that I had two hands. Normally, however, I *cannot* do so. "But all you need is to hold them up before your eyes!"—If I am *now* in doubt whether I have two hands, I need not believe my eyes either. (I might just as well ask a friend.)†

---

* A picture comes to my mind, of a series of slowly ascending, interconnected loops. But this is not quite right. The movement of the *Investigations* does have a kind of circularity, and it does seem to build, at least for a while, to ever greater levels of complexity or mental challenge. Nonetheless, I agree with Abel: The loops keep returning to a few fundamental points.

From among the many notes of Wittgenstein's that have been published since his death:

> I do not explicitly learn the propositions that stand fast for me. I can *discover* them subsequently like the axis around which a body rotates. This axis is not fixed in the sense that anything holds it fast, but the movement around it determines its immobility. (*On Certainty*, §152.)

† *Investigations*, Part II, xi, 188e. *Cf.*, Moore, "Proof of an External World", 145-46:

> I can prove now, for instance, that two human hands exist. How? By holding up my two hands, and saying, as I make a certain gesture with the right hand, 'Here is one hand', and adding, as I make a certain gesture with the left, 'and here is another'. And if, by doing this, I have proved *ipso facto* the existence of external things, you will all see that I can also do it now in numbers of other ways: there is no need to multiply examples.

I can see him when he's writing these lines pacing around his dim little rooms at Cambridge—the rooms he had at Cambridge University—and holding his two hands up in front of his face and looking at them and wondering how he could prove their existence and how he could really doubt it.*

> What am I believing in when I believe that men have souls? What am I believing in when I believe that this substance contains two carbon rings?
>
> Does it make sense to ask "How do you know that you believe?"
>
> A dog believes his master is at the door. But can he also believe his master will come the day after to-morrow?
>
> How did we ever come to use such an expression as "I believe . . . "?⁴⁶

As part of a book I was working on—a book revolving around the current belief that children should be taught to express their feelings (as if it were children rather than adults who struggled most in this regard?)—I became interested in the sensations of amputees. For example, apparently, for some time after amputation amputees continue to feel sensation in what experts observing them from the outside refer to as the "phantom limb." And thus there is also an idea of "phantom sensations" and "phantom pain." Supposing a human being going through such a period (such a traumatic period) were asked how many hands he had. Well, it is quite clear to him—as a result of his present sensations as well as the whole history of his life up until this moment—he has two hands. (We are back to Pyrrhonian skepticism and appearances and how we speak about them.) Would it be cruel to ask such a person (as during a psychology experiment), "Hold your two hands up before your eyes." And if the subject of the experiment (the amputee) then did so? That is, if he made a movement and felt that he had complied with the request, that he was indeed holding his two hands up before his eyes?

A source: An article by Lieutenant Colonel Richard Sherman, who has been the chief of surgical research at a US Army medical center: "Pain after amputation—a lifelong problem?"

* *N.B.*: Abel is wrong about the "dim little" rooms. Apparently for most of his time at Cambridge Wittgenstein lived in Moore's former college rooms, which were at the top of a tower and offered a splendid view of Trinity College. Not finding any furniture, at any price, that he liked, Wittgenstein had his furniture custom made. (Monk, 55-56.)

Marsalina: It is only a matter of time before you crash your hard drive.

Abel: I appreciate your concern, and perhaps it is more warranted than I allow myself to think.

Marsalina: Can I make a little suggestion.

Abel: Sure!

Marsalina: Let's—finally—get to our job, this section 32. I think this might help get us away from this "stuck point." How did it go, *Ein fremd* something. There *is* something nice about that phrase. Say it in German again.

Abel: *Wer in ein fremdes Land kommt. Wer in ein fremdes Land kommt, wird manchmal die Sprache der Einheimischen durch hinweisende Erklärungen lernen.* Who into an alien country coming, gets sometimes the language of the inhabitants from ostensive definitions learning.* It rhymes.

Marsalina: So how about we just say this: The stranger comes into a foreign country, and he points and asks, and he gets some kind of response—or a no-response response—and sometimes he understands what this response in fact refers to and sometimes he does not.

Abel: You know, I've done a lot of thinking about his section—

---

* Perhaps this is the place to note that, during the years Wittgenstein was a schoolteacher in rural Austria, "*fremd*" (strange) was, apparently, "the word most often used by the villagers to describe him". The information and quotation is from Monk, 194, who goes on: Why, the villagers asked, should a man of such wealth and culture choose to live among the poor, especially when he showed such little sympathy for their way of life and clearly preferred the company of his refined Viennese friends? [Who would come to visit him.] Why should he live such a meagre existence?

To say Wittgenstein showed little sympathy for the rural Austrians is understatement at best. These people, he wrote on one occasion, "are not human *at all* but loathsome worms." He told Russell that they were not really people at all, but one-quarter animal and three-quarters human. He wrote another friend, "I suffer much from the human, or rather inhuman, beings with whom I live". (Monk, 212 and 228, citing, *inter alia*, letters to Paul Engelmann of September 9, 1922 and February 24, 1925.) Waugh, 108, quotes Wittgenstein rounding out these remarks, we might say, in an earlier diary entry, from the front during the First World War: "I am nearly always surrounded by people who hate me. And this is one thing which I still do not know how to take. There are malicious and heartless people here. It is almost impossible to find any trace of humanity in them."

Marsalina burst out laughing. You don't say!

Abel, sounding a little hurt: I have. I think even Wittgenstein didn't appreciate how complicated the matter is. The other day I overheard a colleague of mine, married to a Japanese woman, joke that in Japanese there are twenty-five ways of saying yes and only one of them means yes.

Or, for example, imagine that Wittgenstein's stranger shows up in a foreign country and he goes into a pastry shop. That's the way I've worked the thing through in my mind. There's a pastry case, and this man, an American, a Jewish-American—Gershom—he points at an object, a piece of pastry, on the other side of the glass. It looks like what he would call a "bear claw." An "almond-flavored yeast-raised pastry shaped in an irregular semicircle resembling a bear's claw." That's a definition I found.

Marsalina, softly: It's you who is obsessed.

Abel, smiling, I presume: I have another variation in which the guy is in France and he points to what the French call "un pet de nonne"—literally, "a nun's fart"—a dainty sort of doughnut. "*Queesqueso?*" he asks badly. That is, he has some faulty idea of how to say "What is this?"

Marsalina, laughing: Or "What is cheese?"

Abel: . . . in some language that is foreign to him, but not a very good idea, and not a very good idea of either the sounds or intonations of the particular foreign language spoken in that particular pastry shop. And so then the person behind the counter—a fetching young woman, let's imagine—says something that sounds to the stranger like "chabanakongkomuk."[*]

Wittgenstein touches but briefly on the matter of sounds.[†] I don't

---

[*] Luckily for me, and in more than one way, I am a fan of William Cronon's writing on environmental history. And thus, as a result, one day I stumbled, quite by accident, on another reference to this Indian word and was able to have a laugh at Abel's otherwise quite private joke. In *Changes in the Land: Indians, Colonists, and the Ecology of New England* (66), in a discussion of the Indians' and the colonists' ideas of property, Cronon notes that a few Indian place-names did make reference to possession or ownership. One of the more graphic of these is Chabanakongkomuk, which is in what has become Worcester, Massachusetts. Chabanakongkomuk was once a "boundary fishing place," and the name could be translated: "You fish on your side, I fish on my side, nobody fish in the middle—no trouble."

[†] See in particular §20 of the *Investigations*, which includes:

> Someone who did not understand our language, a foreigner,

know if you remember this from learning English when you were a kid, but one of the hardest things to learn when you are first learning a new language is what the sounds are and where the sounds break up into words or into morphemes, pieces of meaning.* Sarah, for example, always says that one of the keys to her learning French as well as she has was the time she put in studying phonetics. This not only helped her sound more like a French person when she spoke, it helped her understand French people when they spoke. But for an English speaker French is relatively easy. Imagine the strange country you come into is China. You're coming from the US to China to try to find if there are any Chinese left who will make sneakers for fifty cents an hour, and you don't know the first thing about the Chinese language except that it's foreign. You're pointing at things and people are returning sounds, but you have no idea they're speaking in tones.

Marsalina: They're trying to tell you to they'd be glad to make your sneakers, but through a subcontractor in Bangladesh.

Abel: Exactly, we might say. Only in my example, in the example I've worked up, when the fetching young woman behind the pastry counter says "Chabanakongkomuk," she means, "You know, you're the third

---

who had fairly often heard someone giving the order: "Bring me a slab!", might believe that this whole series of sounds was one word corresponding perhaps to the word for "building-stone" in his language. If he himself had then given this order perhaps he would have pronounced it differently, and we should say: he pronounces it so oddly because he takes it for a *single* word.

* Following Abel's lead, let us imagine that in a French *boulangerie*, an overly thoughtful native speaker, wishing to be helpful and not complicate matters for an American foreigner, supplies "*du pain*," the name for a genus of baked goods, when one member of the multifarious species—be it *une baguette, un batard, un pain de campagne*, etc.—is indicated. What will be the fate of this bit of learning if, say, it is next used in another *boulangerie*, the foreigner arriving and saying "dupain" (with an American accent = doopan?)?

Or, coming back toward Wittgenstein, suppose the American "learns" that the way to refer to this range of French baked goods is with the simple "*pain*"—the actual French noun being a compound: "*le pain.*" If I may be allowed my own little joke, I would reference the *Investigations*, §246: "What is this supposed to mean—except perhaps that I *am* in pain?" Yet history tells us that with the help of various approximations of the French syllable *pain* many Americans have quite successfully bought bread-like substances in French bakeries.

American to ask for one of those today." Or, "Don't worry, even at the price I'm going to charge you, you can afford it."

There you are, pointing at what you would call, in English, a "bear claw," and trying to ask in this foreign language you are just learning, "What is this?" But the person behind the counter cannot understand you and has her mind on her Groovy Netbeans studies, and she's a sales clerk in any case, not a teacher of Serbo-Croatian, Spanish, Chinese, French or whatever as a second language.* So, as she reaches to fish out one of these "bear claws" and then bags it for you, she is saying, more or less under her breath, this string of sounds that you process as chabanakongkomuk. And, we might say, she thinks that what she has said is something like an English string (which she does not know): "Don't worry, even at the price I'm going to charge you, you can afford it." But even this, her presumption, may not be correct because what is it that she has said? Is it what she *meant* to say or what she has been *heard* as saying?† Has she said, "Don't worry,

---

* Groovy and Netbeans: computerspeak. According to Wikipedia (as of 2010), NetBeans refers to both "a platform framework for Java desktop applications, and an integrated development environment (IDE) for developing with Java, JavaScript, PHP, Python, Ruby, Groovy, C, C++, Scala, Clojure and others." Groovy is "an object-oriented programming language for the Java platform."

The reference to Serbo-Croatian reminds me of something an old college classmate told me about the negotiations on the 1995 "General Framework Agreement for Peace in Bosnia and Herzegovina." Apparently, the Bosnians insisted that these negotiations (to be held at a US Air Force base in the middle of Ohio) include interpreters to render what the Serbs were saying in Serbo-Croatian into Bosnian, and vice-versa. Since, however, the vocabulary and grammar of the two languages were the same—since before the conflict Bosnians imagined that they were in fact speaking Serbo-Croatian—the work of the interpreters became to repeat, word for word, what the one party was saying to the other. (*N.B.*: There may be Bosnians—and Serbians, Croats and Montenegrins—to say that this account is incorrect; I am mixing up four distinct languages, or four dialects in any case. And, we might say, this is true, *since the dissolution of Yugoslavia*. While prior to that dissolution there was only one, Serbo-Croatian language.)

The Yiddish linguist Max Weinreich used to say that "a language is a dialect with an army and navy"—a line he apparently heard from a member of the audience at one of his lectures. In the case of the former Yugoslavia, however, it would appear that the phrase would be "a language is a dialect with a government recognized by the United Nations."

† *Cf.*, Iris Murdoch, from "The Idea of Perfection" (20): "I can decide what to say but not what the words mean which I have said. I can decide what to do but I am

even at the price I'm going to charge you, you can afford it"? Or, "Would you like anything else this morning, Sir?"* This latter being what you, the foreign pastry-buyer, has guessed from the context, from your experience in pastry shops in which it was assumed that you and the sales clerk spoke the same language, for all this earlier clerk may have herself (or himself) been Serbian, Spanish, Groovy or Hmong.†

Marsalina: Which is all to say that learning a foreign language, or learning it from ostensive definitions, ain't easy.

Abel: Listen, I found this, or some version of this, in some Cliff Notes on the *Investigations*:

> We do not understand each other because of a relationship between language and reality; we understand one another because the tool we use for mutual understanding—

---

not the master of the significance of my act."

* There is an essay to be written on this subject, and I will try to avoid writing it in this footnote. We assume that we say something specific, and if our statement seems not to have been understood as we meant it (or as we imagined, wished we meant it), then we assume we have been misunderstood, the fault lying with our interlocutors. From another perspective, however, our statements are like space vehicles, launched from one context toward another context that we may or may not well understand. And if our statements continue to travel or resonate—"to thine own self be true"; "the only thing we have to fear is fear itself"; "the meaning of a word is its use"—they will pass through other contexts. And in each new context our statements—or our words, our phonemes—will be heard differently, will have different meanings. Of course Polonius, Franklin Roosevelt or Ludwig Wittgenstein may protest from their graves: "This is not what I meant when I said that!" But there is a naïveté in this protest. Do we imagine that we can control the meanings of our words once they leave our lips? (And, again, at least of we post-Freudians it may be asked: Do we imagine that the meaning of our words, as they exit our oral cavities, is confined to what we, at that moment or another, were wishing our words might mean?) Please excuse the following R-rated and out-of-date example, from back when I was young, and the female orgasm was much discussed in and out of the bedroom: "When I said that even though I didn't have an orgasm I really enjoyed having sex with you, all I meant was that I really enjoyed having sex with you."

† The Hmong are or were an Asian ethnic group from the mountainous regions of China, Vietnam, Laos and Thailand. As a result of the Laotian civil war, in the 1970s many of the Hmong were driven from their homes, resettling in the United States, as well as in Australia, France, French Guiana and Canada.

language—presumes mutual understanding, just like a car presumes movement or a watch time.[47]

If we use the tool—language—it makes no sense to wonder if understanding between humans, between language users, is possible, just as it makes no sense to wonder if time really exists when we are looking at our watch in order to tell the time. This is not to say that we humans are capable of a level of understanding deeper than that which is choreographed by language; nor that time is necessarily some sort of cosmic ordering principle that transcends the simple fact that according to my watch it is now 3:28 or that it would seem to be time for me to get another cuppa Joe.

As, asking Marsalina if she wanted anything, Abel got up to go get another coffee, I lowered my head, staring down at my table top so that the magical quality of the afternoon, of overhearing this conversation, would not be disturbed by a glimpse of one of the real people involved in it. The human mind being what it is, however, hardly had I acted on this intention, and in acting, in observing my acting, brought this intention into my conscious mind, then I "saw" Abel and Marsalina, in my mind's eyes. He was, though perhaps only in my mind, a lanky man, with a long, thin face and with long black hair hanging down over his ears. It was as if—in this image or set of images that flashed through my mind—he was leaning, hands on the table, over Marsalina, who was a petite, taut, dark-red-lipsticked Afro-Latina woman.

As Abel was just starting for the food-and-drink counter, he said: Don't forget.

Marsalina, as it will appear, having begun to consult the messages on her cellphone: What's that?

Abel: We have been focusing on the problem of understanding others—of understanding a pastry seller—and, secondarily, on the problem of being understood when one speaks. But there is of course a third problem: Others understanding you when *they* speak. And here "understanding" might be a rather tender word. That is, I would like you "to understand" who you are speaking to, who I am, but I also would like you to "show understanding" when you speak.

Marsalina: Go get your coffee.

It was quite a few minutes before Abel returned. The line was long, the service slow, and, it seemed, he'd taken a book, his book on Magellan, to read while he was waiting. While he was still some distance from Marsalina, he began quoting from it, as full of enthusiasm as ever.

Abel: Listen to this! I was just reading this. A list of items Magellan took on his ships. *Reading from the book*: "Twenty thousand noise-makers, little bells. Nine hundred small mirrors. Fifty dozen scissors. Plus some number of colorful handkerchiefs, bracelets, combs, fake gemstones and glass beads."*

So now—*he was finding his place on the bench near Marsalina*—tell me this: Why did he take all this "junk," as we would call it?

Marsalina: To trade with the Indians—the "native Americans," the "indigenous peoples."

Abel: Because to them this was hardly junk. These were marvels. The mirrors possessed magical powers—and perhaps the scissors too. And these marvels were worth vastly more than the gold and silver that these people had in great quantity. One of the things I have been wondering lately is if this isn't one of the foundations of trade: a lack of agreement in meaning.

One of the most famous phrases in the *Investigations*, perhaps *the* most famous, section 242: "If language is to be a means of communication there must be agreement not only in definitions but also . . . in judgments." Perhaps this is just plain wrong. Or rather, in some very basic, very common contexts it's wrong. For my daughter, a package of glow-in-the-dark plastic "Silly Bandz" is worth vastly more, perhaps infinitely more, than the three-dollar allowance-advance that she is going to use to pay for it. For the owner of the stationery shop, it is rather the reverse.† My little American daughter holds up her package of Silly Bandz and smiles at this refugee from the petroleum-based internecine conflict in Algeria, who smiles down on her as he reaches to take my three dollars out of my little girl's hand. And they are smiling and getting along so well and able to communicate with one another in the particular sense of doing business with one another, and this is precisely thanks to their *lack* of agreement in judgments.‡

---

* *Cf.*, Zweig, *Magellan*, 121.

† In *Capital*, 293 (Chapter 7, Section 2), Marx observes that the capitalist does not manufacture boots for their own sake, nor is he even interested in boots' use value (to keep feet safe, warm and dry). Instead of boots the capitalist would as soon produce yarn or horse manure if either of the latter produced as much or more exchange value and profit. "Boots" for the capitalist, we might say, are not "boots" in any of the senses of the word we might find in a dictionary.

‡ William Cronon, *Changes in the Land*, 93-94:

Marsalina, sounding quite grumpy: Gotcha. And this would relate how to a bunch of strangers in a very strange country?

Abel in a self-mockingly plaintive tone and completely ignoring Marsalina's changed mood: Don't you see— Can you appreciate the trouble I'm in? I know you think I'm making a mountain out of a molehill, or deliberately confusing myself, losing myself in complexities and ignoring the text I claim to be trying to understand. But here's a smart guy, a very smart guy—Ludwig Wittgenstein. We might say that his intelligence, his perceptiveness, is a whole 'nother level of magnitude from mine. He's finding connections at a level that I do not even recognize. Or—or "and," I should say—he's finding the disconnections. He is applying all his rage, all his disappointment, all his sense of not living up to what was expected of him, what his father expected of him and his brothers, what the ethical and religious teachings of his culture, of his *Heimat*, made him feel he should expect of himself— He goes after Western thinking, some of the best of Western thinking, and he finds it confused, misguided, *Unsinn, sinnlos, bedeutungslos.**

> Indians first had to learn the uses of European fabrics and metals before they would trade for them; as Verrazzano discovered at Narragansett Bay, this did not always happen automatically. What Indians valued was often less the inherent technical qualities of a material object than its ascriptive qualities as an object of status. (In this, they were not fundamentally different from Europeans who sought to obtain animal skins so as to display personal wealth.) A kettle or metal arrowhead might have virtues that save labor and were desirable in their own right, but these did not become compelling until other Indians owned them and an individual's importance began to be measured by their possession. Indians eventually sought many of the things Europeans offered in trade, not for what *Europeans* thought valuable about them, but for what those things conveyed in *Indian* schemes of value. In effect, they became different objects. Being rare and exotic, European goods could function as emblems of rank in Indian society and as gifts in the exchanges that created and maintained alliance networks.

* *Unsinn*: nonsense; *sinnlos*: without sense, senseless; *bedeutungslos*: meaningless. My sense is that Wittgenstein inherited this condemnation from Moore. *Cf.*, Keynes's memoir, "My Early Beliefs," page 88, where he writes about Moore's method, "according to which you could hope to make essentially vague notions clear by using precise language about them and asking exact questions. . . . 'What

So this, we might say, is a bit disquieting. But you don't have to be a rocket scientist—you can just be me—and you can see that Wittgenstein doesn't have it quite right either. And you can see that, above all—and like everyone else, all the other philosophers—he is not really writing philosophy. Or he's not writing what we thought philosophy was—what we were hoping it could be? Rather more a search for fundamental answers—or fundamental questions at least—than some strangely twisted, or deflected, form of self-expression, of reaction?

> "Yes, but there is *something* there all the same accompanying my cry of pain. And it is on account of that that I utter it. And this something is what is important—and frightful."*

Sounding yet more mournful. "Life, too, is a book in which we have not found the answer." My English professor wife made that observation the other night when I interrupted her nightly reading with my obsessing about Wittgenstein. "Life, too, is a book in which we have not found the answer." Life, too, is a book in which we *cannot* find the answer. In which there is no answer to be found—or where the many answers we find turn out, at best, to be grasping—

"At straws," I believe he was going to say. But he stopped himself—finally, it seemed, grasping that something was not entirely right or the same with his interlocutor. She had been listening to him with at best half an ear. "Did you miss me?" *he asked.*

Marsalina: I was too busy getting sued for sexual harassment by a drag queen.

Abel: What!

Marsalina: I kid you not. By a good drag queen, too. My daughters and I went to see him, laughed our heads off. But he also got in the unfortunate habit of snorting coke to stay awake during government working hours, and then sending confidential communications to his most devoted fan at the *New York Times*.

Abel: So you fired him, so he's suing you for harassment. On what grounds?

---

exactly do you mean?' was the phrase most frequently on our lips. If it appeared under cross-examination that you did not mean *exactly* anything, you lay under a strong suspicion of meaning nothing whatever."

* *Investigations*, §296.

Marsalina: At two o'clock in the morning in some former meat locker on East 14th Street I asked him if he preferred waxing or shaving.

Abel: Marsalina, this is not like you, letting your guard down like that. Whatever were you thinking?

Marsalina, sharply: I was thinking we were friends. I was thinking he was my ace office manager, the person I relied on to let me know which of my dear colleagues were playing what games behind my back while I was locked up in negotiations for weeks at a time.

Abel: This is not good.

Marsalina: No, it's not good. It could be $250,000 of not good.

Abel: The money is nothing—it's not your money in any case—add another 25 cents to the sales tax or something on the phone bill and the guy's happy, his lawyers are happy, your lawyers are happy, but . . . I've got to say it's a blotch, Marsalina.* It's like Bobby Fischer moving pawn to queen three when he should have moved pawn to queen four. It's like Madonna appearing on television and forgetting the outrageous thing she was supposed to do. It's like—

Marsalina, with good humor: It's like a research librarian forgetting that in a fucking library you're supposed to keep your fucking mouth shut!

Abel, laughing out loud: Well, at least the blow to your reputation isn't affecting the richness of your vocabulary.

Marsalina: Let's get back to Wittgenstein, Shakespeare.

Abel: "Adversity's sweet milk, philosophy." *Romeo and Juliet.*†

---

* Abel is suggesting here that the governmental entity for which Marsalina works is financed in part by a tax on people's phone bills, and hence a large legal settlement could be paid by increasing this tax just a bit.

† "Adversity's sweet milk, philosophy," is a perfect example both of how language has its own, verbal, variation on optical illusions, and of Wittgenstein's proposition that language pictures "take us in" (trick us) by pointing to a particular use, and away from other, perhaps equally or more valid uses. We all "know" what is meant here: In adverse moments, when we are feeling down or overwhelmed, philosophy and philosophizing can be a comfort. But (*Investigations*, §65): "to repeat: don't think, but look!" Or (me, here): Don't look, think! Milk is what our mothers give us to help us grow. So is Shakespeare's phrase saying that philosophy is a comfort to us in our adversity, or that adversity gives us philosophy to help us grow, or that philosophy is the milk that helps adversity grow?

But where were we? There is something else I was planning to say when I was coming back with my coffee . . . and thinking about Silly Bandz . . . and (*he was trying to rewind, find what he had been meaning to say*) . . . and life and books—and ran smack into a drag queen!

What, *mamma mia*, was it?

Marsalina, glumly: Ostensive definitions, I think we were talking about ostensive definitions—pastry and ostensive definitions.

Abel, as if still wondering if this was what he wanted to say, and perhaps twiddling a plastic fork that had been lying on the table: We do not see a fork as a fork, as an object with a name.* The word "as" implies an act of interpretation, but we do not interpret what we see except in those cases where we really do entertain more than one possible interpretation. We simply see the fork and pick it up—*there was the briefest hiatus as Abel began to do as he was saying, picking up the fork*—and plunge it into our coffee so that we can cut it into more manageable pieces. The meaning of

---

§113: "But *this* is how it is—" I say to myself over and over again. I feel as though, if only I could fix my gaze absolutely sharply on this fact, get it in focus, I must grasp the essence of the matter.

§114: One thinks that one is tracing the outline of the thing's nature over and over again, and one is merely tracing round the frame through which we look at it.

On one level or at certain moments—most moments—it's obvious, ridiculously obvious, it's the first option, *obviously*: philosophy is a comfort to us in our adversity. But there are those moments—the most troubled and most interesting cases?—when we are not so sure, when we find something in the other options, or in the possibility that all three are true.

See the discussion of illusions, optical and verbal, in the "Third Interpolation," and the discussion of deceptive pictures and pointing in the segments on "decontextualizing" and "pointing" in appendices C and A respectively.

* *Investigations*, Part II, xi, 166e:

It would have made as little sense for me to say "Now I am seeing it as . . ." as to say at the sight of a knife and fork "Now I am seeing this as a knife and fork". This expression would not be understood.—Any more than: "Now it's a fork" or "It may be a fork too". [Wittgenstein's ellipses.]

One doesn't "take" what one knows as the cutlery at a meal *for* cutlery; any more than one ordinarily tries to move one's mouth as one eats, or aims at moving it.

a word is its use.

But no, wait! That's not what I meant to say at all. Now I remember what it was. I wanted to tell you this story that someone at the library told me the other day.

Marsalina: Tell me.

Abel: if you're not too upset about—

Marsalina: Eric. No. It's only money, as you said. Tell me the story you were told.

Abel: When this woman—the woman who told me the story—and her brother were in high school they ended up living in France for a few months. It had to do with their father's job. Her brother, you can imagine, an American boy, had a rather limited palate—was a bit of a food-phobe. And one day they were eating at someone's house and he was concerned about the meat that was on his plate and he wanted to know what it was before he took a bite. To help him the hostess stuck out her tongue and pointed at it. *Und nun können wir, glaube ich, sagen*—and now, I think, we can say that this boy learned the French word for tongue, which nicely is also the French word for language.*

> "*C'est quoi là—là, ce que vous venez de mettre sur mon assiette?*" What's that? What have you just put on my plate?
>
> "*De la langue, de la langue de boeuf.*" It's *some* language, it's some meaty language. "*N'aie pas peur. Mange-la.*" Don't be afraid. Eat up.

Marsalina: It's a miracle we ever understand one another, or want to—could that be your point?

Abel: "Would it not be possible for us . . . to have a feeling of being guided . . . by a spell, feeling astonishment at the fact that we agreed? (We might give thanks to the Deity for our agreement.)"[48]

But actually I think Sarah and I got a bit carried away, playing around with that French tongue story for a paper I was writing for the New School. The reason I brought the story up now is because, in all the many weeks—years—I've been studying the *Investigations*, this is the only example that

---

* "And now, I think, we can say"—the opening words of the second paragraph of §32.

has come to me of someone learning, more or less, a word via ostensive definition. I don't mean that foreigners don't point at things and try to learn nouns in this way, but do they—or how much do they—in fact learn in this way? Whereas this young American—perhaps he didn't learn how to say the word, *la langue*, or learn that this word could also mean language—but we can well imagine that, as a result of that dinner, there was firmly imprinted on his brain an association between a set of sounds, as he misheard them, and a body part.

Marsalina: So what I'm getting for my $135 is that Herr Wittgenstein's first sentence isn't quite right. It's not that this someone will "sometimes learn the language" in this way—from "ostensive definitions," from pointing—it's that on rare occasions he might learn a few bits of language in this way.

Abel: Yes, that's good. And, for another, it's damned hard to learn names in this way. We could feel as if life were too short for a stranger to even learn the names of pastries. And we might add that learning a few names of pastries, or of anything and everything else, is not the same as learning a language.

But I'm afraid that in order to understand the next sentence of our section, we are going to have to look at this matter quite differently.

Marsalina, sounding dazed; losing interest: How's this?

Abel: I'm sorry. I know it's complicated, and may seem pointless besides.

> Here it is difficult as it were to keep our heads up,—to see that we must stick to the subjects of our everyday thinking, and not go astray and imagine that we have to describe extreme subtleties, which in turn we are after all quite unable to describe with the means at our disposal. We feel as if we had to repair a torn spider's web with our fingers.[49]

And so our first thought must be—*All of a sudden Abel shouted loudly*—Why bother!

And then—I suppose because people near him in the cafe had begun to look at him, wondering why he had shouted, worried what he might do next—he began almost whispering, and I had to press my ear to the wooden partition to try to hear. The only thing I can say in Wittgenstein's defense, in my defense, is that there seems to be, nonetheless, something very engaging about this process. And you might say this is my overarching question:

Not what was Wittgenstein talking about, but what is so engaging about his talking?* And I would like to think this is not just a question for me, or for me and Ludwig and a handful of eggheaded people. I would like to think this is a question about human nature or the human predicament.

Marsalina, in a normal tone of voice: My husband never ceases to marvel at what I get out of having coffee with you. But go on, go ahead. Tell me why we have to look at this matter quite differently.

Abel, now speaking normally too: In the next sentence of section 32, which I hope we will get to soon, Wittgenstein says:

> And now, I think, we can say: Augustine describes the learning of human language as if the child came into a strange country and did not understand the language of the country; that is, as if it already had a language, only not this one.

Wittgenstein is comparing our stranger's experience in a foreign country with the experience of a child coming into the strange country of language, let's say.

Marsalina: Or Wittgenstein is saying that Augustine is making this comparison.

Abel: Yes, thank you. You're right of course. And as a rule, we might say,

---

* Along with Abel, I too like to think that Wittgenstein's work touches on many human beings' wonderings about human nature and the human predicament. What is more certain is that his work has come to engage a small army of academics in sifting through it, commenting on it and commenting on previous comments. I am curious as to why some work has this effect—as if the thinker were some kind of intellectual entrepreneur, starting a whole new industry—while other, perhaps equally rich, work continues to stand alone?

Of course the work of the stand-aloners is more likely to be forgotten (if also less likely to be transformed if not betrayed by later interpreters), but still, I think one might come up with some interesting examples of thinkers who have *not* started new industries. I believe John Dewey has been mentioned in this regard, and perhaps a long line of *philosophes* (as opposed to philosophers): Montaigne, Pascal, Diderot, Emerson, Adorno, . . . System builders would seem more likely to create new academic cottage industries, but Wittgenstein was not a system builder. Originality? Iconoclasm? Who was more original or iconoclastic than Montaigne?

Cf., also, Voltaire, "Sur M. Locke," 37: "Aristote qu'on a expliqué de mille façons, parce qu'il était inintelligible". Aristotle's work was explained in so many ways because it was unintelligible.

when Wittgenstein talks about someone else's ideas, it's to point out how wrong they are. Or not just wrong—empty, nonsensical.

So what's wrong here? That is, in Wittgensteinian fashion, we already found something, albeit a very little something, "wrong," let's call it, with the text at hand—with Wittgenstein's text. He underestimates—or seems to underestimate—how difficult it is to learn from ostensive definitions. But what he wants us to do, rather, is to focus on what's wrong with *Augustine*'s text, with *Augustine*'s apparent comparison of infant language-learning with adult language learning.

Marsalina: Does it help if I say that I have no idea what Augustine said about language learning?

Abel: You and everybody else. That is, until Wittgenstein in the *Investigations* ripped Augustine's ostensible picture of infant language learning into tiny little pieces, no one—in almost 2,000 years—seems to have realized that Augustine ever said anything, or made any particular claims, about infant language learning.

We'll get to this soon enough. For the moment, let me ask a different question. Supposing that Augustine did indeed describe the learning of human language as if a child came into a strange country, what did Augustine get wrong, what's the difference between a language-less infant and our Gershom?

Marsalina, as if grasping at straws: Gershom already knows a language?

Abel: Yes. And what does this mean?

Marsalina: I'm afraid I'm fading Abel, I can't keep up with you.

Abel, reaching to pat her arm, I imagine: *Mut!** To me the key words in our section, section 32—the key words besides our stranger coming into a strange land—are "*oft raten müssen*": often guess must. In the text the *raten*—the guessing—is italicized, but to my mind, in my reading, the *müssen*, the compulsion, is more important.

Marsalina: So why "must" Gershom guess? Because otherwise he won't get anything to eat. No pastry for you, you zero. *She laughed.*

Abel, soberly: Good.

Marsalina: Are you patronizing me?

---

* The German word for courage. "Hang in there" might be a good translation in the present context.

Abel: Sorry. And I'll stop torturing you with questions too. Here's the difference between a language-less child and Gershom. Gershom has an idea, a quite developed idea, of the uses of language: to ask for things, to ask questions!* Language, he knows intuitively, allows him to participate in *"vitae humanae procellosam societatem"*—the stormy intercourse of human life.† It allows him to enjoy the sweets, and, along with them, the salts, sours and bitters of social interaction. And Gershom also has a quite developed idea of the structure of human language, that it includes names of things.

Marsalina: That it includes questions and answers. A baby—I'm trying to remember from when *my* daughters were that age— Does there come a point when infants point and ask what things are called, when they consciously try to learn the names of things?

Abel: I don't think so. Or, I should say, my sense is that most children do *not* do this.‡ This is a behavior of adults, and of adults of a quite particular

---

* See *Investigations*, §31: "We may say: only someone who already knows how to do something with it can significantly ask a name."

† Abel is again quoting Augustine, from the same chapter of the *Confessions* that Wittgenstein attacks. As noted previously, however, the sentence that includes this phrase—the key sentence of Augustine's chapter, it would seem—Wittgenstein ignored or intentionally avoided quoting. Abel brings this ignoring up later in the conversation.

‡ In *How Children Learn the Meaning of Words* (MIT Press, 2002), 26, Paul Bloom writes:

> Young children can grasp aspects of the meaning of a new word on the basis of a few incidental exposures, without any explicit training or feedback—in fact, even without any explicit act of naming.

This it to say, *inter alia*, that the disciplined approach Augustine found in his memory of how he had learned to speak his first language, as well as the less disciplined approach of Abel's pastry buyer, may well have been unnecessary, if not counter-productive. (After Benjamin Franklin, and influenced by various calls to vocabulary building that were circulating in the United States of my youth, I made lists of words to memorize. My sense is that, in fact, I learned almost nothing in this way, though clearly, by much reading and writing, I was able to build a substantial vocabulary, and this largely passively, without any deliberate effort on my part.)

Bloom as quoted in Toom, 363. Let me here thank Professor Toom for sending me

kind: adult foreign-language learners. People who take classes or who, when they go to foreign countries, divert themselves trying to pick up some foreign words, trying to have little conversations with the locals.*

Marsalina: And so—we've already come up with plenty of reasons why Gershom guesses wrong—but he guesses right because he already knows a fair amount about this foreign language and about language more generally—about nouns and so forth. Stuff that Augustine's child does not know.

---

a copy of his article, "'I Was a Boy with Power to Talk' (*Conf.* 1.8.13): Augustine and Ancient Theories of Language Acquisition." This article not only informed the present footnote, but also introduced me to a series of excellent, post-*Investigations* articles about what Augustine was in fact saying about language acquisition, and about learning more generally. (See segment on Augustine in Appendix B.)

* *Cf., Investigations*, §3: Augustine "does describe a system of communication; only not everything that we call language is this system."

Second Interpolation

Abel and Marsalina were moving on *to Augustine and the second of the four sentences of the* Investigations' *section 32. But I—loathe to leave Gershom behind, and not seeing, at 62, any particular reason to hurry; not seeing the challenge as Wittgenstein did—as knowing how to go on with my life—but rather as finding ways to keep it from going on too rapidly, relentlessly, without me . . . * Allow me to pause to ruminate a little more on three things*:

- *how "the stranger," or any foreigner, might in fact be able to learn from ostensive definitions;*
- *the miracle of faith;*
- *how infants may in fact learn their first language.*

Abel touched on the fact that, having already learned a language, the stranger "knows," or believes, that in any language things will have names; languages involve the assumption that the world is made up of distinct objects, and languages involve assigning names to these objects.† *But there is an*

---

* Regarding going on, see *Investigations*, §179: "Think how we learn to use the expressions 'Now I know how to go on', 'Now I can go on' and others; in what family of language-games we learn their use." On one basic and often mathematical level, this idea of knowing how to go on refers to rule following, e.g., by a Mr. A and a Mr. B. §151: "A has written down the numbers 1, 5, 11, 19, 29; at this point B says he knows how to go on." On another level, which we might well call more basic, knowing how to go on with one's life is the opposite of committing suicide.

† Lest I appear a little wacky here—for readers who are saying to themselves, "But of course the world is made up of distinct objects!"—I note that for more than a hundred years now philosophers and physicists of several stripes have been arguing (along with many lovers) that the fundamental elements of the universe are not objects but relations. In his book on Lucretius, the French philosopher Michel Serres argues that our privileging of solids, over fluids, stems from Galileo and has limited explanatory power and, perhaps, limited ethical value. As for Wittgenstein, see the first proposition of the *Tractatus*: "The world is the totality of facts, not of things."

We might note that the solid-based science of Galileo and his contemporaries was linked to a desire by the powers-that-were to improve artillery calculations—to

extraordinary piece of knowledge or belief embedded in this first knowledge/ belief: what is true for a stranger, in his Heimat, *is true where other people live, for all cultures. Even in fifteenth century Homonhon (subsequently a part of the Philippines), Magellan found human beings, human beings raised entirely ignorant of Western ways, who were ready and willing to kill other human beings in order to preserve their autonomy, to reduce others to servitude, or to get more stuff or some momentary security. And as for Wittgenstein, because in Vienna when he was growing up there were distinct objects and these objects had names, he assumed it must be the same in England,* mit die Engländer und die Engländerinnen *in whose midst he came to find himself. And similarly he and his Gershom knew there must be ways of physically indicating things (a subset of "body language").*

I discuss this subject at greater length in the segment on Augustine in Appendix B, but I would note here that, interestingly, in the passage from the Confessions *that Wittgenstein excerpts, Augustine describes this way of physically indicating things: "quae fiunt vultu et nutu oculorum certerorumque membrorum actu" (by facial expressions and the movement of the eyes and other parts of the body).*[50] *Augustine also refers to* sonitu vocis (*tone of voice*) *as one of the non-verbal ways that people express themselves, but tones of voice seem not to be so universal. That is, a particular tone of voice may convey quite different meanings in quite different cultures. Take, for example, the differing intonations used to pose questions, or the way that in French and other cultures expressions of thanks offered in a certain tone mean "No" (or "No, thank you"). Thus the chances are greater that the Augustine infant/child, who is being introduced to but one culture, will find useful clues in elders' tones of voice, than that an adult stranger, with one or more already fixed and subconscious systems for interpreting tones of voice, will find useful clues in these newly-come-upon foreigners' tones of voice. This may be a case where a presumption of a universal human language is going to complicate a stranger's task, a case where a little "knowledge" is a confusing thing. But the key point here is that it is on the basis of the assumption of universality that the stranger is able to learn rightly or wrongly bits of foreign language and make his or her way, however*

---

understand solids and forces better in order to gain a military advantage. Thus now, as we would seem to be entering an era of cyber-warfare, we might conclude that not only will a lot of money continue to be invested in computer science, but all this investment and interest will make their way into our metaphysics and ontology, into our fundamental understandings of the universe, into our understandings of what is fundamental about our universe.

awkwardly or incorrectly, in a foreign culture and language.

Whole books might be written, and likely some have been written, about misunderstandings arising in a "mixed marriage"—a marriage of people from two different cultures. And of course even if you marry the girl or boy next door, there is a mixing and clashing of subcultures, and you will likely be struck at certain moments, realizing how different you are or s/he is and how you have misunderstood one another. The other side of this coin is that a marriage is nonetheless made in all these circumstances; the partners "grow together" and reach many understandings, even if some smaller or larger portion of these are misunderstandings. *It is the partners' naive presumption (in the first days of love) that they might and indeed do understand one another correctly, and on a very deep level, that allows them to join together and reach some understandings and come to realize the depth of their misunderstandings.*

It is easy enough to call this the miracle of faith, and thus a whole 'nother dialogue or essay threatens: on what Wittgenstein may have to say about this miracle and about how dependent we are on it, no matter how atheistic or anti-organized-religion we claim to be.* *The but slightly smaller point for the moment is that our "life in language," as Wittgensteinians call it—our life as a social animal, we might say—is built on faith, on the slender stilts of a faith that we can indeed understand one another, that even before we begin speaking to one another we have a great deal in common. (Think similarly of the faith of an ant that the ant just in front of him is justified in his faith that the ant just in front of her is justified in his faith that . . . "And what I shall assume you shall assume / For every atom belonging to me as good belongs to you."*†)

Wittgenstein occasionally reminds his readers, in one way or another, that it is perfectly possible we have very little in common until we begin speaking, *to include speaking to ourselves. But the miracle of language (to include of the faith it demands) is that it not only depends on, it also reifies this sense of there being a universal human experience (e.g., of pain). And language does this work independently of whether in (a very hard to imagine) a-linguistic*

---

* Abel already quoted from *Investigations*, §234:

> Would it not be possible for us, however, to calculate as we actually do (all agreeing, and so on), and still at every step to have a feeling of being guided by the rules as by a spell, feeling astonishment at the fact that we agreed? (We might give thanks to the Deity for our agreement.)

† Whitman, *Leaves of Grass*, Song of Myself [1].

existence human beings would have the same or similar experiences. To put this another way, what is universal in our experience is language; in language we find (as infants or foreigners or native adults) shared experiences. We find there are others in our world who, it seems, müssen/*must share our experiences, understand us and be understandable by us. And we are ever enthralled by this discovery, by this phenomenon—enthralled to the point that even philosophers but rarely reflect on the slenderness of the stilts on which this house of cards is built.**

---

* *Investigations*, §118:

> Where does our investigation get its importance from, since it seems only to destroy everything interesting, that is, all that is great and important? (As it were all the buildings, leaving behind only bits of stone and rubble.) What we are destroying is nothing but houses of cards and we are clearing up the ground of language on which they stand.

Certainly there is a way of reading the *Investigations*, a way that Abel would sympathize with, a reading in which Wittgenstein keeps repeating to us: "Look at the stilts. Look at the walls—the cards." Look at the building materials of our culture, of our "knowledge": They are not solid slabs, but like cards leaning together on top of stilts. Don't waste any more time thinking, look! Look at the accumulation of human knowledge in libraries, and now in databases, on flash drives, on servers. The bigger a stilt-house gets the harder it is for the residents to see the stilts. The size of the house—the number of cards it contains, the weight of all this data, information—may make those inside quite ignore any questions about stability or durability.

Cf., Wittgenstein's Viennese contemporary Stefan Zweig, *The World of Yesterday* (1-2):

> When I attempt to find a simple formula for the period in which I grew up, prior to the First World War, I hope that I convey its fullness by calling it the Golden Age of Security. Everything in our almost thousand-year-old Austrian monarchy seemed based on permanency, and the State itself was the chief guarantor of this stability. The rights which it granted its citizens were duly confirmed by parliament, the freely elected representative of the people, and every duty was exactly prescribed. Our currency, the Austrian crown, circulated in bright gold pieces, an assurance of its immutability. Everyone knew how much he possessed or what he was entitled to, what was permitted and what was forbidden . . . . In this vast empire everything stood firmly and immovably in its appointed place, and at its head was the aged emperor; and were he to die, one

Searching for an analogy I find myself regurgitating, as it were, a bit from a not very good book I found on the airplane I took to New York. The bit described how Hollywood dealmakers routinely lie to and cheat one another, and then they go out and play tennis together. What Wittgenstein is saying is that both Bilder, both pictures, have validity: the selfishness and greed as well as the camaraderie; our isolation and alien-ness, our foreign-ness to one another and to all around us, our failure to empathize and to find "real friends," and also our shared experiences, our mutual understanding, our friendships of necessity, as my 10-year-old niece calls them.

In "The Crack-Up," F. Scott Fitzgerald, wrote about the challenge of trying to hold two opposed ideas in the mind while retaining the ability to function.* To me, this well describes one of the principal reasons people have so much trouble reading the Investigations, and why so many readers, distinguished philosophers included, reduce the book's contents with one-sided interpretations: It is very hard to keep in mind, to believe, that Wittgenstein is calling attention to both sides of the coin—the vase and the woman's face in a popular optical illusion; the man going uphill and sliding downhill in one of the many optical illusions Wittgenstein offers in the Investigations. (See the segments in Appendix A on "pointing" and on "the exception.") Or to touch on an example I often use with my students: Science has taught us that the

---

    knew (or believed) another would come to take his place, and nothing would change in the well-regulated order. No one thought of wars, of revolutions, or revolts. All that was radical, all violence, seemed impossible in an age of reason.

And now Zweig (v) on what fate had in store for this Golden Age and its citizens:
    Each one of us, even the smallest and the most insignificant, has been shaken in the depths of his being by the almost unceasing volcanic eruptions of our European earth. I know of no pre-eminence that I can clam, in the midst of the multitude, except this: that as an Austrian, a Jew, an author, a humanist, and a pacifist, I have always stood at the exact point where these earthquakes were most violent. Three times they have overthrown my house and my existence, severed me from the past and all that was, and hurled me with dramatic force into the void, into the "I know not whither" which I know so well.

* What Fitzgerald, writing of personal psychological struggles, meant by this observation—the use he made of it—was quite specific and rather different from the use I am making of it here. His next sentence is: "One should, for example, be able to see that things are hopeless and yet be determined to make them otherwise."

Earth goes around the Sun, and not vice-versa, but of course we are reminded every day that the Sun goes around the Earth. A first-rate intelligence can not only accept both of these Bilder, s/he can work with them, think about what it means that both of these pictures are valid. And this acceptance of the opposition, of an opposition, of opposition, opens our eyes to a broader vista, to the possibility of many other possibilities.

Non-Euclidian geometry could offer a good example here, but if I may, I would offer the example of a "text-to-self" composition my niece Atalanta wrote in fifth grade. She was asked to compare something in a book with something in her life. First, she described a character in a novel (The Conch Bearer): *a girl, Nisha, who grew up poor in Kolkata (Calcutta) and was surprised to discover, when she finally left the city, that there could be such greenery in the world.* Similarly, once taken from Chicago to the Grand Tetons, Atalanta had been surprised by the scale, let's call it—by a natural world so much more grand and imposing than the human constructions that rise like a wall at the end of Lake Michigan. But, "at least for me," she wrote, "this one surprise made me wonder what the next surprise was going to be. Nisha and I both discovered that the whole world is not like our personal bubbles. This opened up our imaginations and we then discovered the nearly endless possibilities of life on Earth."

As for how infants may learn their first language, just about all I know is that theories, or hypotheses, abound. Nonetheless, I put together the following paragraphs in the hopes that they might spur some reflection. In a major work of philosophy from 1960—Word & Object—Willard van Orman Quine, borrowing from the then highly regarded behaviorist B.F. Skinner, proposed a model of infant language learning that is quite different from the name-based, Augustinian model that Wittgenstein's section 32 may put in our minds (for all that Wittgenstein rejects this as a model of infant language learning).[51] Skinner's approach to language has not been "without critics," as Quine notes rather understatedly. Nonetheless, I believe, the following picture remains insightful.

The picture is of an infant, babbling along, perhaps simply for the oral and aural pleasures of making sounds, of moving her tongue in her mouth and feeling vibrations and air currents—and without the least idea that verbal communication might help her get what she wants. At the first stage, at least, the child has no idea that she, like Augustine's child, might "by cries and broken *accents and various motions"* express thoughts or have her way.*

And we might imagine further that the child babbles something that sounds vaguely like "Papa," which is a typical first word not only because it is easy for a child to say and one of the first language-like sets of sounds that many children do in fact say, but also because this is why fathers are referred to as Papas—because it is so relatively easy for an infant to say "Papa."† So the child babbles something like "Papa," and Papa's face lights up with pleasure. He kisses his child and calls out happily, "She's said her first word—Papa!"

Noam Chomsky, who made a chunk of his reputation from his brilliant attack on Skinner's view of language, argued with great force that it would not be possible for a child to learn language so quickly if he did not already have a great deal of it pre-programmed, as it were, in the structures of his brain.‡ But there is insight, too, in viewing the matter from the opposite extreme: It is no harder or easier to acquire language than it is to be colonized by an imperialist power. It is not so much that others—including elders and pastry shopkeepers—try at times to teach us; more importantly, they continually presume that our utterances fit within a certain phonetic system and grammar and have meaning—meanings that they are already prepared to understand, within their *phonetic system and grammar,* within their *understanding of the world and of their and their interlocutors' places in it.* They *have a language pre-programmed for us, if you will*—for infants, indigenous peoples, the lower classes. They continually task themselves to identify "our" grammar and

---

* " . . . *cum gemitibus et vocibus variis et variis membrorum motibus edere vellem sensa cordis mei, ut voluntati pareretur, nec valerem quae volebam omnia nec quibus volebam omnibus,* . . ." Longing by cries and broken accents and various motions of my limbs to express my thoughts, that so I might have my will, and yet unable to express all I willed. (See the final pages of this book for the whole of Book I, Chapter 8 of the *Confessions,* here excerpted.)

† We might assume that in every culture the nicknames for important relatives and important nurturers of infants are derived from sounds that are easy for babies to say.

‡ The Chomsky attack on Skinner appeared in his "Review of Skinner's *Verbal Behavior.*" Apparently Chomsky, subsequently defending his attack from attack, said that the review was particularly directed at how Skinner's variant of behavioral psychology "was being used in Quinean empiricism and naturalization of philosophy." (Quotation appeared in Wikipedia article on Chomsky, accessed April 2011.)

meaning as theirs. Or, more precisely, they identify a meaning that accords with their mood, desires, views, intentions, self-interests. And they feed these sounds, grammar and meaning back to us.* "Papa" being what "I" wish to be called, and what I wish to be "your" first word, "Papa" is you have indeed said.

How many of others' actions, speech acts included, have been studied and classified by anthropologists? How many of an infant's actions, sleeping habits not excepted, are not turned into language (including body language) by her elders? Her least babbling is made phonetic, grammatical, meaningful. Excuse my repeating myself, and yet again: Our life in language is built on faith that we can indeed understand one another, that even before we begin speaking to one another we have a great deal in common.

And, returning to Gershom—who I, personally, picture not as a tourist in a pastry shop, but standing alone in an arid, empty patch of Egypt—we can note that it is often much the same for an enthusiast trying to learn a second language and for a thirsty child trying to tell a sandy expanse from a shimmering lake. Imagining he has a better grip on the language than he does, in the pastry shop Abel's Gershom may point to a pastry and attempt to ask how much it costs, and the salesgirl, noticing that one set of sounds that she has heard is akin to the nominative noun used to identify the pastry, may return this name—e.g., Napoléon—and the stranger will—müssen—take it from there. If, however poor his pronunciation may be, the stranger gets the leafy, creamy pastry he wants, he counts this morpheme, this seemingly meaningful combination of sounds, as successfully learned. Napoleon.

Furthermore, Augustine states that he learned the language of his elders in order to have his way—to better get what he wanted from them (only to find that other humans had wills too!).† But in the process his elders

---

* See also the discussion of the development of the self in Fonagy, Gergely, Jurist and Target, e.g., from page 11: "In general we might say that the self as agent arises out of the infant's perception of his presumed intentionality in the mind of the caregiver." And there is an idea in Melanie Klein (a forerunner of Fonagy et al.) that one role performed by a good parent is to deliver an infant's feelings back to the infant in a more intelligible and manageable form—and a good psychotherapist is thought to do the same for patients. See, for starters, Craib, 68 and 55, citing Donald Winnicott's work and Wilfred Bion, *Second Thoughts* (Heinemann, 1967).

† *Investigations*, §338: "After all, one can only say something if one has learned to talk. Therefore, in order to *want* to say something one must also have mastered a language; and yet it is clear that one can want to speak without speaking. Just as

channeled his infant fluidity, not only by telling him what words to use or what words he was using, but also by telling him what his will was—and that a will was something he had. ("The poor thing, he's hungry.") Or, to use more Wittgensteinian language, the ostensive definitions provided by the elders were not so much names of things as externally provided definitions of the infant Augustine's will, and it was through these definitions that the infant came to have a will, or, at the very least, came to focus on the fact that something he had could be called and thus thought of as a will—or as a wanting (the concept of "will" being as yet way beyond him).* And thus, Augustine says,*

> *non enim eram infans qui non farer, sed iam puer loquens eram . . . vitae humanae procellosam societatem altius ingressus sum*
>
> I was no longer a speechless infant, but a speaking boy . . . launched deeper into the stormy intercourse of human life

Indeed, the very next chapter, after this one in which Augustine learns to speak, begins with him storm-tossed: "But, O God, my God, I now went

---

one can want to dance without dancing."

Wittgenstein's middle proposition seems true only if in "want to say something" the "something" is something specific. One can imagine a child who has not mastered any spoken language wanting to be a part of a conversation and without having anything specific to say. As for master speakers, adults and others, often we speak without having much of anything to express besides our child-like desire to be part of the conversation, of a conversation. I note, and hardly for the first time, Georg Simmel's observation that conversation in its purest and most sublimated form "wants to be nothing but relation." People who have something specific they want to say gum up the works and are ostracized. Georg Simmel, "Sociability," 53.

* If we need another example here, and an expanding of the discussion, I would call attention to how pop music lyrics (or, in earlier ages, poetry verses) have shaped adolescents' and pre-adolescents' feelings. They do not simply give prominence to some of the things we are feeling, they also tell us what we *should* be feeling, what feeling—for instance, about a member of the opposite or same sex—should feel like. And similarly, teachers and texts tell us what we should be thinking, and it can take a graduate student several years to separate himself (or herself) from what he has been taught, and to begin, or re-begin, to think for himself. It can take all of us, *qua* lovers, seeking to love in a more honest or fulfilling way, ... It can take years, if not decades, to separate ourselves from what the culture has taught us about love, and about our feelings more generally. And, once separated . . . ? We come face to face with the void?

through a period of suffering and humiliation....

I was sent to school to learn to read. I was too small to understand what purpose it might serve and yet, if I was idle at my studies, I was beaten for it, because beating was favoured by tradition....

I begged you [God] not to let me be beaten at school. Sometimes, for my own good, you did not grant my prayer, and then my elders and even my parents, who certainly wished me no harm, would laugh at the beating I got....

We [boys] enjoyed playing games and were punished for them by men who played games themselves. However, grown-up games are known as "business," and even though boys' games are much the same, they are punished for them by their elders. No one pities either the boys or the men, though surely we deserved pity, for I cannot believe that a good judge would approve of the beatings I received as a boy on the ground that my games delayed my progress in studying subjects which would enable me to play a less creditable game later in life.

(3)

Augustine describes the learning of human language

In the cafe Abel and Marsalina were now taking up in greater earnest the second sentence of section 32, where Wittgenstein brings Augustine in. Before giving readers Abel and Marsalina's words, I would note that during this stage of their conversation, even more than previously, Abel and Marsalina both go off on tangents, and on tangents of tangents. Readers may find their patience tried. They may say to themselves something on the order of, "Are these people really talking about anything at all?"

I take this to be a reasonable question, not only in this particular case, but as regards many human conversations and texts. So I would not skip over this aspect of human experience, of our "life in language." I also think that in their bumbling, human way, Abel and Marsalina end up taking themselves and us with them, into some interesting rooms.

The Metropolitan Museum of New York comes to mind. Sometimes a tourist or local might go there in order to see a particular exhibition or to visit one of the galleries. The musical instruments, let's say. But also, some rainy day when you can't think of anything else to do, you might go up to the museum and just wander—from American furniture to arms and armor to the arts of Africa and Oceania. Because of the way the human mind works, at the end of your day you might—to yourself or in conversation with someone else—synthesize your experience, your wandering. Perhaps (if you were the artist Robert Irwin) you could conclude:

> The art world is highly invested in the idea that . . . [an] object can be moved from one environment to another without its being critically altered, which then gives rise to the illusion that it can be moved from culture to culture, that it has the ability to transcend its cultural specificity, which in turn gives rise to the ultimate illusion that . . . there exist certain objects isolated and meaningful enough to be transcendent, . . . that they are, as it were, timeless.*

---

* Weschler, 148, quoting Irwin.

> *And here would be a very intelligent synthesis, but also one that did not quite reflect your particular experience, or, more generally, the human experience, which is much more akin to wandering down various paths than to getting anywhere in particular.*

In any case, Abel began by again reciting the English text of Wittgenstein's second sentence:

> And now, I think, we can say: Augustine describes the learning of human language as if the child came into a strange country and did not understand the language of the country; that is, as if it already had a language, only not this one.

Marsalina: Well, I can see I'm in trouble yet again because now I don't know anything about Augustine, besides that he was a saint.

In a droning voice, Abel launched into a biography of Augustine: Augustine of Hippo (354 to 430 C.E.) was a Latin-speaking philosopher and theologian who lived in the Roman Africa Province. His writings were very influential in the development of Western Christianity. "*Macte virtute; in orbe celebraris, Catholici*"*—

Marsalina interrupted, making some sort of cutting or stopping gesture with her hands, I imagine. Stop, Abel. I'm only mortal, we're only mortal. I feel like I made a commitment to help you understand 108 words from one philosopher . . . We have to stop somewhere, I have to stop somewhere.

Abel: "*Die Erklärungen haben irgendwo ein Ende.*" Explanations come to an end somewhere.[52] Presumably we don't like that. It puts such a stark, ineluctable, frightening limit on everything. And yet, presumably because we are mortal, because mortality is home to us, we also get frightened when there are no limits. We have to stop somewhere, . . . Or? Immortality would threaten?

Marsalina: You know what's wrong with you?

---

* This is a famous line from a letter from Jerome to Augustine (classified as Jerome letter 141 or Augustine letter 195). "Macte virtute; in orbe celebraris, Catholici te conditorem antiquae rursum fidei venerantur atque suspiciunt." You are renowned throughout the whole world; Catholics revere and look up to you as the restorer of the ancient faith.

Abel: Talk about a subject lacking limits!

Marsalina, quietly but with warmth: It's as if I think I'm talking about one thing, and you make me feel like in fact I'm talking about something else. And so it's as if I didn't really know what I was talking about, as if perhaps I never really know what I am talking about. And so—

Abel: Wait, stop, before you say anything more. *Again the sound of rustling papers, Abel searching for something.* Let me read you something from one of the great interpreters of Wittgenstein, Stanley Cavell, a Harvard professor. *Abel read from Cavell's "Notes and Afterthoughts on the Opening of Wittgenstein's Investigations"*:

> The assertions of Augustine's memories are not, rhetorically, accosting, or insisting, as, say, Socrates's interlocutors are in stopping him on the street with their accostive certainties. On the contrary, we need not see at once anything to stop or to puzzle a philosopher, anything he might be finding remarkable about Augustine's words. I note that I had read Augustine's *Confessions* before reading *Philosophical Investigations*, and I remember wondering . . . over his passages concerning time, but not over his passages concerning the acquisition of language. So if there is something disturbing or remarkable about these words, then I am prepared to find that that is itself a remarkable fact about them. As if to suggest: one does not know, in advance, where philosophy might begin, when one's mind may be stopped, to think. . . . If we are stopped to philosophize by *these* words, then what words are immune to philosophical question?[53]

Marsalina: There you go again. I'm trying to talk about something specific, about a psychological experience, and you bring in yet another quotation and turn my psychological experience into a philosophical question. Or, at other times, you turn what seems to be a philosophical question into a psychological matter. The word "pain"—Wittgenstein's pain—your pain—mine. Why don't I just say, "You don't know what the hell you're talking about, Mr. Abel Danziger! Mr. Ludwig Wittgenstein."

Abel: Why don't you? And I'm sure Wittgenstein responded similarly when people got similarly upset with him. And of course there is little more frightening than a leader—even just the leader of a discussion—who has more questions than answers.* In our fear, we might well want to kill such a leader, eliminating him and his uncertainty right along with him. "What you're saying is intolerable!" And so we are intolerant.

Marsalina: Back to Augustine or whatever before we end up in outer space.

Abel: We are in outer space, my dear. Spinning like a top on our little ball of matter and rocketing around a not particularly distinguished star like a very speedy tether ball on a very, very long rope. And so . . .

Marsalina, with a certain impatience: And so what?

Abel: And so let me propose that to explicate the second paragraph—our last three sentences!—let's adopt a different way of proceeding than the one we followed for the first paragraph. Let's first briefly review the experience of the Augustine infant/child which Wittgenstein is comparing to the stranger's experience of paragraph 1, but now let's look at the analogy of someone coming into a strange land from a child's perspective. "Little by little I began to realize where I was and to want to make my wishes known to others, who might satisfy them. But this I could not do—" I'm quoting from a part of Augustine's *Confessions* that Ludwig may have skipped over. Perhaps he could have proposed that here was something that might be called a "private language"—a collection of language-like signs that do not do as much signifying as an infant, or an adult, might wish. These signs may give us—we infants, we adults—a certain satisfaction—the satisfaction that comes from getting something off our chests—along with the dissatisfaction that comes from no one seeming to understand what we are trying to say, what we feel—from we ourselves not understanding what we feel, what we are trying to say, that we are trying to say something. But this the infant Augustine could not do because his wishes were inside him.

> My wishes were inside me, while other people were outside, and they had no faculty which could penetrate my mind. So I would toss my arms and legs about and make noises, hoping that such few signs as I could make would show my meaning, though they were quite unlike

---

* Bouwsma, "The Blue Book," 181:

> And now it would be natural to say that since the author [i.e., Wittgenstein] is manifestly aware of these questions, and must know that these questions cry out and have been crying out for centuries for answers, that he does not answer is a bad sign.

what they were meant to mime.

From Wittgenstein's perspective, this model, Augustine's model, is false, misleading, because it implies that, prior to acquiring language, or to being acquired by it, a human being could have a way of making something of his or her experience, of having hopes and meanings. Nonetheless—and I think this is interesting—nonetheless, and even if we should agree with Wittgenstein about the falseness, still we can, if you will, feel Augustine's pain.* And we can recognize, too, that this is not just a predicament of infancy, of human beings who have not learned how to talk the talk—

Marsalina: Or walk the walk.

Abel: Yes, they are just, like so many of us, crawling the crawl. But I had been hoping that at this point—when we got to the second paragraph of our text—we were going to get up off the mat, as it were, and adopt what we Americans like to call a "positive attitude."

Marsalina: It's not?

Abel: You mean, it's not positive? or, it's not an attitude? I suppose I'd say it *is* an attitude, a type of posturing, but not a positive one. That is, the positivity has always seemed to me only skin deep, or only whitened-teeth, trained-smile deep. Underneath lies the slough of despond, a bottomless pit of despair, and of sinning against—betraying—one's own self.

Marsalina: Aren't we in a sunny mood today!

Abel: In another lifetime I am going to write a book *In Praise of Negativity*. I've been making notes and numbering them, like Wittgenstein. Did it ever occur to you, for example, that, from a scientific perspective, from an electromagnetic perspective, positivity is positively repellent and attracts the negative?

Marsalina: I might be a case in point.

Abel laughed out loud. You're sharp, very sharp.

Marsalina: That's what my boyfriends—my colleagues—say, but it's not usually a compliment. Let's go back to cell block 32. How many words was it again?

---

* "I feel your pain" is a line attributed to President Bill Clinton. Wikiquote traces this to a response of Clinton's to AIDS activist Bob Rafsky at the Laura Belle nightclub in New York City on March 27, 1992.

Abel: 102 words in German, 108 in English.

Marsalina: So how many can we have left?

Abel: Do you mean, "When will we be done, for Godsakes?" Or, say, "How much oxygen do we have left?"

Marsalina: Either one.

Abel: In fact, I think we've slipped out of cell block 32 to the recreation yard.

Maraslina: How's that?

Abel: We've finally gotten to the excerpt from *Lieder* I, *Kaputt* 8 of Augustine's *Confessions*, the excerpt with which Wittgenstein begins section 1 of his *Investigations*.* In less than an hour, Marsalina, we've managed to get to the very first page of the book!

Marsalina: *Magnifico.*

Abel, reading:

> When they (my elders) named some object, and accordingly moved towards something, I saw this and I grasped that the thing was called by the sound they uttered when they meant to point it out. Their intention was shown by their bodily movements, as it were the natural language of all peoples: the expression of the face, the play of the eyes, the movement of other parts of the body, and the tone of voice which expresses our state of mind in seeking, having, rejecting, or avoiding something. Thus, as I heard words repeatedly used in their proper places in various sentences, I gradually learnt to understand what objects they signified; and after I had trained my mouth to form those signs, I used them to express my desires.†

---

* I.e., *Liber* I, *Caput* 8—Book I, Chapter 8.

† In 2009 the classical scholar Tarmo Toom offered a more modern rendering of this passage:

> My grasp [of language] made use of memory: when people gave a name to an object and when, following the sound, they moved their body towards that object, I would see and retain the fact that their object received from them this sound which

In our section 32, second sentence, Wittgenstein has stated that Augustine's description of infant language learning—the description appearing, or seeming to appear, in this excerpt—it's as if a child (a *Kind*) came into a strange country and did not understand the language of the country. Why? Again, we're reprising, reviewing some of what we've already discussed.

Marsalina, with a smile in her voice: I see, since we're "reprising," and with a positive attitude, we'll let the girl provide the answers.

Abel: Gender mainstreaming—that's what my friends at the UN call it.

Marsalina: While the world is passing men by. You're like horses after the invention of the automobile.

Abel: Oooh-la.

Marsalina: In any case, do you know what I want to say—about those words you read me, from Augustine?

I imagined Abel shaking his head. He didn't know.

Marsalina: Well, don't you think—I mean, I'm sure you *do* think—this is a very odd child.

Abel: Well, he was a saint, or became one.

Marsalina: Yes, fine, perhaps that explains it. But otherwise, are we really supposed to believe that an infant child is sitting there, observing carefully what his "elders" are saying, what objects they are referring to, and he is storing this data in his mind like a computer, or like one of these superlogical adults you come across sometimes.

Abel: Like a computer programmer, perhaps. A person who, in lieu of connecting with people, makes a life—a perfectly good life, we might want to say—among what he and his homologues in other cubicles call "code." A person who believes that all of life can be reduced to, or can be, has been, built up out of such code—be it HTML or CGAT (DNA code).* There is a code for sickle-cell anemia, a code for the ocean, a code for love. "*L'universo e' scritto in linguaggio matematico,*" as Galileo put it. The

---

       they pronounced when they intended to draw attention to it.
       . . . I gradually gathered the meaning of words, occurring in their places in different sentences and frequently heard.

* I.e., DNA is "written" in four nitrogenous bases: cytosine, guanine, adenine and thymine.

universe is written in mathematical language—is defined by, or perhaps simply is, a set of equations.⁵⁵

> We are in the grip of calculations. From the square footage of our homes, through our iron levels, the resolution of our TV screens, the memory of our computers, right up to the financial cost of global warming—everything that concerns us gets turned into numbers. We turn the body into a weight, intelligence into a test result, the past into a genetic code and our anxieties into insurance policies and risk assessments. Here is what we mistakenly call realism: this obsessive resorting to numbers, without which our perceptions as well as our thoughts have come to seem invalid.*

Marsalina: You're losing me again, and I am still wondering about this child, the baby Augustine. It seems to me that, as you would say, we have two options.

Abel: And what would those be?

Marsalina: Well, we could decide that the adult Augustine, the *Confessions* writer, was fantasizing a bit, or was "*un-sinning*," wasn't that one of your Wittgenstein words? He has some adult idea of language learning that he wants to put forward, and he's imposing it on this little child, half-imagining that this is what he himself was really like when he was little. I suppose, giving a saint the benefit of the doubt, he did not mean for us to take him so literally, to look so carefully at what he was saying. He was trying to make a more general point about how children learn by listening to adults. But of course a child—there's no way a child could know all these things.

Abel: Well, we do have Chomsky. I'm afraid it's been a while since I've read any of his books, but as I recall, his idea is that we humans can only learn language as fast and as well as we do if we have a built-in "language acquisition device" which includes some sort of proto-grammar. And also, I presume, this device would have to include some sort of subconscious system for understanding the relationships between the grammatical

---

* I'm taking what my students call a Webucated guess here. I think this could be Abel's—or his wife's?—translation of cover copy from Isabelle Sorente's *Addiction générale*.

categories and between sounds and meaning. So then—*rete mirabile!*—an infant—little baby Augustine, for example—uses bits of experience, things he hears, reactions to things he utters, to transform his innate proto-language into this non-proto, this "real" language that he is now learning to speak.*

Marsalina: Very nice, but, excuse me, this is not what Wittgenstein is trying to get at.

Abel: No, or I don't think so. That is, one is always teetering on a seesaw with Ludwig. Is he trying to "ac-cent-tchu-ate the positive," to see the half-full aspect of the glass?† Is he trying to say, "Look at all we must have in order to learn language, and, more generally, in order to be able to communicate with one another, to be able to understand one another, as we certainly can"? Or is he throwing mud, showing what fools we are, showing that we don't know what the hell we're talking about it? "My aim is: to teach you to pass from a piece of disguised nonsense to something that is patent nonsense."‡

---

* *Rete mirabile*—"wonderful net," or network. Perhaps that was exactly what Abel wished to say: An infant's capacity for language is like a wonderful network or net, for catching things, being caught, getting caught up in. Wikipedia-ing, I find that the term *rete mirabile* is also used to refer to a complex of arteries and veins lying very close to each other, something found in some vertebrates, and also, we might say, in infants.

† "Ac-cent-tchu-ate the Positive" is the title of a pop song, written during the Second World War by Harold Arlen and Johnny Mercer, and subsequently performed by Bing Crosby, The Andrews Sisters and Ella Fitzgerald, among others. Mercer said he got his starting phrase—"you got to accentuate the positive and eliminate the negative"—from the African-American preacher and spiritual leader Father Divine. Two verses:

> You've got to accentuate the positive
> Eliminate the negative
> Latch on to the affirmative
> Don't mess with Mister In-Between [Mister Wittgenstein?]
>
> You've got to spread joy up to the maximum
> Bring gloom down to the minimum
> Have faith or pandemonium
> Liable to walk upon the scene

‡ *Investigations*, §464. Brian McGuinness, in discussing Wittgenstein's writing in his biography of the "young Ludwig" (304), uses the felicitous analogy of systole and diastole.

Marsalina: The emperor has no clothes.

Abel: Is it the emperor, the philosopher, our distinguished President, or the whole rag-taggle lot of us? You know—you work in Brooklyn, I don't know if the President ever goes to Brooklyn—but here in this black hole of money and power, we often suck 'im in. And not just the President, but his whole asteroid belt of limos and SUVs, with the gun tips sticking out of the windows and the whirling gunships overhead, and the lines of police on motorcycles like in Dr. Seuss. Watching, you can have a feeling of the power of the man and of the office—to be able to command such protection, and when your average Minister of Foreign Affairs is making his or her way to the airport with only one or two cars, three or four guns. But then there is also a feeling of weakness: to need all this protection, and to be in hiding somewhere behind one of the hundreds of tinted, bullet-proof windows, punching buttons on a Blackberry to find out the half-time score of a basketball game, or to tell his girlfriend he'd like to be her tampon—or eating her sandwich without the crust, . . .*

Marsalina: If we dug deep enough we'd find a point here? Something to do with something we were talking about?

Abel: Is this disguised nonsense or patent nonsense? Do we take refuge in language and, say, in our whitened smiles and bullet-proof glass, or by these means are we, the real us—the real frightened, insecure, desperately pretending us—revealed? A leader might be able to lead a dozen knights across a field to attack another dozen knights, but to run a huge country,

---

* There are a host of references here. The Dr. Seuss comment refers to *And to Think That I Saw It on Mulberry Street*. ("It takes Police to do the trick / To guide them through where traffic's thick . . . They'll never crash now. They'll race at top speed / With Sergeant Mulvaney, himself, in the lead.") The "tampon," I presume, is a reference to an amorous telephone conversation between Prince Charles and his future princess, Camilla Parker Bowles, in which Charles expressed a desire to live inside Camilla's underpants. And the sandwich with the crust cut off refers to a supposed taste of President George W. Bush's. Apparently—or was this just leftwing gossip? or a rightwing press agent's creation to show Bush to be a man of the people? or part of Bush's acting the part of a man of the people? or part of Bush's acting because for him, as for most people, "just being himself" was too hard, or too painful or frightening? In any case, apparently at least on one occasion orders were given that crustless peanut-butter-and-jelly sandwiches should be waiting for President Bush in a hotel room where he would be stopping in his travels. As, presumably, such sandwiches had been waiting for him in his first-grade lunch box. I take this—this childishness—to be Abel's point in recalling this story.

with a budget in the trillions, nuclear weapons and all the rest—no. This clearly is a charade, and we're all caught up in the charade because we're deathly afraid that if we actually looked and saw our president and ourselves in all our nakedness, . . .

Marsalina: It would be frightening.

Abel: It is frightening!

Marsalina: Which bring us to my option 2.

Abel: Which is?

Marsalina: Well, I guess it is that it would be frightening if the emperor was not wearing any clothes, or might not be wearing any. Or certainly a leader with more questions than answers, like you said. It might be frightening to think that I'm spending my days and nights in stuffy, windowless hotel rooms arguing with other people about who's to get 10 cents more, who 10 cents less. And now, in the midst of this chaos, this charade, you're trying to tell me that this philosopher and saint—Saint Augustine—who we've been reading, looking up to, taking orders from all these years—he didn't know what the hell he was talking about? Imagining that—what? 1 year old?—he was able to studiously observe how words were used "in their proper places." When he couldn't have yet learned that were proper or improper places to take a dump—never mind places for nouns, the names of things. You've gotta be kidding me, Augie baby.

Abel, with a big smile, I assume: And yet, again, here is one of the great classics of the Western canon, of Western literature and thought. A book that has been read by countless students and scholars over many centuries, and as far as we know, until this one Austrian—Ludwig Wittgenstein—came along in the twentieth century, no one said, "Hel-lo, anybody home?" "If you're talking nonsense here, Augie baby, what other bridges are you trying to sell me?"

You know, in fiction writing there is this idea of "suspension of disbelief": in order to relax into the story, the myth, we have to turn off some part of our critical faculties and accept that a prince might well marry a commoner or that Lolita's mother was not in fact prostituting her daughter to get Humbert Humbert to marry her. It's the same thing in philosophy. Here we are in philosophy "ostensibly" trying to get to—or get at?—the truth, but in order to engage whole-heartedly in this ostensible pursuit we need to turn off some part of our critical faculties, we have to accept as true something that, if we stopped to reflect, we would not in fact accept.

I find this in so many of the classic works of philosophy I pick up. Early in the work, there's a claim made—and usually it's featured as obvious, "everyone agrees that" such and such. And—sometimes, not always, I presume, but sometimes—something about the claim or about this "everyone agrees that," "it's so obvious" line, something makes me stop and ask myself, but does everyone believe this? do I believe it? is it believable?* The worm of doubt creeps in, and the rest of the book, the rest of the argument, is, as it were, ruined for me. The book becomes at best a kind of historical or psychological document. This is what someone once wrote; this is a text or human being that has been taken very seriously, for some reason that is not directly or not entirely explained by the text itself, which is founded on at least one unsupported, if not ridiculous claim.

Marsalina: Which is presented as "so obvious."

Abel: Exactly. What did Paul Krugman say? I was just reading this. There's "a certain level of misunderstanding," he said. In fact, "important people have no idea what they're doing."[56] He was talking about world leaders, I believe, but certainly begging the question as to whether *New York Times* columnists or Nobel Prize-winning economists or world-renowned philosophers—

Marsalina: Or research librarians.

Abel: Certainly, right up there at the top, research librarians. Remember all those "sexy" bumperstickers—nurses do it with a hypodermic needle? loggers do it with a chain saw? Research librarians do it with allusions.†

Marsalina: One of your little jokes. Homemade.

---

* An example I found in Hume, *Treatise of Human Nature,* Introduction, 45 (the fifth page of the text):

> For nothing is more certain, than that despair has almost the same effect upon us with enjoyment, and that we are no sooner acquainted with the impossibility of satisfying any desire, than the desire itself vanishes. [My underscoring.]

† Unlikely that either of Abel's examples appeared on bumperstickers back in the day when such bumperstickers were in vogue. On a website offering an extensive compilation, clearly going beyond the old bumperstickers, I did not find Abel's examples, or anything about loggers, but there were plenty of more likely possibilities, such as: "Nurses do it with care," "Lawyers do it in their briefs," and "Librarians do it by the book." (http://www.dkgoodman.com/doitm-r.html#top and http://www.dkgoodman.com/doitg-l.html#L — consulted in 2011.)

Abel: Yes, thank you. But my point is—I can say this about myself, my profession: It's as if we're never finding anything out *for ourselves*, but always for someone else.

He began self-mockingly riffing off some lines in Matthew Arnold's poem "The Buried Life":

>And we have been on many thousand lines
>And we books and articles by thousands find
>The triumph, satisfaction, the chest-swelling pride!
>Hour upon hour, day after day,
>For professors countless, if unheralded they,
>While hardly, the humble librarians, have we
>For one little hour—

Marsalina: Earth to Abel, come in please.

Abel: I know. I'm making a mess of a beautiful poem.

Now he recited from the poem correctly, and with feeling:

>And we have been on many thousand lines,
>And we have shown, on each, spirit and power;
>But hardly have we, for one little hour,
>Been on our own line, have we been ourselves—
>Hardly had skill to utter one of all
>The nameless feelings that course through our breast,
>But they course on for ever unexpress'd.
>And long we try in vain to speak and act
>Our hidden self, and what we say and do
>Is eloquent, is well—but 'tis not true!

Just this very morning I managed to track down the original German text of the petition some German businessmen sent to Hindenburg in November 1932, asking him to appoint Hitler Chancellor. Document 3901-PS, exhibit USA-837, in *Trial of the Major War Criminals before the International Military Tribunal*, Nuremberg, 14 November 1945 - 1 October 1946; Vol. XXXIII, Official Text, English Edition, Documents and Other Material in Evidence, Numbers 3729-PS to 3993-PS.

I may have some of the numbers wrong, but the frightening thing is that I probably don't. They've made a home for themselves in my brain like bubble-gum under a lunch counter. Weirder, I have the strange feeling of somehow—and this very morning—having—finally? in May 2009?—stood up to the Nazis, spoken out against the Holocaust, because I found this document for a professor of history who, for all I know, wants to use it as part of his proof that the Germans weren't so bad after all, they didn't really *want* to kill the Jews, they just wanted to make some money during difficult economic times, improve their P/E ratios.

We—we Americans—are obsessed with sports because in sports, at least, the goal becomes crystal clear: winning. Winning at basketball, winning at baseball, winning at figure-skating. And but rarely—when an athlete gets cancer or a coach gets caught breaking the rules, something like that—do we pause to ask ourselves whether either this particular winning or winning itself is a very worthy goal? Or whether the Saints winning, or the Patriots or the Giants, has anything to do with us. Or whether, perhaps—this is *never* asked—whether the point of all this winning, and losing, is not to distract us from the fact that we, too—it's not just our leaders and our librarians—have precious little idea what the heck we're doing or why. We don't know if it's important to be winning or losing, *and* we don't know if we are, in fact, winning or losing. Or perhaps we do know that last part—we're *looo-zers*, those miserable creatures on whom we cannot heap enough scorn. Winning is everything, we've been taught to believe, and we're losing.

Excuse me for bending your ear here, but to me at least there's an important point buried in here—an important point not only about "us" and "everything," but also about Ludwig Wittgenstein and his *Investigations*. I don't know that much about how cons work, but I think that if I did I could make the connection.* The con gets the mark to accept as absolutely true something that is in fact implausible, and then everything builds from there. Even though winning is as hypothetical, let's call it, as everything else, it—winning—is everything, the only thing, and you can't give up. No pain, no gain.

Marsalina: Even though you're not even getting paid minimum wage, you can own a home and get tax deductions too—until your mortgage "balloons" and the sheriff's deputies are dragging your sorry-ass mattress out to the curb.

---

* Apparently some of Wittgenstein's fellow Viennese philosophers, such as Otto Neurath, came to regard Wittgenstein as a con man. (Edmonds and Eidinow, 159.)

Abel: It's a beautiful country.

Marsalina: I am assuming you know it's hardly just *this* country. My—

Abel, laughing: But surely another country can't have THIS pain!

Marsalina: I'm afraid— It's my sense that a good deal of what keeps people all over the world "together"—what keeps nations together and keeps individual brains, psyches together—is this thing you're calling a con. "If it sounds too good to be true, it is true." We don't need the reality—we can't have the reality—this phrase can't be true—but we have to believe that it is.

Abel: "Hey, you never know."

Marsalina: What's that?

Abel: An ad for the lottery. "The meek shall inherit the Earth." An ad for the Bible. If only everyone could just shut up and accept that everything labeled "sure thing," "so obvious" and so forth is in fact true. The meek shall inherit the Earth and winning—inheriting like little Luki Veetki!—is everything.* If only truth were whatever we claimed it to be. Or, in fact, perhaps this is precisely what the truth is. "Wars produce many stories of fiction, some of which are told until they are believed to be true."† We might revise Wittgenstein's the meaning of a word is its use: in fact, *repeated use* is the key. The truth of a proposition stems from, depends on, its repeated use. Be our truth that the world was created in seven days or that only the strong survive, and we and all the organic life around us are consequences of this law being enforced by the Abdominal Snow Hand day after day for 4 billion years.‡

---

* The "Veetki" is Abel's expansion of Ludwig Wittgenstein's childhood nickname "Luki."

† Ulysses S. Grant, *Memoirs*, Chapter 67: Negotiations at Appomattox, 555.

‡ I am guessing that the Abdominal Snow Hand is here taking the place of Adam Smith's "invisible hand" by which we promote larger social ends which were no part of our self-interested intentions. In *The Wealth of Nations*, Smith provides this example:

> It is not from the benevolence of the butcher, the brewer or the baker, that we expect our dinner, but from their regard to their own self interest. We address ourselves, not to their humanity but to their self-love, and never talk to them of our own necessities but of their advantages.

Perhaps what happens when we sense that it's just a fantasy, or just claims, just propositions—when we hear an assertion that makes us a little suspicious, like Augustine's about how as an infant he first started down the road toward conversing with God—perhaps what happens is that some part of our unconscious, something like the internal "censor" Freud talked about, something in any case, intervenes to try to stop us from stopping and asking ourselves, "Is this really true?" "Could this really be true?" Or are we just floating on a bunch of hot air, on a plane to nowhere? If this "censor," or whatever we should call it, is in fact successful, as he or she usually is, we accept the con and are thereby freed to go on with the pursuit of truth or money or conversations with God or whatever, free and happy in the knowledge that at the end of this rainbow what we want and what will be are One. Speak and it shall be given. I suppose this could be what's in an infant's head when or she first begins speaking.*

Marsalina, as if having tuned out somewhere in the middle of Abel's wanderings. Or, more exactly, it was as if, like a skin diver or a whale, she had plunged below the surface of the conversation. Her own thoughts had continued on their way as she swam on, out of sight, and now, breaching, she began speaking from the point at which she, alone, had arrived. All the various things people say when they think they are in love. When they are telling themselves, "This must be love!"

There was a quietness. I imagined Abel a bit stunned by this unexpected intervention and by the hard, emotional, scornful edge in Marsalina's voice.

Marsalina began again: A lot of people are simply not capable of love. I don't know how that idea has gotten into my head, but it seems to be stuck there. A lot of people are simply not capable of love. People have their careers. Maybe they have someone at home to bump into in the

---

See Book IV, Chapter 2 for the hand, and Book I, Chapter 2 for the butcher, et al.

* In fact, "speak and it shall be done," and variations on this line, come to us from the Old Testament (Ezekiel 12:25), where this is presented as a power not of humans but of God. Or might we think of this as wishful thinking on God the father's/God the infant's part? E.g., from the King James Bible: "For I *am* the Lord: I will speak, and the word that I shall speak shall come to pass: it shall be no more prolonged: for in your days, O rebellious house, will I say the word, and will perform it, saith the Lord God." In the case of many infants, though not all, it can be said that they come to discover that no matter how they speak the house remains rebellious, does not bend to their wills.

kitchen when they're getting their coffee and cereal. Someone to talk to about their careers, or to sit next to them watching their favorite television show. I see the people in my building who have nothing but a little dog to dress up in the wintertime and take outside twice a day to shit. Which shit they carefully, dutifully, lovingly pick up. Every day, a few more bags of loving shit.

I imagined on Abel's face some contortion of sympathy and concern. Perhaps he reached to touch Marsalina and she shrugged him off. She wasn't done speaking.

Marsalina: There's something else I wanted to say. There are quite a few things I want to say, but let me start with this. Thanks to your Mr. Wittgenstein you seem to have stumbled upon the extraordinary fact that communication between human beings is not always that great. There are a lot of things people are unable to say—maybe they don't have the words, maybe they are afraid of getting fired or left alone, maybe they are alone, there really isn't anyone to hear what they want to say. You don't need to go to a pastry shop in Yerevan to realize this.* This is something people—ordinary people—are dealing with every day, in offices, at their homes.

Another break. Marsalina seemed to be touching on aspects of life, aspects of her own life, that she did not have much experience talking about. She was not speaking with the confidence or fluidity she had before. More than that: I had the sense she was using some version of what Wittgenstein or a Wittgensteinian would call a misleading analogy. That is, I had the sense now—and also later on, long after the conversation was finished and I had time to reflect—I had the sense that there was a "THIS pain," but Marsalina wasn't ready to talk about it or didn't know how to talk about it, had not yet "found the words," as we say. So instead Abel and I got this sort of misleading analogy, as if—if I may wax Abelian—as if Gershom, back in the pastry shop, were trying to learn the Aboriginal name for bear claw by pointing at a cheese Danish.

Abel: I'm listening.

Marsalina: I'm just going to say this for now. A big part of my job, of labor relations, is listening carefully to the bullshit people are saying. Listening

---

* Yerevan (or Erevan) is the capital of Armenia and one of the world's oldest continuously-inhabited cities, dating back to the eighth century BCE. After the First World War, Yerevan became the capital of the Democratic Republic of Armenia as survivors of the Armenian genocide settled in the area.

to the bullshit and responding to it as if it were ice cream.

Abel: Example please.

Marsalina: "If this is all I take back to the membership they'll have my head" might mean: "If you can make it look like we forced you to concede to this deal, we're good with it."

And so, Mr. Wittgenstein, here's a language game for you. When you respond—when I respond—I respond both to the words that have been spoken and also to what was not spoken but was really meant. The union president says, "If this is all I take back to the membership they'll have my head." I say, "Well, just because we like your head so much, Frankie, we're prepared to go to the press with such and such an offer."

My side puts an offer on the table that is much worse than what I have just proposed and, more or less, gotten agreement on. Both sides plan to meet again in two days, which gives Frankie and his boys and girls enough time to shoot their mouths off to the media, hold a big rally. Two days later my side "caves in." We agree to the offer we had aready proposed, the offer Frankie said his members would reject.

Abel, admiringly, lovingly and mockingly: Nice. And to think that the end result is that working people end up with a little less and labor lawyers with a little more. Language games can be such a wonderful thing.

Marsalina, still speaking softly, but regaining her former force: Fuck you too, Abel. If I'm not mistaken, your union's the one that was forced to accept only 18 paid holidays a year—Christmas, Yom Kippur, Martin Luther King and Obi-Wan Kenobi. Talk about working people taking it on the chin.

Abel: We simply don't believe in discrimination, to include discrimination against people getting to spend an afternoon talking philosophy with an old friend, or getting to sleep in sometimes, having whole days with nothing planned in advance. Having spaces in their brain that are not so taken up with to-do lists and urgent irrelevancies and pushing and shoving to get to be the chief assistant to the assistant chief . . . There's actually some room for random, unexpected thoughts. Or for some kind of thinking at least.

Marsalina: At the taxpayers' expense.

Abel: Seriously, Marsalina, this is what's so screwed up about THIS country. Eighteen paid holidays is a violation of the natural order of things, but not making $1 billion a year speculating in the capital markets or raiding pension funds or selling people electronic products they don't need and that within the year will be sitting in some landfill adding their toxicity to the previous years'. People hear—some boot-licking employee of a media mogul hears—that some union has negotiated 18 paid holidays for its members, and it's an outrage. That librarians—or better, schoolteachers—are paid a fifth or a tenth or a hundredth of what the lawyers or p.r. flacks or corporate raiders and financial speculators make: this is not an outrage, it's somehow part of the natural order of things.* And it's time to fire all the teachers. Obviously they've failed us, because instead of learning to pay our teachers well, we have learned to give thieves million-dollar bonuses and tax breaks. And no one ever says, "Eighteen paid holidays a year, that sounds good! Everybody should have that!" "Defined benefit pension plans, what a great idea! Why did we ever decide that it was better to get rid of them?" "Let everybody have health care—now there's a good idea." "Let's make sure the food we eat is not poisonous." Eureka! I'm a genius! What an incredible idea!

Marsalina: If I'm not careful, you're going to start quoting Marx again.

Abel: I might. And we might have to throw out everything we've said heretofore and focus on the extent to which trying to decipher Wittgenstein, and many other activities like this, are first and foremost ways of not confronting the social realities. Instead of actually thinking about the lives we are living. Between a rock (capitalism) and a hard place: capitalism. Workers of the world unite. You have nothing to lose but your cellphones. "The philosophers have only *interpreted* the world . . . ; the point, however, is to *change* it."[57] There's some Marx for you. Instead of addressing the lives we are living, we tell ourselves that we must, or must first, think on a deeper level. What does the word "life" mean? "As if our logic were, so to speak, a logic for a vacuum," or, let's say, for a so-called "flight attendant" or "balloon mortgage."

---

* It would seem the word "flack" comes from the German acronym for *Fliegerabwehrkanone* ("airplane defense cannon") or *Flugabwehrkanone* ("flight defense cannon"), from whence the word came to mean "anti-aircraft gun" and then "anti-aircraft fire." From there it took a few decades to get to flack as "adverse criticism," and from there to the public-relations professional who is paid to fabricate and deploy anti-adverse-criticism fire—thereby himself, or herself, becoming "a flack." (From Wiktionary entries for "flak" and "flack," consulted April 2011.)

* I assume Abel was not trying to put down flight attendants, but rather to get at ideas like flight/escape, or a logic for people who have intentionally stuck their heads in the clouds. The logic-in-a-vacuum sentence may be found in the middle of *Investigations*, §81. What might be called a Marxist reading of Wittgenstein is offered as a segment of Appendix C.

(4)

So, als käme das Kind in ein fremdes Land

There was a pause which I used to run to the bathroom as fast as my legs could carry me—and every step of the way cursing the pinched bladder of an aging man. When I got back Marsalina was asking where "we" (she and Abel) had left their infant saint.

Abel: On the rug, trying to get all his elders words *"locis suis posita"*—placed in their places. Here is an idea of right and wrong (or proper and improper, if you prefer). A place for every word and every word in its place.

Marsalina: So how do we get from here back to our Gershom, how do we make the connection: the child on the rug, the man in the pastry shop?

Abel: The confection, you mean. Or the *con*fection.

Marsalina: Control your infant self for a moment at least. Presumably what Wittgenstein is saying is that the two people, the Augustine child and the stranger coming into a strange country, they both faced—or might appear to face? *only* appear to face?—many of the same challenges: that is, to guess what objects were being indicated and to guess which sounds were names for those objects.

Abel: Very good, Marsalina! You're blossoming into a philosopher right under my very eyes.

Marsalina: You're a good teacher.

Abel: Sarah says that too, watching me with Celeste: I've "missed my calling." Ah well. If that's all I've missed.*

---

* One observer has said of Wittgenstein:

> He was an absolutely marvellous mimic. He missed his vocation: he should have been a stand-up comedian. In his funny Austrian he could do all sorts of mimicry of accents, styles, ways of talking. He was always talking about the different tones of voice in which you could say things, and it was absolutely gripping. I remember one evening he got up from his chair, talking in this funny voice, and said something like, "What do we say if I walk through this wall?" And I remember realizing that my knuckles were going white gripping my armchair. And I really thought that he was going to go through the wall and

In any case, we now have our Wittgenstein saying that it is as if the Augustine child already had a language, only not the one he was learning. Is this just because the stranger does? That is, is Wittgenstein claiming that since they're alike in several respects, the child and the stranger may be assumed to be alike in this one?

Marsalina: No, of course not. Let me think.

Abel: Do you mean, let you think without speaking? Or think—talk to yourself? Or is the expression "let me think" really a request for time—say, for the subconscious to do mysterious work? To which the name "thinking" is applied?

Marsalina: How can I answer one difficult question when I'm being bombarded by a dozen others?

Abel: Sorry. "Why I dislike holding to one point is that it injures the *tao*. It takes up one point and disregards a hundred others."*

Marsalina, ignoring Abel's last remark: It's what we already said: the names. That's the issue. Can I say that's the whole issue, or the crux of this section or something like that? I mean, it seems to me that what Wittgenstein is saying is how, if the child did not already have a language, how could it know that things that were being physically indicated and spoken about had names?†

> that the roof was going to fall in. That must have been part of his spell: that he could conjure up almost anything. (Peter Gray-Lucas, quoted in Edmonds and Eidinow, 24. My underscoring.)

* Mencius; as quoted in Goody and Watt, 338, citing I.A. Richards, *Mencius on the Mind* (Kegan, Paul, Trench, Tuber, 1932), 35.

† Abel and Marsalina's task *might* have been easier if they had started at the beginning of Wittgenstein's book. In the very second paragraph, right after he quotes three sentences from the *Confessions*, Wittgenstein writes:

> These words [i.e., Augustine's], it seems to me, give us a particular picture of the essence of human language. It is this: the individual words in language name objects—sentences are combinations of such names.—In this picture of language we find the roots of the following idea: Every word has a meaning. This meaning is correlated with the word. It is the object for which the word stands.

I.e., it is this "picture" of language, a conception popular at Cambridge University

But how can the child know that there are names if he has no language? Or—what fun! I feel like I'm getting it!—isn't Wittgenstein saying—or trying to call our attention to the fact that learning that things have names and learning language—or one's first language—somehow go hand in hand?*

---

during Wittgenstein's time there, that Wittgenstein is *ostensibly* trying to combat.

* If I might here pause to do a few mental stretches, I would first note that Lacan, among others, took one, Wittgensteinian step farther the view of our life in language that Marsalina has just outlined. "*C'est le monde des mots qui crée le monde des choses, d'abord confondues dans l'*hic et nunc *du tout en devenir.*" It is the world of words that creates the world of things, initially mixed up in the here and now of universal becoming. ("Fonction et champ . . . ")

Secondly, I would note that, as regards children, present-day child development experts say that up to a certain age a child does not distinguish himself from others, his mother most notably. We might say that the infant has things mixed up, but, in fact, he has no things. He is lacking both an idea of "other" and an idea of "not other," and without these the world can have no definition, and no objects. An infant has the 1 or *is* the 1, but he has no 2, and thus no 3, 4, 5 . . .

So then, thirdly, let us note the timidity in Lacan's "*d'abord confondues.*" This phrase—in contrast to the closing "*du tout en devenir*"—suggests that initially there are, say, tables, chairs and beds, or at least stars, stones and apples; it's just that without words we cannot tell them apart. Or perhaps we have a kind of kaleidoscopic view, with bits combining and recombining, boundaries ever shifting or shiftable. Students of the past—of Homeric Greece and well before, of the Neanderthals and Cro-Magnons, speak of the "fluidity" and "permeability" of our minds during these ancient times. This seems a grasping at a false sense of security, a wish that there really be something—somethings—outside our language.

I find myself coming back, as I often do, to a philosophical question that was greatly energized by an article of Quine's ("On What There Is"). Along the way to making other points, Quine floats the idea that all possible object(s) deserve only one name—e.g.: "possible object."

> Take, for instance, the possible fat man in that doorway; and, again, the possible bald man in that doorway. Are they the same possible man, or two possible men? How do we decide? How many possible men are there in that doorway? Are there more possible thin ones than fat ones? How many of them are alike? Or would their being alike make them one? Are no two possible things alike? Is this the same as saying that it is impossible for two things to be alike? Or, finally, is the concept of identity simply inapplicable to unactualized possibles? But

Am I a genius or what? Give me another question!

Abel: I'm afraid it's not going to be sufficiently challenging now that you're high on self-expression.

Marsalina: You mean my next answers are going to be as full of themselves as my last ones.

Abel: No cause for shame there. Sartre wrote on amphetamines. Was this because he knew that it's all a confidence game, or that it doesn't matter as much what you write as that you write a lot?

Marsalina: Sartre, schmarte. My speciality is Wittgenstein! *She laughs.*

Abel: OK, we've made it to sentence 3. Just two or three or four more questions and you're off the hook. Wittgenstein says it's as if the child could already think, only not yet speak. "*Als könne das Kind schon denken, nur noch nicht sprechen.*"

Marsalina: You're right, too easy. It's as if the child could—or did—already

---

what sense can be found in talking of entities which cannot meaningfully be said to be identical with themselves and distinct from one another?

From this perspective, it seems to me, it is also the case that prior to language there is/was only one possible object. In the beginning—to include in the beginning for a child—there is just the 1 (the One). There is no idea of plurality or of objects, nor is there any denial of plurality or of objects. All is One. And similarly there is, if you will, a secondary beginning point at which there is light—light is One—but there are no points of light (e.g., no stars). There is no discontinuity and thus no continuity; no discreteness and hence no indiscreteness. A word like "stars" identifies a later moment at which, with the help of language, this Oneness is no more, or when it has become, like life in the womb for an adult, an imagined experience, an imagined wholeness, to long for and regret having lost, when the light has, if you will, been blasted into bits.

"After great pain, a formal feeling comes." There come to be stars, or stars come to be part of our worlds, our experiences. And, interestingly, these emanations from astral bodies come from so far away and at such different distances from us that what we are seeing at a precise moment in a specific night sky is the seeming evidence of physical processes that occurred in very different eons. And yet for us, it is all happening now, "in the sky tonight" . . .

Luckily I can claim to be wandering too far off the track and thus avoid trying to prove claims that, in fact, stretch my mental capacities to their breaking point. I can pull in my wings, bow my head and sit back down, stretched at least. ("After great pain": Dickinson, poem 122 or 341.)

think that things had names.

Abel: And, last line, "'think' would here mean something like 'talk to itself'". "*Und 'denken' heiße hier etwas, wie: zu sich selber reden.*"*

Marsalina: Harder. I suppose the point is that the child—or the fake child, Augustine's obviously embellished memory—was telling itself these things we've been calling thinking. I mean, it told itself, "Things have names," "My elders are indicating things and referring to them with sounds." But I don't see where Augustine says this.

And what about subconscious "thinking"—or whatever you want to call it? Even the adult stranger, he doesn't have to—in fact, unless he's a linguist or a philosopher he's not going to say to himself or to others that things have names, or that such and such is the way people physically indicate things—"ostensively"—and so forth. All this knowledge is . . . Can I call it "sub-linguistic"?

Abel: We might need some term like that. And, if you insist, we could come back here tomorrow to discuss Wittgenstein's later work as a response to Freud's discovery of the unconscious—assuming that something beyond consciousness can be discovered and that some of your nails have come undone.† There's a nice line in Part II of the *Investigations*: "*Ich habe jetzt*

---

* Notes from a 1946 seminar have Wittgenstein asking about what it meant to speak to oneself? "Is this something fainter than speaking? Is it like comparing 2+2=4 on dirty paper with 2+2=4 on clean paper?" (And which, we might ask, would be the clean, which the dirty?) Edmonds and Eidinow, 8, quoting notes taken by Kanti Shah at Wittgenstein's seminar of October 25, 1946.

† Two paragraphs from Ray Monk that well encapsulate one aspect of Wittgenstein's conception and speak to this question of an unconscious. The distinction between two types of proposition, Monk writes (468):

> lies at the heart of Wittgenstein's entire philosophy: in his thinking about psychology, mathematics, aesthetics and even religion, his central criticism of those with whom he disagrees is that they have confused a grammatical proposition with a material one, and have presented as a discovery something that should properly be seen as a grammatical (in Wittgenstein's rather odd sense of the word) innovation.
>
> Thus, in his view, Freud did not discover the unconscious; rather, he introduced terms like "unconscious thoughts" and "unconscious motives" into our grammar [our language] of psychological description. Similarly, Georg Cantor did not dis-

angenommen, daß ich selbst nich träume." I have assumed here that I do not dream myself.* I have assumed here that I do not have my own nails. We might take this as a commentary on the whole of the *Investigations*. I-Ludwig have assumed—because otherwise how could "I" write a book?—that compared to everyone else I have a privileged perspective, I have knowledge, even if it is only, like Socrates's knowledge, the knowledge that I don't know. But this is, of course, a fantasy. If what I-Ludwig am saying is—if by some incredible stroke of luck it happens to be—true, and whether I ever come to know of this luck or not, the implication is that I am as lost and found in the life of language as everyone else. I have assumed here that I do not dream myself, but of course I do.†

It's nice, too, that the German word for "dream" (*Traum*) comes, like our "trauma," from the Greek word for a "wound" or "damage." One wonders how many Germans wake up feeling refreshed.

But I'm afraid I'm going to let you down. We've come to the end, our last line: "It's hard to surrender life at the approach of inevitable death." Well, actually, that's not our buddha, Ludwig, that's *the Buddha*. *The Sutra of 42 Sections*, perhaps the closest to perfection that a writer has ever come.

The Buddha said: "There are twenty things which are

---

cover the existence of an infinite number of infinite sets; he introduced a new meaning of the word 'infinite' such that it now makes sense to talk of a hierarchy of different infinities. The question to ask of such innovations is not whether these "newly discovered" entities exist or not, but whether the additions they have made to our vocabulary and the changes they have introduced to our grammar are useful or not. (Wittgenstein's own view was the Freud's were and that Cantor's were not.)

* *Investigations*, Part II, vii, 157, 157e. *Cf.*, Alice Crary's introduction to *The New Wittgenstein*, where she proposes (1) that Wittgenstein traces "the sources of our philosophical confusions to our tendency, in the midst of philosophizing, to think that we need to survey language from an external point of view." Our difficulty (from Wittgenstein's perspective) is, Crary writes (6), "one of coming to recognize that the idea of such a point of view creates the *illusion* of understanding".

† I.e., I am beginning with an assumption I know to be false in the hopes that in this way I can arrive at some true thoughts? In mathematics the pursuit of such hopes is called *reductio ad impossibile* or *reductio ad absurdum*—proof by contradiction.

hard for human beings.... It is hard to come into contact with things and yet remain unaffected by them.... It is hard to refrain from defining things as being something or not being something.... It is hard to help others toward Enlightenment according to their various needs. It is hard to see the end of the Way without being moved.

Pardon me. I'm taking refuge in superficial erudition; the wiles of a librarian.

Marsalina: But I demand nothing more from you than superficial erudition. As his timesheet attests, my husband doesn't spend a lot of time in these kinds of conversations. And, I might add, he is nonetheless routinely called upon to say—to say with confidence—how words are being used and how they should be used in the future.

Abel: "So we do *sometimes* think because it has been found to pay."* But

---

* *Investigations*, §470. The context is provided by §466-69:

> What does man think for? What use is it?—Why does he make boilers according to *calculations* and not leave the thickness of the walls to chance? After all it is only a fact of experience that boilers do not explode so often if made according to these calculations. But just as having once been burnt he would do anything rather than put his hand into a fire, so he would do anything rather than not calculate for a boiler.—But as we are not interested in causes,—we shall say: human beings do in fact think: this, for instance, is how they proceed when they make a boiler.—Now, may not a boiler produced in this way explode? Oh, yes.

And thus §467:

> Does man think, then, because he has found that thinking pays?—Because he thinks it advantageous to think?
>
> (Does he bring his children up because he has found it pays?)

And §469:

> And yet one may say that thinking has been found to pay. That there are fewer boiler explosions than formerly, now that we no longer go by feeling in deciding the thickness of the walls, but make such-and-such calculations instead. Or since each calculation done by one engineer got checked by a second one.

And thus to §470: "So we do *sometimes* think because it has been found

let me see if I can't get back to one of your earlier points. I suppose one way of looking at it is as the source of Jerry's great talent. That is, we can imagine that he has a lot of fancy clients and a high hourly rate not because he went to Williams and Yale, or because of the people he met at those schools, or because of the prestige and campaign contributions of his firm, his willingness to turn a blind eye to certain harsh realities, let's call them, but—

Marsalina: Wake me up when we get to Albuquerque.

Abel: OK, excuse me. But my point, nonetheless, is that your super, Jerry, knows, as—

Marsalina: We'll just let that one go.*

Abel: *Danke vielmals.* (Thanks a million.) My point is that your husband knows "without thinking," without talking to himself, when, for example, his clients should and when they should not worry about the legality of their various machinations—their various efforts to move money from other people's columns into their own. I, by contrast, have to talk to myself, often for days, about many *seemingly less significant*—or at least lower-dollar-value—decisions, and even then, and to a large extent therefore, I am constantly making mistakes. But your Jerry, at least as I am imagining him, he does not have to go through the time-consuming and error-introducing process of putting his "thoughts" into words. And similarly, neither children nor adults need to have ever verbalized that things have names in order to be able to learn names. Nor do children or adults need to recognize consciously that something is being physically indicated. Our stranger in a pastry shop does not say, even privately to himself, "The pastry shopkeeper is pointing to a bear claw."

Marsalina: Or nun's fart.

Abel: *Le lutin.* That's what Sarah and Celeste call it. There's *le lutin*, the goblin who gets into our butts and makes foul smells and percussive sounds.

Marsalina: In my household it's Con Ed.† "Will somebody please call Con to pay."

---

* In New York City, "Super" is a short form of "superintendent," or of "apartment-building superintendent"—a colloquial way of referring to the person who looks after the trash, the boiler, the cleanliness of the common spaces.

† ConEd is a large public utility which sells gas and electricity to New Yorkers.

Ed!"

Abel: Wittgenstein apparently once said that a serious philosophical work could be written that would consist entirely of jokes, however . . . He wasn't joking.[58]

Marsalina: Which is what makes his remark laughable.

Abel: You really don't need me.

Marsalina: Have you been thinking I did?

Abel, in a dreamy tone (or a mock dreamy tone? I'm not sure): Let's just say there was a time . . . When you bought new shades for my windows.

Marsalina: I just didn't want the whole neighborhood to see you naked.

Abel: Just you.

Marsalina: I don't know what the hell you're talking about! And I can only hope you've been keeping this fantasy to yourself.

Abel, with a Cheshire cat smile, I imagined: Don't worry, your secret is safe with me.

Marsalina: Abel, there is no secret. I want you to tell me there is no secret. And I don't want you to be giving anyone—did you hear that—*anyone* the impression there is.

Abel: Yass boss. And now if you could stop yapping and finally let me say what I've been trying to say.

Marsalina burst out laughing: That's too good! I should stop yapping.

Abel: I know, you think I've been doing a fair amount of talking too, but—

Marsalina: I think *what?* You're something special, my friend.

Abel, with a mock mournfulness: I'm afraid I'm going to have to take that as a compliment. I was hoping to be able to do a little useful summing up.

Marsalina: Do your summing up, big guy. Twenty-five words or less.

Abel: Wittgenstein—you may remember him—"as if the child could already think, only not yet speak." Not, already could speak, only not yet think, by the way. I don't know why he never took up that possibility. In many ways it seems the richer field. I might have some good examples ready at hand.

Marsalina, laughing: I'm not sure you have any words left, however. You'll have to let the yapping bitch take over. The point is, your friend

Wittgenstein's point is: thinking may not be at all necessary for language learning, but if thinking involves words, we learn to think as and because we learn language.

Abel: *Mazel tov*. And if, *Bat Mitzvah* girl, the rabbi could get a word in here, I would add that Wittgenstein may also be suggesting that, because thinking is language-based, the specific language we learn—the language of our elders—shapes or establishes a range of possibilities for our thinking.

Marsalina: And so when Wittgenstein says "'think' would here mean something like 'talk to itself'"?

Abel: The point here may be precisely that thinking is *not* talking to oneself, or not simply that.*

No, this can't be right. Perhaps we have to say something like: There may well be non-linguistic mental processes, but we can sense the content or import of them only indirectly—only insofar as they are manifested in behaviors: in statements, physical expressions, actions, all of which are mediated by and come to be understood through our life in language. And, more generally, there are various penumbrae of phenomena, let's call them—sublingual unidentifiablenesses onto which many of us project names like "knowledge," "belief," "understanding." As with your husband's rapid "thinking," or knowing what to do and say "without thinking," so in other cases we only get an idea of these penumbrae in the effects—ideas, statements and so forth—that they seem to engender. The bottom line is clear, but how the hell did we get there? After how many machinations, how much denial and wishful thinking?

Marsalina: You've reminded me of a joke. Here, listen, Abel, I'll tell you a joke. Two guys are sitting in a bar, and one says to the other, "What was the greatest invention of the twentieth century?" Have you heard this one?

I imagine Abel shook his head, No. I had not heard the joke either.

Marsalina: Good. One of the union reps told it to me and I told it to Jerry

---

* I like to think that Wittgenstein is not "teetering on a see-saw," as Abel proposed earlier, but rather, he is simultaneously interested in both sides, the up and down, the yes and no, and even more in the possibility that we function and dysfunction without being able to distinguish up from down, without being able to establish which is right, or what is right, of if rightness is a useful criterion for our evaluations. And without our even recognizing—most of the time, except in moments of crisis, when capacity really matters, or seems to really matter—our incapacity.

and now he's telling everybody; it's become his favorite joke. The one guy says, "What was the greatest invention of the twentieth century?" and the other guy says, "I dunno, the credit card."

"No, seriously," the first guy says. "The airplane, television, nuclear weapons, antibiotics, computers—which do you pick?" Which do *you* pick, Abel?

Abel: Me? The greatest invention? Safe sex. Assuming there is such a thing.

Marsalina: *Bzzzt.* Wrong. The thermos.

Abel laughed, an easy, happy laugh.

Marsalina: I knew you were going to like this joke. So the second guy says, "The thermos! What's so great about the thermos? It keeps things hot, keeps things cold."

"Yes." This is the kicker, the punch line. "Yes, but how does it know?"

I heard her slap Abel playfully.

Abel: Have you ever thought of throwing over labor relations and becoming a philosopher?

Marsalina: What do you mean, a philosopher? A comedian.

Abel: Philosopher, comedian, it's just semantics.

Marsalina: I guess you could be a comedian too. We could be a team.

Abel: Burns and Allen, Marte and Danziger.

(5)

Und verstehe die Sprache des Landes nicht

Abel and Marsalina are about to enter a sort of philosophical thicket—a spiny, and perhaps also wooden, tangle of Wittgenstein, Augustine, Lacan, Plotinus, Lucretius, and God only knows who all else. In preparing the references for this part of the conversation, I found myself writing footnotes of such length that they threatened to drown out Abel and Marsalina. I decided, therefore, to move all this explication and commentary to Appendix B. Readers who like to have their background material in advance—those with a tendency to read an editor's introduction before plunging into an author's work—may wish to pause now to see what this appendix has to offer. It is divided into segments: Plotinus first, then Augustine and Wittgenstein. The segments are not free-standing, but knit together. The final segment includes my deepest plunge toward a psychobiographical understanding of Wittgenstein and his Investigations.

Marsalina: I told my secretary I was going to the beauty parlor, so I'd better show up tomorrow with some ostensible nails.

Abel: Going to the beauty parlor—that's a reasonable excuse for leaving work at 2 o'clock in the afternoon?

Marsalina: Anything is a reasonable excuse when you've spent the previous evening singing the praises of a vice-president who's just been pushed over the side.

Abel: Meaning?

Marsalina: Rewarded for decades of not always honest or competent service with new golf clubs and early retirement.

Abel: "America has a genius for great and unselfish deeds."*

---

* This is a quotation from Ronald Reagan/Pope Pius XIII, courtesy, I presume, of one of Reagan's speechwriters. Apparently, as part of his remarks at the First Annual Commemoration of the Days of Remembrance of Victims of the Holocaust, April 30, 1981, Reagan said:

> [I]t was the Pope [Pius XIII], at the end of World War II, when the world was so devastated, and yet, we alone remained so strong, who said: America has a genius for great and unselfish

Marsalina: Which is why I need to get my nails done.

Abel: Perhaps more sharpened than polished.

Marsalina: Ah, but you don't understand—the polish hides the blood.

Abel: Now I understand my low mood when Sarah comes back from the beauty parlor. It's not—or not just—that I find nail polish unattractive, I—

Marsalina: You're afraid.

Abel: I think I am. I think that's a good way to put it—afraid, or maybe just jealous. The polish seems much more important—and gets so much closer—than me. But . . . In any case, as regards this afternoon's program of work, I hate it to say it, but there's one more thing I need to mention.

Marsalina: What's that?

Abel: You can tell this to your manicurist: Wittgenstein quoted Augustine out of context.

Marsalina: That's sure to catch her attention, and particularly since she's Korean and the only English she has learned in her first eight years here is "Policegidtip."

Abel: Kriegsüberwachungsamt.*

Marsalina: If you say so.

---

  deeds, and into the hands of America, God has placed an afflicted mankind.

Reagan and his speechwriters may well have also used this phrase on other occasions.

* Perhaps Abel was alluding to the possibility that some force was interfering either with the manicurist's ability to communicate, or with Marsalina's ability to understand her. At the time of the First World War, the Kriegsüberwachungsamt, or KÜA, was the censorship department of the war office in Vienna. I have read that one of its challenges was dealing with the cheerful letters prisoners of war were sending back from Russia to their families in Austria-Hungary. Although the prisoners' treatment by the Russian authorities was horrendous, and thousands of the prisoners were dying of typhoid, diphtheria and other illnesses aggravated by little food, little heat, overcrowding, beatings, forced labor, lack of sanitation and medical care, and so forth, . . . The prisoners were ashamed to have been taken prisoner (rather than dying nobly in battle); they did not want to upset their families; *and* they had to get their letters past the Russian censors. Waugh (75) records the KÜA issuing the following order on Christmas Eve 1914:

Abel: Kriegsüberwachungsamt—chabanakongkomuk—policegidtip—at some level isn't one string of sounds as good as another?*

> Letters have been received lately from our prisoners of war in enemy countries. In some of these letters the writers describe life in captivity in a very favourable light. The spreading of such news among the troops and recruits is undesirable. The military censors are therefore to be instructed that such letters from our prisoners of war as may, by their contents, exercise an injurious influence are to be confiscated and not delivered to their addresses.

It sounds straight out of *Catch-22*. Waugh gives as his source Alon Rachaminov, *POWs and the Great War: Captivity on the Eastern Front* (Oxford, 2002). In 1914, for example, 96,000 prisoners of war were brought to Omsk in Siberia. By August 1915, 16,000 of them were dead (Waugh, 81).

* On some level, the answer may be no. That is, going back to the Stoics, to the pre-Socratics and likely before, we have had an idea that there must be some connection between the sounds of our words, or of some of our words, and the phenomena to which they refer. In the *Cratylus* (428D-E), Plato has Socrates attribute to the eponymous pre-Socratic philosopher the idea that "the correctness of a name consists in displaying the nature of the thing it names." For the Stoics, in the beginning of the word, of language, natural sounds mimicked some characteristic features in the things that provoked these sounds. Such onomatopoetic sounds, in turn, helped to identify particular things when these sounds were made again. Eventually, the natural sounds developed into vocabularies and languages as these were conventionally imposed in various linguistic communities by people less attuned to the rational order (λόγος) of the world and more neglectful of the link between "primary sounds" and things.

The Stoics were greatly interested in etymology, believing that it offered a way to get back to this original connection between language and the world. Or, borrowing from a phrase of Quine's which is discussed in Appendix B, we might say that the Stoics, and many others, have hoped that in a connection between sounds and things we might indeed find at which edges the human-made fabric of language touches experience.

There is more on Stoic views of language learning in Appendix B. The quotation from the Stoics given here is from Toom, 362. He in turn cites James Allen, "The Stoics on the origin of language and the foundation of etymology," in Dorothea Frede and Brad Inwood, eds., *Language and learning: Philosophy of language in the Hellenistic age*; Proceedings of the Ninth Symposium Hellenisticum (Cambridge University Press, 2005): 14-35; and Michael Frede, "Principles of Stoic Grammar," in John M. Rist, ed., *The Stoics* (University of California Press, 1978): 27-76. It is worth noting that, in addition to "rational order," the Greeks used the word λόγος (*logos*) to refer to a range of phenomena, including words, speech and

Marsalina: Have we been reduced to that level?

Abel, smiling, I imagine: Nice, very nice, Marsalina. And I wonder if "that level" isn't the one we began with—when we were just out of the womb, or still in it perhaps. Language begins as a sort of wall of sounds—or perhaps it is like all the different sounds one might hear in the jungle. That a baby might hear in the jungle? But while being held in his mother's or father's arms. And then slowly he begins to find or imagine consistencies, patterns, or these are shown to him by his parents. And he tries, too, to imitate some of the sounds.

In any case, what I have wanted to do was to read you all nine sentences of the chapter of Augustine's *Confessions* from which Wittgenstein took his excerpt. We might say that he, Augustine, is focused on the next step, after we make our way out of the jungle of undifferentiated sounds.

> Passing hence from infancy, I came to boyhood, or rather it came to me, displacing infancy. Nor did that depart (for whither went it?) and yet it was no more. For I was no longer a speechless infant, but a speaking boy. This I remember; and have since observed how I learned to speak.* It was not that my elders taught me words (as, soon after, other learning) in any set method; but I, longing by cries and broken accents and various motions of my limbs to express my thoughts, that so I might have my will, and yet unable to express all I willed, or to whom I willed, did myself, by the understanding which Thou, my God, gavest me, practise the sounds in my memory.†

---

reason. As if there were a family resemblance among all these uses of λόγος.

* Going carefully through the tenses of the Latin verbs and noting the phrase *huc pergens* (to this time), the classicist Gillian Clark states, *contra* Wittgenstein, that Augustine "can remember being a child who speaks; <u>he does not claim to remember how he learned to speak, but has realised what happened</u>." This is consistent with Pine-Coffin's translation: "I can remember that time, and later on I realized how I had learnt to speak." I believe, however, that these interventions are attempts to square Augustine's conception of memory with what we moderns take memory to be. See Appendix B for more on this head. In any case, Augustine is clear that his "memory" of how he learned to speak was based on his adult observations of infants.

† I suppose Abel chose this particular translation—from the nineteenth century and by an Anglican reformer (E.B. Pusey)—because it popped up in a Google

This "practice" strikes a false note to me. It is not a word that accords well with my idea of infancy. A more recent translation uses the phrase "my memory prompted me," which is not a whole lot easier to swallow as regards an infant just learning to speak. Less charitable souls than we might imagine that Wittgenstein waited to begin his excerpt until this whole idea of a, say, 1-3-year-old trying to figure out how to express his thoughts was done with—otherwise the misleadingness of the analogy and of Augustine's reconstruction of his early childhood would have been too obvious.

The sentences Wittgenstein came to excerpt "my" nineteenth-century translator, E.B. Pusey, translates as follows:

> When they named any thing, and as they spoke turned towards it, I saw and remembered that they called what they would point out by the name they uttered. And that they meant this thing and no other was plain from the motion of their body, the natural language, as it were, of all nations, expressed by the countenance, glances of the eye, gestures of the limbs, and tones of the voice, indicating the affections of the mind, as it pursues, possesses, rejects, or shuns. And thus by constantly hearing words, as they occurred in various sentences, I collected gradually for what they stood; and having broken in my mouth to these signs, I thereby gave utterance to my will.

And then there is the last sentence of the chapter, which Wittgenstein did *not* use:

> Thus I exchanged with those about me these current signs of our wills, and so launched deeper into the stormy intercourse of human life, yet depending on parental authority and the beck of elders.

Marsalina: Now I see what devious tricks you've been up to. There was no

---

search. (At the end of the present piece, readers may find Pusey's translation of the whole chapter as well as R.S. Pine-Coffin's translation from the 1960s.) The Latin being translated by Pusey here—*prensabam memoria* (I would grasp with my memory)—is the reading of a highly regarded ninth-century edition of the *Confessions*, which itself was originally published five hundred years earlier. Another edition has *pensabam* for the verb. Thus, translating: I would weigh, or I would consider, in my memory.

need to use an analogy to deduce that the Augustine child was thinking before he could speak. Augustine says it—the child had thoughts and resolved to learn to speak in order to better express them. And the passage itself—this practicing of sounds—suggests that thinking *is* something like talking to oneself, but perhaps in a different language.*

Abel: And—never mind specific questions of language learning—Augustine's picture of infancy—of a small, pre-linguistic child analyzing his situation and resolving on a way of improving it and practicing privately in order to be able later to perform well in public—does not accord at all with our views of infancy, and it is hard to imagine Augustine's idea according with the views of infancy prevalent in Europe when Wittgenstein was preparing his *Investigations*. And once we fully appreciate that Augustine is remembering being an infant, we cannot help but feel that his memory is, to use a phrase Wittgenstein uses in another context, "*ein seltsames Gedächtnisphänomen*" (a queer memory phenomenon).⁵⁹

Another line from Cavell, a very nice way of viewing Augustine's description, I think, a much gentler way than Wittgenstein's. He—Cavell—is writing about how his daughter learned something, and how he learns from this, from her, from a child, that

> What we learn is not just what we have studied; and what we have been taught is not just what we were intended to learn. What we have in our memories is not just what we have memorized.†

Abel adopted momentarily a grandiloquent, summing-up tone. "What we have been taught is not just what we were intended to learn"—there's a whole lesson—can I say?—a lesson for parents right there. But my point for the moment is much more academic: If one reads all nine sentences of Chapter 8, Book I of the *Confessions*, instead of just the three Herr

---

* Please see the segment on Augustine in Appendix B, wherein it is explained, *inter alia*, how in Augustine's conception an infant has two or three languages before s/he learns to speak with words.

† "Excursus on Wittgenstein's Vision of Language", 177. Nor, I might add, or explicate, are our memories limited to things we have in fact experienced.

Cf., as well, Augustine, *Confessions* X:8 "Great is this power of memory, exceeding great, O my God, a vast and unlimited inner chamber. Who has plumbed its depths?"

Wittgenstein provides, one is much less likely to take this passage seriously as a description of remembering, of learning or of language learning, *tout court*. The passage is clearly also about other things—the will and the clash of wills, "*vitae humanae procellosam societatem*," the stormy intercourse of human life—the "mob of emperors, all whistling," to quote Sir Waldo.

Abel recited:

> Each man woke in the morning, and with an appetite that could eat the solar system like a cake; a spirit for action and passion without bounds; he could lay his hand on the morning star: he could try conclusions with gravitation or chemistry; but, on the first motion to prove his strength,—hands, feet, senses, gave way, and would not serve him. He was an emperor deserted by his states, and left to whistle by himself, or thrust into a mob of emperors, all whistling . . . [60]

What writing! English—American—has been all downhill since Emerson.

Marsalina: So then your question is: Why didn't Wittgenstein give us the whole chapter?

Abel: Why even in section 1—the very opening of his book—didn't he just give us all nine sentences? Because, one might well think, it would not have served so well as a "misleading analogy." We would have been less likely to get or feel confused.*

Marsalina: So this is your point: Wittgenstein is at least as involved in creating misleading analogies—presumably for instructional purposes—as he is in trying to counteract how they mislead us.

---

* Of course it might also be said that Abel is taking Augustine out of context by focusing on only one chapter, and also to the extent that he is reading this chapter as if Augustine were in dialogue with modern philosophers and modern views of infancy and language learning. It is easy enough to say that every bit of language—and no matter how lengthy the bit may be, be it the compilation of every book Google's machines and minions have translated into packets of O's and 1's—is taken out of context, or contributes to the making of its own context. As a result of Wittgenstein's *Philosophical Investigations*, Augustine's chapter became a commentary on infant language-learning, something that it was not otherwise. (*Cf.*, Karl Popper: "History is affected by discoveries we will make in the future." As quoted in Edmonds and Eidinow, 1.)

Abel: Actually, I am inclined to go a step further, although here I believe I am exceeding the range of the *Investigations*. Misleading analogies are all we've got. As the French psychoanalyst Jacques Lacan put it, speaking is about getting it wrong—and love about giving something you haven't got to someone who doesn't exist.*

---

* Cited in Adam Phillips, "On Love," 39. In a French text, Elisabeth Roudinesco, *Lacan, envers et contre tout* (Seuil, 2011), 99, I found « L'amour c'est donner ce que l'on n'a pas à quelqu'un qui n'en veut pas. » Love is giving something you don't have to someone who doesn't want it.

One evening while I was at work on this book I was having dinner in Chicago with a good friend of mine, an old friend with whom I have had many intimate conversations, a banker at the tail end of a divorce, her second divorce. At some twist in our conversation I found myself quoting Abel quoting this line of Lacan's, but my friend could not make heads or tails of it. I launched into a rather lengthy and, we might say, aggressive explanation, an explanation that I can only hope was of some use to my friend, but which I think, in any case, may be useful to others.

"Imagine, for example," I said, "someone who has spent her whole life nurturing other people in the hopes that eventually someone, just one person, would get the message: 'I need nurturing too.' After so many years without it, she really needs it, but she doesn't quite, or doesn't yet, realize that this is what she needs. She thinks rather that she likes to cook and entertain, and give massages, and buy fancy presents.

"So she meets a man who she feels understands the real her, this her—or even just this need—that she herself doesn't understand, that she is using a good deal of her energy to hold just below the surface of her consciousness. This person who is in her heart, but not in her words.

"She and this man get married and for many years she takes care of him—but not really, because her every act of caring is, more importantly, a message: 'Please take care of me,' 'Please care for me.' And this is a message her husband cannot, will not hear. He has thought he was marrying quite another women: a woman who liked to cook and entertain and give massages, and buy him fancy presents with all the money she earned working long hours in corporate America. Nor does he find much real caring in all her acts of caring because subconsciously he hears, he feels, the message, the request, the need these acts contain. He hears, we might say, what he does not want to hear. He might even hear a call to that side of himself that has long wished to give, but is afraid that in giving one little thing he might be giving away not just his autonomy, his individuality, but his whole self. Afraid, he closes his ears and stays late at his lab with another woman whose requests and needs are harder for him to hear, and so her attentions to his needs—or to what he feels are his needs—are easier to accept."

Marsalina: Nice.

Abel: Very nice. But, you know, more than 1,500 years earlier Plotinus was already way beyond this: thinking is getting it wrong. Or translating, let's call it, as we begin to work with the One, the absolute, Truth and Beauty, and so forth—as we begin, with our thoughts, with our language, to describe and analyze, we lose track of what was before us—of where and what we were, previously. As the whole, the One, becomes an object of intelligent examination, it becomes not a whole but a thing, a thing with qualities, and these qualities are like rhinestones fascinating the eye, theories fascinating the mind, and so . . .

Perhaps it's like when you look in a microscope and something you had seen as a whole—a cell, for example—now has many parts, and if you increase the magnification you see yet more parts, and you can keep doing this well beyond the point where the whole of the something is no longer visible, it no longer fits in the space of the lens, and in your mind it has given way before your interest in, your fascination with, one or another of the parts. What was one—or, in a larger sense, the One—has been blown to bits, or, say, enlarged into bits. And even if these bits could be glued together with miracle glue and miraculous dexterity, or science or philosophy—state-of-the-art technology—they would still not be the pre-thinking, pre-linguistic whole. If I say, "I love you"—and may I say that I do love you, Marsalina—still these words deform what I feel, or make my feelings into something else, for all I have no way of knowing how I felt previously, or if I felt previously, before sacrificing to the possibility of knowing on the altar of language.[*]

But we also have to recognize that this misleadingness, this getting it wrong, the deformations of language and of human interaction more generally—this is what is creative. "By sanctifying our faults we create."[†]

Here, we might say, there's a whole lot of Lacanian loving going on. And we might find ourselves asking, what ever happened to "real love"?

[*] More analogies: The photograph as compared to the moment photographed, the recording of Ravel's "La valse" as compared to hearing the piece played "live," as compared to waltzing yourself—or to being Ravel, or to being in the crisis depicted by the piece, the collapse of Europe in the first half of the twentieth century. (See Schorske, 3-4, and Ross, 120-21.)

[†] Jean Cocteau, interviewed for the *Paris Review* in 1964. "The *first* time a thing appears it disconcerts everyone, the artist too. But you have to leave it—not re-

This is the source not only of the wonders of literature and music, it is the source of the diversity of life, the source of organic life itself. If the language—the sequences of proteins—that is genetic code never fails to replicate itself "correctly," or is never forced to make mistakes as a result of external stressors; or if the more fundamental morphemes of atomic and molecular structure resist all deformation—we're nowhere, let's call it.* We're not just stuck in endlessly repeated circumstances, there were never any us or circumstances or sticking or unsticking.

Now we've left Plotinus for Lucretius—the streams of history, the flux of time. *Again a scrambling for a piece of paper, a quote*:

> If it were not for the swerve, everything would fall downwards like rain-drops through the abyss of space. No collision would take place and no impact of atom on atom would be created. Thus nature would never have created anything.[61]

It is the swerve, the deviation from the norm, the taking of the wrong, the misleading path, that is creative and thus essential to life—because it leads to accidents, collisions. Thus we might say, *contra* our Austrian, *contra* Wittgenstein: This was our real paradox—not that any course of action could be determined by a rule, but that only by departing from the rules can we live, can we collide and collude and create.† Perhaps "every course of action can be made out to accord with the rule," but this

---

touch it. *Of course* you must then canonize the 'bad.' For the good is familiar. The new arrives only by mischance. As Picasso says it is a *fault*. And by sanctifying our *faults* we create. (Italics in original text, which is in English, although the conversation appears to have been in French.)

* In his youth Wittgenstein apparently once remarked that religious belief gave people the courage not to care what might happen—for to someone with faith, nothing *could* happen. (Monk, 67.) By this I understand Wittgenstein to have been making Abel's point inversely. If the universe functions according to the dictates of a higher power, there are no accidents, no deviations from the norm, nothing happens that was not supposed to happen, we and our thoughts and actions—foreordained incidents in the whole—count for extremely little.

† And, I might add, only by departing from Vienna and its rules, and the rules of Karl Wittgenstein. The larger point raising its head here: Would anyone want to say that departing from home, rebelling or exiling oneself, is essential for creativity? Or, more exactly, does creativity lie in the swerve, in the departure from home, however slight this departure may be? Then we shall be encouraged to say that such creativity is connected to things like intolerance, rebellion, denial, escape.

is to lose the forest for the trees, this is to miss the more essential point, or points.

Marsalina: Oh, Abel, you win. I don't know if you're smart or a pretzel, but I can't keep up with you.

Abel, clearly speaking through a big smile: Will you credit me then with having given an object lesson in Wittgenstein's technique? As a philosopher nicely put it: the reader soon feels

> as though he were being turned round and round and then as though this world of words were whirling past him. There seems to be no increment, nothing upon which one can fix his grasp and tell his friends, "This I have found."[62]

Marsalina, sounding as if her mind were elsewhere: Something like that.

Abel: And so, your anxiety level mounting—never mind "increments," verities however small—you are ready to grab hold of the first mirage that you see. Whereupon your problem becomes that the nearest mirage is Wittgensteinian "philosophy," which even he is not quite sure is philosophy. If "we call our investigations 'philosophy,' this title, on the one hand, seems appropriate, on the other hand it has certainly misled people."[63] "*Philosophie dürfte man eigentlich nur* dichten." (Philosophy ought really to be written only as a *form of poetry*.)*

I am often reminded of something I learned in my one summer in the wild, out of Greenwich Village—at a sleep-away camp next to a sheep farm: Be careful around electrified wires, test them with the back of your hand. Should you touch them with your palm—with an open hand and an open mind, can I say?—your natural reaction will be to close your fist, to hold tight to the surging current until, in some potentially deadly spasm, it shakes you free.

Marsalina: Lovely.

---

* Wittgenstein, *Culture and Value*, 24e, note from 1933-34, as translated by Marjorie Perloff in *Wittgenstein's Ladder*. I suppose I have to say here that Plato's view seems to have been, rather, that philosophy could be written—could only be written?—as a form of theater.

Third Interpolation

A T THIS POINT *Marsalina shook herself free to go to the bathroom, promising to come back to say good-bye. Hearing Marsalina heading my way, I quickly stuck my nose in Kripke—in my book.*

While Marsalina is freshening up—or not freshening up at all, it may come to seem—I am going to take this opportunity to identify what seems to lie near the molten core of Ludwig Wittgenstein and his Investigations. *As usual, I will not be brief, but once finished I will let Abel and Marsalina's voices carry us the rest of the way. I promise.*

First off, while not dismissing the obsessional, arid, academic quality of many of Wittgenstein's concerns, I would like to again join with Abel in putting the focus on other voices in the Investigations. *One of these voices can be heard as if speaking from the bottom of Wittgenstein's heart* (in corde suo, *as Augustine would say), and another speaks of fundamental problems of everyday human existence. A third voice speaks of fundamental problems of Wittgenstein's social circumstances, of his family and his times, of the problems that contributed—along with his mother, his sister and Francis Skinner, have I forced myself to write?—to Ludwig's lifelong, obsessive, passionate search for rules.**

The Investigations' *Preface, written in 1945, begins with Wittgenstein stating:* "The thoughts which I publish in what follows are the precipitate of philosophical investigations which have occupied me for the last sixteen years" *(i.e., from 1929). He goes on to write of "the darkness of this time," i.e., of 1945 or of the years from 1929 to 1945. In his biography Monk says that in Wittgenstein's mind this darkness was "directly attributable to the worship of the false idol of science against which his own work had been directed since the early 1930s." He quotes from a note made by Wittgenstein in 1947*:

> Science and industry, and their progress, might turn out to be the most enduring thing in the modern world. Perhaps any speculation about a coming collapse of

---

* As regards Ludwig's relationships with his mother, his youngest sister Gretl (Margarete) and Francis Skinner, see the segment on Wittgenstein in Appendix B.

science and industry is, for the present and for a *long* time to come, nothing but a dream; perhaps science and industry, having caused infinite misery in the process, will unite the world—I mean condense it into a *single* unit, though one in which peace is the last thing that will find a home.*

From a political perspective, and from the perspective of the United States, the period of the creation of the *Investigations runs from the beginning of the Great Depression to the end of Second World War. From a Germanic perspective, in 1929 Hitler was in love with his niece, a year away from his first electoral triumph, and in 1945 he was committing suicide in his Führerbunker amid the ruins of Berlin. The Allied forces were stumbling upon the remains of the concentration camps and sending pictures of the starving inmates to newspapers and magazines.*

A key period for me is November 1932 to February 1933. During these three months many of the leaders of German big business decided to throw their weight, and some of their money, behind Hitler and Göring—not because most of these businessmen were necessarily anti-Semitic, but rather on account of their interest in "that tranquility required for business revival".† Perhaps the

---

* Monk, 485-86; quoting *Culture and Value*, 63e. See also another note made in 1947 (*Culture and Value*, 56e):

> It isn't absurd to believe that the age of science and technology is the beginning of the end for humanity; that the idea of great progress is a delusion, along with the idea that the truth will ultimately be known; that there is nothing good or desirable about scientific knowledge and that mankind, in seeking it, is falling into a trap. It is by no means obvious that this is not how things are.

A few pages on, when we get to Wittgenstein's picture of the old man with the stick, perhaps this passage will be recalled. I cannot think of a better example for my upcoming proposal that the man is going both uphill and down.

† The quoted phrase is a translation of a phrase from the *Deutsche Allgemeine Zeitung*. The translation appeared in the *TIME* magazine of November 28, 1932, with *TIME* identifying the quoted newspaper as one of the "news organs of Biggest Business"; as quoted in Ferguson and Voth, "Betting on Hitler," 112. The historian Henry Ashby Turner, Jr., refers (68) to German big business's "respect for constituted authority," a phrase that could also be used to explain the United States' historic support for any number of ruthless dictators around the globe.

business leaders could see or had been told that the Nazis were going to spend

---

From a business perspective, constituted authority is essential, and a lack of tranquility anathema. (See, for example, the history of Marsalina's native Dominican Republic. Pons, 357, writes: "Although U.S. diplomats in Santo Domingo tried to prevent the coup d'état, once confronted with the accomplished fact they accepted [the soon to be savage dictator] Trujillo, saying that they preferred him *as a guarantor of political stability and as a better alternative to revolution.*" My italics.)

Readers may not be surprised to learn that debates have raged among historians regarding the role of big business in the reign of Nazism (and of Vichy France). In crafting the sentence in the main text about the "key period," I have tried to temper my own economic-determinist perspective (for all it has been ingrained in me by observing world events for quite a few decades now). I suppose I hold out a quixotic hope that my crafting may have produced something non-controversial. What I have read regarding the historiography relating to this period, however, suggests that even my choice of commas could be contested.

Let me in any case close with an anecdote, let's call it, found (on page 109) in the economists Ferguson and Voth's recent analysis of the extra profits reaped by large German businesses whose leaders "bet" on Hitler. On February 20, 1933, a week before the Reichstag fire and two weeks before the elections that (with some help from the fire) were to bring the Nazis fully to power, leading financiers and industrialists participated in a meeting at Göring's residence in Berlin.

After giving a speech attacking Communism and declaring private enterprise to be incompatible with democracy, Hitler left the conclave. Göring laid out plans for winning the upcoming national elections, observing that "the sacrifices asked for . . . would be so much easier for industry to bear if it realized that the election of March 5th will surely be the last one for the next 10 years, probably even for the next 100 years." Schacht then presided over the establishment of a campaign fund totaling three million Reichsmarks for the electoral campaign.

Hjalmar Schacht was a wealthy former banker, and former president of the Reichsbank, who was to become, under Hitler, chairman of the Reichsbank and then minister of the economy. He has been credited with overseeing a Keynesian economic program, including large public works programs supported by deficit spending, that revived the German economy and brought the Depression-era unemployment rate down from about 30 percent to an extremely low level. The disbanding of the labor unions, the declining wages, and the encouragement of cartels and monopolistic price-fixing would have to be factored into the equation—into an evaluation of Nazi-era economic policies.

Ferguson and Voth give as the source for the anecdote and its quotation: *Trials of War Criminals Before the Nuernburg Military Tribunals Under Control Council Law No. 10, Vol. 6, Case No. 5, The "Flick Case": United States against Frederick Flick, et al.* (United States Government Printing Office, 1952).

heavily on public works, dissolve the labor unions, purge the civil service of Left-leaning staff, and thereby usher in a period of high employment, expanding profits and a 25 percent decline in real wages. (Here indeed is the sort of tranquility that promotes business revival! A tranquility that lasted about six years, before giving way to a savagery, a lust for killing and destruction such as the world tries not to see very often.*)

In any case, I can imagine the welter of feelings Wittgenstein must have had during The Blitz, when Germans were bombing and preparing to invade his adopted country, and then again when the English and Americans were bombing German cities, and when British and American forces from the west and Russian forces from the east were overrunning the German-speaking lands, Vienna included.

Far away in Brazil, in 1941 or 1942, shortly before he committed suicide, Stefan Zweig wrote in German words that may be translated

> People talk with such ease about bombing, as if it were an everyday affair, but when I read that houses have

---

* I am reminded of a standard feature of my quarterly telephone conversation with Max, my family's wealth manager. Can't you see that the world is going to hell in a handbasket! I tell him. How are we going to preserve our assets, let alone make money, when all the wheels come off the capitalist bus? Or when global-warming-induced "natural" catastrophes and the global interconnectedness of business combine to produce a series of financial shocks that so destabilize and bankrupt major governments that war comes to seem the only answer. (There are historians to argue that economic problems forced Hitler to go to war in 1939, and that war was also the way the American government found to finally pull the United States out of the Great Depression. For our children's sakes, may a different script be written as regards the consequences of twenty-first century income inequalities.)

Max's calm answer to all this is that, as a wealth manager, he is concerned with the immediate prospects for the economy and for markets, and with "looking about three-to-five years down the road." This could explain why he has a good job as a wealth manager, and I have a good job as a professor of the humanities at what used to be called a "cow college." And we can also say that from a perspective of superior returns on investment over the short and medium term, Germany's business leaders were right to throw their weight behind Hitler. He may have killed some Jews and communists, and driven yet more Jews out of business, but the economy took off, and, as Ferguson and Voth have recently shown (101), at least at the outset when Hitler and Göring were greatly in need of support, "firms supporting the Nazi movement experienced unusually high returns, outperforming unconnected ones."

crumbled, I crumble too.*

Around the same time, Wittgenstein was writing (*in some combination of German and English*):

Was die namen der Sprache bezeichnen, muß unzerstörbar sein: denn man muß den Zustand beschreiben können, in dem alles, was zerstörbar ist, zerstört ist.

What the names in language signify must be indestructible; for it must be possible to describe the state of affairs in which everything destructible is destroyed.†

Alles, was zerstörbar ist, zerstört ist. *Everything, that destructible is, destroyed is. Imagine how sad you must be to have written this, with the people of your* Heimat, *your home town—instead of welcoming you home for Christmas—wanting to kill you as a Jew and leave your body to rot in the same ditch with the bodies of your sisters and of the only one of your brothers to have made it past the last war.* Alles, was zerstörbar ist, zerstört ist. *The history of both Austria-Hungary and Germany, and of the Wittgenstein family, in the first half of the twentieth century, in the course of Ludwig's lifetime.*‡

---

* I encountered this sentence in an eloquent French translation by Jean-Jacques Lafaye et François Brugier: "Les gens parlent si facilement de bombardement, mais quand je lis que les maisons s'écroulent, je m'écroule moi aussi avec les maisons." (Zweig, *Montaigne*, 8-9.)

† *Investigations*, §55. See also this line from Wittgenstein's 1929 "Lecture on Ethics": "I can only describe my feeling by the metaphor, that, if a man could write a book on ethics which really was a book on ethics, this book would, with an explosion, destroy all the other books in the world." A comment from a student of Wittgenstein's at Cambridge: Wittgenstein was "like an atomic bomb, a tornado." See also from Hilter's *Mein Kampf*: "[I]n my earliest youth I came to the basic insight which has never left me, but only became more profound: *That Germanism could only be safeguarded by the destruction of Austria*." (As quoted in Monk, 385; italics as in Monk. "Tornado" from Edmonds and Eidinow, 11, quoting Wasfi Hijab.)

‡ It might be said that the story and chief interest of Waugh's *The House of Wittgenstein* is how an immense fortune, built in a generation, may quickly lose its immensity (though apparently Karl Wittgenstein's descendants continue to live comfortably off the wealth he acquired and shrewdly invested). A bit of the immense pile went to extravagant living, some was given away, thrown away or not well husbanded, and much was simply taken by the Nazis, as previously described. As regards the giving or throwing away, Waugh (108) says that, although at the time of the First World War the Austrian army's mortar cannon were "the fin-

Wittgenstein's Russian teacher, Fania Pascal, has recalled once proposing to Wittgenstein that they discuss (as a way of learning Russian?) the growing Nazi aggressiveness and the weak English response to it. Ludwig's response: "I am as much ashamed of what is happening as you are. But we must not talk of it."* (Interesting that the emotion confessed here is shame.)

A FOOTNOTE *in the* Investigations, *the lines in the book that have become central to my understanding of it*:

> I see a picture; it represents an old man walking up a steep path leaning on a stick.—How? Might it not have looked just the same if he had been sliding downhill in that position. Perhaps a Martian would describe the picture so. I do not need to explain why *we* do not describe it so.†

---

est heavy howitzers" being produced, Ludwig, then a young soldier in the army, thought they could be better made. So he gave 1 million kronnen to build a larger, better weapon. The money was never used for this purpose, but rather, it seems, was consumed by the hyperinflation of the 1920s. In 1946, Ludwig's sister Margarete sold paintings her husband had collected in Paris: a Matisse still life, portraits by Toulouse-Lautrec, Gauguin and Modigliani, a Picasso. This collection would come to be worth hundreds of millions of dollars or more, but selling these paintings when and how she did netted Margarete $56,705. (Waugh, 260; Monk, 7, on how the descendants continue to live comfortably off Karl's accumulation.)

* Fania Pascal, "Memories of Wittgenstein," 40. See also Monk, 389:

> The first mention in Wittgenstein's diary of the crisis facing Austria during the early months of 1938 occurs on 16 February. "Can't work", he then wrote: Think a great deal of a possible change of my nationality. Read in today's paper that a further compulsory rapprochement between Austria and Germany has taken place—But I don't know what I should really do. [My underscoring.]

† *Investigations*, footnote which has been connected with §139, p. 50e. For an alternative reading of this picture, see Affeldt, "On the Difficulty of Seeing Aspects." There (in footnote 10) he makes a connection between the picture of the man and the picture of a galloping horse in Wittgenstein's discussion of aspects (*Investigations*, Part II, xi, 172e):

> When I see the picture of a galloping horse—do I merely *know* that this is the kind of movement meant? Is it superstition to think I *see* the horse galloping in the picture?—And does my visual impression gallop too?

On first reading, these words may well feel comforting. It would seem that what Wittgensteinians call our "life in language"—here our life in visual language—offers us certainty, even where skeptical examination might lead us to think there was none. There is something zauberhaft *(magical, enchanting) or even* unheimlich *(eerie, uncanny) in how we are able to understand things—pictures, words, concepts—that on closer examination do not seem so clear. We might hear in Wittgenstein's last sentence echoes of the dismissive remarks of self-described realists, realist philosophers included. Of course if we wanted to waste our time we could wallow in skepticism, wonder if the guy was really walking up hill or if the African-American ex-con whose gun and blood were found at the scene of the crime really was the murderer, or if instead of the Sun going round the Earth, the Earth went round the Sun. But, in fact, wouldn't all this wondering be perverse or just a waste of time? We are not really confused until we insist on being confused—or until, for example, in a time of crisis, in the midst of a divorce, say, we really are confused, we don't know if we're going uphill or down, we can't "find our feet." But those times pass, or we end up in a mental hospital. As Stanley Cavell wrote, "Everyone knows that* something *is mad in the skeptic's fantastic quest for certainty."*[†] *I.e., Cavell is hinting at a question which proves not so easy to answer. What is this "something"?*

I must here recall a childhood memory of Wittgenstein's. In a bathroom in his childhood home, in his father's palace in Vienna, some plaster

---

I.e., Affeldt is here proposing a non-skeptical reading of the picture of the old man with the stick. He is heading only one way: uphill.

* *Investigations*, §142: "It is only in normal cases that the use of a word is clearly prescribed; we know, are in no doubt, what to say in this or that case. The more abnormal the case, the more doubtful it becomes what we are to say."

† *Disowning Knowledge*, 8. We could get wrapped up in a whole 'nother dialogue based on Cavell's many, challenging reflections on skepticism. See, for example, this from "Declining Decline", 37-38:

> Suppose that Descartes discovered for philosophy that to confront the threat of or temptation to skepticism is to risk madness. Then since according to me the *Investigations* at every point confronts this temptation and finds its victory exactly in never claiming a final philosophical victory over (the temptation to) skepticism, which would mean a victory over the human, its philosopher has to learn to place and to replace madness, to deny nothing, at every point.

had fallen from the wall, and Luki saw this pattern as a duck, but it frightened him because it also looked like a monster in a Hieronymus Bosch painting. We would seem to have stumbled on a source, if not the source for the adult Ludwig's interest in optical illusions.* (Cf., this beginning of one of the notes published in Culture and Value: "*I am often afraid of madness. Do I have any reason for assuming that this fear does not spring from, so to speak, an optical illusion: taking something to be an abyss right at my feet, when it's nothing of the sort?*")

It seems to me also that for the child Ludwig—and for the child Ludwig who lived on in the adult's mind (as child selves live on in all of us)—the old man with the cane was yet another such, frighteningly dual, unstable image. He was *sliding downhill, and he* was *waddling, duck-like uphill (and we might note that going uphill is often harder, if less frightening than sliding downhill). From a child's perspective, the reason we do not need to explain why* we *do not describe the man as sliding downhill, or even talk about it, is obvious (painfully obvious, an adult could say). I can hear the thin, childhood voices of my niece and nephew saying to me—in response to my too-probing questions—once the questions were about a nightmare, another time about a conflict, a humiliation at school—"This is not something I would like to talk about," "Can we please talk about something else?"*

And so, let us adults return to Wittgenstein's note about the old man again and, with courage, pause at the assertion that the picture could have looked just the same if the man were sliding downhill.† *And we might reflect*

---

* Optical illusions in the *Investigations* include the duck/rabbit of Part II, xi, 166, a convex/concave step (Part II, xi, 173), and what Wittgenstein calls a "double cross" (Part II, xi, 176): a white cross on a black ground that could as easily be a black cross on a white ground.

The *Investigations* is also—like most every text?—full of sentences that might be thought of as functioning like optical illusions, with their meanings capable of being turned inside out, and then outside in again. A famous one is §109: "*Die Philosophie ist ein Kampf gegen die Verhexung unsres Verstandes durch die Mittel unserer Sprache.*" Philosophy is a battle against the bewitchment of our intelligence by means of language. This could be interpreted—has been interpreted—as meaning either that philosophers use language to combat bewitchery, or that philosophers battle bewitchments caused by language itself. (See, Affeldt, "Captivating Pictures", 258.)

Please see as well the discussions of pointing and of the exception in Appendix A.

† See Heraclitus: "The path up and down is one and the same." (As translated in

further about how at times, and not just in the midst of personal upheaval, we are fooled—and not only by pictures, but also by people who appear honest, trustworthy, loving and so forth. By philosophers quoting other philosophers, or by bankers peddling mortgages, for example.

And why are we deceived by such people—by, say, the heading-uphill impression we may have of a colleague? Sometimes it is because we are told to believe, or because everyone believes and we do not want to "stick our necks out." Often it is, as Abel and Marsalina discussed, because we so want to believe. We certainly wish human behavior were not so relentlessly self-interested. We wish we could trust absolutely the people we work with, and sleep with. We wish to be able to relax in happy and easy agreement with our fellow men and women, and with "nature," the larger world around us. We wish to find pure love. We wish to find peace—"the peace of repose, the peace of the Sabbath, the peace which has no evening."* "The real discovery is the one that . . . gives philosophy peace, so that it is no longer tormented by questions . . . "†

And so could it be this—this desire for the peace of questionlessness—that has led Wittgenstein to say there is no need for him to talk about the "flip

---

Barnes, 103, citing Diels-Krantz reference B60.) This would also seem the place to note that the translation of the German "*Bild*" as "picture" has occasioned some discussion in the secondary literature. In *Wittgenstein's Vienna* (see 31 and 183), Janik and Toulmin trace Wittgenstein's use of the word back to Viennese cultural debate and German science, and in the process encourage translations such as "model" or even "artifact." A *Bild* "is for Wittgenstein something which we make, or produce, as an artifact."

Toward the conclusion of "The Availability of Wittgenstein's Later Philosophy," Cavell, in comparing Wittgenstein's and Freud's work, proposes translating *Bild* (or *Bilder*) as "fantasies." From page 72: Both Wittgenstein and Freud are "intent upon unmasking the defeat of our real need in the face of self-impositions which we have not assessed, or fantasies ("pictures") which we cannot escape." (I have deleted citations of the *Investigations* included in this sentence.)

Thus, we might think of our certainty that the man is heading uphill (or only uphill) as an artifact of our minds (and of our language, our culture), or as a fantasy. In "fact," the man is simultaneously heading uphill and sliding down. And the shower is an artifact for cleansing and for mass murder, ethnic cleansing. And—imagine a child building with different colored blocks—our artifacts and fantasies are the materials with which we make up an understanding of our world.

* Augustine, *Confessions*, XIII: 35.

† *Investigations*, §133.

side," if you will, of his picture of the man with the cane? Or is it because one of his particular, peculiar, extraordinary rhetorical strategies is to point readers in a misleading direction—as if thereby to create a special, quiet space, right at the back of their brains, for silent, deeper contemplation?* Or is his refusal to explain a failure of nerve on his part, or, perhaps, because it is not the therapist's job to lead us over the cliff (or into the empty, electric box of high anxiety), but simply to help us appreciate its existence and how frightened it can make us feel? In his Memoir, Malcolm summarizes one of Wittgenstein's themes: "We are constantly deceived by mental pictures which are in themselves correct." I take this "we" to be all-inclusive; that is, Ludwig too.†

Apparently Wittgenstein thought of using as the epigraph for the Investigations the famous line from one of Bishop Butler's sermons on morality: "Everything is what it is, and not another thing".‡ (It might be said that we now have a colloquial variant: "It is what it is.") As regards the old man with the stick, it would seem that what *is* is that he might be headed up or down. We are deceived by what Descartes called la précipitation et la prévention: by judging too hastily while not discounting our prejudices (e.g., our wishful thinking).⁶⁴

And yet it also needs to be said, again, that something *is mad in the skeptic's fantastic quest for certainty*. To put this another way: On account of our prejudices and hasty judgments, our wishful thinking, we go through life in a fog, misunderstanding; and without our prejudices, hasty judgments and wishful thinking we would never escape that electric box, we would be paralyzed, unable to go through life at all.

We do not see a fork as a fork: we simply see the fork and dig in to our supper. The word "as" implies an act of interpretation, and we do not interpret

---

* Please see the discussion of pointing (pointing as a way of misleading) in Appendix A.

† Malcolm, *Memoir*, 54. I take the process to be yet more inclusive: We are also ourselves constantly, and often intentionally, creating mental pictures which are misleading, and which often have as their primary purpose misleading ourselves. And here, in the parade of misleaders of others and misleaders of themselves, Ludwig looks to be in the front ranks.

‡ Butler, originally from *Fifteen Sermons*, Preface, §39. This Preface is reproduced in the Butler volume containing the fifteen sermons cited in the "Works Cited" of the present text. The segment on Hume in Appendix C comes back to Butler's statement and a footnote gives the context in which Butler made it.

what we see except in those cases where we really do entertain more than one possible interpretation.

"C'est quoi là—là, ce que vous venez de mettre sur mon assiette?"

"De la langue, de la langue de boeuf." It's some language, it's some meaty language. "N'aie pas peur. Mange-la." Don't be afraid. Eat up.

I CAN'T RESIST PAUSING *to offer another delicious anecdote. This one comes from Wittgenstein's mentor G.E. Moore, the great champion of common sense, from a tour Moore made of American university campuses. During a lecture at the University of Michigan in Ann Arbor he pointed to a ceiling and declared, by way of illustrating what he knew with certainty: "There is a window in the roof." To emphasize the importance he attached to this particular example, he then declared: "If I didn't know this, when I said it, I never know anything of the kind."*

As it turned out, however, there was no window in the roof. "What looked like a window," Moore was informed later, "merely covered an opaque portion of the dome."[65]

It seems to me that in this case Moore was lucky or unlucky (depending on how one wishes to view the matter). Most of the time is it not the case that other people are unable to point out our errors to us, or out of malice or politeness they refrain from doing so? And for our own parts, we have such a need of being sure, of something at least, that we ignore most all the hints that our beliefs are rather less well-grounded than we are sure they are.

Amid all this, it is worth keeping in mind that Wittgenstein's greatest philosophical interest was ethics. His work can be seen as a series of extraordinary, failed attempts to find a way to talk about ethics—or to find any rules.* In the first of his two published books he wrote, "[I]t is impossible

---

* I find myself reminded of anecdotes regarding the disorder of the Austro-Hungarian military forces at the beginning of the First World War. It is said that in the first days these forces shot down several of their own airplanes, so the order was given not to shoot at any airplanes. And meanwhile the commander of the armed forces could not decide whether he wanted to first fight the Serbians or the Russians, and so he had masses of new recruits travelling back and forth on the railroads between the two fronts. Waugh (see 69-70) describes how "one train, packed

for there to be propositions of ethics."⁶⁶ In a 1929 "Lecture on Ethics" he apparently said:

> Ethics so far as it springs from the desire to say something about the ultimate meaning of life, the absolute good, the absolute valuable, can be no science. What it says does not add to our knowledge in any sense. But it is a document of a tendency in the human mind which I personally cannot help respecting deeply and I would not for my life ridicule it.⁶⁷

Ethics involves value judgments, not simply accepting the pictures we are given and the standard views, or readings, but asking if these views, and indeed the pictures themselves, are right or wrong.* *And we can only make such judgments if we possess what Mesoamericans called* neltilitztli tzintliztli, *some fundamental truth or true basic principle—some basis for deciding whether the man, or "man" in general, is going uphill or down, if we are on the right path or wrong. But this we lack, and have in its place the* Übereinstimmungen*—the*

---

with soldiers, was returned to the very station from which, days earlier, it had departed amid the clamor of trumpets, bunting, waving hands and fond farewells."

May I be allowed to use these anecdotes as analogies for the delicious paralysis, if you will, that is the *Investigations*. We would announce the rules, our ethics, if only we could be sure that, as a result, we were not going to be shooting down our own planes. If the result of our shooting down other people, other arguments, is that our ability to survive, let alone fly, is undermined, . . . Where are we?

The shuttling back and forth between the two fronts reminds me of the *Investigations*' internal dialogue. Besieged on both sides, we come to be defined above all by our shuttling, and by the inevitable insufficiency of our defenses.

Apparently the soldiers of the Austro-Hungarian Army spoke ten different languages. Readers of Appendix B will find that in Augustine's model, even young children who have learned only one *spoken* language in fact make use of three or four, and since Freud psychologists have been exploring the possibility that the self is a kind of small village, made up of several, competing interests and voices (e.g., the id, ego and super-ego, or the "false self" and the "true self"). From this perspective, the problem is not only insufficient defenses, but also managing the complexity.

* This is not the place to write a survey of the various conceptions of ethics that have been set down on paper over the last several millennia. Nor am I qualified to write such a survey. It has, however, seemed necessary to at least nod in the direction of David Hume and of those who would say that Hume put to rest many of the concerns about the lack of foundations for ethical thinking that I am raising here. This nodding is done in the segment on Hume in Appendix C.

agreements—*found in our language and in our* Lebensformen—*our forms of life.** The English have their agreements, their shared beliefs, and the Germans have theirs, and the Russians theirs, and the Arabs, and the Israelis, and so forth. And at times others' agreements can seem quite awful, inhuman even, and at times, if less often, we may feel the same about our own cultures. And at times there is war and some of the agreements are adjusted, let's say, while others are left soaked in tears and blood.†

---

* In a footnote many pages ago I noted the divergent interpretations of this core term in Wittgenstein's writings. I noted that for me culture plays a large role, though hardly the exclusive role, in the creation of our forms of life. Here we have the difference between "sex"—biologically determined—and "gender"—culturally determined. Being a female involves, for many female adults, ovulating, and this is a significant component of females' form of life. Being a woman in the twenty-first century United States, however, also involves the possibility of taking "the pill" or of insisting that a male partner use a condom, and this is also a significant aspect of the form of life of women, and of men, in our times. And expressions of all this—of the ovulating and of "the pill" and so forth—are embedded deep within our language, not only in terms such as "safe sex," but much more basically. Please see the writings of scholars in this field, and I would note again Bourdieu's explorations and explanations of his conceptions of "habitus" and "champs." (Briefly, *les champs*: external expressions of power relations in the society that guide people's behavior; *habitus*: internalization within the mind and the body of these relations and their dictates, in such a way that this *habitus* organizes the individual's perceptions and actions. See Wacquant, "The Structure and Logic of Bourdieu's Sociology.")

But I would not to my own self be being true if I did not also again come back to other side of this coin. Which is the efforts of philosophers to find something more solid, less ever-evolving, less relative, in Wittgenstein's conception of *Lebensformen*. Since I believe that Wittgenstein is also working with a two-sided coin, or working both sides of the street, it is not surprising to me that if one dips into his writings one can find evidence for either position one may wish to take. That is, for either "my" more culture-based definition of *Lebensformen*, or for Wittgenstein referring rather to *etwas animalisches* "something animal"—i.e., to females as opposed to women. (This phrase is from *On Certainty* §359: "But that means I want to conceive it as something that lies beyond being justified or unjustified; as it were, as something animal.")

Finally, I would call attention to one of Bearsley's observations (232), which I accept as conclusive and concluding: "Nowhere does Wittgenstein give an explanation of what he means by this important term"—i.e., *Lebensformen*.

† I have long been curious about this activity of negotiating international treaties, which do serve a regulatory function, but only until a real conflict breaks out, at

And so, and before getting back to Abel and Marsalina, allow me to propose, and with a certain brutality, how various threads—Wittgenstein's times, his homosexuality and Jewishness, his interest in ethics, the old man with his cane—may be knit together. I see a picture of Jews and homosexuals, along with gypsies, socialists, anti-Nazi political activists, Eastern European counts and any remaining intellectuals, being led off a train; children separated from parents, husbands from wives, some sent to find freedom in work, some sent, first, to take a shower. Might a Martian object, "This is not a shower, this is a gas chamber!" I do not need to explain why* we do not describe it so. "Remember, you're doing the right thing," Richard Nixon—raised a Quaker!—apparently told his chief of staff on Easter Sunday, 1973. "That's what I used to think when I killed some innocent children in Hanoi."*[68]

> "[T]his is how it is—" I say to myself over and over again. I feel as though, if only I could fix my gaze absolutely sharply on this fact, get it in focus, I must grasp the essence of the matter.†

---

which point they are, as we say, not worth the paper they are printed on. In a segment of Appendix A I touch on Carl Schmitt's idea of *die Ausnahme*: the exception. "The norm is destroyed in the exception." "What always matters is the possibility of the extreme case taking place, the real war." But here, in the present case, yes, the real war matters, but something else seems to matter too: this coming to provisional agreements, as if to pretend that the real war will not take place, or simply because this coming to agreements is another thing human beings like to do, besides killing one another. (Schmitt, *Political Theology*, 12, and *The Concept of the Political*, 35.)

* *Arbeit macht frei*: Work makes you free—the slogan over the entrance to Auschwitz and other concentration camps. In his book on *Fin-de-Siècle Vienna* (146 and 197), Carl Schorske notes other, earlier variations on this expression, with which, we might say, the Nazi version was in dialogue: *Wollen macht frei* (desiring makes you free) and *Wissen macht frei* (knowledge makes you free). The latter was the great slogan of the Austrian liberalism Hitler so wished to wipe off the face of the Earth. (And we might note further that Freud's approach to psychotherapy is in dialogue with this Austrian idea of knowledge making one free.)

† *Investigations*, §113. I assume that I am not alone in having the experience, in the course of visits to psychotherapists, of hoping that by fixing my gaze on dynamics of my childhood, or of my marriage, my wife's death, I would both grasp the essence of these matters and, further, rid myself of their hold over me. To date, and I am in my seventh decade, this has not been the case. To the point where, if in this regard I retain any hope, it is only that in giving up all hope—*through* giving up all hope?—such a miracle might come to pass. But this is also to set the stage for a further and likely richer set of reflections, perhaps taking off from the

"*What has to be accepted, the given, is—so one could say—forms of life.*"[69]

"**W**HAT DOES IT MEAN *to know what a game is? What does it mean to know it and not be able to say it?*"[70] What does it mean to know what murder is and not be able to say it! What does it mean to know what injustice is and not be able to say it? I hear echoes of Plato and Socrates: What does it mean to not know what the agathon—*the highest good—is?*[*] What does it mean, and what may be the effect, of not knowing what arete (*excellence, virtue*) is? What would it mean to be a courageous warrior without knowing what andreia (*a warrior's courage*) is? And so forth.

> We have the feeling that the ordinary man, if he talks of "good", of "number" etc., does not really understand what he is talking about. I see something queer about perception and he talks about it as if it were not queer at all. Should we say he knows what he is talking about or not?

> You can say both. Suppose people are playing chess. I see queer problems when I look into the rules and scrutinise them. But Smith and Brown play chess with no difficulty. Do they understand the game? Well, they play it.[†]

---

commonplace "be careful what you wish for."

* See the discussion of "The Good" in Appendix C.

† Monk, 356, quoting Rush Rhees' notes of Wittgenstein lectures in 1936, as reprinted in *Philosophical Investigations* VII, no. 1 (January 1984): 1-45. *N.B.*: In this extract, Wittgenstein distinguishes himself from "the ordinary man," and it is the ordinary man who "knows" and the unordinary one—the higher class one, I believe we must say—who is skeptical. Again, it would seem that the real subject here might be the gap between human beings, in this case between the great mass of ordinary ones, and "we," the elite: Wittgenstein and his coterie of disciples at Cambridge. And thus I would ask how far we, or Wittgenstein, have come from Plato and his Socrates stopping Athenians in the agora and showing them that in fact they do not know what they think they know? They do not know what "the good" or "number" or "courage" means.

For me what is being called into question here (though not only here) is how to read the famous line from section 242 of the *Investigations*: "If language is to be a means of communication there must be agreement not only in definitions but also

Consider for example the proceedings of what we call "games". I mean board-games, card-games, ball-games, Olympic games, and so on. What is common to all of them?—Don't say: "There *must* be something common, or they would not be called 'games'"—but *look and see* whether there is anything common to all.⁷¹

Now consider for example what we call a "shower." I have days when I think that this is, more or less, the whole of the Investigations; *this is where Wittgenstein, and perhaps all of us, got stuck; this is the point he keeps coming back to over and over again. I do not mean the Holocaust, though certainly this is a place . . . Can we say that the Holocaust—and so many other, similar horrors*: *Rwanda, Armenia, Hiroshima . . . If all this had not occurred, we might possibly feel that we knew, as Wittgenstein puts it—and as Beckett, too, was putting it at around the same time—How to "go on"?*

For "I know" seems to describe a state of affairs which guarantees what is known, guarantees it as a fact. One always forgets the expression "I thought I knew".*

In the post-Holocaust, post-Hiroshima period, we continue to go on, of course. And it is not that we have forgotten how to walk, and, as Sartre noted, in our walking, in our actions, we make values spring up like partridges.† *We are not lacking for "shoulds," for* Regeln und Bestimmungen,

---

. . . in judgments." It seems to me that what Wittgenstein is saying in passages like the one under discussion here is that he himself did *not* find agreement in judgments. He found that most people, "ordinary" people, agreed with one another and were able to communicate with one another therefore, but he did not share their judgments and, thus, could not really communicate with them, but only with the few people with a particular desire to agree with him and with the interest, leisure and intellectual perspective to try to understand what he was saying.

I find myself reminded again of others of Wittgenstein's comments about "ordinary" people—e.g., the rural Austrians he went to teach ("not human *at all* but loathsome worms") or the soldiers with whom he served in the First World War: "It is almost impossible to find any trace of humanity in them." (As noted much earlier, these quotations come from Monk, 212 and Waugh, 108.)

* Wittgenstein, *On Certainty*, §12. As noted in a previous footnote, for Wittgenstein on "going on," see, *inter alia, Investigations*, §151 and §179.

† "*Mes actes font lever des valeurs comme des perdrix*", *L'être et le néant*, 73. See also, from the previous paragraph of Sartre's text: "*La valeur tire son être de son exigence et non son exigence de son être.*" Values are created by demands rather than demands

rules and regulations. In our increasingly complex societies we have more rules and regulations than ever. What we have lost is our confidence—our misplaced confidence, it would seem to have been—that there is a right way to go, that we might know the right way, that good will come from obeying, that either the rules or the obeying are necessarily good—not simply expedient, but good (agathon, summum bonum, neltilitztli tzintliztli).*

> *Du denkst, du mußt doch einen Stoff weben: weil du vor einem—wenngleich leeren—Webstuhl sitzt und die Bewegungen des Webens machst.* (You think that after all you must be weaving a piece of cloth: because you are sitting at a loom—even if it is empty—and going through the motions of weaving.)[72]

> . . . *là où je suis, je ne sais pas, je ne le saurai jamais, dans le silence on ne sait pas, il faut continuer, je ne peux pas continuer, je vais continuer.* (. . . where I am, I don't know, I'll never know, in the silence you don't know, you must go on, I can't go on, I'll go on.)†

So is the *hypothesis* possible, that all things around us

---

being created by values. Sartre's larger interest here is in the extent to which we human beings use unthinking obedience as a way of avoiding confronting our capacity to choose and the incumbent responsibilities—as a way of avoiding taking responsibility for our lives, let alone for others' lives. I note that the inverse perspective is also valid: In order to feel a greater sense of efficacy in the face of death, human beings get caught up in making trivial, irrelevant decisions, or in ruminating over "decisions" that in fact we lack the power to make or would only make one way, "decisions" in which there is an "only choice" that we are inevitably going to make. This explains in part the mania for shopping: There is reassurance in seeming to be able to make seemingly meaningful but in fact insignificant choices.

* See segment on "The Good" in Appendix C.

† The concluding phrases of Samuel Beckett's *L'Innomable* (*The Unnamable*), 1949; English as translated by Beckett himself. See also "Waiting for Godot," Act II:

> Vladimir: There's nothing we can do.
> Estragon: But I can't go on like this!
> Vladimir: Would you like a radish?
> Estragon: Is that all there is?
> (And they go on.)

don't exist? Would not that be like the hypothesis of our having miscalculated in all our calculations?[73]

Views from the deck of our brave new world.

WE OFTEN TAKE COMFORT *in the fact that it looks to all appearances like the man with the stick is heading uphill, that computers and cellphones—and automobiles, airplanes, antibiotics, the "green revolution" in agriculture—have made our lives easier, more efficient, richer. It's so obvious, only idiots or philosophers would even think there was any question about such things. And it is yet more comforting to us that most everyone around us agrees with us. Yes, of course, he's heading uphill, we're heading uphill.*

> I'm pretty sure living standards will continue to surge, as they have for everybody for a century or more. Gizmos will get cheaper. New technologies will sprout. Luxuries will be considered necessities. . . . For about 4,000 years living standards barely budged. Then, in the 18th or 19th century they began to take off and the upward ascent has been miraculous. People at the poverty line live better, materially, than kings and queens 200 years ago. Once human creativity was unleashed during the industrial revolution there's been no going back.*

---

* David Brooks in Brooks and Gail Collins, "In Praise of Progress," *New York Times* on-line, July 28, 2010.

Regarding going back, this from *Bloodlands*, historian Timothy Snyder's revision of our understanding of the larger holocaust that occurred in Eastern Europe in the 1930s and 1940s: the Soviets and Germans invaded Poland together, and carried out a policy of *de-Enlightenment*. Reasoning from different ideologies, but drawing similar conclusions, the Germans and Soviets killed some two hundred thousand Polish citizens between 1939 and 1941, disproportionately the educated people who represented European culture and might have led resistance. On the German side, the *Einsatzgruppe* and *Einsatzkommando* who did the killing, Snyder writes, "were in some sense killing their peers: fifteen of the twenty-five Einsatzgruppe and Einsatzkommando commanders had doctorates." (Snyder, 415 and 126.)

It might be said that this movement was defeated, and so, from a longer-term perspective, there has been no going back, the old man is still heading uphill. But how would we fit into this analysis such phenomena as: the persistent attacks on American intellectuals and intellectualism since the end of the Second World War;

All this may be said, and indeed has been said in one form or another for hundreds of years and with a repetitiveness that seems at times to be begging the question. But we might say that a difference between now and 200 years ago—or between before and after the assassination of the Archduke Franz Ferdinand on June 28, 1914— We are less sure. It has begun to occur to some people (to many more Europeans than Americans) that the old man could well be sliding downhill. And would it be better—certainly for polar bears! and for homo sapiens too?—if he were heading downhill?

Allow me to quote at length from Wittgenstein's Viennese contemporary Stefan Zweig in order to fill out a picture of how, during their lifetimes, the man appeared to slide downhill—or rather, fall off a summit.

> In its liberal idealism, the nineteenth century was honestly convinced that it was on the straight and unfailing path toward being the best of all worlds. Earlier eras, with their wars, famines, and revolts, were deprecated as times when mankind was still immature and unenlightened. But now it was merely a matter of decades until the last vestige of evil and violence would finally be conquered, and this faith in an uninterrupted and irresistible "progress" truly had the force of religion for that generation. One began to believe more in this "progress" than in the Bible, and its gospel appeared ultimate because of the daily new wonders of science and technology. . . . At night the dim street lights of former times were replaced by electric lights, . . . Thanks to the telephone one could talk at a distance from person to person. People moved about in horseless carriages with a new rapidity; they soared aloft, and the dream of Icarus was fulfilled. . . . Hygiene spread and filth disappeared. People became handsomer, stronger,

---

the declines in reading and in our investment in our public education system; the persistent banning of books; the rejection of the experts' view of global warming, . . . ? Symptomatic of all these phenomena, I would say, is this connection of gizmo-devising with human creativity, as if our certainty that we have not arrived at another Dark Age were based on the pleasant, energy-efficient lighting of a billion LED screens. This may indeed be what human creativity is all about—gizmos and self-deception—but there have been eras and subcultures that have had much higher aspirations. The Vienna of Ludwig Wittgenstein, Stefan Zweig, Sigmund Freud, Gustav Mahler, Gustav Klimt, for example.

healthier, as sport steeled their bodies. . . . [A]nd all of these miracles were accomplished by science, the archangel of progress. Progress was also made in social matters; year after year new rights were accorded to the individual, justice was administered more benignly and humanely, and even the problem of problems, the poverty of the great masses, no longer seemed insurmountable. The right to vote was being accorded to wider circles, and with it the possibility of legally protecting their interests. . . . Small wonder then that this century sunned itself in its own accomplishments and looked upon each completed decade as the prelude to a better one. There was as little belief in the possibility of such barbaric declines as wars between the peoples of Europe as there was in witches and ghosts. Our fathers . . . honestly believed that the divergences and boundaries between nations and sects would gradually melt away into a common humanity and the peace and security, the highest of treasures, would be shared by all mankind. [We're a long way from gizmos here!]

It is reasonable that we, who [by the early 1940s had] long since struck the word "security" from our vocabulary as a myth, should smile at the optimistic delusion of that idealistically blinded generation, that the technical progress of mankind must connote an unqualified and equally rapid moral ascent. We of the new generation who have learned not to be surprised by any outbreak of bestiality, we who each new day expect things worse than the day before, are markedly more skeptical about the possible moral improvement of mankind. We must agree with Freud, to whom our culture and civilization were merely a thin layer liable at any moment to be pierced by the destructive forces of the "underworld."[74]

All this said, I will also note that the Holocaust was not something Wittgenstein dwelt on publicly; perhaps not even in his own thoughts or subconscious. (Was it something that, long before the news was broadcast,

Wittgenstein already knew about, from growing up in his family, in Vienna, from serving on the front lines in the First World War, from negotiating with the Nazis to exchange his sisters' lives for gold?)

Wittgenstein was obsessed rather—and as only a veteran of trench warfare could be?—by what we will call the gap between people, and by the gap between us and understanding, between his wish to be good and do good, to act and write with integrity, and by his inability, our inability, to know what the good or even integrity in fact is—besides social conventions, ever-evolving social conventions.* Like some bridges, language and other social conventions not only span the gap, they make it harder for us to appreciate the gap, to see the rushing water below. And thus we are comforted and confused, we are lost to our lostness.

Among other things, it is my strong suspicion that social conventions—and philosophers', sociologists' and others' wonderings and research as regards language and social conventions more generally—also serve another function: to hide another gap or series of gaps: within us, between voices within our selves, between our self-images and the standards we have for ourselves and our behavior. "Just improve yourself, that is all you can do to improve the world," Wittgenstein was known to tell his friends.[75] Or, as he put it in a youthful letter to his mentor, Bertrand Russell:

> I can't think about logic today. Perhaps you regard this thinking about myself as a waste of time—but how can I be a logician before I'm a human being! Far *the most important thing is to put my own house in order!*[76]

Such ideas are hardly unique to Wittgenstein and may have a good deal to say for themselves. But what is striking is that it is hard to say that this approach worked for Wittgenstein himself. Certainly over the years he improved his philosophical ideas, in the sense of taking them further, perhaps approaching as close as a human being can to the kernel of what "he" had to say—to what his circumstances had to say through him. But if self-improvement, or becoming *a* human *being*, involves becoming *a* better person. . . . Well, what

---

* Wittgenstein, *On Certainty*, §94:

> I did not get my picture of the world by satisfying myself of its correctness; nor do I have it because I am satisfied [with] its correctness. No: it is the inherited background against which I distinguish between true and false.

would we mean by that?

If we limit this betterness, this humaneness to a conventional idea of being more respectful of others, of their autonomy and their equal claims on being who they are, . . . It would be easy enough to say that this is a task, a way of viewing other people, on which Wittgenstein made absolutely no progress, and this perhaps thanks in part to his obsessing about the task of improving himself (rather than, say, his relations with *others).**

> I have suffered much, but I am apparently incapable of *learning* from my life. I suffer still *just* as I did many years ago. I have not become any stronger or wiser.[77]

One of his ideas—an appealing idea—was that a writer or philosopher could not write truly if he were not being true to himself and about himself. And Wittgenstein had the further idea—certainly right—that to be so true required a good deal of courage, perhaps more than he himself had. But he tried his best. He tried in various ways to confess his sins—and not in the Catholic way or in the post-Freudian way, to a disinterested professional, but in the traditional Jewish way: to people he had harmed (the Austrian school children he had beaten) and to his friends. Above all he wanted to confess that he had not always told the truth.† *He had lied about how many Jewish grandparents*

---

* If we accept Perry Meisel's previously noted characterization of Wittgenstein as a melancholy narcissist, we might ask what a narcissist's interest could be in improving a self that is, in a certain sense, perfect, beautiful, or perfectly fascinating?

† The following letter exemplifies the superficiality of many of Wittgenstein's confessions. I note that such behavior can help a person avoid what really concerns him or her; however, it may also keep these "real concerns" just below the surface, easy to find, easy to come out. As if the person were saying, "What is important I am not confessing, but confession is important to me, because there is something important I wish I could confess, but I cannot." We play a similar game with many of our negative statements. "I am *not* upset." "It's not that I don't want to talk to you, it's just that . . . "

The letter, from October 1938, as quoted in Monk, 412-13:

> Dear Mrs. Stewart,
>
> I must apologize for an untruth I told you today in Miss Pate's office. I said that I had seen Mrs Thompson recently in Birmingham; & only when I came home this evening it occurred to me that this wasn't true at all. I stayed with the Bachtins a few weeks ago in Birmingham & I *tried* to see Mrs Thompson & we had a talk on the phone; but I wasn't able to see her.

he had (saying one rather than three). To avoid trouble with the law, he had lied to a court about the extent to which he had beaten his students.

    We might say of such confessing, however, that it is the kind of endeavor that always comes up short. Somehow the act of confessing, of being brutally honest with ourselves, includes withholding, denying, lying. In confessing how we have lied we lie about something else, or leave this something else, like a sleeping dog, lying. In Wittgenstein's case, as in anyone's, one might easily make a list of non-confessed "sins"—the sadism of his behavior toward Francis Skinner might be near the top. His feelings about his mother, and how, by not coming to terms with these feelings, he, and his mother, were unable to maintain any relationship after his father died. THIS, we might say, was the real Bild—the real picture or fantasy—in which he was held captive—the feelings about his mother than he could not confess even to himself. And THIS too: the desire to be completely honest and truthful when complete honesty and truthfulness are chimera.*

    Human beings did not adopt the habit of speaking because it offered us a means of mutual deception, but so that each of us might make his [or her] thoughts known of another. I am glossing a line in Augustine's Enchiridion.[78] Two millennia ago it seemed such a simple process. But now I think we can see the gap that separates Wittgenstein—and Freud, Lacan and all of us after so many centuries of "progress"—from Augustine. Now we of course wish that our life in language were simple, that we might be sure what our thoughts were, that they were our thoughts (and not something we were parroting or saying for another, or for a self we wished we were). We wish that deception, self-deception most definitely included, weren't often the point, that love did not so often involve giving something we haven't got to someone who doesn't quite exist.

    In "The Ghost of the Tractatus," the philosopher Anthony Kenny takes the idea of getting things wrong to what is both its end and starting point: how we get ourselves *wrong*, misread ourselves. Kenny's argument is that Wittgenstein's later statements regarding his first book, the Tractatus, misrepresented it.[79] I think it fair to say that many professors of literature

---

    When I talked to you this afternoon what was in my head was that I had seen Mrs Thompson at your house before she went to Birmingham. Please forgive my stupidity.
                  Yours sincerely, L. Wittgenstein

* See the segment on Freud in Appendix C.

would find nothing surprising in this claim. While they certainly recognize the privileged position from which a writer or other artist views her or his own work, they do not expect the artist's reading to be superior to or as accurate or profound as others' readings. In our personal lives (to say nothing of the world of politics and the law) we often have a sense that other people are misrepresenting themselves, and this may occasionally cause us to wonder how often we misrepresent our own selves. Often this is not in order to get ahead, but it is certainly in order to get away with something, to pass for someone we are not. Sometimes, for example, afraid to take on new challenges, we try to pass for someone less capable than we are. Or, to get a promotion: more capable.

Another example: I believe the current view is that about 50 percent of United States citizens are, as Abel might say, mixed laundry—that is, "Mischlinge" (mixed race): have some African ancestry. If this is the case, then more than 100 million of us are passing for "white" when we may in fact qualify as "black." And parents pass as happily married "for the sake of the children." Employees pass as committed to corporate goals that they could care less about, if they have even given these goals—or goals more generally?—any thought. And so forth.

In L'être et le néant *(Being and Nothingness) Sartre made rather a large deal of* "mauvaise foi," *with which a self misrepresents itself—its thoughts and feelings—to itself and others; when we are not to our own selves being true. But, as Sartre himself outlines, we should not underestimate how difficult, if not impossible, the alternative is. That is, how difficult if not impossible it is to be who we are. (Which is also to say that it becomes quite difficult to nail down what this being who we are might mean.) At the very least we may say that it is the incompletable work of a courageous and self-focused lifetime to try to locate and hear clearly the voices of the true selves within us, to not always be acting and speaking with at least some degree of* mauvaise foi.

Cavell at the end of one of his essays proposes that "ignorance of oneself is a refusal to know."[80] *To me this seems both headed in the right direction and a tremendous underestimation of how hard it is, of how much confidence it takes not to so refuse, and of how limited our expectations of self-knowledge must be. "Man is a great depth," Augustine wrote. "There is in man an area which not even the spirit of man* knows of."[81]

In an essay I once made an analogy to closing, opening or leaving open doors within the mind. No one, I am sure, leaves all the doors open. And if, let's say, there are three really significant doors—a door to the cold storage?

a door to the boiler? a door to the sky?—well, these, . . . Very few of us are interested in opening many of these even a crack, even momentarily. Most of us are too busy/keep ourselves too busy to think about any of our psychic doors— for all we know/refuse knowing that they are there.

If Socrates and Montaigne did not already make this point clear to us—about this valiant but futile, or futile but valiant work of a lifetime— certainly the combination of Wittgenstein's writings and writings about him does. He spent a lifetime trying to strip away layers of self-deception, along with layers of philosophical confusion, so that he might say what he really had to say or accept its unsayability and be silent, stop philosophizing. Using a mathematical concept, as he himself often did, we might say that he found that the gap is infinite between the limit of a function (e.g., self-knowledge) and the products of the function (the rungs of a mental ladder climbed in the pursuit of self-knowledge). With the help of language one can try and try to understand and express what one finds in corde suo, in one's heart, and one will keep coming up short. It could be that beings—of some other species or on some other planet?—should *be silent when they cannot speak truly, but for human beings here on Earth silence is not an option, and nor is speaking quite truly.*

S O THAT, IN A HARD NUTSHELL, is the first of my final remarks. The second and last one will involve taking the unusual step of objecting to something before it has been said. That is, I am going to object to something that Abel is going to say after Marsalina comes back from the bathroom. Abel is going to say that one of Wittgenstein's underlying motivations was a need to try to reduce the size, or the relentless pressure, of his superego, of guilt.* Using a sort of Freudian shorthand, we might say this problem was related to a domineering "father." That is, on the first level, Karl Wittgenstein was, everyone says, domineering by nature (and I imagine him as the sort of person who—like an overstoked boiler?—is running at such speed and with such intensity that those around him may feel always lagging and lacking, if not also a bit frightened). On the second level, there was something in Vienna and in Austrian culture, or

---

* See Kierkegaard, *Repetition* (in *Repetition* and *Philosophical Crumbs*), 60:

> The whole of my being shrieks in self-contradiction. How did it happen that I became guilty? Or am I not guilty? . . . What a miserable invention is human language, which says one thing and means something else!

in Germanic culture more generally, that was like an oppressive father, and this, too, Ludwig was escaping from. And when he got to England he found new father figures—Russell and Moore—to do battle with and to try to escape from—to Norway and in the interior monologue of the Investigations *and of the many notes from this latter period of Wittgenstein's life.**

The argument I would advance, however, is that Karl and Vienna (and Russell and Moore) were not, if you will, oppressive enough. No, stop. It sounds as if I am on the way to saying, "Spare the rod, spoil the child"; "Spare the dogmatism, spoil the student"; and this is not what I want to say. I want to say that if the rod has not been spared, or more simply, if there has been, as Zweig describes, a great sense of order and security, and then these are in childhood or youth taken away, . . . Now you have a problem, now you have a desperate searching for Ordnung und Regeln, *of* Regeln und Bestimmungen—*order and rules, rules and regulations*. Vienna with the empire collapsing around it, and the Palais Wittgenstein with the sons committing suicide—they simply did not offer Ludwig the order, or sense of order, he had, as a young child, been led to expect and depend on.

It is also often noted, in writing about Vienna at the end of the empire, that its great artists—painters, musicians, architects and designers—rebelled against the hypocrisy and ornamentation, the degraded values and aesthetics of the Doppelmonarchie. But what do we find in this rebellion? In the strict minimalism of Adolf Loos's designs (and of the Viennese home Ludwig helped design for his sister, and of the furniture he had made for his Cambridge rooms) are not the rules much stricter, more "Spartan," than those that prevailed, or that had been exhausted, previously?† Schönberg's music can

---

* See Appendix C for my argument (after Tom Regan) that scholars have been underestimating the extent to which Wittgenstein's work is a response to and a moving on from Moore's work. And may I note an advantage of having a father like Karl Wittgenstein—assuming you are able to survive! Having such a father may lead a child to be drawn to other strong men and to know how to build relationships with them.

† Monk, 240: "When [Wittgenstein] played music with others, . . . his interest was in getting it right, in using his acutely sensitive ear to impose upon his fellow musicians an extraordinary exactitude of expression."

As regards the house Ludwig helped design for his sister, Monk reports (237):

> The house was designed with little regard to the comforts of ordinary mortals. The quality of clarity, rigour and precision

be (and is) considered revolutionary, but this is revolution in the Jacobin sense: after revolting against the authority of an aging father, replacing his regime with something stricter, harsher, more demanding (of the composer and his audience in Schönberg's case; more demanding of the rulers and the ruled in Robespierre's).*

As regards Ludwig's father and home life, yes, Karl once was by nature an extremely domineering father, but after his sons began committing suicide, what authority did he retain in the eyes of those still remaining? Or in his own eyes? What could undermine a father's authority more than to have his sons kill themselves? Biographies of Ludwig note that while Karl insisted on having his first sons taught by tutors at home, after Hans's apparent suicide and Rudi's public one, he sent Paul and Ludwig away to school. (A message Ludwig received loud and clear, and recalled throughout his life: if he was to have a future, to survive, he had to get away from home. This was something even his home, his father, appeared to believe.†*)*

In a meditation on Descartes, Jacques Derrida proposed, as if for

---

>which characterize it are indeed those one looks for in a system of logic rather than in a dwelling place. In designing the interior Wittgenstein made extraordinarily few concessions to domestic comfort. Carpets, chandeliers and curtains were strictly rejected.

Ludwig's sister Hermine commented:

>Even though I admired the house very much, I always knew that I neither wanted to, nor could, live in it myself. . . . [A]t first I even had to overcome a faint inner opposition to this "house embodied logic", as I called it, to this perfection and monumentality. (As quoted in Monk, 237.)

* Adolf Loos, "Ornament and Crime," 169:

>It is easy to reconcile ourselves to the great damage and depredations the revival of ornament has done to our aesthetic development, since no one and nothing, not even the power of the state, can hold up the evolution of mankind. . . . But in economic respects it [ornament] is a crime, in that it leads to the waste of human labor, money and materials.

† *N.B.*: In his youth, Karl himself ran away from home, to New York, where he scrounged a living as a waiter, bartender, violinist, teacher. And he had also rebelled in being the only one of his siblings to marry a Jew, against his father's express wishes.

Descartes and many another philosopher. "*Je ne philosophe que dans la* terreur, *mais dans la terreur* avouée *d'être fou.*" *I philosophize only in* terror—*in the confessed terror that I might be mad. This is also to say that philosophy involves, as it certainly does, trying to find more order, more logic in our wild world than is really there.** *Or further—that philosophy involves trying to find a logic that, we know in our hearts, is not, cannot be there.* "[M]uß die vollkommene Ordnung auch im vagsten Satze stecken." *I am quoting Wittgenstein a little out of context, but in what, I believe, was his larger context.* "*There must be perfect order even in the vaguest sentence.*"† "[*T*]*he clarity that we are aiming at is indeed complete clarity.*"‡ *And if not? And given that there is not perfect order or complete clarity, and that there cannot be?*§

What I am proposing, with this leg up from Derrida, is that Wittgenstein's paramount problem was not too much authority—Abel's

---

* *Cf., Culture and Value*, 37e: "Within all great art there is a WILD animal: *tamed.* All art has man's primitive drives as its groundbass."

† *Investigations*, §98:

> On the one hand it is clear that every sentence in our language 'is in order as it is'. That is to say, we are not *striving after* an ideal, as if our ordinary vague sentences had not yet got a quite unexceptionable sense, and a perfect language awaited construction by us.—On the other hand it seems clear that where there is sense there must be perfect order.—So there must be perfect order even in the vaguest sentence.

I once heard a translator of speeches in the United Nations Security Council talk about how, when diplomats begin speaking about the most sensitive aspects of their or their countries' behavior, their grammar and diction breaks down. In such cases, the translator proposed, an accurate translation would be equally vague and even technically incorrect and inscrutable. I take this to be an example of the perfect order of vague sentences.

‡ *Investigations*, §133. Wittgenstein there goes on to say that "complete clarity . . . simply means that the philosophical problems should completely disappear." Simply?! In Appendix B I will write about our more general desire that all our legitimate/illegitimate questions disappear.

§ "It is my task, not to attack Russell's logic from within, but from without. That is to say: not to attack it mathematically—otherwise I should be doing mathematics—but its position, its office." *Remarks on the Foundations of Mathematics*, Part V, §16, 174e. In my psychobiographical mode, I consider it significant that this remark, and this challenging of the authority of mathematics, was being done during the Second World War, when the whole notion of authority was in crisis.

upcoming idea of an overlarge superego—but the threat of chaos (of suicide and world war and global financial crisis and the wanton killing of anyone with Jewish ancestry and of Eastern Europeans more generally).* *The problem— obviously—was the lack of* Ordnung, *and the use of* Regeln und Bestimmungen *to rationalize mass murder. Abel underestimates the extent to which it was the breakdown of authority that upset, or obsessed, Ludwig.*

*We are here edging toward a discussion of the psychology of fascism, which I will leave to others more schooled in this subject than I. What I will propose, focusing on Ludwig, is that a modern society of course has powerful rules—explicit ones and implicit ones. Many of these rules become internalized, self-enforcing, through guilt and anxiety, but there are also police, teachers, government and civic leaders pronouncing the rules and acting to enforce them or to see that they are enforced. But now suppose there comes that French-revolution/God-is-dead/collapse-of-the-*Doppelmonarchie *moment or set of moments—which lead to the realization that the only enforcer left on Earth is "me." "Little ol' me," I find myself wanting to write. "My" head is full of rules, inherited rules; my behavior has been organized by these rules; but now I look around me and there's no one left to enforce these rules or to defend them. It appears that everything—the rules and the punishments—depends on me! (It was not for nothing that one of Wittgenstein's ongoing struggles was with his desire to masturbate, because in this case it was all too clear that the last and only remaining line of defense against himself was himself.)*

It is one thing to have a large superego if you have faith in its

---

* Snyder (411) calculates that in the 1930s and 1940s, 14 million Eastern European civilians were victims of "deliberate killing policies" of Stalin and Hitler. This count includes:

> 3.3 million Soviet citizens (mostly Ukrainians) deliberately starved by their own government in Soviet Ukraine in 1932-1933; three hundred thousand Soviet citizens (mostly Poles and Ukrainians) shot by their own government in the western USSR . . .; two hundred thousand Polish citizens (mostly Poles) shot by German and Soviet forces in occupied Poland in 1939-42; 4.2 million Soviet citizens (largely Russians, Belarusians and Ukrainians) starved by the German occupiers in 1941-1944; 5.4 million Jews (most of them Polish or Soviet citizens) gassed or shot by the Germans in 1941-1944; and seven hundred thousand civilians (mostly Belarusians and Poles) shot by the Germans in "reprisals" chiefly in Belarus and Warsaw in 1941-1944.

authority, in the wisdom of the church, state and parents who installed this superego in a large corner of your brain. But when this authority is too weak or has been proven to be misguided or, worse, has come to doubt itself—here are grounds for getting really upset! Now we are like a child throwing a tantrum.* *I want someone to stand up and say No! You are going to do this and not that! This is what you must do and must not! And the more I yell and scream, the more I realize there is no one. There is no one left standing. No one who can play that role, no one who will play that role—not even my chosen mentors, Bertrand Russell and G.E. Moore, and Ludwig Boltzmann who committed suicide before I could come study with him, and my older brothers too. Now I am really in a rage, and there seems to be no reason for anything. "Father, why have you forsaken me!"*†

> Who tricked me into this whole thing and leaves me standing here? Who am I? How did I get into the world? Why was I not asked about it, why was I not informed of the rules and regulations but just thrust into the ranks? . . . And if I am compelled to be involved, where is the manager—I have something to say about this. Is there no manager? To whom shall I make my complaint?‡

Many years ago I remember hearing of a paradigm in some theory of child development. The idea was that in a child's life there is a moment (or in most cases it must in fact be a series of moments, of repeated confrontations)— when the child challenges authority, her or his parents. Let's say the child refuses to take a bath, saying simply, challengingly, "I don't want to." According to the paradigm, the parent may—will—respond in one of three ways, which I will illustrate as follows:

---

* Or like Nietzsche, his father dying on him when he was just a baby? There is no God! God is dead! God has died on me, on us. Can there be any greater outrage? (And I think, too, of all the boys and girls growing up these days without fathers, or alienated from their fathers.)

† A common translation of words spoken by Jesus while on the cross, as reported both in Matthew 27:46 and in Mark 15:34. The King James version of the latter passage reads: "And at the ninth hour Jesus cried with a loud voice, saying, Eloi, Eloi, lama sabachthani? which is, being interpreted, My God, my God, why hast thou forsaken me?" This can be read as one of the voices of every child, forsaken at birth, at weaning, the first day of school, of work, of marriage, and when unable to avoid her or his mortality.

‡ Kierkegaard, *Gjentagelsen* (*Repetition*), *Fear and Trembling and Repetition*, 200.

(1) "OK, if you don't want to, you don't want to. I'm not going to fight with you. I have other things to worry about, your bath is not that important to me, so what if you go to bed dirty, I don't have the strength to fight with you."

(2) "Get your f---ing butt in that bath this minute or I am going to pick you up and put you in there! I don't care if you don't want to take a bath. I don't even care if you don't need a bath. I said you're going to take a bath, and so you're going to take a bath, and now."

(3) "Please, let's not fight about it. You know, when people are dirty they need to get clean. People don't like to be around people who are dirty. People who are dirty get sick."

I have to say that it has been my observation (watching other people with their children) that #2 often works the best. It gives a young child a tremendous sense of strength and confidence and security to know that his parents are strong and have such confidence in their decisions, to know that the rules are the rules and can't be bent. That said, when the paradigm was presented to me, it was with the idea that option 3 was best because it allows the child to preserve his or her autonomy. S/he, as an independent decider, is being appealed to in the hopes that s/he will make the decision the authority believes is right. From this perspective, the problem of the overly authoritarian parent (#2) is that the child may feel like a nobody; her or his will counts for nothing. The problem of the insufficiently authoritarian parent (#1) is that the child may feel all alone (a stranger in a strange land)? Just when he was ready to fight somebody, to test her or his will, the other disappeared on him, there was no other will out there. To me, this describes the predicament in which Wittgenstein found himself, in his home with his father and mother and 30 servants; in Vienna with the empire collapsing; and even at Cambridge with the great Russell and Moore giving way before the force of his criticisms. Here is an incredible loneliness and confusion. Here are grounds for grasping desperately, obsessively for rules, and for coming up empty every time.

Couldn't there have been someone, when I threw my first tantrum, or the second—or perhaps later when I was talking too much, not letting anyone else speak—couldn't there have been someone to grab me by the arms—to hold me, that would have been part of it—and to just put me in the bath or tell me that, for the moment at least, I was going to shut up?

Reading about Wittgenstein's adult life, I have the sense that he kept searching for people who could both stand up to him—to his arguments, his self-obsession, his unfeeling comments, his not letting others speak—someone to stand up to him and *stay in the game with him, want to keep playing with (that is, keep arguing with him and talking with him about his concerns, hearing his strong opinions). Someone who was not overwhelmed by him, as Russell and his longtime lover, Francis Skinner, were, but did not keep him at arm's length either, as Moore did.*

I WOULD TAKE THIS *a step or two further, and then, again, let Abel and Marsalina takes us home. And it has also become apparent, as I have been editing and rewriting these words, that this will be the occasion to take a step or two backwards, to recall some of the earlier moments of this intellectual journey before it must come to an end.*

As Wittgenstein's biographer Ray Monk remarks, and as many another have suggested, Wittgenstein was completely absorbed in the philosophical problems he took up after Russell and Moore, or posed for himself. These problems "were not a part of his life, but the whole of it."[82] *This has not been seen as entirely positive. Russell observed of his mentee: "He has not a sufficiently wide curiosity or a sufficient wish for a broad survey of the world."*[*]

---

[*] Monk, 73; quoting a letter from Russell to Morrell, March 6, 1913.

As it has been to Descartes, the word "solipsism" has been applied to Wittgenstein. (From the *Tractatus*, 5.62 and 5.63: "That the world is my world, shows itself in the fact that the limits of language (the language which only I understand) mean the limits of *my* world. . . . . . I am my world.") And one might speak as well—and particularly in light of the present text!—of self-indulgence. But then we might wish to ask, self-indulgently, what purpose does the solipsism or self-indulgence serve? It is hard not to escape the conclusion that it is just one of the many ways—heroin being another, and cattiness, and gambling, fantasy football, watching television, and studying the particular effects of *this* chemical on *that* organism—ways of avoiding having to see other things—the deeper, larger, stronger.

I find myself recalling some comments on neediness made by the psychoanalyst, and composer, Emmanuel Ghent in his article on "Paradox and Process." What appears to be neediness—or, we may say, what appears to be self-indulgence—may, in fact, be an expression of a real need, say an urgent, even desperate need to be "heard," e.g., by a father figure such as Bertrand Russell. (And we will leave Abel's father and my own out of it.) This neediness—this urgent need, say, to talk

What I would propose first, as a thesis in a dialectical process, is that Wittgenstein's narrow and inward focus hamstrung his philosophical understanding. And, further, insofar as one accepts this point, one may be led to question that large segment of philosophical endeavor that has involved searching for the truth within, that has embraced the belief of Socrates and Descartes (among others) that truth is innate and requires only (!) the right method and hard work to be found.*

At the outset of this text I quoted Augustine: "Do not go out. Go in to yourself. Truth dwells in the inner man." By following these instructions, however, Wittgenstein (whether he ever read these words of Augustine's or not), . . . How do I want to put this? It is not that Wittgenstein ignored that his ideas were products of his circumstances. At the outset I also quoted, in a footnote, the lines published in Culture and Value—*where Wittgenstein proposed that his originality belonged "to the soil, not the seed." But, we might say, Wittgenstein was more than content to leave the matter there. He—willfully, obsessively (and desperately?)—got so caught up in the seed, in his seeds and their various sprouts (his behaviors, ideas, feelings), he had little time to think about the soil. And, again, one often feels that this was the overarching goal: not to think* about *the soil, be this his family, Vienna and Austria more generally, or the First World War, or the rage, the murderous self-hatred—or was it just a willingness to kill for money and power?—which consumed Europe for much of Wittgenstein's adult life. Here I would also recall again Fania Pascal, Wittgenstein's Russian teacher, proposing to Wittgenstein that they discuss the growing Nazi aggressiveness, and Ludwig's response: " . . . we must not talk of it." There is too much earth in the soil.*

---

about logic, or about Wittgenstein, or, perhaps even, about the Holocaust?—is well designed to keep the real need from being known—above all by oneself.

* *N.B.*: This was among of the beliefs that Descartes did not doubt when he put his mind to doubting everything. Other things he continued to believe in while he was doing his best to doubt everything: the value of doubting, or of reasoning; his ability to reason; his ability to be sure—without thinking, as it were—what thinking was. Edmonds and Eidinow (230) give Wittgenstein a lot of credit for unmasking Descartes's project and thereby overturning several hundred years of philosophy and emancipating Descartes's followers from "the slavery of the search for rock-bottom certainty". Throughout the present work I have been presenting a more complex and, I believe, more descriptive picture, in which certainties, but certainly not our desire for certainty, have been shaken by many phenomena of the past 100 years or so—Freud, Wittgenstein, the Holocaust and the atom bomb among them.

I am sure that many of my readers have had the experience of being given—say by a child struggling with a shoe—a knot to entangle, and of themselves getting entangled in the process, finding in it both unwanted annoyance and a kind of satisfaction—that one might forget about everything else in one's life and just work on this one diabolical knot. "How on God's earth did this get so tangled up, Jonah"—you might say to the child, as if you did not already know the answer. "How many times have I told you, you have to untie your shoes every time you take them off. And you don't just pull on the ends. That only works if they've been tied correctly. Otherwise you have to pay attention, pull the laces apart. Just pulling you make it worse." And all the while, while you're talking, your fingers and mind are engaged in a sort of mini-epic struggle with those laces, until finally—and with such a nice little surge of satisfaction—you've succeeded, the knot is undone. (And then, all of sudden you realize, glancing at your watch—you've spent all this time on the laces, now Jonah's late to school or tennis or whathaveyou. It might have made more sense for him to wear another pair of shoes or to try, as he usually did, to slip his shoes on without untying the laces.)

I have gone on at some length with this example, because it seems to me to well describe Wittgenstein's adult life. As if he spent the better part of it untying a knot or two (which he had inherited from Bertrand Russell and G.E. Moore). Was there ever a moment when he looked up and said, "Oh my God, all this time, the world has been hurtling on without me, I've missed so much, there's so much I should have done, might have done"?

A thought experiment, as physicists call it: Let us suppose that logic (the knot) had been but a part of Wittgenstein's life, and a larger part had been given over to thinking about the source of his interest in logic—that is, to thinking about "the soil" and how it had influenced, was influencing the particular growth of his seed. He might have found inspiration for this work in Augustine's Confessions or in Freud's writing, and also in the writings of another Germanic, semi-Jewish refugee in England: Karl Marx. I have yet to come across evidence, however, that Wittgenstein, despite his fantasy of emigrating to the Soviet Union, ever paid Marx much attention.* Nor is there much evidence that Wittgenstein tried very hard to learn much of anything from other writers or books. McGuinness proposes that Wittgenstein

---

* Monk, 486, describes Wittgenstein looking through a book on Rush Rhees' bookshelf: Max Eastman's *Marxism: Is it Science?*. That's all I've found so far. (Again, please see Appendix C for my Marxist reading of Wittgenstein.)

"read intensively, rather than read widely," and occasionally in Wittgenstein's letters one finds him recommending books to friends.* Nonetheless, a reader of Wittgenstein texts and biographies might easily come to the conclusion that, as for influential books, there had been, above all, two: Otto Weininger's at least half-crazed, homophobic and anti-Semitic Geschlecht und Charakter (*Gender and Character*), and Tolstoy's Gospels in Brief, *the book Ludwig apparently read over and over again while at the front in the First World War, a book that reduces Christ's life and teachings to five messages, e.g.: "Do not seek delight in sexual gratification." (This being a delight of which the young Tolstoy, like the young Augustine, had been quite fond.)*

I have been struck by this description of a room in Wittgenstein's Cambridge quarters:

> When you entered his room for a lecture, you found some fifteen or twenty wooden chairs and one deck chair facing the fireplace, before which stood a black anthracite stove. To the right below the window a trestle table with papers. On the mantlepiece a low-powered bulb on a

---

* In his biography of the "young Ludwig," McGuinness (33-34) states: "Of what works and writers he came to know actually in childhood, we have only strong indications. The great writers—Goethe, Schiller, Moerike, Lessing—he turned to all his life.... He read intensively, rather than read widely: he would return again to a passage or poem that 'said something to him'.... Naturally enough, therefore, his notebooks abound in quotations from Goethe and Schiller."

On page 37, McGuinness writes: "Ludwig all his life had [Karl] Kraus's habit of taking his opponent at his word and reading from a single ill-judged sentence a whole moral character." Perhaps the present text suggests that I myself am not lacking in this tendency. My interest for the moment, however, is in what this comment suggests about Wittgenstein's reading habits. My sense from all I have read about him is that reading "serious" literature or scholarly work (as opposed to detective stories) did not account for many hours, or perhaps even minutes, in his days. This is not to say, however, that reading was unimportant in his life. Rather the opposite: he read bits—or molehills, let's call them—and out of these molehills made mountains (e.g., he built the *Investigations* up from three sentences in Augustine's *Confessions*.)

I recall reading this way when I was young. My experience was that when I struck a molehill I had to put the book down and start writing or go for a walk or go find someone to talk to, because I became so worked up, so elevated, as it were, by the mountains my mind was making. This is not to say that my mountains were as extraordinary as Wittgenstein's.

retort stand. Behind you a bookcase with two or three books.*

It is this "two or three books" that strikes me. If you were to come to my office at the college—or to the offices of the great majority of my liberal arts colleagues—you would find the book shelves and window sills and table tops, and perhaps chairs and floor as well, overloaded with books. Or—now that I stop to think about it, I wonder if this isn't a Bild, *a fantasy, of mine, or "ein seltsames Gedächtnisphänomen" of professors' offices when I was just starting out. Now you will find a computer certainly and, let's say, a varying number of books.*

In any case, I believe that this is what I have to teach, what I try to teach, above all: a love of books, of reading. I always tell my students at the end of each term to write me, at any point in their lives, about books they have been reading, and it is one of the greatest pleasures of my life these days to receive these letters.

And so I am struck, too, by this line which, as it were, pops out at me from one of Wittgenstein's notes: "Reading the Socratic dialogues one has the feeling: what a frightful waste of time!".† And this, too, from the philosopher and literary critic I.A. Richards, a contemporary of Wittgenstein's:

---

* The description of Wittgenstein's room is from Gasking and Jackson, 50. See also Monk, 443, writing about Wittgenstein's life during the Second World War. A young colleague, Roy Fouracre, would visit Wittgenstein in his room: "The room, like his rooms at Cambridge, was completely bare, and Fouracre was surprised to see no philosophy books at all, but only neat piles of detective magazines."

That psychobiographical voice in my head will not be silent. "Can we at least *ask* if people, like Wittgenstein, who have a great interest in detective stories are not also quite interested in secrets and in finding out who committed the crime. That there has been a crime is quite clear; it's often right there on page 1. But who, ultimately, is to blame?"

† *Culture and Value*, 14e. The rest of the note: "What's the point of these arguments that prove nothing and clarify nothing." As usual, what is being criticized by Wittgenstein has a good deal in common with his own approach—for example, all the questions and answers in Plato, the explorations of how words are used, recognitions of the limits of human understanding . . .

See also a comment of Wittgenstein's quoted by Monk (476-77): "I have recently been reading a fair amount; a history of the Mormons & two books of Newman's. The chief effect of this reading is to make me feel a little more my worthlessness."

In those days at Cambridge, you had no assigned reading. You had no apparent awareness . . . in lectures that others had ever thought about these matters before. Whitehead, Russell, Moore, McTaggart, and the rest were all prophets, as it were, of various kinds. They would occasionally make a reference to someone—but it was in order to controvert.[83]

Wittgenstein of course was in one sense a much greater teacher than I, but I remain struck that his method—like Descartes's and Socrates's, interestingly enough—had no room for books. We might say that this was because Wittgenstein—again like Socrates and even Descartes to some extent—saw the much greater value of conversation, of rigorous conversation. But, as has been noted, Wittgenstein's conversation was basically an internal dialogue, a public internal dialogue that aggressively shut other voices out. And, more generally, we might note a particular limit of conversation among people who are disinterested in books, or in learning from others who are not party to the present conversation (be this because they lived long ago or simply because they do not happen to be there when the conversation is taking place).* Such people are also ignoring what may well be the more important "truth": the pleasures of reading great books.†

---

* *Cf.*, for a broader, anthropological perspective, Goody and Watt, "The Consequences of Literacy" (344, 310-11 and 340), wherein it is proposed, *inter alia*, that the literate "cannot discard, absorb, or transmute the past in the same way." A member of a non-literate society (and also a non-literate individual today?) "has little perception of the past except in terms of the present; whereas the annals of a literate society cannot but enforce a more objective recognition of the distinction between what was and what is." Thus, inversely, advantages of a less literate approach are suggested.

Along the way the authors (this was fifty years ago) propose that radio, cinema and television

> do not have the abstract and solitary quality of reading and writing, but on the contrary share something of the nature and impact of the direct personal interaction which obtains in oral cultures. It may even be that these new modes of communicating sight and sound without any limit of time or place will lead to a new kind of culture: less inward and individualistic than literate culture, probably, and sharing some of the relative homogeneity, though not mutuality, of oral society.

† To be accurate, I would note that, in contrast to Wittgenstein and Descartes,

So, returning to the thought experiment: Imagine a Wittgenstein who showed respect for and interest in book learning—in what voices from the past might be saying, instead of just how a few odd bits might serve as a foil for present ruminations. Imagine a Wittgenstein who allowed his concern with what was happening in the world around him to play a much larger role in the conscious processes of his mind. Imagine a Wittgenstein who was able to engage in conversation with others in ways that accepted their equal standing in the world, their equal right to contribute their thoughts to the conversation and to lead it down the particular paths that interested them. Imagine—being yet more demanding of poor Luki—that he had been able to make the connections between seed, soil and plant the principal subject of his investigations, so that his work became not an (extraordinarily successful!) attempt to escape the world as he had found it, but to understand—not on a philosophical level, but on a human, psychological level—the very human need to escape, the circumstances of human existence that lead to the need for escape, and the joys and comforts and traps and misery that can be found in various means of escape.* Would

---

Socrates, who lived at the dawning of books, did not scorn the wisdom and poetry of his predecessors, but often (at least in Plato's fictional dialogues) used them as a kind of diving board—a jumping off point—for his questions and observations. And as for M. Descartes, I cannot help but note that he took the bold step of publishing his first book, *le Discours de la méthode*, not in Latin, like most every other scholarly book of his time and place, and going back many centuries, but in French, so that "even women" (who were not taught to read in Latin) might understand it. The conclusion would seem to be that Descartes was not entirely against book learning, nor entirely afraid of how the teachings of others encumber and obscure the true understanding with which each of us is born. Rather, it would seem that what Descartes was really against was people learning from any books or teachings but his own.

"Even women" from a letter from Descartes to P. Vatier, February 22, 1638, as quoted in Denis Moreau's "Introduction" to the year 2000 Livre de Poche edition of the *Discours*, 20, fn 2. Descartes's phrase: "[J]'ai voulu que les femmes mêmes pussent entendre quelque chose". Note that Descartes was not referring to all women; in the seventeenth century more than 80 per cent of the French population was illiterate.

* To be fair, I should note that there are those, perhaps particularly Steven Affeldt (after Stanley Cavell), who read Wittgenstein as doing just this. E.g., in "The Difficult of Seeing Aspects" Affeldt writes that Wittgenstein's focus

> is on what becomes of ordinary individuals when they are led
> by circumstances—which need not be at all dramatic or "phil-

this not have— Or let me, rather, put it this way: Could this have produced a greater level of understanding than Ludwig's compulsive putting his fingers on knots in academicians' logic and in their understanding of language?*

That, as advertised, was my "thesis." And now the antithesis: It also deserves saying that it was the narrowness and inwardness and intensity of Wittgenstein's focus that allowed this one human being to tunnel so deep, into caves never before explored by the human mind. And it deserves saying, too,

---

osophical"—to stop to think and undertake to express themselves about some ordinary matter. His focus, that is, is not on moments when we explicitly understand ourselves to be stepping back from our ordinary lives but on the emergence of philosophical emptiness precisely in the course of those lives. And one of his central discoveries, as Stanley Cavell was the first to emphasize, is that "we may at any time . . . be speaking without knowing what our words mean, what their meaning anything depends upon, speaking, as it were, in emptiness." We may at any time, that is, and without realizing it, be in the midst of philosophizing—not as a special activity, but as ordinary, recurrent, human emptiness. (Affeldt cites Cavell, "Notes and Afterthoughts", 133.)

* Somewhere in here we also need to make room for a third source of learning: what are sometimes called "life experiences." That is, experiences that do not directly involve reading or reflection. For all this is a very large and rich source, it may not be as large as one might think insofar as reflection is at times directly involved in our learning from our life experiences.

Is there not a line, perhaps in one of Melville's or Conrad's novels, "the sea was my Shakespeare"? I have not been able to track it down. Nicely, one of the most quoted lines attributed to Augustine is "The world is a great book, of which they that never stir from home read only a page" (and variations thereon). But it seems unlikely that Augustine ever said or wrote anything like this. On a website I find a comment perhaps made by/perhaps attributed to a distinguished Augustine scholar, James Joseph O'Donnell: "Augustine does not speak of his travels or what he learned on them, and he hated travel itself. He dismissed the inquisitive observation that tourists practice as culpable curiosity, which he regarded as a great sin."

> Some people read books in order to find God. Yet there is a great book, the very appearance of created things. Look above you; look below you! Note it; read it! God, whom you wish to find, never wrote that book with ink. Instead He set before your eyes the things that He had made. (Augustine, Sermon, Mai 126.6; as quoted in *The Essential Augustine*, 123.)

that he likely did not have much choice in the matter. Edmonds and Eidinow quote from a recollection of Wittgenstein's oldest sister, Hermine:

> I told him . . . that imagining him with his philosophically trained mind as an elementary school teacher, it was to me as if someone were to use a precision instrument to open crates. Thereupon Ludwig answered with a comparison which silenced me, for he said, "You remind me of someone who is looking through a closed window and cannot explain to himself the strange movements of a passer-by. He doesn't know what kind of storm is raging outside and that this person is perhaps only with great effort keeping himself on his feet."[84]

And so now we must do our best to make it to a synthesis, which I take to lie in the following observation, which I believe was richly, touchingly exemplified by Abel and Marsalina's conversation at a New York Barnes & Noble in 2009. For all the narrowness, inwardness, obsessiveness, academic-ness and so forth of Wittgenstein's work, what gives that work its intellectual and emotional power, what continues to engage new generations of readers—and despite all the arid (mis)uses that have been made of Wittgensteinian texts and ideas—is that Wittgenstein reaches toward the heart of human experience. To return to one of the very first points Abel made: When Ludwig writes "Wer in ein fremdes Land kommt" (Who into an alien country coming), he is not only speaking about language and the learning of language, and he is not only speaking about the fundamental experience of his life—as a child coming into the Wittgenstein family and as a young man taking refuge in England and in analytic philosophy—he is talking about one of the fundamental experiences—emotional experiences—that we all have, in coming into the world, and into the particular worlds into which each of us come.

Now, recalling words that, over the several years I have been preparing the present text, have come to seem like old words, even ancient words of wisdom, I would reprise something Abel said, in reference both to Wittgenstein's section 32 and to Moses's naming his son Gershom. I quote Abel:

> . . . we might have to recognize, that—oddly, paradoxically—what we may share above all is our isolation, or this feeling of aloneness. We may be united in our being strangers to one another . . .

In my mind Abel is touching here, and perhaps as nearly as we can touch, the great gift one Ludwig Wittgenstein had to offer his contemporaries and all of us who have come after him and who, even as we must come up short, do our best to read with an open mind. "We may be united in our being strangers to one another." And, I would add that we are also united in wishing—and we may be wishing more for this than for any other thing, more than for immortality even—wishing that this strangeness, this distance between us, this gap might not be.

(6)

As if the child already had a language

Marsalina, returning from the bathroom: You know, Abel, I will say that I feel somehow purified by this discussion we have had, and I have to think that for that I have both you and Wittgenstein to thank.

Abel: We're like a high colonic.

Marsalina: Only I suspect that for his part Mr. Wittgenstein was never vulgar.

Abel, on his way to reciting from section 28 of the Investigations: The ostensive definition of the number two—

> "That is called 'two'"—pointing to two nuts—is perfectly exact.—But how can two be defined like that? The person one gives the definition to doesn't know what one wants to call "two"; he will suppose that "two" is given to *this* group of nuts!

Marsalina: He didn't write that!

Abel: He did. And so you see, I have simultaneously put to bed any number of questions about Ludwig Wittgenstein:

> (a) He could be vulgar;
>
> (b) He was a homosexual; and
>
> (c) What has heretofore been most in doubt: Wittgenstein had a sense of humor!*

---

* It is said that one of Wittgenstein's fellow Cambridge philosophy dons used to read each sentence of his lectures to his students twice. Except for the jokes, which he read three times. That, said one of his students, was only way you could tell what was a joke.

This professor, C.D. Broad, a non-Wittgensteinian, was not liked by Wittgenstein. As a practical joke, Joan Bevan, the woman to whom Wittgenstein said his supposed last words about his wonderful life, once told Wittgenstein, then, at the end of his life, a guest at her house, that Broad would be coming round for tea. This was just a joke, but when Wittgenstein discovered the truth (Broad not coming for tea), he "went into a deep sulk, refusing to speak to his hostess for two days." (Edmonds and Eidinow, 70-71.)

Marsalina: And to think that I once had a cup of coffee with you.

Abel: But was it the cup or the coffee you had? Or was it you who was had? No, seriously, there is something I need to point out here. There is something important that you were on the verge of establishing with your "Mr. Wittgenstein was never vulgar."

Marsalina: What was that?

Abel: You were establishing a negative pole, if you will, something that cannot be said about Wittgenstein and the *Investigations*.* Perhaps "It was not written in Chinese" would have done as well as "Mr. Wittgenstein was never vulgar."† What I've been wondering as we've been talking and trying to establish what this section 32 really is about—I've been wondering if it might have been easier, quicker if we had started by establishing such a negative pole. "Section 32 is not about love." Or perhaps that is debatable, for all neither "love" nor "affection" appears anywhere in the *Investigations*.‡

All that said (in fun), I also note that there is plenty of evidence that Wittgenstein had a sense of humor, when he wanted to.

* It might be said that Bouwsma uses a variation on this strategy, and with excellent results, in his review of "The Blue Book." His "negative pole" is constructed over half a dozen introductory pages. By way of example I cite the following from near the beginning: "This book (i.e., "The Blue Book") contains no introduction, no conclusion, no chapters, no chapter headings, no helpful title." (Bouwsma, *Philosophical Essays*, 177.)

† Yes, seconding Abel, the latter proposition would seem to be incorrect. Apparently, for example, the following was among Wittgenstein's favorite expressions (and perhaps as a stranger he misunderstood how vulgar it was?): "Don't try and shit higher than your arse." He apparently applied this expression to philosophers who he felt were on the wrong track. (Edmonds and Eidinow, 16.)

As for the Chinese, I am reminded of this Wittgenstein note from August 21, 1914, which was reproduced, with a slightly different English translation, as the very first note in *Culture and Value*: "When we hear a Chinese talk we tend to take his speech for inarticulate gurgling. Someone who understands Chinese will recognize *language* in what he hears. Similarly I often cannot discern the *humanity* in a man."

‡ "Postponing loving until knowledge has been acquired means substituting knowledge for love." Freud, "Leonardo da Vinci and a Memory of his Childhood," I, 54.

Please see Appendix A's discussion of pointing, including of a possibility raised in a footnote to the *Investigations* (below §30): Suppose, to explain the word "modest"

"Section 32 is not about lemonade?"

Marsalina: I'm tired, though, Abel, and I'm sure your lovely wife and daughter are waiting eagerly for you to come home. So just answer one more question for me, and then let's call it an afternoon.

Abel: *Mit Vergnügen*. With pleasure.

Marsalina: During this little discussion we have learned a lot from Wittgenstein and had a good time doing it, yet from time to time I've sensed this undertone of hostility on your part. It's as if you thought Wittgenstein was guilty of some crime or that he was getting off too easy. Didn't he just write a few books?

Abel: So did the Gospel writers, and look what a mess they got us into! Your point is a good one, though, and I wish I could say this was just my attitude toward Wittgenstein and not something more generalized—a hostility toward many great minds. My personal analysis, for what it's worth, is—surprise, surprise—two-fold. On the one hand, I am sure it's the old father/God thing. What good is all Wittgenstein's genius and authority if he cannot save me? Worse, he makes me work so hard to understand what he's saying. And why go to such trouble unless there is some hope that one might at least save oneself, that one might find the magic formula hidden in the riddles of this man who wrote that "the riddle does not exist"?* But no amount of studying can transform Wittgenstein from a human into a god, and the harder one studies the more one is forced to recognize that there can be no magic formula, not even in great philosophical works. Salvation is just one of our mirages.

As if that weren't enough, there is what I think of as the problem of the over-large superego. Perhaps you could just have carved on my tombstone, "Here lies Abel, whose life was a futile attempt—" Don't laugh. "Whose life"—my life—was/is "a futile attempt to escape feelings of inadequacy and guilt. And thus, being an intellectual, he sought above

---

to someone whose English was weak, one pointed to an arrogant man and said "That man is not modest"?

* *Tractatus*, §6.5.

A comment about Wittgenstein in his early days studying philosophy at Cambridge: Wittgenstein "is reading philosophy up here, but has only just started systematic reading; and he expressed the most naive surprise that all the philosophers he once worshipped in ignorance are after all stupid and dishonest and make disgusting mistakes!" Monk, 50; quoting from David Pinsent's diary, May 30, 1912.

all to show that greater intellectuals than he were inadequate and guilty too. And in the process—when he realized what he was doing—he felt even more inadequate and guilty."

Marsalina: *Pobrecito.* But if you're going to be doing all that carving, please don't leave out how you also gave a series of aging females a sense that they were still worth talking to, if not getting naked with.

This was rather a lot for Abel, and for a few moments he was sputtering, like a poorly tuned motor on the back of a row boat. Then—at least in my imagination—Marsalina reached and touched his arm. "Don't worry," she said, "you can keep your underpants on."

Abel: You're too fast for me.

Marsalina: I'm too fast for you! It's more than an hour now I've been doing my damndest to try to keep up!

Abel, perhaps now reaching to touch Marsalina: And I appreciate it. I really do. If I was a professor or a graduate student, I might have more people to talk with about these things, but as a cutting-edges-and-corners "information professional"—*his voice took on a droning, reciting quality*—combining traditional duties with tasks involving quickly changing technology, to say nothing of my wide knowledge of a wide variety of scholarly and public information sources and my abreastness of trends in publishing, cyberspace and the media, and how I tailor programs and systems in order to ensure that— And also, I should mention how the better part of each day after day is spent looking up or resetting the passwords students have forgotten and telling them to go left to get to the bathroom.

I'm desperate! *He laughed.* And meanwhile, did I finish answering your question about my "undertone of hostility."

Marsalina: I knew we had gotten off the track somewhere.

Abel: It's actually more interesting than you might have imagined, because while I don't know anything about Wittgenstein's relationship with his father, I am sure I am not the first to say that Ludwig, too, suffered from an over-large superego. In fact, my sense is that he suffered much more than I have—more than most of us in this age of guilt. Apparently he once said that a way in which the notion of immortality can acquire meaning is through the feeling that one has duties from which one cannot be released, even by death.[*]

---

[*] Malcolm, *Memoir*, 71. Another tortured, beautiful note, from the very end of

So here then is my question for you: Did Wittgenstein not champion or explore this observation of Augustine's regarding language because one of his overriding objectives was to get out from under feelings of inadequacy and guilt by calling our attention to the shortcomings of great thinkers?*

Wittgenstein's life: "God may say to me: 'I am judging you out of your own mouth. Your own actions have made you shudder with disgust when you have seen other people do them.'" (*Culture and Value*, 87e.)

* It might also be noted that, at least since Socrates and Diogenes of Sinope (a.k.a., the Cynic), it has been traditional for ambitious philosophers to build their reputations on exposing weaknesses of the reigning philosophies and philosophers, their immediate teachers often included. One might indeed make a distinction between a small set of great philosophers and a much larger set of ordinary ones solely on the basis of the individuals' relative willingness to condemn illustrious predecessors and contemporaries. The ordinary are identifiable by their habit of having a kind word for all, even for those in the back of whose arguments a dialectical knife is being twisted.

In the extreme version of the more aggressive practice, the up-and-coming philosopher, rather than stabbing and twisting, simply wipes the table clean, asserting that before him people weren't really doing philosophy or didn't know what philosophy really was, or didn't even know the meaning of the words they were using. (And, even better, along the way the aggressive, and without a hint of self-mockery, note the difficulty of the task now before them—i.e., of reinventing philosophy having abjured the possibility of anyone helping them. Descartes, for example, feels "comme un homme qui marche seul et dans les ténèbres"—like a man who walks alone in the dark. Indeed!)

Among the extremists may be found not only Socrates, Descartes and Nietzsche, but also G.E. Moore and the man who came to inherit his chair at Cambridge: Ludwig Wittgenstein. Thus before Moore "no one had even conceived the problem of ethics correctly", and Wittgenstein, in Moore's wake, made more or less the same claim, if more extremely, and without, it would seem, laughing at the absurdities not very hidden in this chain of events.

I would also note another nice irony. For all Newton said he had been helped by the shoulders of giants, and for all Newtonian mechanics lives on in physics classes, often in the natural sciences when a new theory carries the day, an old one is overthrown, confined to the dustbin of history, with scientists losing all interest in studying the past error. In the natural sciences there is only the present Truth and the possibility that future research will expand or modify it, or show it, too, to be wrong. In philosophy, however, for all philosophers may claim to be emerging from the quicksand of idiots and idiocy—and for all the school of "analytic philosophy" birthed at Cambridge by Moore, Russell and Wittgenstein

And it isn't too difficult—reading Wittgenstein's texts and reading in the memoirs and biographies—it isn't too difficult to decide that his strategy was to call attention, relentlessly, to the shortcomings of all and sundry. One of his disciples remarked on Wittgenstein's ability to "find out the weak spots of another human being and to hit out hard."[85]

Here (*more paper rustling*), let me read you something. Listen to what Bertrand Russell wrote about the effect on him, at the time one of the leading philosophers in the world, of being subjected—of allowing himself to be subjected—to Wittgenstein's criticism of his work. "I [Russell] saw he [Wittgenstein] was right,

> and I saw that I could not hope ever again to do fundamental work in philosophy. My impulse was shattered, like a wave dashed to pieces against a breakwater. I became

---

(and prefigured by Bishop Butler well before them) has belittled the study of the history of philosophy—and for all for more than a thousand years intellectuals were interested in only one of Plato's dialogues—and for all the "modern" philosophers, while resuscitating Plato, scorned Aristotle and medieval philosophy . . . The work of Emerson, Hume, Heraclitus, Rousseau, Marx, Cratylus, Cusa, Nietzsche, Montaigne, Lucretius, Aristotle, Kierkegaard, Voltaire, Sextus Empiricus, Butler, Augustine, Kant, Plotinus, Pascal and even Sidgwick and Moore will not die. Lovers of wisdom continue to find insight and succor in old texts and ways of thinking. Shall we say that philosophers who mock and condemn their predecessors fail to notice what they do when they are awake, just as they forget what they do when asleep?

The question just above is from a translation of a statement that appears in one of the fragments that has come down to us from Heraclitus (Barnes, 101, citing Diels-Krantz reference B1). The quote from Descartes is from *Discours de la méthode*, Seconde partie, 86. The quote about no one conceiving of the problem of ethics correctly comes from a *Guardian* review of Moore's *Principia Ethica*. A little more:

> Mr. Moore's mission . . . takes the modest form of assuring almost all other philosophers since the world began that they have never even conceived the problem of ethics correctly, much less succeeded in solving it. And so he sweeps the gross absurdities of Aristotle, Kant, and other triflers into the waste-paper basket, tosses Christianity on top of them, and finally leaves no on outside that useful receptacle except a fragment of Henry Sidgwick and himself, a result which may be gratifying to the University of Cambridge but must be distressing to the rest of the world. (As quoted in Regan, 19.)

filled with utter despair. . . I *had* to produce lectures for America, but I took a metaphysical subject although I was and am convinced that all fundamental work in philosophy is logical. My reason was that Wittgenstein persuaded me that what wanted doing in logic was too difficult for me. So there was no really vital satisfaction of my philosophical impulse in that work, and philosophy lost its hold on me.*

To me there is something very sad—or enraging—about this.† Of course, Ludwig might well have been right: Russell's work, or Russell's work during that time, was garbage. Or perhaps it wasn't so bad, but it wasn't great; there was nothing in it of lasting value. It didn't meet Ludwig's standard: either do great work, read or listen to the great works of others, or commit suicide. But how do we know what Russell might have written if he had been encouraged during this transitional time? And what right does one human being have to shatter another's impulse? On what basis does any individual decide that God has decided to speak through him, ruling on the worthiness of another man's, or woman's, path?

Marsalina, with a certain timidity: I suppose we often do something like this though, commenting on people we don't like, or political opponents. And then there are all those—Jesus, for example—who have indeed spoken as if God were speaking through them. You're describing a whole profession: preaching.

Abel: I suppose I am. You're right. I need to do some rethinking. But not re-feeling. I still feel there's something deeply wrong here. What is that line from Yeats? *Abel recited from memory, glorious memory*:

> I, being poor, have only my dreams;
> I have spread my dreams under your feet;
> Tread softly because you tread on my dreams.‡

Marsalina: That's beautiful Abel. I can't help feeling, though, that you

---

* Letter from Russell to Morrell, 1916, reproduced in Russell's *Autobiography*; as quoted in Monk, 80-81.

† And I am reminded of Wittgenstein's cruel treatment, aforementioned, of his close friend/lover, Francis Skinner: convincing him to go to work as a mechanic in a factory, rather than pursue a promising career in mathematics.

‡ William Butler Yeats, "Aedh wishes for the Cloths of Heaven."

are turning against your beloved Wittgenstein. Are you suggesting that because of his insensitivity, his enthusiasm for criticizing other people . . . Are you suggesting that this in some way invalidates his work?

Abel: I guess to what extent and how are my questions. And I raise them, I hope, not simply because of my own raging superego's desire to belittle a great man—

Marsalina: If you do in fact have a raging superego, something I am inclined to doubt.

Abel: And I certainly would not want to suggest that I identify with Wittgenstein in the sense of feeling that he and I are similar people. If his work speaks to me—as it certainly does—it must be because it speaks to something more general, something rather widely shared by human beings, some aspects of the human predicament.

Marsalina: Well, all this must be in Ludwig's favor.

Abel: Yes, certainly. But here's where I'm at. Here's where I'm at in my Magellanic voyage, eating my own sandals so I can keep on sailing across the seemingly interminable ocean of section 32 of the *Investigations*.* In the Preface to the book, Wittgenstein writes "*Daß das beste, was ich schreiben konnte, immer nur philosophische Bemerkungen bleiben würden*" (The best that I could write would never be more than philosophical remarks); and "*ist . . . dieses Buch eigentlich nur ein Album* (this book is only an album). Suppose that instead he had written, "What follows is first and foremost an attempt to use philosophy"—or, better, "to use criticism of others' ways of thinking—to assuage my feelings of inadequacy and guilt"? How would you have read the ensuing pages? Or would you have read them at all?†

Or that sounds a little stupid now that I say it out loud. How

---

* I.e., Magellan and his crew ended up eating leather (along with rats, maggots and sawdust) to try to stay alive as they traversed the Pacific, the expanse of which was unimaginable to them. Their ideas of oceans were based on the Atlantic and Indian oceans. To reprise a phrase used earlier, they were lost in their lostness. By the time they reached Guam at least twenty men had died from complications due to starvation.

† Nietzsche immediately comes to mind in this regard. Imagine that one or another of his works (*Die Fröhliche Wissenschaft*? *Der Antichrist*?) had opened with a brief discussion of his feelings about his pastor father having died when Friedrich was very young? Readers who have gotten this far may be able to anticipate my response: Bring it on! Here's a book I would like to read!

about this: It is said that Wittgenstein got the idea for his "picture theory of language"—never mind what that is—while in a trench on the eastern front in the First World War, looking at a schematized picture of the possible sequence of events in an automobile accident in Paris.* Supposing he had put all this together: the scene at the front, his feelings about being a soldier, perhaps about to lose his one life in that trench; and then telescoping, or withdrawing, to feelings by looking at pictures of an automobile accident—a record of a tragedy that happened to someone else, to a stranger in a strange land—to an enemy, or to someone in enemy territory at least, in France. And then imagine Ludwig withdrawing from there back to a further distance, a further level of abstraction, to the picture theories that were being tried out in the physical sciences. Supposing he had made a truly heroic effort in trying to pull together these three or more levels of human experience and of human reactions to life. Instead of escaping, I'm afraid I have to say, into some picture theory of language, however brilliant this theory may be. In fact, I think we can say that the brilliance of the theory is a distraction or diversion. It encourages us— and perhaps this is what it does above all, like an inspired performance of Beethoven's Ninth—or would this be an uninspired performance?— which encourages us to take our minds off our predicament and off how we respond to it. Wittgenstein is encouraging us to mistake the forest for one extraordinary human-made tree. What an extraordinary theory—or basketball dunk on television—or symphony or song. Isn't this what it's all about in the end—diversion, escape?

I hope I am saying this with some empathy in my voice. To have been a soldier at the eastern front in the First World War must have been living hell. I certainly have read things about life in the trenches on the western front, in Belgium and northern France.†

---

* See Wright, "Biographical Sketch", 7-8. I think Abel's point comes across better if I do not offer an explanation of Wittgenstein's picture theory of language, or of its previous use in German scientific texts.

† From the diary of Ernst Jünger, at the time a nineteen-year-old German lieutenant:

> You cower in a heap alone in a hole and feel yourself the victim of a pitiless thirst for destruction. With horror you feel that all your intelligence, your capacities, your bodily and spiritual characteristics, have become utterly meaningless and absurd.

Marsalina, gently: OK, Abel, I hear you. But do you mind if I ask why you didn't give me this speech an hour ago?

Abel, shaking his head, I imagine: The best excuse is that I did not know that this is what I had to say. It's taken an hour with you—it's thanks to your willingness to listen to my babbling, and so patiently, . . . So I think . . . *There was a halting quality to Abel's voice; it was an emotional moment for him.*

He went on: "*Und nun können wir, glaube ich, sagen.*" And now I think I can say that I have reached *an* understanding of section 32 at least. Is that nothing? "Is whispering nothing? Is leaning cheek to cheek? Is meeting noses? Kissing with inside lip?"*

> While you think it, the lump of metal that will crush you to a shapeless nothing may have already started on its course.

From the recollections of Mary Borden, an American working as a nurse at the front:

> We receive these bundles. We pull off a blanket. We observe that this is a man. He makes feeble whining sounds like an animal. He lies still; he smells bad; he smells like a corpse; he can only move his tongue; he tries to moisten his lips with his tongue. . . .
>
> He is only one among thousands. They are all the same. They all smile as if they were grateful. And often they apologize for dying. They would not die and disappoint us if they could help it. Indeed, in their helplessness they do the best they can to help us get them ready to go back again.

Jünger, *The Storm of Steel: The Diary of Ernst Junger* (Zimmermann & Zimmermann, 1985; a translation of the original German); Borden, *The Forbidden Zone* (Heinemann, 1929); both as quoted in Groom, 194-95 and 179-80.

* From the speech of the jealous Leontes in Shakespeare's "The Winter's Tale" (Act I, Scene ii).

>   Is whispering nothing?
> Is leaning cheek to cheek? Is meeting noses?
> Kissing with inside lip? . . .
>   Is this nothing?
> Why, then the world and all that's in 't is nothing;
> The covering sky is nothing; Bohemia's nothing;
> My wife is nothing; nor nothing have these nothings,

Marsalina: It's about babbling and listening—your section 32.

Abel laughed: Babbling *and* listening. Very good, Marsalina.

If this be nothing.

(7)

Als könne das Kind schon denken

I have concluded that it was at around this point that Marsalina put her hand in Abel's and the two of them sat there, hand in hand. There was another pause, a pause I am not going to intrude upon with any more of my own commentary. Then Marsalina spoke, in a new tone as it were.

Marsalina: Speaking of listening . . . *She paused.* I think you may be leaving out something important.

Abel: What's that?

Marsalina, softly: You've talked a lot about Wittgenstein, and a fair amount about yourself too, of course. You've thanked me—and more than I deserve—for listening to you and helping you. But you haven't asked why. You haven't asked why have I sat here so long with you, struggling with a few paragraphs in a book?

Abel, sputtering: No . . . excuse me . . . Marsalina . . . excuse me.

Marsalina: Don't worry about it Abel. I'm not blaming you. But I do want you to ask me why. Why, Marsalina, have you sat here so long? What have you been waiting to say?

Abel: Yes, Marsalina, why have you sat here so long? What have you been waiting to say? Please tell me—and excuse me.

Marsalina: Have you ever wondered, Abel, what you're going to make of all this—of life, I mean—when you get to the end? I don't mean: Have you ever come up with some glib words. I mean, have you ever really found yourself wondering—wondering so you can't sleep—imprisoned in wondering—without any words?

You've just spent almost two hours in a cafe talking with me. Many more hours, days, reading Wittgenstein, reading about Wittgenstein. There are my nails that for some reason need doing, the marathons I run, hours just running until I'm in such pain the next day I can hardly walk.*

---

* "If you can't find happiness in stillness, find it in running! But what if I am too tired to run? Don't talk of collapse until you break down. Like a cyclist I have to keep pedalling, to keep moving, in order not to fall down." (Wittgenstein diary entry, April 9, 1942; as quoted, as translated, in Monk, 442.)

Abel: I hear you. This is something you've been thinking about? This is what you wanted to talk about, and I didn't get the message and made you listen to me rant and rave about Wittgenstein?

Marsalina: Well, I wouldn't quite say that. I would say that it was easier to listen to you, to talk with you about Wittgenstein, to try to figure out something reasonably figureable-outable.

Abel: Something for which the words, at least, were clear.

Marsalina: You know, a few weeks—it seems like a few months ago—Jerry got me to watch *2001: A Space Odyssey* with him. I think what got to me was the scene where HAL turns off the oxygen and chemicals—other chemicals—going to the astronauts who are sleeping in the "hibernators," and then Dave, the last person alive, pushes the bodies in their tubes out into space. And also the slowness of HAL's own death, or brain death, when Dave starts turning him off, and we hear HAL speaking and then singing, not unlike an elderly person, slowly dying in a hospital bed. The idea that came to my mind—that's been in my mind ever since—perhaps it's the reason I called you. I suppose it is. At the end—assuming we still have enough brain cells left to think with—is it just going to seem to have been futile, a waste of time and breath? "Futile"—perhaps it's not that I have no words. Perhaps it's that I only have this one.

I imagined Abel squeezing her hand and looking into her eyes, trying to pass empathy from his eyes to hers.

Marsalina: The arguments, the jockeying for position, the lists, staff evaluations—now this sexual harassment suit. The driving up to the country house and back from the country house. For all I really like it up there, once we get there and unpack and before we're packing the car to drive back again.

You know what it is, or what it might be, Abel? It goes back to something I was saying—when I was attacking you for always changing the subject. It's as if the things that seem to matter so much at the moment don't really matter. That's almost the sign that they don't matter: that they seem to matter so much. And what does matter, or what may matter, is what lies in between, in the cracks.*

---

* *Investigations*, §129:

The aspects of things that are most important for us are hidden

Abel, softly: "Step on a crack, break your mother's back."

Marsalina, smiling, it seemed: I remember that. And it's funny, too, that you brought up that thing about the therapist, because just the other day I was wondering, maybe it's time, and to go for myself, to say what I think, what I remember, what I have not forgotten, all the things . . .

Her voice trailed off. And then returned: What do you think? I suppose it's the real reason I called you.

Abel: To . . . Not to find out what I think. I'm happy to hear you're thinking of trying . . . I don't want to say "therapy" because of its implications of disease and cure. I'm happy to hear you want to talk about what you think and feel and remember. And I'm sorry you're feeling this . . . this sense of futility.

Marsalina: I don't know if I used the right word. I don't know what I want to say. I don't know where to begin. And if I begin will I ever shut up?

Abel, momentarily losing "his feet": Are you . . . ? Is that a question?

Marsalina: It could be a question. It could be a sense of a bottomless pit. That's scary.

Another quietness. I imagined Abel nodding, agreeing, waiting patiently.

Marsalina: I wish there were a simpler, more direct way of living. That's one thing. I wish I could say what I really want to say. There's another. Before it's all over and I've been slidden—is that a word?—never mind, it is now—before I've been slidden into outer space, or six feet under, I want to say a few things! I wish I had the guts. The way you do—without any censoring or strategizing or worrying about how ridiculous— Or is this, is this right now the right thing to say? What could be the consequences? Are they what I'm after? What the fuck am I after? pardon my French. I wish I felt some good could come of it, out of really talking for once. Would that be really having a conversation?

Abel: It could—

---

because of their simplicity and familiarity. (One is unable to notice something—because it is always before one's eyes.) The real foundations of his enquiry do not strike a man at all. Unless *that* fact has at some time struck him.—And this means: we fail to be struck by what, once seen, is most striking and powerful.

Marsalina: Besides just getting some things off my chest.

Abel: That could—

Marsalina: My colleagues—my husband!—would laugh, hearing me talk like this. They think of me as so outspoken. But—*she laughed*—they've never had a coffee with you and Wittgenstein.

Abel: "Yes, a key can lie for ever in the place where the locksmith left it, and never be used to open the lock the master forged it for."*

Marsalina: Say that again?

Abel, repeating: "Yes, a key can lie for ever in the place where the locksmith left it, and never be used to open the lock the master forged it for."

Marsalina, softly, slowly: That does seem a little bit like what I was trying to talk about. That's from Wittgenstein?

Abel nodded, I imagine. My New School professor had heard something on the radio, on a show about religion on NPR, something about how we are people in search of a mystery.† And so he was proposing—or asking, really—in the course of discussing the *Investigations*—could it be that we are a people in search of a mystery, or could it be that philosophers get tangled up in their questions, to avoid having to use or even see the key?

Marsalina, plaintively: And you think this might apply to me too?

Abel: Well, that would be presumptuous on my part. And I don't think that you get tangled up in questions or are in search of a mystery.

Marsalina: But I'm still not using the key.

Abel: I suppose I would say that I think you can see the lock and the key, and that heretofore you have kept your distance. Let sleeping keys lie.

---

* *Culture and Value*, 1946, 54e.

† The only thing I could find in this regard was a comment by Arlene Sánchez-Walsh, a scholar of Latino Pentecostal and Evangelical spirituality, made to Krista Tippett, the host of the show "Being" on National Public Radio (NPR). The specific show, "Reviving Sister Aimee," was broadcast on June 9, 2011, so this would seem not to have been Abel's professor's source in 2009, though perhaps Sánchez-Walsh had also made this rather general comment earlier.

I would also note that in "The Difficult of Seeing Aspects," Affeldt suggests that Wittgenstein regarded "the sense of the mysterious as, in part, produced by a flight from the remarkable." E.g., of the remarkability of our life in language.

Marsalina: And what about you?

Abel: What about me? That's too easy! I'm back there with the questions and the mysteries. The things that are too complex to figure out—and particularly if we can find a lot of irrelevant junk to throw in, in case the task should not seem complex enough.

I'm sure it's not just me, but, still, I'm very impressed by all the little questions I come up with in the course of a day. How should I lock my bike so it will be most secure? Which sweater do I want to wear? Caf or decaf? Halal chicken from the Bangladeshi street vendor or Swiss enchiladas from the Mexican take-out?* What strikes me is that the specific answers don't really matter very much, if at all; it's like—just as I have a need for caffeine and protein, I may have a need to answer a certain number of questions every day.

Marsalina: It helps you to ignore the real questions of your life—is that what you're saying?

Abel: The real ones or perhaps just the semi-real ones. How are Sarah and I are going to put Celeste through college? Or why am I not chaining myself to the White House fence to protest the use of drones to do our bombing for us, and genetically modified organisms to do our farming for us, and campaign contributions to do our governing for us, and "social media" to do our connecting for us, and . . .

Marsalina: Or about your relationship with Sarah, for example.

Abel: About my relationship with Sarah for a very good example, though I take that also to be a remark about your relationship with Jerry. That that might be one of the things in the lock box.

Marsalina: So I guess what you're saying is that all I have to do—or all we have to do—and Jerry and Sarah, too—is to screw up our courage.

Abel, quoting Lady Macbeth:

> But screw your courage to the sticking place,
> And we'll not fail.[86]

Marsalina: Please stop interrupting me, Abel.

Abel: I'm sorry. Please go on.

---

* Halal chicken, prepared as prescribed by Moslem law. Swiss enchiladas: i.e., *enchiladas suizas*.

Marsalina: It just seems like a matter of having the courage to pick up our keys, open our locks, let all the demons out. And then maybe we—maybe even our friend Ludwig would have been—demon free.

Abel: Of course then there'd be all our demons running around in public, and with no clothes on, as it were.

Marsalina, persistently serious about this point: Don't run away yourself, Abel. Tell me this—or help me think about this—can you think of anyone who seems to have indeed picked up their key, opened their lock?

Abel: No, of course not. And—wait—don't get mad at me—I am not making a joke. Just because the task is obvious—just because it may, in various guises, present itself to some of us several times a day—this doesn't mean that more than two or three people in the whole course of human history have ever picked up the key and opened their locks. Ludwig Wittgenstein certainly *not* among them.*

There's a fairy tale, perhaps you know it—Bluebeard?

I imagined Marsalina shaking her head no. She didn't know it.

Abel: There are a series of rooms, deeper and deeper underground, and a series of keys. You might say that most all of us have opened a lock or two, descended a floor or two down into our psyches, but only half a dozen people have made it to bottom floor, and only two or three of those dared open that door.†

---

* Wittgenstein, somewhat in synch with Abel, but with his own, much more Wittgensteinian than Abelian twist:

> You see, I know that it's difficult to think well about "certainty", "probability", "perception", etc. But it is, if possible, still more difficult to think, or try to think, really honestly about your life and other people's lives. And the trouble is that thinking about these things is not thrilling, but often downright nasty. And when it's nasty then it's most important. (Letter to Norman Malcolm, November 16, 1944; quoted in Monk, 475.)

† My sense is that Abel is not referencing the original fairy tale, "La Barbe bleue" by Charles Perrault, but rather some later version, such as Bela Bartok's opera "*A kékszakállú herceg vára*" (Duke Bluebeard's Castle; libretto by Béla Balázs). With help from the Wikipedia entry on Bluebeard's Castle, accessed in June 2011, here is the story:

> Judith and Bluebeard arrive at his castle, which is all dark.

Marsalina: And what do you think they—the two or three—found?

Bluebeard asks Judith if she wants to stay and even offers her an opportunity to leave, but she decides to stay. Judith insists that all the doors of the castle be opened, to allow light to enter into the forbidding interior, insisting further that her demands are based on her love for Bluebeard. Bluebeard refuses, saying that they are private places not to be explored by others, and asking Judith to love him but ask no questions. Judith persists, and eventually prevails over his resistance.

The first door opens to reveal a torture chamber, stained with blood. Repelled, but then intrigued, Judith pushes on. Behind the second door is a storehouse of weapons, and behind the third a storehouse of riches. Bluebeard urges her on. Behind the fourth door is a secret garden of great beauty; behind the fifth, a window onto Bluebeard's vast kingdom. All is now sunlit, but blood has stained the riches, watered the garden, and grim clouds throw blood-red shadows over Bluebeard's kingdom.

Bluebeard pleads with her to stop: the castle is as bright as it can get and will not get any brighter; but Judith refuses to be stopped after coming this far, and opens the penultimate sixth door, as a shadow passes over the castle. This is the first room that has not been somehow stained with blood; a silent silvery lake is all that lies within, "a lake of tears." Bluebeard begs Judith to simply love him, and ask no more questions. The last door must be shut forever. But she persists, asking him about his former wives, and then accusing him of having murdered them, suggesting that their blood was the blood everywhere, that their tears were those that filled the lake, and that their bodies lie behind the last door. At this, Bluebeard hands over the last key.

Behind the door are Bluebeard's three former wives, but still alive, dressed in crowns and jewelry. They emerge silently, and Bluebeard, overcome with emotion, prostrates himself before them and praises each in turn, finally turning to Judith and beginning to praise her as his fourth wife. She is horrified, begs him to stop, but it is too late. He dresses her in the jewelry the wives wear, which she finds exceedingly heavy. Her head drooping under the weight, she follows the other wives along a beam of moonlight through the seventh door. It closes behind her, and Bluebeard is left alone as all fades to total darkness.

A misleading analogy if ever there were one?

Abel: My personal theory is that, above all, or beneath all, they found themselves in a highly unusual place. A place beyond—beneath?—anyone's imagining.

Marsalina: And that's all? That's all I get, Abel, for all the hard brain work I've been doing this afternoon!

Abel: You wanted . . . a key, I guess. Rather than *your* key, you wanted mine, or Wittgenstein's—the master's key, or, even better, the "master key," "the master," as locksmiths say. Seems a little passé, a little patriarchal or phallocentric—this looking for a master—wouldn't you say?

Marsalina: Frankly, I don't know what to say. Or what I *would* say is that I wasn't expecting for you to just leave me, Abel, in a "highly unusual place." Somewhere beneath my imagining.

Abel, hesitantly, apologetically, paraphrasing a bit from Plato's Cratylus: "If I'd attended Prodicus's fifty-drachma course . . . But as I've only heard the New School's one-drachma course, . . .⁸⁷

There was a pause, as if for the feelings of coming up short to sink in. It was not long, however, before Abel spoke again, and with his sprite-like enthusiasm and tone returning: I'll tell you what. If you still have a moment I'll tell you a love story, a Wittgensteinian love story.

Marsalina, glancing at the time on her cellphone, I imagine: If it's not *too* long.

Abel: So here it is, in the abridged edition. Setting: The stacks of a university library, somewhere between the B358s and the B3376s.* An *unheimlich*, white-blonde and beyond-the-pale, Jewish-American, middle-aged man of about my size and demeanor runs into a not unattractive Canado-Senegalese young woman, a graduate student who works part time at the circulation desk.† He asks her what she is studying—in graduate school,

---

* B358: library call number for works about Plato; B3376 for works about Wittgenstein.

† *Unheimlich*: eerie. Or, in this case, perhaps "eerily" would be the correct translation. As for being "beyond the pale," this is more complicated. The word "pale" derives from the Latin "palus", meaning stake, or, synecdochically, a fence. According to Wikipedia (consulted July 2011), the phrase "beyond the pale," as used to refer to unacceptable behavior, comes from the Pale in Ireland (*An Pháil* in Irish or the English Pale: *An Pháil Shasanach*). This was the part of Ireland that was directly under the control of the English government in the late Middle Ages

that is.

Marsalina: And she says, "Not middle-aged married men."

Abel: Worse, "fashion marketing."

Marsalina: What's so bad about that?

Abel: Fashion marketing—now you need a master's degree to sell clothes? And the first thing—perhaps the only thing—you're taught is misleading at best: marketing is not selling. Selling is what we used to do, forcing people to buy things they didn't need. But now we identify their true needs and meet them. For example, you may have noticed all the young women wearing vaguely Grecian sandals these days, or the newfound willingness, *voire* enthusiasm, of *homo sapiens* to pay money for T-shirts that serve as advertising for the companies selling the T-shirts.

Marsalina: I'm missing the big problem here. Your attractive friend likes clothes and wants to earn her living selling them or marketing them, either way.

Abel: Yes, and at some point after our little conversation I realized this, and I thought to myself, she cares about clothes and I care about Wittgenstein, these are just two different ways of going through life . . .

Marsalina: Without having to use the key.

Abel: Yes, that's more or less what I was thinking. But then the Wittgenstein in me got me wondering about the word "care." I thought of something Sarah sometimes says: "Tell me again why I care?"—meaning "I don't care." And I thought about the compound: "care about." We like to feel we "care about" other people.

Marsalina: And they about us.

Abel: And they about us, most definitely. But it is an odd locution, if you stop and reflect: "care about." It reminds me for some reason of hovering, as if caring involved a kind of hovering. And what about the difference

---

and, on a reduced scale, for a few centuries thereafter. Presumably, however, Abel is referring (or is also referring) to the Pale of Settlement (or *Черта оседлости* in Russian): the region of Imperial Russia in which permanent residency by Jews was allowed (much of what today is Lithuania, Belarus, Poland, Moldova and the Ukraine, along with parts of western Russia). Approximately 2 million Jews emigrated from the Pale between 1881 and 1914, most of them—Abel's ancestors presumably among them—came to the United States, to New York.

between "caring about" and "caring for"? It seems to me that when we're "caring for" we're doing a lot more caring than when we're "caring about."

Marsalina: A good description of the "liberals" in my neighborhood. They think that "caring about" is a worthy substitute for "caring for." In fact, they aren't caring people at all. What they really care about is getting invited to dinner parties with people who've sold more books or won more awards than they have, or who have played basketball with the President.

Abel: You see what a slippery slope this fashion marketer and her caring about clothes got me on.

Marsalina: Did she even that say that, that she "cared about" clothes, or fashion?

Abel: No, of course not. But maybe what I heard—or what my middle-aged marriedness heard—was that she cared more about clothes than she ever could about me.

Marsalina: If ever a man was in need of philosophy!

Abel: Yes, exactly. And what was interesting to me—the reason I've been bending your ear with this little story—was that it did not take too long for my Wittgensteinian reflections on the difference between "caring about" and "caring for" to lead me to think about my caring about and my caring for Sarah and Celeste. And I thought that for me what all this means is that what happens to them happens to me too. This "I" that physically at least seems to lead an autonomous existence—this "I" that may not be able to sufficiently "understand" these other people— But this otherness is also a fiction, if perhaps a useful fiction. Sarah, Celeste and I are, for the moment at least, One. A very complicated One—if a One is allowed to be complicated—but a One nonetheless.

Unlike Wittgenstein or Moses or his son, while I may be a stranger to myself, I am not a stranger in a strange land; I have a home, however in need of physical and psychological fumigation it sometimes seems to be. For Wittgenstein there is "something" accompanying his cry of pain. And "this something is what is important—and frightful". "Only whom are we informing of this?" Wittgenstein goes on to ask. "And on what occasion?"*

---

* *Investigations*, §296. The whole text, a fragment of which Abel had quoted earlier, is:

"Yes, but there is *something* there all the same accompanying

I had the sense that tears were coming to Abel's eyes. His voice was choked as he now said: For me the "somethings" are less important than the someones, the whoms. Sometimes it is my cry, and, more often really, it is their cries that I hear. And certainly this is important, and at times frightful, but of course more of the time it is comforting—that they are there, that I can hear them and help them, that they can hear me and help me.

If that means "Have I reasons?" the answer is: my reasons will soon give out. And then I shall act, without reasons.*

Yes. The answer is: my reasons will soon give out. And then I shall act without reasons! "We fail to be struck by what, once seen, is most striking and most powerful."†

I have this thing with Celeste when either one of us gets sick. We call it "Siamese medicine." The one who is well sits or lies where the one who is sick can touch them, say, while we're both reading, or she's reading and I'm listening to the radio. The point—the cure—is just the physical contact. Like Michelangelo's man and God. Like you and me right now. It is not so much that the health of the healthier one flows to help cure the disease of the sicker one; the warmth, and just the fact, of the contact is soothing and healing—for both people. This is as close to health as—

There was the ringing of a cellphone that seemed to be coming from somewhere very close to my left hip. Marsalina answered it and quickly agreed to a meeting, and then said to Abel: That was my manicurist. It's now or never.

With that they both got up and there was—a long hug, I'm sure it was. My head was again bent to my book, my eyes tightly shut, as against tears.

---

        my cry of pain. And it is on account of that that I utter it. And this something is what is important—and frightful." Only whom are we informing of this? And on what occasion?

* *Investigations*, §211.

† *Investigations*, §129.

(8)

And "think" would here mean something like "talk to itself"

Years have passed since I first heard and scribbled down Marsalina and Abel's conversation. Years that have been spent attempting, through reading and writing, to . . . Not so much to make sense of the conversation, or even to explicate it for others or for myself, or to take Abel and Marsalina's thoughts and feelings a step further. My sense is that, above all, I have wanted to live, however temporarily and fancifully, in the possibility that such a conversation represents. That the people around me might be exploring their thoughts and feelings in this way, with such vigor—that Marsalina and Abel's conversation might not seem an unusual event. That someday I might—or might again—have such a conversation with someone?

But now . . . Some force within tells me it's time to move on. Essays, books—and friends—set aside while I worked on the present text are now pulling at me, making me feel a little annoyed—with myself above all, for not being able to put this conversation behind me and indeed move on.

In that Barnes & Noble, likely soon to be rendered verflossen (bygone) *by the* schöpferische Zerstörung—*by the creative or not so creative destruction that is capitalism—by online booksellers and e-books and* Die Endlösung (*the final solution*): *the appropriation of language by advertising, public relations, television* animateurs (*animators*: Emcees)—*I heard Marsalina, as she was leaving the cafe, calling back in Abel and my direction*: You know what my boss would say after such a lengthy presentation?

I shook my head and imagined Abel shaking his too.

Marsalina: "Next time number the pages."

We all laughed out-loud at that. And Abel now stood with his head above the partition so that not only could he see me, if he wanted to, but Marsalina could see him blow her a kiss as he called out, cheerfully: Fuck you, too, my dear. And good luck with your nails. Don't forget to tell the Koreans what I said.

Marsalina: What—or which—was that?

Abel: Wer in ein fremdes Land kommt, wird manchmal die Sprache . . .

Marsalina, walking quickly past the shelves of games and magazines and on toward the escalator landing, may not have heard him. She did not reply. Abel turned away from the partition—to gather his papers and books, I supposed.

I, too, gathered my things and myself. I put on the re-shelving shelf the commentaries on Wittgenstein—the book by Kripke and other books that I had not read. I packed up my scribble-covered portfolio reviews and risk-reward matrices.

In the midst of these activities, I found myself trying to decide: Should I walk back to my hotel or go over to the Knickerbocker for a good ol' American steak? Refrains of the Investigations *came back to me: "How can a rule show me what I have to do at this point?" And, "Man fragt sich: 'Wo soll das enden?'" One asks oneself: "Where is this going to end?"*[88]

Appendix A

Pointing, The Exception, Gaps and Scaffolding

Pointing[*]

In both its German and English versions the *Investigations* is overflowing with pointing in the sense of pointing with a finger (or glance) at something, and also with points (tiny dots and purposes and of arguments), and with ostensive definitions and arrows that point. While in German all this activity requires several nouns,[†] in the English translation, the word "point" and variations thereon can be, and are, used over and over again—so often, in fact (almost 100 times), that there have been points (moments) when I have wondered if perhaps Wittgenstein or Anscombe (his student and translator) were having some fun seeing how many times and different ways they could use the word "point."[‡] Or were they, more seriously, offering "point" as a leading example of a word with a large family of resemblances (a large family of somewhat similar uses)? For the moment I will point to one section in particular, §454:

> How does it come about that this arrow → *points*? Doesn't it seem to carry in it something besides itself?—"No, not the dead line on paper, only the psychical thing, the meaning, can do that.—That is both true and false. The arrow only points in the application that a living being makes of it.

---

[*] I have Professor Affeldt's article on "On the Difficulty of Seeing Aspects" to thank for bringing my attention to this matter of "pointing." I would not, however, have him made responsible for my, likely iconoclastic views on this matter.

[†] My German-English dictionary offers half a dozen different German nouns as equivalents for one or another use of the English "point." E.g.: *Punkt* (dot), *Spitze* (of a pencil), *Zeitpunkt* (moment), *Stärke* (someone's strong point), *Thema* (thing to be discussed), *Pointe* (of a story), *Zweck* (purpose).

[‡] Among the additional uses of the word "point" in the English translation: to point with a gun and at examples and to possible uses; point of view; point of light, point in a discussion or to stare at; to make a point of (reading slowly); to bring someone to the point of; to be to the point or point out; a needle point; a pointer.

Let us ruminate briefly on Wittgenstein's example. How does it come about that this arrow → points to the right and not to the left? And what about the times when an arrow seems to point to the left, but actually points to the right? Or the times when we are sure that *it* points to the left and yet this somehow means that we are to go right? An obvious example is when a road sign gets turned or when an old sign has not been removed, and thus misdirects us. But of course parents, too, point their children in certain directions, and often the children realize that if they are going to survive, let alone thrive, they need to go in a quite opposite direction. (Karl Wittgenstein and his sons come to mind.)

For quite a different example, I note that some women (and men) dress in ways we call "sexy," and this—say, the revelation of a goodly portion of a woman's breasts—may put thoughts of sex in a man's head (or a woman's), and s/he may think quite specifically that this particular person would be a good person to have sex with. Abel used an example of very short skirts that seemed to him to point quite directly to sex—or to *le sexe d'une femme*, as a French person could say, referring to the *les organes génitaux extrernes* (the vulva). And yet it may well be that sex (the act rather than organs or fantasies) is not what a woman wearing a short skirt or low-cut dress has in mind. She may be pointing in the direction of sex without having the least intention of herself heading that way. With some (many?) women and men it may be that the ability and willingness to dress in a sexy fashion is linked to, indeed depends on, disinterest in the activity that the look calls to mind.* (Similarly I have known politicians who were

---

* I cannot not cite here Sartre's discussion of mauvaise foi in *L'être et le néant*. See in particular (89-91) his example of a woman who, without realizing what she is doing, abandons her hand to a man who is trying to seduce her. "She talks about life, about her life. She shows her essence, that she is a person, a thinking person. And all the while the divorce of body and soul has been achieved. Her hand rests inert between the warm hands of her partner. It is neither consenting or resisting—a thing."

I must also confess that the example of the sexy dressers came to my mind because of my niece Atalanta's interest in Lady Gaga. This led me to read an interview that had been done with this celebrity, the former Stefani Joanne Angelina Germanotta. "I have this weird thing," she told *Vanity Fair*'s Lisa Robinson, "that if I sleep with someone they're going to take my creativity from me through my vagina." That is, she is rather afraid of the sex act. And yet to me, in my highly limited knowledge of Lady Gaga, she is someone who intentionally appears in public in sexually provocative, outrageously revealing outfits. (Now we are on to Sartre's

in private quite shy, uncomfortably shy, tongue tied, and it seemed for this reason that they had chosen to make their lives in public, pressing the flesh, giving speeches.)

Another example, to bring to yet another plane this discussion of how we can have difficulty knowing what to make of what seems to be indicated—ostensibly, ostensively. One day when I was working on this segment I got into a taxi on the back seat of which someone had left a cellphone. This led me to tell the driver that I had no idea what to do with this abandoned phone—how to contact the abandoner—because I myself had no cellphone. "Oh," the driver said, "then you must have no worries." (He later told me how throughout his workday his wife would call him with one concern after another.)

"No," I replied. "It's just the opposite." (The arrow only appears to be pointing left.) "People with cellphones are constantly distracted from their worries. But me, I have to live with mine."

In fact, though, I quickly realized, perhaps the arrow was pointing left after all. If my worries were all that great, or if I lacked the inner resources to accept these worries into my consciousness and to deal with them more or less successfully at that level, . . . Well, I would have a cellphone (or drink a little more wine than I do, play the ponies, bite my nails . . .). That I do not have a cellphone and few bad habits besides philosophy is a sign that my worries are not that great. (As befits a man who inherited a little money, has a Harvard Ph.D. and tenure, and no children.)

In any case, it seems to me we now have a good idea of the problem with arrows—or, better, with humans, to include with our life in language, our symbols and cellphones and worries and many another phenomenon all wrapped up together.*

---

example (94) of the waiter who, in being, on the job, a waiter, acts the part of a waiter, without for all that himself being a waiter.)

* Apparently, crucial to the development of relatively simple and supple writing systems was the supplementing of logograms with phonetic symbols. An example that is offered in the scholarly literature is of the Sumerian sign for an arrow ("*ti*") which, by what is called "phonetic transfer," came also to stand for the homonym *ti* meaning life, a concept not as easy to express pictographically. (Goody and Watt, 312.)

So then, coming back to Wittgenstein, I note that, in addition to points, the *Investigations* is full of similes, analogies, invented language games that all seem to be *pointing* toward phenomena that Wittgenstein would like us to pay more attention to; telling aspects of our life in language. But the question—the question that was brought to my attention by Affeldt's article on "aspects" (a major concern of Part II of the *Investigations*)— the question is whether Wittgenstein's pointing is indeed *toward* the phenomena that seem most important to him, or whether Wittgenstein is, at least in some (many?) cases, pointing *away* from what he considers important? As a mother or father bird may fly *away from* its nest as a way of trying, via misleading, to protect her or his young.

In *Wittgenstein's Poker* it is reported that in his youth—and would one have to be young to say such a thing?—Wittgenstein apparently told an editor that his book, the *Tractatus*, consisted of two parts: the written part and the unwritten part. "And it is precisely this second part that is the important one."[89] I.e., what was important was all that could not be said about ethics, or the fact of this inability—the human inability—to speak in meaningful ways about ethics. As if most everything the book seemed to be pointing toward, and that generations of scholars have taken from it—the truth tables we all learned in school, for example— All this was not the point.

For his part, Affeldt is interested, and for somewhat different reasons than mine, in the discussion of the language game Wittgenstein offers in the very first section of the *Investigations*. Here is Wittgenstein's text:

> <u>Now think of the following use of language</u>: I send someone shopping. I give him a slip marked "five red apples". He takes the slip to the shopkeeper, who opens the drawer marked "apples"; then he looks up the word "red" in a table and finds a colour sample opposite it; then he says the series of cardinal numbers—assume that he knows them by heart—up to the word "five" and for each number he takes an apple of the same colour as the sample out of the drawer.—It is in this and similar ways that one operates with words.—"But how does he know where and how he is to look up the word 'red' and what he is to do with the word 'five'?"—Well, I assume

that he acts as I have described. Explanations come to an end somewhere.—But what is the meaning of the word "five"?—No such thing was in question here, only how the word "five" is used.

Notwithstanding the phrase I have underlined, Wittgenstein himself, in section 2, points out that what he has, at least ostensibly, been pointing at with this first example is *not* human language. "That philosophical concept of meaning [given in §1] has its place in a primitive idea of the way language functions. But one can say that it is the idea of a language more primitive than ours."

So a reader—and particularly a reader who was not caught up in the discussions of language and meaning going on at Cambridge University when Wittgenstein was a student and teacher there—may well find himself asking why Wittgenstein bothered to develop and present this clearly artificial and apparently not-analogous analogy? Among other things, were an author to think that a reader's trust and faith in his authority were important, or that clarity was a goal, . . . ? Would you begin your book by urging readers to think of one use of language and then suggest, in the very next paragraph, that this example—an example that appears to come from the author—does not well describe the language the readers *thought* he was talking about/pointing toward: their language, our language, human language.

In the subdivision I have come to in my own Wittgenstein studies, I have come to feel the language games he invents are akin to various other kinds of language games with which highly verbal people like to amuse themselves: e.g., devising palindromes or believable-though-false definitions for obscure words. But this is not the answer to my question about Wittgenstein's tactics that I wish to write about. Rather I would focus on Affeldt's answer, which seems to me much richer than my own gut response.

> Wittgenstein [in §1, with the apples] has deliberately crafted a jarring example in which language use appears lifeless and mechanical, and has done so, at the opening of his investigations, precisely to call to mind (by contrast) the vitality of our life with words . . . He aims to call all of this to mind for at least two reasons. First, it must form a touchstone for any adequate philosophical reflection

on language. But second, and for present purposes more importantly, he wants to allow us to recognize the reality of our life with words as remarkable.

What, for present purposes, interests me most in these phrases is the "call to mind (by contrast)." This suggests that, at least in this case, at the outset of the *Investigations*, Wittgenstein is pointing toward or at something (the lifeless, mechanical example) in order, in fact, to have us look away from it: at life-full, non-mechanical, human language.* But this is also to say that in seeming to point in one direction, he is in fact pointing in another, in the opposite direction. As if when you, traveling, a visitor, a stranger, asked a local resident how to get somewhere, he gave you quite detailed directions *and* you were to know from this—from the level of detail? from something in his tone of voice or the way he was looking at you—that you were to do the opposite of what he had just described.†

"But wait," an attentive reader objects, "Wittgenstein himself, in section 2, as you have yourself described—Wittgenstein himself tells you that his 'detailed directions,' as you call them, are wrong, or will not get you where you want to go."

"Yes," I say. "So you ask a man for directions and he takes some care to give you directions, detailed directions, and then he tells you that they will not get you where you want to go." Here we have arrived at the paradox Bertrand Russell made so much of. "The Cretans, always liars, evil

---

* *Investigations*, §185: "Such a case would present similarities with one in which a person naturally reacted to the gesture of pointing with the hand by looking in the direction of the line from finger-tip to wrist, not from wrist to finger-tip."

† Or what might we make of statements of grand ideals, e.g., that we Americans and our government are dedicated to "life, liberty and the pursuit of happiness," or one of the famous lines in Matthew (16:26): "For what is a man profited, if he shall gain the whole world, and lose his own soul?" Such statements might be said to be like arms that point toward the stars, and an eye might follow the path backward, from fingertip to shoulder, and discover things at least as true: e.g., the dedication of Americans and the United States to making money (with life, liberty and happiness often be damned), or to the problem of keeping one's soul (being true to one's ideals) but not having enough to eat or becoming alienated from one's less scrupulous fellow citizens. It seems to me that here we have opened another door on the Wittgensteinian subject of illusions, optical and verbal.

beasts, idle bellies!" wrote Epimenides, a Cretan.* But, with Wittgenstein and the *Investigations* at least, the matter is taken a step or two further insofar as more not-analogous language games are offered, and indeed the number of words devoted to these is rather greater than the number devoted to saying what human language is indeed like. So it is as if you, the stranger in our example, were to ask for directions and were given directions and then told these were not quite right, or worse, and then you were given more directions, similarly qualified.

I am reminded of the old "Down East" (Maine) comedy routine "Which Way to Millinocket?".

> Narrator: "I was standing outside Sutherland's IGA store one morning, when I heard a flivver approaching down the street toward me."
>
> Sound effects of an old car sputtering to a stop, then a visitor's, stranger's voice: "Which way to Millinocket?"
>
> Narrator: "Well, you can go west to the next intersection, get onto the turnpike, go north through the toll gate at Augusta, 'til you come to that intersection . . . well, no. You keep right on this tar road; it changes to dirt now and again. Just keep the river on your left. You'll come to a crossroads and . . . let me see. Then again, you can take that scenic coastal route that the tourists use. And after you get to Bucksport . . . well, let me see now. Millinocket. Come to think of it, you can't get there from here."[90]

But we are not trying to get completely lost here. And so I would come back to Wittgenstein's question "How does it come about that this arrow → *points*?" At many moments in the *Investigations* Wittgenstein says/reminds his readers that this is something we just know; it is a given of our "form of life." One such moment, which in the main body of this

---

* From a poem by Epimenides (circa 600 BCE), often known by the Latin translation of the title, "De oraculis/peri Chresmon," and perhaps preserved through history above all on account of the quite other use that the apostle Paul, in his usual Paulish way, made of the poem, e.g., in Titus 1. There the poem is quoted in 1:12, but the moral drawn in 1:15: "Unto the pure all things *are* pure: but unto them that are defiled and believing *is* nothing pure; but even their mind and conscience is defiled."

book I discussed at length and rebelliously, has to do with the picture of the old man with the stick. How do we know that "his arrow"—his body—is pointing up the hill rather than down? "Might it not have looked just the same if he had been sliding downhill in that position. Perhaps a Martian would describe the picture so. I do not need to explain why *we* do not describe it so."

This clearly is one voice in the *Investigations*; the voice of common sense we might well call it. But there are other voices. And particularly, and particularly for our present purposes, there is this other voice that goes beyond simply disagreeing—that goes beyond simply insisting, as I did in discussing the man with the stick, that the old man might well be sliding downhill. This other voice is telling us—through examples such as the shopkeeper with the apples *and also directly*—that pictures and pointing are deceptive. "This is the point at which I go wrong."[91]

Language gives us pictures, Wittgenstein proposes. And so, I might add, do the media, celebrities, politicians, professors of humanities. What is to be done with these pictures, how they are to be used, remains obscure. Quite clearly, however, this must be explored if we want to understand what we are saying.

But the picture seems to spare us this work: it already points to a particular use. <u>This is how it takes us in</u>.*

"Takes us in": tricks us. (Or are we so many stray cats?) Language is tricking us. Pictures, *Bilder*, analogies are tricking us. Much as magicians trick us. They trick us by pointing, by directing our attention to the wrong thing, to what is, at best, irrelevant. They point at something—or at more than one thing—and thus make it more difficult, much more difficult for us to see what's really going on.

In the very first section of his *Investigations*, in the space of four paragraphs, Wittgenstein, I would argue, uses language and variations on pointing to mislead his readers two or three times. First he points at a section in Augustine that he quotes out of context and for all—or because—this is not one of the sections of the *Confessions* that really interests him. (See the discussions of Augustine and Wittgenstein in Appendix B.) Then

---

* *Investigations*, Part II, vii, 157e. My underscoring. The previous few sentences were also adapted from this passage in the *Investigations*. The exact quotation is given in the segment on "decontextualizing" in Appendix C.

Wittgenstein offers a language game of his invention—an engaging, intriguing game—in order, it would seem, to say above all that this game has little or nothing to do with language.

And so, my next and final question for this segment. If Wittgenstein's arrows, as many another's arrows, are not pointing at what they seem to be pointing at, can we know at what they are in fact pointing? Can they tell us—call attention to—anything at all? Or, to put this another way, if arrows are not, or are not consistently, "really" pointing at what they are pointing, when can they be thought to be pointing at anything at all?*

> Could one define the word "red" by pointing to something that was not red? That would be as if one were supposed to explain the word "modest" to someone whose English was weak, and one pointed to an arrogant man and said "That man is not modest". That it is ambiguous is no argument against such a method of definition. Any definition can be misunderstood. But it might well be asked: are we still to call this "definition"?[92]

What did Abel say at the very beginning of his conversation—or at the moment that first caught my ear? It's the Garden of Eden, complete with red apples and forked-tongue philosopher? With such assurances did Magellan and his crew set out to go east by going west, and with none but Magellan possessing a map, and that one quite wrong?

From one perspective, the point we have arrived at in our own voyage is simply that of students struggling to understand a difficult text, and sorely tempted to conclude that the reason we cannot understand is because the text makes no sense. The emperor has no clothes! But what makes our present pass more interesting is that we are not simply talking about Wittgenstein. "Life, too, is a book in which we have not found the answer," as Abel's wife's, Sarah Campbell, put it.†

---

* I am reminded of a boy I knew when I was growing up. He used to take a stick or pencil and point it repeatedly at a wall or a tree trunk, with his back to the rest of the world. His family called this "pointing," and it was thought to be essential to this boy in some way—to his psychic equilibrium, to helping him organize the various bits whirling in his mind perhaps.

† See also from Thoreau's Journal, March 16, 1852:

> Spent the day in Cambridge Library . . . The Library is a wil-

So we might make it through and over this pass, I will quote at length here from Affeldt's "On the Difficulty of Seeing Aspects and the 'Therapeutic' Reading of Wittgenstein":

> It is a central part of Wittgenstein's ambition in *Philosophical Investigations* to reveal not only *that* we recurrently turn toward emptiness, but concretely and specifically *why* we do so. He wants to bring to light and depict in as compelling a manner as he is able the various human drives, cravings, anxieties, fantasies, perversions, wishes, and the like that lie behind and are manifest in the turn to philosophical emptiness. Surely part of why he wants to do so is that he seeks to understand and depict at least some of the complexities of our human nature as currently constituted. (This is not a merely intellectual interest in a type of philosophical anthropology. A man as tormented as Wittgenstein must also have been seeking to better understand himself.) However, more importantly, Wittgenstein must work to bring to light the aspects of our nature manifest in the emergence of philosophical emptiness because they are exactly what must be treated in genuine Wittgensteinian therapy. His therapy, that is, cannot merely treat symptomatic emptiness. It must treat the aspects of human nature that recurrently produce this emptiness.
>
> Accordingly, while Wittgenstein does want to calm the

---

derness of books. The volumes of the Fifteenth, Sixteenth, and Seventeenth Centuries, which lie so near on the shelf, are rarely opened, are effectually forgotten and not implied by our literature and newspapers. When I looked into Purchas's Pilgrims, it affected me like looking into an impassable swamp, ten feet deep with sphagnum, where the monarchs of the forest, covered with mosses and stretched along the ground, were making haste to become peat. Those old books suggested a certain fertility, an Ohio soil, as if they were making humus for new literatures to spring in. I heard the bellowing of bullfrogs and the hum of mosquitoes reverberating through the thick embossed covers when I had closed the book. Decayed literature makes the richest of all soils.

restless and tormented voice of philosophical emptiness, he *must* also provoke it, call it forth. He must do this, in part, because it is his only means of discovering and investigating the aspects of human nature requiring his treatment. But he must also provoke the voice of philosophical emptiness because it is in and through that voice being called forth from each of us, in the encounter with Wittgenstein's text, that we discover ourselves to harbor the drives, cravings, anxieties, and the like that its emergence reveals. It is only in and through the voice of emptiness being called forth from us that we recognize our need for Wittgenstein's therapy and that it can begin to work upon us.

And so, where are we? What is on the other side of the mountain?

In the complexity, *voire* confusion of his pointing, Ludwig is indeed pointing at something that *seems* quite fundamental: the complexity and confusion and perhaps even desperation of our pointing, and our confusion (and desperation?) *tout court*, and in the midst of so many signs, natural and human-made.

This does not mean that we do not "go on." This means, as Abel so rightly concluded, that our reasons, confused or simply exhausted, no longer able to find their feet, give out. Explanations do, indeed, come to an end. And even though and when our reasons do give out, this will not and indeed cannot stop us from acting, to include killing one another, but also trying to love, without reasons.*

> "How am I able to obey a rule?"—If this is not a question about causes, then it is about the justification for my following the rule in the way I do.
>
> If I have exhausted the justifications I have reached bedrock, and my spade is turned. Then I am inclined to say: "This is simply what I do."[93]

Or as Emily Dickinson described:

---

* Or Philip Roth, more pessimistically, in *American Pastoral*, 64: "The picture we have of one another. Layers and layers of misunderstanding. The picture we have of *ourselves*. Useless. Presumptuous. Completely cocked-up. Only we go ahead and we *live* by these pictures."

> We grow accustomed to the Dark—
> When light is put away—
> As when the Neighbor holds the Lamp
> To witness her Goodbye—
>
> A Moment—We uncertain step
> For newness of the night—
> Then—fit our Vision to the Dark—
> And meet the Road—erect—
>
> And so of larger—Darkness—
> Those Evenings of the Brain—
> When not a Moon disclose a sign—
> Or Star—come out—within—
>
> The Bravest—grope a little—
> And sometimes hit a Tree
> Directly in the Forehead—
> But as they learn to see—
>
> Either the Darkness alters—
> Or something in the sight
> Adjusts itself to Midnight—
> And Life steps almost straight.[94]

It is the duality, the ambivalence, of Dickinson's "almost straight" that Wittgenstein would have liked most of all.

The Exception

Allow me to apologize in advance for the particularly choppy, or stew-y, nature of this next segment. This is, in fact, the last of the writing and thinking I have done for this book, and it has shown—it has helped me to accept—it's time to put the cap back on the pen. "*Le diffus ne parvient à choisir sa voie, à hiérarchiser. . . . Le prolixe, lui, ne sait pas s'arrêter ; . . . dans la crainte du silence, du vide : les bavards sont des anxieux.*"* (The scattered never chose their route, never rank and order their thoughts. As for the verbose, they don't know how to stop. Afraid of silence, of the void, the talkative are anxious.)

But still, a moment good Sirs and Madams . . . While Wittgenstein was doing his hard thinking in England and Norway about how human

---

* Duchesne and Leguay, *Dictionnaire des subtilités du français*, 111.

beings use language under ordinary circumstances, another Germanic thinker, Carl Schmitt, who came to be a Nazi party member and ideologue, was developing a rich theory of *die Ausnahme*: "the exception." "The norm is destroyed in the exception," Schmitt proposed, and, "What always matters is the possibility of the extreme case taking place, the real war."[95]

> Precisely a philosophy of concrete life must not withdraw from the exception and the extreme case, but must be interested in it to the highest degree. . . . The exception is more interesting than the rule. The rule proves nothing; the exception proves everything: It confirms not only the rule but also its existence, which derives only from the exception.[96]

Schmitt was focused, though not exclusively, on political philosophy and legal theory, and, as many before me have noted, he has potent arguments to make in those contexts.* But his perspective can also be applied to our more personal lives and to considerations of language and meaning. In this regard, I would note that the workings of the exception can be thought of in two separate ways. One of these ways I associate with Schmitt, as well as with various moments in Wittgenstein's texts.† However, as in my slow, stumbling way, I have, I hope, come to

---

* I recommend in particular Giorgio Agamben's *Stato di eccezione*, published in the United States as *State of Exception*. I would also note that in a passage in *Gjentagelsen* (*Repetition*) Kierkegaard proposed that the exception, for all it is "an offshoot" of the universal, "explains the universal" in explaining itself. The last lines of the first chapter of Schmitt's *Politische Theologie* (*Political Theology*) are a quotation from this passage in *Gjentagelsen*. An English translation: "The exception . . . thinks the universal with intense passion." (See *Fear and Trembling and Repetition*, "Concluding Letter," 226-27.)

† *Cf.*, from *Investigations*, §142:

> It is only in normal [ordinary] cases that the use of a word is clearly prescribed; we know, are in no doubt, what to say in this or that case. The more abnormal the case, the more doubtful it becomes what we are to say. And if things were quite different from what they actually are—if there were for instance no characteristic expression of pain, of fear, of joy; if rule became exception and exception rule; or if both became phenomena of roughly equal frequency—this would make our normal language-games lose their point.

The German of the key phrase: "*würde, was Regel ist, Ausnahme und was Aus-*

better understand Wittgenstein, it has seemed to me that he *also* had a particular and more unique interest in the other way that the exception does its work. In the present segment I will first present what I am going to call the Schmitt-o-Wittgensteinian (SOW) perspective and then the more uniquely Wittgensteinian (MUW) perspective.

In the first case, which Schmitt's use of the word "war" brings to mind, there is a temporal split; the non-exceptional and the exception do not occur at the same time; the exception does its work through memory and anticipation, across spans of time. For the most part we go about our normal lives, accepting and following the rules and using words without wondering what they mean, imagining our lives are defined by these rules and words, and assured that our experiences and our relations with others and with our selves make sense because these rules, words, relations and human beings are governed by this normalcy. But then, in extraordinary moments, "real wars" take place and much that we thought we knew is upended or discarded. We find ourselves with quite another view of how people really are, what words mean, what really matters to us. And perhaps above all, we may find ourselves disturbed—at times paralyzed—by this sense that what we thought we knew is proving to be so incorrect, and so who is to say that our wartime understandings, or our divorce-time or grief-time or stock-market-crash-time understandings, are any more correct? As I have suggested previously, losing ourselves in our lostness is easier than we usually imagine.

Much of the time, it may come to seem, people do know when we are in pain—just not when it really matters! (Or seems to.) Much of the time we feel that we are well understood (whether we are or not), but, it may seem, the exceptions come when more than ever we are in need of understanding and of being understood. At such crucial moments it can seem that we or everyone else or something in any case is wrong or confused. And there are other exceptional times, too: Times when we reflect on past events and feelings and realize, or imagine, that what we once thought was one thing, one feeling—pain—really was, or now seems to have been, something else—pleasure?

Not to go too far out on a limb, or into the stew pot, but . . . Think, for example, of sadomasochistic "games"—not the ones people play "for fun" or sexual release, though they may be confusing enough, but

---

nahme, zur Regel"—if rule became exception and exception rule.

rather the ones played unwittingly and unawares. Until much later—the exceptional moment—when the thought occurs: "I" was abusing/being abused; I was denying the other/denying myself. More exceptionally, a few people—the more courageous ones?—may admit to themselves—at times with horror—that they had found pleasure or release in the abuse or denial. And again, not with toy whips and chains.

So then, adding ancient Greeks to the mix here, I note that exceptional events, exceptional insights, exceptional uses of words, exceptional texts can brings us to, and threaten us with ἀπορία (*aporia*): the situation in which (as Kierkegaard put it) "thought ceases and speech is silenced, when explanation retreats in despair," when we no longer even know what we want to say.* Perhaps as a result of some unexpected cards life has dealt us, or as a result of trying (too hard?) to understand either why (why me? why these cards?) or what (what cards are they really?). . . we are completely stumped.† Words—like "love" or "exception" or "*aporia*," words whose meaning we thought we knew—may now seem almost meaningless, and thus we may come to feel that even in our more normal moments we did not know what we were talking about or what other people were saying to us.‡ (This is one way of reading Adorno's

---

* Kierkegaard, *Repetition* (in *Repetition* and *Philosophical Crumbs*), 69. The Greek word *aporia* may be literally translated "resourcelessness."

† Socrates's idea was that once we reached this state, and *only* at this point, real learning might begin. (See, for example, the dialogues *Alcibiades I* [often attributed to Plato], 127D-E, and the *Meno* 84C.) Plato—devilishly?—calls Socrates's idea into question, as the interlocutors Plato chose for his Socrates were distinguished in real life by their incapacity, pre- or post-*aporia*, to learn much, or much that sticks with them, from talking with Socrates.

‡ In the case of the word "shower," which under exceptional circumstances has included among its family resemblances "gas chamber," . . . ? Can we hope that if the murderers had stopped to appreciate their life in language and had tried to come to some understanding of the words they were so effortlessly using, . . . of if they had come to appreciate the meaninglessness at which their life in language had arrived . . . ? Might there have been fewer victims of the Holocaust? Probably not. Here the lack of clarity, the euphemistic use of words like *Dusche* (shower), was part of the final solution, *Die Endlösung*. And all we may be left with, linguistically and epistemologically, is a certain longing to know, in exceptional circumstances if not more generally, the "real names" of things—and *before* these things or words are used on us or by us, and for all we may recognize the contingent nature of all our real names.

famous comment, or not-quite comment: "There can be no poetry after Auschwitz."*)

And thus in this sense the exception has its great effect in extraordinary moments and in how we respond to such moments, *and* insofar as, through memory, history, anxiety and imagination, our daily lives, our unextraordinary moments, are shadowed, haunted, eaten away at by past or anticipated exceptional occurrences and by how we have responded—by what the extraordinary has taught us, rightly or wrongly, about the possible, about ourselves, about the sources and extent of understanding. In the wake of exceptional events (including exceptional thoughts and feelings) we continue to go about our daily lives as ever—we must go on—but, you might say, we do not take the goings on quite as seriously as before. We have trouble shaking off a sense of irony, of living a charade, or a little off kilter. (Life cannot look the same, for example, words cannot mean the same thing since my wife died.)

In the course I teach on the exception I offer a set of fictional, yet, I'm afraid, still harsh examples. Imagine, for example, a married couple, quite happily married in most every way. But once, long ago, the husband got drunk, and he was angry with his wife about something, and he hit her. Just once, and without breaking a bone or even smearing her mascara. Or perhaps the aggression was not physical, but psychological, and it was the wife who was the aggressor.† Perhaps she had much the larger salary;

---

* Presumably, the now famous English line comes from a 1951 Adorno essay "Kulturkritik und Gesellschaft" ("An Essay on Cultural Criticism and Society"), which appeared in English translation in the collection *Prisms*. The English translation there (page 19), however, is "to write a poem after Auschwitz is barbaric," and this is an honest rendering of the German: " . . . *nach Auschwitz ein Gedicht zu schreiben, ist barbarisch, . . .* " Adorno, however, wrote or said variations on this phrase on at least a few other occasions. And thus one sees other versions in English as well, e.g.: "No lyric poetry after Auschwitz." (The particularly interested might see the comments by Frederik van Gelder, of Frankfurt University: http://www.marcuse.org/herbert/people/adorno/AdornoPoetryAuschwitzQuote.htm.)

† It occurs to me just now, rewriting this segment for the umpteenth time, that perhaps this example is not as fictional as I have imagined. That is, I now recall that my girlfriend when I was in graduate school used to throw dishes at me. I was about a foot taller than her, so I suppose I was more surprised than threatened. I don't recall ever being injured. What was being established, though, through this exceptional behavior, there in what she liked to call our "no prospects apartment" (Prospect Street, Cambridge, Mass.)? That I was impenetrable, or sufficiently

the husband had been raising the kids at home and painting old-fashioned landscapes which sold poorly. And one night, angry with him, the wife threatened to leave, to leave him without even credit in the Social Security system, and taking the children as well, as women with "good" lawyers have done. It was something the wife wished—even as the words were escaping her lips—how she wished she were not saying these words! She apologized profusely, got on her knees to demand that her husband forget the whole thing, forget every word of it. But the words had been said.

These are relationships in which the exception, the extreme case, has been made explicit. It has occurred and had its effects, to include implanting an anxiety: that it might happen again, or its promise might be fulfilled. And so we might say that the participants in these relationships have the advantage of living more truly (if also more enveloped in the fog of anxiety). Somewhere in the backs of their minds they retain a clear picture of Thanatos, of the death instinct, as Freud's English translators have called it—of human destructiveness, self-destructiveness most definitely included. Amid the warmth, comforts and joys of their relationships, these couples also sense the violence and alienation that lies in wait, like a wolf in the woods.

Another set of examples: parents who have left their spouses, broken up families, or who have broken off communication with one of their own parents. Somewhere in their minds waits the possibility that their children, too, might one day make the same exceptional decision, leaving, breaking off communication. (Again I apologize for the harshness of these examples. Augustine was much more gentle in referring to the "*vitae humanae procellosam societatem*," the stormy intercourse of human life.)

And so now for what I am calling the MUW perspective, in which there is no temporal split, in which, we might want to say—Wittgenstein might have said—there is nothing exceptional. This is rather the given: at every moment, and notwithstanding what we may have experienced or not experienced, we live with warring meanings, with warring possibilities,

---

tough, absolutely reliable? or did not care enough to fight back? That it did not matter what she did; that, like a young child, she could behave as if actions had no consequences? A lot was being said, that much is certain.

none of which can be eliminated. There is the fact (coming back to a point Abel made) that we do not need to know what a fork is in order to eat with one.* And there is the fact that

> It is possible to imagine a case in which I *could* find out that I had two hands. Normally, however, I *cannot* do so. "But all you need is to hold them up before your eyes!"—If I am *now* in doubt whether I have two hands, I need not believe my eyes either.⁹⁷

There is the fact that we have found and find almost constantly such comfort in language. It connects us with other people. It gave us new means of sharing and daily gives us a feeling of sharing our troubles and our joys. It gave us new means of working together to try to increase our physical security at least. And there is the sense, too, in which language has opened up broad vistas for our anxiety to explore, and wandering/wondering into these territories (or caves, up these mountains—pick your analogy) we find that our wandering/wondering will not end, cannot end. And this may frustrate the less courageous and frighten whoever's left.†

---

* Again, Part II, section xi, 166e, of the *Investigations*:

> It would have made as little sense for me to say "Now I am seeing it as . . ." as to say at the sight of a knife and fork "Now I am seeing this as a knife and fork". This expression would not be understood.—Any more than: "Now it's a fork" or "It may be a fork too." [Wittgenstein's ellipses.]
>
> One doesn't "*take*" what one knows as the cutlery at a meal *for* cutlery; any more than one ordinarily tries to move one's mouth as one eats, or aims at moving it.

† I find myself curious to read a psychobiography of Shakespeare. Perhaps someone of a Freudian bent has speculated on Shakespeare's early childhood. It seems to me that something happened, something that at a young age got him in touch with insecurity, unreliability and doubt, and at a very deep level. As Cavell has pointed up, in so many plays Shakespeare shows us how easy it is to lose our grip on what is happening, on who the people around us are and what their feelings for us and our feelings for them are. And yet, from a Shakespearean perspective, we must constantly fight against this tendency—and for all it may lead us to great truths, or to great half-truths.

"The Winter's Tale" (Act II, Scene i) and Leontes again:

> How blest am I
> In my just censure, in my true opinion!

Here the split between ordinary and exceptional is not temporal; it is we who are split between the two possibilities, between our know-how and the limits of our understanding (and between our sharing and our enmity and isolation). Life and language are so easy, we know *without thinking* how to use words or how they are being used AND it's all so difficult: If we try to understand, to grasp the meanings of words, to grasp what is happening to us, to grasp who we are dealing with and who we ourselves are. It can indeed be "as if we had to repair a torn spider's web with our fingers."* Again, in this case, this is *not* exceptional; this is our everyday experience, in which our ordinary "know how" is constantly shadowed by our inability to know. To lean on the line from Kierkegaard quoted in a previous footnote: as our sharing may be explained by our isolation, and by our vulnerability, so, too, our know-how is explained by our ignorance. The passion inspired by the limits of our understanding—by a need to understand that outstrips our ability, and by a concomitant need to deny these limits even to the point of our embracing denial and ignorance— All this has led to our know how. But neither know-how nor passion are knowledge.†
And, again, we live with this "fact," if I may call it that, on a daily basis.

> Alack, for lesser knowledge! how accursed
> In being so blest! There may be in the cup
> A spider steep'd, and one may drink, depart,
> And yet partake no venom, for his knowledge
> Is not infected: but if one present
> The abhorr'd ingredient to his eye, make known
> How he hath drunk, he cracks his gorge, his sides,
> With violent hefts. I have drunk,
> and seen the spider.

We have to fight against losing our grip, or learning what we are absorbing, because this may take us down the road to madness, murder included. "Explanations come to an end somewhere," Wittgenstein writes, without noting that this is what, in English, we call a "dead end."

* *Investigations*, §106. Abel quoted this section at greater length in Section (2) of the main text.

† I prepared a lengthy critique of the sociologist Anthony Giddens's "positivist" reading (my term) of Wittgenstein—as an example and discussion of what I think is wrong with this type of reading, for all it is perhaps the most popular (most conventional) reading of Wittgenstein. For better or worse, I have decided to spare readers this text, which came to wander over more than a dozen pages. Instead, a brief résumé here.

ONE OF THE BRITISH child psychoanalyst Donald Winnicott's phrases was: "fear of breakdown is the fear of breakdown that has already been experienced."[98] This is easy enough for us to appreciate, for example, in Oedipus's case: he was deathly afraid of doing irreparable harm to a relationship that his father had long ago destroyed. And from this perspective, we may perceive a temporal split, between what happened when Oedipus was a baby—or, indeed, before he was born—and how in young adulthood he responds to fears and desires that may be traced back to these early events. But there is also a sense in which there is no split: for all or most all of us, unresolved Oedipal conflicts are part of our present lives, and this not necessarily because of things that have happened or been said, but because of the dynamic we find ourselves caught up in, inevitably, as children and as parents. I think Winnicott's phrase can also be used to explain the MUW perspective as regards the exception. It is not that we have been wounded, threatened or baffled by exceptional events. Rather, we live with anxiety born of the fact that the insecurity of our life in language is *not* exceptional, it comes with language and with the comforts life in language offers. We are afraid of chaos and madness, that there might be nothing solid to cling to.

Both the positivist and skeptical camps see Wittgenstein calling attention to the same human capacity: our being able to "go on"—for example, our being able to use words in ways that often seem to be understood by others and reify an idea of common understanding. It may be said, and I believe this is one of Wittgenstein's points, that for a social animal this is an essential, even wonderful capacity. The positivists, however, leap from this to the conclusion that such "practical knowledge" (to use Giddens's term) is sufficient, and they find in Wittgenstein a "tool kit" for using this knowledge to build up, in however painstaking a fashion, an understanding of how the world works. (See Giddens, *The Constitution of Society*.) Skeptics, by contrast, are more likely to focus on the passages in the *Philosophical Investigations* and elsewhere that point to the insufficiency of such knowledge, the limits of "practical knowledge."

In discussing the alternations and two-sidedness of Wittgenstein's work, Abel used the image of a see-saw. With this in mind we might say that Giddens is sitting on the positive end of the see-saw, and he has so much company over there that his posterior, at least, is well grounded. The skeptics on their end are rather more up in the air. But, again, I would join with those who, like Abel, stress that Wittgenstein moves between both ends of the board, or is the see-saw itself. See, for example, Cavell, "Declining Decline," 32: "The *Investigations* lends itself to, perhaps it calls out for, competing emphases in its consideration of human discourse—an emphasis on its distrust of language or an emphasis on its trust of ordinary human speech."

We are afraid because there is nothing solid to cling to.

To slip two lines from Baudelaire out of their original context and into translation, and with my underscoring added:

> We pass among forests of symbols
> Who watch us <u>as if</u> they were our best friends.*

AN EXAMPLE that merges the SOW, MUW, Winnicottian and Thorniobaudelairean perspectives, and thus may approach the heart of what I am trying to talk about in this segment. A woman says matter of factly to her husband or boyfriend sitting next to her on the couch, "My therapist says that our relationship lacks intimacy." Here is an unexceptional word ("intimacy"), and not even a particularly exceptional conversation. The man hearing this may think he knows what is meant and may reach out verbally or physically to his partner, his beloved, with the intention of having what he thinks would be an intimate conversation or, say, of holding hands with her in an intimate manner (perhaps without speaking, listening to her breaths and his own). But this action on his part, and her reactions to it, may cause him to realize or to wonder if, in fact, he does not know what she or her therapist means by this word "intimacy." (And this might also lead him to wonder what the word means to him.)

Does she mean that *she* would like their relationship to be more intimate? Or might this word "intimacy" mean that his partner is in fact looking for a way to end the relationship without feeling that the ending was her fault? (We are back to the problem of pointing discussed in the previous segment.) Has her therapist, perhaps unwittingly, or for the $135 or $195 per hour, offered her this intimacy as a way out, intimacy being a shortcoming that is commonly associated with men? (And thus, if there is to be blame, and the problem is labelled intimacy, the break-up would not be the woman's fault.)

---

* "Correspondences." This is my translation/borrowing from the first verse, which reads:

> La Nature est un temple où de vivants piliers
> Laissent parfois sortir de confuses paroles ;
> L'homme y passe à travers des forêts de symboles
> Qui l'observent avec des regards familiers.

In the ensuing years subsequent events offer this man various and conflicting interpretations of what his partner meant by "intimacy," or of what she might have meant, of how meanings were, intentionally or unintentionally, revealed as a result of the word's use. He may well feel a certain longing, a great longing, to have known what was meant that evening on the couch. He may feel that this exceptional moment of lack of clarity, or such *mauvaise foi,* has defined his whole, now past relationship, and perhaps his life more generally. The moment may hold up a sort of mirror and reflect back to him images of his past "intimate" relations and questions about people and words.

From the SOW perspective, he—and she?—has learned (useful or not useful) lessons from an exceptional experience. From a MUW perspective there is nothing exceptional about a word like "intimacy" or about not knowing what it means. If anything exceptional has occurred in this example it is the exceptional realization of what the ordinary involves, of the confusion in which we live.

We might say that from the perspective often associated with Wittgenstein's later work, our life in language offers us a picture of a happy couple enjoying their happiness. The connection between this happiness and reality may be tenuous at best, but that does not make it any less happiness. (And might we write lines for a sunnier Wittgenstein? "Yes, there is *something* there accompanying my feelings of joy, and this something is what is important—and soothing?) This picture, this happiness depends, however, on our capacity to deny or ignore the ever-present possibility (or alternative), to deny not only Thanatos, but also the limits of our understanding, the limits even of our denials, of skepticism.

As, in the extreme case, with so many people who, physically at least, survived the horrors of the world wars, as with a student of mine who as a teenager lived through the genocide in Rwanda and who cannot forget so many scenes, to include picking through piles of limbs to try to identify dead relatives, . . . Our going on depends on our ability to consign both our exceptional experiences and the limits of our everyday (mis)understandings to special corners of our minds.

The gaps within

In an otherwise insightful philosophy article I found a variation on this issue, a variation that is often found in the Wittgensteinian literature.

> A familiar task for any supporter of Wittgenstein is that of showing how his criticism of philosophical fantasies leaves intact undeniable realities. For example, his assault on a private language does not deny that we have sensations.

"No!" I wrote in red pen in the margin. Wittgenstein's critique, being more about questioning than answers, leaves little intact.* Wittgenstein shows that (faced with the exception, with the chasm of not understanding) we cling to certain beliefs and forms of life as if they were undeniably correct, because they *must be* undeniably correct or we would not know how to go on. His assault on private language does not deny that we have sensations, but nor does it assure us that we do. What we have is a language of sensation—of pain, for example, or joy.

In my "third interpolation" I noted that Anthony Kenny takes the idea of getting things wrong to what is both its end and starting point: how we get *ourselves* wrong, misread *ourselves*. Kenny's argument is that Wittgenstein's later statements regarding his first book, the *Tractatus*, misrepresented it.[99] This opens a large door, revealing or reminding us that when we are talking about *inter*personal misunderstanding and gaps, we could just as well be talking about *intra*personal ones, about the misunderstandings and gaps within us. This is both a large subject and a large part of Wittgenstein scholarship and debate that I am here only going to skip across, as on rocks across a rushing river.

---

* *Cf.*, Bouwsma, 180 and 181:

> And as for those readers in general who want answers to their questions and who, if they already have answers, want better reasons, the author gives neither better reasons for the old answers nor any answers, and those readers who keep their questions may be considered either fortunate or unfortunate, as the case may be. . . .
>
> And now it would be natural to say that since the author is manifestly aware of these questions, and must know that these questions cry out and have been crying out for centuries for answers, that he does not answer is a bad sign.

My 10-year-old nephew says there is nothing that worries him about going to sleepaway camp for the first time. Would we want to say, therefore, that there is nothing that worries him about going to sleepaway camp for the first time?* This sharp pain at the tip of my finger for a few instants just after it has been pricked: Is this pain not, in fact, like a moment in a conversation, like my nephew's comment about camp—an expression of feelings, but not the feelings themselves? Where is this pain? (Where is Theo's, my nephew's, anxiety?) Is it there in my finger, or moving along neural pathways between finger and brain, or all in my head?† If, very worried about my mother, I accidentally prick my finger and "feel" nothing—do not even notice the pricking—has there been no pain? "*Sag nicht, du habest sie unbewußt gehabt!*" Don't say you had [certain mental experiences] unconsciously!‡

For Christmas, some of my students gave me a boxed set containing all of Leonard Bernstein's "Young People's Concerts" with the New York Philharmonic. (What a nice present!) Bernstein therein (in 1958, it would have been) proposes to his young audience in Carnegie Hall that music expresses and inspires emotions—well-known emotions like joy and love and sadness, but also emotions for which we have no words. He seems to be headed toward saying that this is music at its greatest, its most profound, when it touches emotions that cannot be spoken of, which can be felt but not identified or known. But what are these—unknowable, can I say?—emotions?

Let me put this another way (and coming back to one of the first footnotes of this book). In the seventeenth century Descartes proposed as self-evident that there can be nothing in our minds of which we are not aware.§ By the early twentieth century Freud had convinced some of us

---

* The inverse, from a description of a politician who has just won a crucial, historic vote in an assembly: "He looks emotional; he looks like he's on the verge of tears; there is no reason to think he's pretending or, like the consummate actor he is, if he is pretending, that he's not feeling what he's pretending to feel." Cercas, 320.

† See Wittgenstein's discussions in *The Blue Book* (7 and 16), of the locality of thinking. From 16: "It is correct to say that thinking is an activity of our writing hand, of our larynx, of our head, and of our mind, so long as we understand the grammar of these statements." That is, so long as the statements are made within contexts which our culture has established as appropriate for such statements.

‡ *Investigations*, §171.

§ Descartes, Quatrième réponses—Réponse à l'autre partie (De Dieu); *Médita-*

(rightly or wrongly) and worried many another that, in fact, there could be a great deal in our minds of which we are not aware, and, in fact, much of our behavior and feelings is channeled by these subconscious contents—and all the more channeled because we are not aware of these subconscious contents.* Shortly thereafter, Wittgenstein, hardly uninfluenced by Freud, insisted, in his own way and using much different language, that of the unconscious we must be unconscious; the unconscious is unknowable, and consciousness involves language. We are not only able to express but also to identify pains (rightly or wrongly) because we understand (rightly or wrongly) some kind of pain language, be it the language of blood oozing from a cut, the tears and lamentations of a parent whose child has died, or the words of a philosopher.

> "What would it be like if human beings showed no outward signs of pain (did not groan, grimace, etc.)? Then it would be impossible to teach a child the use of the word 'toothache'."—Well, let's assume the child is a genius and itself invents a name for the sensation!—But then, of course, he couldn't make himself understood when he used the word.—So does he understand the name, without being able to explain its meaning to anyone?—But what does it mean to say that he has 'named his pain'?—How has he done this naming of pain?! And whatever he did, what was its purpose?[100]

And what was this pain? we need to go on and ask. If there is no language for a feeling, is it felt? If Theo when he seems to be anxious reads—will not lift his nose from a book—a book that he has likely read three times before, if not ten, and that he has chosen for this reason, for the familiarity of the text . . . But he does not fret or say he is anxious. He does not find any use for this word "anxious" or offer any other external expression of any mood besides a slightly flattened affect, a slight absentness

---

tions métaphysiques, 337, 356 and especially 369, where Descartes proposes that there is nothing in our minds that is not a thought, and it is impossible to have a thought that we are not conscious of (i.e., when we are thinking it).

* Yes, I know, Freudians these days object to the term "subconscious" on the grounds that Freud had some objection to its German equivalent. However, among other things, in this particular sentence the phrase "unconscious contents" would be confusing, and "contents of the unconscious" awkward.

or vagueness, willed isolation. Is he anxious? Or does he "just feel like reading," as he would say? Or is the act of reading one of the common ways human beings express their anxiety (and even if they themselves don't get the message?).

We might think of an intermediate case in which one tries to express a feeling—for example, a feeling of unhappiness within a family—but no one, no one in one's family or outside it "wants to hear about it," as we say. As per the Stevie Smith poem Abel quoted, in which "it was too cold always," family members may tell themselves that "you," the person in pain, are waving not drowning, or that you are only pretending to be drowning (or reading), fantasizing that you are drowning.* In such situations, isn't it often the case that the feeling of the person in pain or her means of expressing it atrophies or gets buried deep in her unconscious, and it becomes as if she no longer felt, or could no longer feel, this thing. To quote another poet, Yeats: "Too long a sacrifice / Can make a stone of the heart."[101] So now what about a feeling that can never be voiced even once because there is no language for it? Or what about the anxiety that Theo does not quite feel perhaps because he has not yet fully learned the uses of the word "anxiety"? What sorts of stones are these?

A seemingly undeniable reality here is this Wittgensteinian "life in language" and how inescapable it is, and how it is an ever-evolving cultural construct, and always at one remove from any underlying "undeniable reality," should there in fact be one. While Wittgenstein does not deny that we have sensations, he also points out that we cannot be sure that we do either. (Or, if you prefer a less aggressive reading, we cannot be sure what our sensations are.) We have language. Lots of language! Wonderful language!

> [I]f we construe the grammar of the expression of the sensation on the model of "object and designation" [e.g., a pain and its expression] the object [the pain] drops out of consideration as irrelevant.[102]

We share in our designations of pains, and may even find pain in and through these designations, but as for whether there is some object,

---

* "Certainly," a voice in a Wittgensteinian interior dialogue would say, "there are people who are hypochondriacs and people who we call 'needy,' by which we mean that their needs are a kind of bottomless pit, or bottomless in a different way than less needy people's needs."

or set of neural events, that corresponds to this word "pain" that English speakers use, or whether each of us has our own various sensations which we learn to describe with this commonly recognized description "pain," and which we may even come to feel as the commonly recognized thing "pain"; or whether, on the contrary, the description has imposed feelings upon us that were quite other or did not exist prior to the evolution of this language— We cannot know. What was love before "love"? Or before "*Liebe*," "*amour*," "*eros*," etc.? Or before neuroscientists armed with CAT scanners began equating (or confounding) our feelings with electrochemical events in various parts of our brains.

> Of course, if water boils in a pot, steam comes out of the pot and also pictured steam comes out of the pictured pot. But what if one insisted on saying that there must also be something boiling in the picture of the pot?"[103]
>
> "But you will surely admit that there is a difference between pain-behaviour accompanied by pain and pain-behaviour without any pain?" [Or between love behavior and "true love"?]—Admit it? What greater difference could there be?—"And yet you again and again reach the conclusion that the sensation itself is a *nothing*."—Not at all. It is not a *something*, but not a *nothing* either! The conclusion was only that a nothing would serve just as well as a something about which nothing could be said. . . .[104]

Scaffolding

Wandering about New York City, I have found myself stopping to look at the omnipresent scaffolding, hastily erected so that facades can be scrubbed, bricks re-pointed, windows replaced. The scaffolding is relatively strong and reliable—periodic fatal accidents notwithstanding—because of the materials (steel) of the construction; because of the configuration, the relationships between the pieces of material; and also because the scaffolding is resting comfortably on what we call solid ground. Of course there are moments—during and after earthquakes, for example—when we are impressed that the ground is not as solid as we had imagined, but—in reflecting on Wittgenstein—I am more struck by the absence of anchors, holes, rods deep into the earth, etc.. That is, there is no connection between the scaffolding and the ground, except for the connection of metal touching concrete (sidewalk) and, above all, the connection made by the weight of the scaffolding, and of the human workers, tools, bricks and buckets that the scaffolding comes to bear.* The heavier the human stuff above ground, the more solid the connection to the usually solid ground, even though the human and the non-human are not tied together in any way.

So then, explicating my own analogy, can we say that the construction that is language, our life in language, culture, science and so forth—all this gains solidity not only from the strength of the materials with which it is constructed and from the strength of the relationships of the materials, but also from the weight of this construction. As if to say that the sheer accretion of culture over the ages gives a solidity—which we might call truth?—to this construction, to our culture.† And this for all that—as we build higher and higher, using fancier materials and architectural techniques, cantilevering and so forth—our connection

---

* Here is a good example of the distinction I was making in the segment on the exception. Abel and I have been impressed by how human understanding gives way at exceptional moments—earthquakes, holocaust, divorce. Schmitt's point is that the possibility of these exceptional moments and how we have behaved during such moments in the past is always with us. These things haunt us and define us, I might say. But Wittgenstein, in my reading, is focused on the fact that the scaffolding is *never* anchored to the ground. There is nothing exceptional about this. This is our common everyday experience. We may, we do choose to ignore this, to go about our repointing and repainting without worrying—or with worrying, if we prefer. But this does not anchor our scaffolding or reduce the risks in the midst of which we go about our lives—the risk of dying being at the top of the list. It simply means that we can and do function in spite of those risks and of their un-eliminatability. From this perspective, why talk of *die Ausnahme*, the exception? This is life.

† I am reminded of Abel's quotation from Ulysses S. Grant ("Wars produce many stories of fiction, some of which are told until they are believed to be true"), and of Abel's conclusion, or proposition: "The truth of a proposition stems from, depends on, its repeated use." One of many possible examples, this from David Lindberg's *The Beginnings of Western Science* (358): "[T]he ignorance and degradation of the Middle Ages has become an article of faith among the general public, achieving the status of invulnerability merely by virtue of endless repetition." Lindberg (137) also reports that in antiquity several calculations of the Earth's circumference were made, some of them quite accurate. But an inaccurate calculation (about three-quarters of the current figure for the Earth's circumference) was picked up by Ptolemy and from him by Columbus, becoming the basis for the latter's calculations of the distance between Spain and the Indies.

to the ground may seem increasingly tenuous? Of course there are times when—

Lower E. Side scaffold shock

Parts of our culture, either our scaffolding or what it is bearing, collapses. (Although our life in language seems never—or never yet?—to have collapsed.) And there are times when—

> *tandis qu'on raisonne*
> *Des foudres souterrains engloutissent Lisbonne,*
> *Et de trente cités dispersent les débris,*
> *Des bords sanglants du Tage à la mer de Cadix.*
>
> while we are theorizing
> The wrath of the earth engulfs Lisbon
> And scatters what remains of thirty cities
> From the bloody banks of the Tagus to the sea
>   of Cadiz.*

There are times when earthquakes of one sort or another shake our faith in the solidity of the ground on which we have built and remind us of the rather limited nature of our connection to this ground.

And there are those, myself included, who may comment—or yell and scream—"but it's only scaffolding, that's all it is!" To which Wittgensteinians of a certain stripe might well answer—and, if my analogy is correct, they might well be answering with good reason—"But now you are ignoring how reliable scaffolding can be!" Most of the time.

Back in Chicago, after dinner I lie down on my big white couch in my big, empty apartment in the middle of a continent, and I am amazed by how at peace I can be. The sound of the fan; two girls talking on the street corner outside. I find my mind recalling the time when Philippe Petit strung a wire between the "twin towers" of the World Trade Center, walked out into the middle of the air, lay himself down and looked up at the sky.

---

* Voltaire, "Poème sur le désastre de Lisbonne" (307); my translation. The headline—"Lower E. Side scaffold shock"—is from a June 3, 2011 *New York Post* story about a scaffold that collapsed (Mongelli, 6).

Appendix B
Explanations and reflections regarding Plotinus, Augustine and Wittgenstein

---

The at least initial motivation for this appendix was to provide background information to flesh out Abel and Marsalina's conversation as regards:

- *Plotinus's conception of what Augustine later converted into The Fall.*

- *Augustine's ideas, many of them inherited from the Stoics, regarding language, as contrasted with Wittgenstein's ideas on this score.*

- *Wittgenstein's reading of Augustine.*

Although the appendix is divided into separate segments, they have been designed to flow from one to the other, and they keep coming back to the ostensible undertaking of the book as a whole: exploring section 32 of Wittgenstein's Philosophical Investigations.

A word of warning for the squeamish or more austere: In the segment devoted explicitly to Wittgenstein, this appendix includes my deepest descent into the rich loam or mud or quicksand of psychobiography. Of course I would not be engaging in this descent if I did not feel . . .

There is much to be said for the simple swimmer, mask-less, fin-less and even goal-less. Think of leisurely breaststrokers gliding along a surface, finding relaxation in so doing, and also, likely without even realizing it, avoiding the equipment, training, risk, expenses and other complexities of scuba diving, which might be seen as distractions that keep a swimmer from seeing clearly or of being clearly. With this in mind, I must confess that in my scholarly life I do a lot of scuba diving, and am fascinated to come across strange fish, coral formations, the wreckage of old ships.

Plotinus

There may be little more taxing, intellectually, for the brain of a human being living in the twenty-first century than trying to read Plotinus, even in translation. I am prepared to say that this fact suggests another: Plotinus has a lot to tell us which we would do well to try to understand. And another: On the path toward understanding Plotinus it is easy for we moderns or post-moderns to get lost. It is also the case, though Abel ignores this, that Augustine's thinking and writing were more influenced by Plotinus than by anyone else.* And thus there is a sense in which, while Wittgenstein seems to have thought that in critiquing Augustine he was undermining Plato . . . Plato may have been less involved than Plotinus.†

In any case, Abel's daring leap into Plotinus sent me to a far and dusty corner of my bookshelves—to Plotinus's *Enneads* and to a Sorbonne

---

* Brown, 91, suggests that Augustine's getting to know a group of Platonists—followers of Plotinus first and foremost—was more important to his intellectual and personal development than his confessed conversion under a fig tree. (Although even there, books were to blame. In Book VIII, Chapter 12 of *The Confessions* Augustine writes that in the garden he heard the voice of a child urging him "*tolle lege, tolle lege*"—pick it up, read it; pick it up, read it—and the passage of the Bible that he read (Romans 13:13) told him to give up womanizing for Jesus.)

Quoting from Brown, 94-95:

> As with many immensely fertile thinkers, it is difficult to imagine Augustine as a reader. Yet, what happened at this critical time [in his life], and in the years that follow, was a spell of long and patient reading, apparently aided by some discussions. Such reading included treatises of Plotinus, one of the most notoriously difficult writers in the ancient world. It was a reading which was so intense and thorough that the ideas of Plotinus were thoroughly absorbed, "digested" and transformed by Augustine. Ambrose, who also read Plotinus, patently ransacked his author: it is possible to trace literal borrowings from Plotinus in the bishop's sermons. For Augustine, however, Plotinus and Porphyry [Plotinus's interpreter] are grafted almost imperceptibly into his writing as the ever present basis of his thought.

See Brown's chapters on "The 'Confessions'" and on Augustine and "The Platonists." A terminological note, quoting Brown, 91: "We call this movement 'Neo-Platonism,' but the participants called themselves 'Platonists,' *Platonici*, pure and simple—that is, the direct heirs of Plato."

† Pierre Courcelle (168 *ff.*) has proposed that Augustine's first-hand knowledge of Plato was confined to a portion of the *Timaeus* translated by Cicero. That is, most of Augustine's Platonism was third-hand, via Plotinus translated from Greek into Latin. Augustine was also influenced by the Platonism of the gospel according to John. (Brown, 98, re John.)

professor's commentary on the *Enneads*—books I had not touched in decades. I cannot say that my re-reading led me to feel complete confidence in Abel's interpretation of Plotinus's theories. I believe the interpretation I am going to offer here involves a little less leaping.

The highest realm for Plotinus is The One, followed by The Intelligence (the home of potentiality), something akin to what Plato's Socrates referred to as the *eidos*: the "something" through which all the separate essences (e.g., the essence of horse-ness, fork-ness, redness) can be seen to be not manifold, but one and the same.* Below this realm is The Soul, which in turn gives way to, or overflows into, individual souls, which may ultimately plunge "deep into the body" and the realm of the senses. In asserting their independence from the realm of The Intelligence, these individual souls give individual forms (*eide*, the plural of *eidos*) to matter.†

The Sorbonne professor, Émile Bréhier, wrote of the soul being "plunged in the body, in life and in the forgetting of its own nature."[105] He is touching on an idea in Greek thought, long before Plotinus, of *t'alethe*— the true things, the forms. This phrase comes from the word *aletheia*—

---

* The explanation in this segment comes from *Enneads* IV, V and VI. Let me also thank three other texts for assistance here, particularly as regards *t'alethe*: Plato's *Meno*, Werner Jaeger's *Paideia*, and Martin Mueller's "Children of Oedipus."

† *Cf.,* Augustine's proposal that a human being is "*anima utens corpore*": a soul using a body. (Augustine, *On the Moral Behavior of the Catholic Church* I, 27, 52; as quoted in *The Essential Augustine*, 67.)

See also Aristotelian hylomorphism, the idea that objects are composites of *morphe* (form) and *hyle*, a purely Aristotelian term which has been translated as "material" or "matter"; it is eternal and has no properties of its own. See Peters, pages 88-91, on *hyle*, where he also discusses Plotinus's use of the term. Peters writes (point 5, page 89):

> For Aristotle the composition of an individual, a Socrates or a Callias, is an extremely complex procedure that may be conceived as the imposition of a succession of increasingly specific *eide* [providing the *morphe*]. Each of these forms is imposed on a progressively more informed matter, and so there are distinctions in *hyle* ranging from a first matter (*prote hyle, materia prima*), the substratum of the form of the primary bodies [i.e., earth, air, fire and water], through a series of more highly informed matters down to "ultimate matter" (*eschate* or *teleutaia hyle*), the matter of this individual existent [e.g., Socrates].

"unconcealing" or "unforgetting." So inverting, the soul, in becoming separated from The Intelligence, becomes separated from the truth; it un-unforgets the truth—i.e., forgets its own nature. The individual soul, an Augustinian might say, is necessarily corrupt.

In Abel's interpretation—and, in quite another sense, in Augustine's interpretation—a key feature of all this is this idea of descent—from the perfection and wholeness of The One to individuality, to imperfection and, ultimately in Plotinus and then Augustine, to evil. "Life here below in the midst of sense objects is for the soul a degradation, an exile, a loss of wings," Plotinus proposed. Each individual soul "steps <u>down</u> into its own individuality." (My emphasis.) The individual souls become

> preoccupied with sensation [the material world] and its impression. Much they perceive is contrary to nature [the higher realms] and troubles and confuses them. This is so because the body in their care is deficient, hedged about with alien influences, filled with desires, deceived in its very pleasures.[106]

This is beginning to sound more like my life and Wittgenstein's, and perhaps like the "getting it wrong" that Abel speaks about. It is also absolutely essential to Augustinian thinking, and thus to the history of the Roman Catholic Church and, indeed, to the history and present of Western Europe and of the many lands and peoples Western Europeans have colonized and partially converted to their ways and beliefs.

From Peter Brown's biography of Augustine:

> The "soul" of Plotinus is very much a cosmic, archetypal soul; its "Fall" merely forms the shadowy background of the human condition. . . . With Augustine this "fall" [what we, after Augustine, have come to call "The Fall"] is intensely personal: he sees it as a field of forces in the heart of each man, an agonizing weakness that forced him to flee from himself, . . . The profound, abstract intuitions of Plotinus have come to provide the material for a new, classic language of the unquiet heart.

Brown now offers some lines from the *Confessions*, Book IV, chapter 7, lines in which Augustine recalls, from his youth, his grief at the death of his best friend (young, yet dying of a fever). I have chosen to quote these lines from Pine-Coffin's translation:

> What madness, to love a man as something more than human! What folly, to grumble at the lot man has to bear! I lived in a fever, convulsed with tears and sighs that allowed me no rest nor peace of mind. My soul was a burden, bruised and bleeding. It was tired of the man who carried it, but I found no place to set it down to rest. Neither the charm of the countryside nor the sweet scents of the garden could soothe it. It found no peace in song or laughter, none in the company of friends at table or in the pleasures of love, none even in books or poetry. Everything that was not what my friend had been was dull and distasteful. I had heart only for sighs and tears, for in them alone I found some shred of consolation. But if I tried to stem my tears, a heavy load of misery weighed me down. . . . Where could I go, yet leave myself behind? Was there any place I should not be prey to myself? None.

One cannot help but be fascinated that Wittgenstein did not write about passages in the *Confessions* such as this one, which would seem to speak so directly to his sense of himself and of the endless struggle of his life. (And, interestingly, driven by his grief, Augustine leaves home: the Wittgenstein solution.) But Wittgenstein instead wrote at length about three of Augustine's sentences about language learning, three sentences snatched from their context. For the moment, however, our ostensible subject is Plotinus; I am providing background for Abel's use of Plotinus's ideas. And so, getting back to work, I note that for Plotinus, and for Abel's Plotinus, falling, the descent of the soul toward evil, its dismal consequences notwithstanding, was an essential process—a life-giving, creative process, we may call it.

> The One must not be solely the solitary. If it were, reality would remain buried and shapeless since in The One there is no differentiation of forms. No beings would exist if The One remained shut up in itself. . . . Likewise, souls must not play the solitaries, their issue stifled. Every nature must produce its next, for each thing must unfold

seed-like, from indivisible principle into a visible effect.*

Inspired by Plotinus, Abel says that his words, ineluctably, "deform" what he feels—e.g., his love for Marsalina. His words make his feelings into something other than what they first were, and, he goes on, leaving love in his wake: "[We] also have to recognize that this misleadingness . . . the deformations of language and of human interaction more generally—this is what is creative."

Again, to me this seems to involve a rich leap or two, on a path into fertile, overgrown woods. I also believe that deeper in these woods one might come to the thought that with this word "creative" Abel was unnecessarily confining a truth of the matter, and ignoring what might be considered a more Plotinian perspective, as well as a rich paradox that lies close to the very heart of the *Investigations* and of Wittgenstein's later work more generally.

My attention to this confinement was called by another three sentences: three sentences in Ray Monk's biography of Wittgenstein. Monk was discussing how one of Wittgenstein's acquaintances—or listeners, perhaps we should call them—later recalled that Wittgenstein had taught him two important things: (i) that things are as they are, and (ii) to seek illuminating comparisons to get an understanding of how they are. Monk writes:

> Both these ideas are central to Wittgenstein's later philosophy. Wittgenstein, indeed, thought of using Bishop Butler's phrase: "Everything is what it is, and not another thing" as a motto for *Philosophical Investigations*.†

---

* Plotinus, §6-§8 of the fourth *Ennead*, on "The Descent of the Soul."
† Butler, originally from *Fifteen Sermons*, Preface, §39. This Preface is reproduced in the Butler volume in the "Works Cited" of the present text. From §39: If the observation that "benevolence is no more disinterested than any of the common particular passions"

> be true, it follows that self-love and benevolence, virtue and interest, are not to be opposed but only to be distinguished from each other, in the same way as virtue and any other particular affection, love of arts, suppose, are to be distinguished. Everything is what it is, and not another thing. The goodness or badness of actions does not arise from hence that the epithet "interested" or "disinterested" may be applied to them, any

And the importance of illuminating comparisons not only lies at the heart of Wittgenstein's central notion of "the understanding which consists in seeing connections", but was also regarded by Wittgenstein as characterizing his whole contribution to philosophy.[107]

Indeed, Wittgenstein recognized that one of his great intellectual gifts was his ability to come up with similes—with analogies, ingenious, illuminating comparisons.* (And he was certainly right about this!)

So is Wittgenstein playing a double game—or might an illuminating comparison be between him and a magician? With one hand he urges us not to think but *look!*—look at what is, and see it for what it is and not another thing. With the other hand he is offering us ingenious and

> more than that any other indifferent epithet, suppose "inquisitive" or "jealous" may or may not be applied to them, not from their being attended with present or future pleasure or pain, but from their being what they are, namely, what becomes such creatures as we are, what the state of the case requires, or the contrary. Or in other words [and for example], we may judge and determine that an action is morally good or evil before we so much as consider whether it is interested or disinterested.

* See, *inter alia*, a line in *Culture and Value* (19): "What I invent are new *similes.*" This appears (in a collection of notes Wittgenstein did not intend to publish) in the midst of a curious passage about how "the Jewish mind does not have the power to produce anything" original, though, "It is typical for a Jewish mind to understand someone else's work better than he understands it himself."

See also Malcolm's notes (50) from a 1946 Wittgenstein lecture:

> What I give is the morphology of the use of an expression. I show that it has kinds of uses of which you had not dreamed. In philosophy one feels *forced* to look at a concept in a certain way. What I do is to suggest, or even invent, other ways of looking at it. I suggest possibilities of which you had not previously thought. You thought that there was one possibility, or only two at most. But I made you think of others. Furthermore, I made you see that it was absurd to expect the concept to conform to those narrow possibilities. Thus your mental cramp is relieved, and you are free to look around the field of use of the expression and to describe different kinds of uses of it.

So "it" is no longer what is, but may indeed be another thing, or any number of other things?

delightful comparisons that inevitably, whether Wittgenstein has wished this or not, take our minds off the "is" and on to the comparison, and the ingeniousness and delight. And so, as regards Abel's speech on Plotinus and the creativity of our misunderstandings and deformations, I would say, Yes—yes, Abel—our misunderstandings and deformations are creative, but our explanations are also misunderstandings and deformations. "The aspect of reaching that is coming up short" would be a way of describing this paradox, and the effects of that reaching-coming-up-short. *Cf.*, for example, Augustine, *The City of God*:

> For that which specially leads these men astray to refer their own circles to the straight path of truth, is, that they measure by their own human, changeable and narrow intellect the divine mind, which is absolutely unchangeable, infinitely capacious, . . . [T]hus they cannot conceive God, . . . *

The "is," the thing in itself, is hardly the same as an illuminating comparison of it or of a description, definition or explanation of the thing, or a collection of "family resemblances" and so forth. Compared to the thing in itself (presuming such a thing exists), all these approaches to it are *other things*.† To use vaguely Plotinian terminology, in seeking to

---

* Augustine, *City of God*, XII:17. In this passage Augustine himself cites 2 Corinthians 10: " . . . they measuring themselves by themselves, and comparing themselves among themselves, are not wise."

For another, less caustic version of the same idea, see a comment of Marco Polo to Kublia Khan, as imagined by Italo Calvino in *Invisible Cities* (86): "Every time I describe a city I am saying something about Venice. . . . To distinguish the other cities' qualities, I must speak of a first city that remains implicit. For me it is Venice."

† *Cf.*, the famous "Seventh Letter," attributed to Plato:

> There is an object called 'circle.' Its name is the word I have just uttered. Next comes its definition, compounded of nouns and verbs; for the object named 'round' and 'circumference' and 'circle' the definition would be 'the thing whose extremities in every direction are equidistant from its center.' Third, there is the representation, which can be drawn and rubbed out or turned on a lathe and later destroyed; none of these things can happen to the real circle, to which all these three refer, because it is something quite different from them. Fourth, there

understand being, in employing the means at our disposal to understand being, we fall away from it. We certainly come to understandings, but the gap between these and knowledge of the thing in itself remains, and remains unbridgeable by language. I, though not Plotinus, would also say that the gap remains unbridgeable more generally, by any means. We may live in this "is," but it appears to us like "the like," if you will. We may live in the "is" and experience it as a series of analogies which fall short. And this "is" human life.

Abel speaks about how language is a bridge between human beings. We might also—with a child's eye?—see a bridge as holding two sides, two banks of a river, apart. Or, at least, a bridge can make manifest to us the distance between the two banks. And so it is with language and what we would understand on the other side of the language bridge that separates "us" and "it" (or separates two us-es, two I's). I suppose my analogy suggests that via language we could indeed cross from ignorance to knowledge, from "us" to "it," and from "me" to "you." All it takes is a little leap—the leap of faith?—the leap from bridge to land, from me to you, you to me.

> The clarification I offer to those who understand me is that after they use my propositions like steps and climb up them, they recognize the propositions are nonsense. It is like throwing away a ladder after you have climbed up it.*

Without worrying o'er much about how you might get down, get home for supper.

And now we have a very good example of what one of the most famous phrases of the *Investigations*—"*die Verhexung unsres Verstandes durch*

> is knowledge and understanding and true belief about these things; these must be classed together, because they reside not in sounds or in physical shapes but in souls; clearly then they must be distinguished both from the real circle itself and from the three instruments first mentioned.

* My translation, or gloss if one prefers, of the first two sentences of the penultimate section of the *Tractatus* (6.54). The third and last sentence of the section might be imagined to prefigure my bridge analogy: They [those who understand me] must surmount/transcend/get over [*überwinden*] these propositions; then they will see the world correctly.

die Mittel unserer Sprache"—is pointing toward.* The bewitchment of our intelligence by means of language (in Anscombe's translation). Language, in providing a means (good or bad, inaccurate or accurate) of understanding some aspect of circumstances, bewitches us into thinking, into feeling that this understanding is knowledge, or is something like knowledge, or must lie on the road to knowledge. And thus we are not any closer to or further from knowledge than we may have been previously, and we are also now more confused.† From a Wittgensteinian and Augustinian perspective, as from a Pascalian one, all this is worthless unless one also realizes that one is nowhere—or just on a bridge, a suspension bridge—unless and until one can take that little leap of faith.

It is also fair to say that of these three—Wittgenstein, Augustine and Pascal—Wittgenstein was the least inclined to actually make the leap. Was this because he saw how wide the gap in fact was? Because he was not at all sure life was better on the other side or down below?

Augustine

The philosopher of science Thomas Kuhn wrote about how puzzling Aristotle's approach to mechanics had been for him until one "memorable (and very hot) summer day" when he was finally able to see the subject from Aristotle's perspective. This led Kuhn to a maxim which Wittgenstein, being of an earlier, more self-enamored generation, was better able to formulate than apply—e.g, to his reading of Augustine. "When reading the works of an important thinker," Kuhn wrote:

> look first for the apparent absurdities in the text and ask yourself how a sensible person could have written them. When you find an answer, . . . when those passages make sense, then you may find that more central passages, ones you previously thought you understood, have changed their meaning.‡

---

* N.B.: This is assuming the original being, the being without language, could have been confused; that is, assuming that confusion, too, does not depend on our life in language.

† *Investigations*, §109; a footnote in the Third Interpolation discusses opposing translations that philosophers have offered of Wittgenstein's section 109.

‡ Kuhn, xii. Passage includes a footnote: "More on this subject will be found in

Beautiful. And given Abel and Marsalina's focus on Augustine's memory, we might start right there: with how much different Augustine's idea of memory was from ours.* Or start right here (in the *Confessions*):

> In my memory, too, are all the events that I remember, whether they are things that have happened to me or things that I have heard from others. From the same source I can picture to myself all kinds of different images based either upon my own experience or upon what I find credible because it tallies with my own experience.
>
> . . .
>
> How, then, did these facts [facts not related to sensations] get into my memory? Where did they come from? I do not know. . . . From this we can conclude that learning these facts, which do not reach our minds as images by means of the senses but are recognized by us in our minds, without images, as they actually are, is simply a process of thought by which we gather together things which, although they are muddled and confused are already contained in the memory. When we give them our attention, we see to it that those facts, which had

---

T.S. Kuhn, 'Notes on Lakatos,' *Boston Studies in Philosophy of Science* 8 (1971): 137-46."

As regards Wittgenstein, *Cf.*, *Investigations*, Part II, xii, 195e:

> I am not saying: if such-and-such facts of nature were different people would have different concepts (in the sense of a hypothesis). But: if anyone believes that certain concepts are absolutely the correct ones, and that having different ones would mean not realizing something that we realize—then let him imagine certain very general facts of nature to be different from what we are used to, and the formation of concepts different from the usual ones will become intelligible to him.

* Readers might cut their teeth on this, from *On the Trinity* X: 11:

> Since then these three, memory, understanding, will, are not three lives but one life, nor three minds but one mind, it follows certainly that neither are they three substances but one substance. Since memory, which is called life, and mind, and substance, is so called in respect to itself, but it is called memory relatively to something.

been lying scattered and unheeded, are placed ready to hand, so that they are easily forthcoming once we have grown used to them.[108]

This would seem to a go a long ways toward explaining why and how Augustine wrote that he remembered how he learned to speak. One may also remember what one has not experienced. This is part of the wonder that is human memory.

This being a book about Wittgenstein, however, we are not going to follow Kuhn's complete program as regards Augustine. Rather, by touching on a few matters, I will raise some basic questions regarding language and learning, outline the divergence of Wittgenstein's and Augustine's conceptions, and give an idea of the confusion that has been fertilized by Wittgenstein's taking a rather un-Kuhnian approach to Augustine, e.g., in section 32 of the *Investigations*.*

The philosopher Myles Burnyeat speaks of Wittgenstein's "creative misprison" (translating: mis-taking) of Augustine, and of "his Augustine"—i.e., Wittgenstein's Augustine, as opposed to Augustine's Augustine, or Burnyeat's.[109] But this is also to say that there is an Abel's Augustine, and a my Augustine, and yours, and my Wittgenstein and my Burnyeat, *und so weiter*. We do not have to go very far down this path before we realize that in a universe of mis-takings, or of competing individual interpretations, it will be hard, it *is* hard (e.g., for a misled consciousness) to evaluate Wittgenstein's or anyone else's uses of language, to include one's own.

Burnyeat also proposes that Wittgenstein is responsible for having made the *Confessions* passage famous "as the precipitate of some 800 years of Platonist philosophizing."[110] That is, Wittgenstein was not using this passage simply to discuss/attack/embrace—to undermine because he wants to embrace?—one author's view of language and language learning;

---

* It is my pleasure to thank several classical scholars—Patrick Bearsley, Myles Burnyeat, Gillian Clark and Tarmo Toom—for such education as I have received in this regard, education received from the articles cited here in footnotes and endnotes, and in the "Works Cited" section. I additionally thank professors Clark and Toom for e-mailing me copies of articles of theirs that I had not been able to obtain via the libraries to which I have access. I would also note that all of these articles, by all four of these scholars, were inspired by Wittgenstein's (mis)reading of Augustine, which moved the scholars to go back to the original sources and to try to correct the record.

he is trying to undermine, blow to smithereens, befriend in his peculiar way—a whole, extremely influential school of philosophy. And, nicely, this attempt has also helped renew our interest in some of this school's teachings.

Inside out vs. outside in

For those who would try to see this passage through Augustine's eyes and mind, and as opposed to through Wittgenstein's, phrases from the *Confessions* that Abel quotes are key. "My wishes were inside me, while other people were outside." I would "show my meaning." In other words, for Augustine, the process was from the inside out. I believe this continues to be the majority or conventional view. There is something inside us, inside each individual, that we wish to express, need to express. For example, a baby needs to tell others that he is hungry! And thus, at least in Augustine's view, he, the *infans,* learns language because, as a young child observing those around him, his elders, he gets the impression that language is going to be useful, if not essential, to achieving this objective: to his getting what he needs and wants, to getting fed in so many ways.* And, as we shall

---

* The British child psychoanalyst and essayist Adam Phillips (in "Self-Made Aristocrats") has noted that Wittgenstein was "unusual for a philosopher because he so often writes about the difficulties a child has growing up in a family." Interestingly, Wittgenstein shared this concern for children's experiences with Augustine. Phillips goes on to say about Wittgenstein:

> His wish to clarify the world as he finds it, . . . turns the figure of the philosopher into a kind of child who wants to understand what is going on in his family, as opposed to the child who takes refuge from his family in a fantasy life [e.g., the fantasy life of metaphysics and metaphysicians]. For Wittgenstein, this is the difference between working out what people are using words to do in a more or less shared family life and being a metaphysician living in a world (or a system) of you own making.

The richness of this observation notwithstanding, I think Wittgenstein was indeed living in a fantasy world largely of his own making. Like many of us academics, he was in a certain sense trying to understand his origins, the family in which he grew up and his feelings, but while also trying to keep these things at a very long arm's length. I know, for example, of a man who was raised in a wealthy but psychologically disconnected home by an Irish servant. This woman was not only the great source of warmth and caring of his childhood, she may have been the only

soon discuss, there is also another suggestion in Augustine: Little does the *infans*, so busy at his language learning, know what else language is going to get him into!

From Wittgenstein's perspective, it does seem—seem powerfully, while perhaps only seeming—that there is indeed something on the inside—THIS pain!

> [D]eep inside me there's a perpetual seething, like the bottom of a geyser, and I keep on hoping that things will come to an eruption once and for all so that I can . . . into a different person.*

> Anyone who listens to a child's crying and understands what he hears will know that it harbors dormant psychic forces, terrible forces different from anything commonly assumed. Profound rage, pain and lust for destruction.†

We might say, however, that in Wittgenstein's schema, children's and adults' desires—needs—to express this something . . . To use an analogy I offered in a footnote to Part (4) of the main text, all THIS is on the other side of the glass.

On the mirrored side where language is, where all expression is, *for Wittgenstein the most fundamental process is not inside out but rather outside in*. The first step in "self expression," as we call it, is learning—taking in—what expressions our culture uses for self expressing. Language imposes itself upon us, and we cannot help taking this language in and using it to return to the outside world our bits of self expression.‡ Which is to say that

---

one. The boy went on to study the settlement patterns of Irish immigrants to the United States.

* Letter from Wittgenstein to Russell, December 1913; as quoted in McGuinness, *Wittgenstein: A Life*, 192. Ellipsis in the original. This may, *inter ali*a, well describe a feeling of an infant in the midst of a tantrum.

† Wittgenstein, *Culture and Value*, 2e (note from 1929).

‡ Seeking an analogy, I find myself reminded of how the Microsoft Word program, which I try, not always successfully, to steer clear of, imposes its ideas of correct spelling, grammar, punctuation and document formatting on what one tries to write. The program does not win every battle, and just as writers and speakers (all of us!) influence the evolution of language, so one might become a Microsoft programmer or beta-tester and help shape what will be imposed on future program users. But the point of this analogy—*approximative*, like all anal-

this external language, internalized, comes to shape our experience, both our sense of our pains and our attempts to communicate them to others, be all this correctly or incorrectly. *Cf., Investigations*, §244:

> How do words refer to sensations?—There doesn't seem to be any problem here; don't we talk about sensations every day, and give them names? But how is the connexion between the name and the thing set up? The question is the same as: how does a human being learn the names of sensations?—of the word "pain" for example. Here is one possibility: words are connected with the primitive, the natural, expressions [Augustine's *verbis naturalibus omnium gentium*] of the sensation and used in their place. A child has hurt himself and he cries; and then adults talk to him and teach him exclamations and, later, sentences. They teach the child new pain-behaviour.
>
> "So you are saying that the word 'pain' really means crying?"—On the contrary: the verbal expression of pain replaces crying and does not describe it.

And I would also fill in the blanks here: crying and the word "pain" replace feelings without describing them.

Infans, puer, Kind, Brustkind

The next major distinction I want to make between Augustine and Wittgenstein has to do with the divergent interests they brought to the subject of language learning. Before making this point, however, I want to call attention to a confusion or series of confusions underlying Wittgenstein's reading of Augustine's three sentences from Book I, Chapter 8. In the main text I quoted a portion of Book I, Chapter 8 of the *Confessions* that Wittgenstein had ignored:

> non enim eram infans qui non farer, sed iam puer loquens eram . . . vitae humanae procellosam societatem altius ingressus sum

---

ogies—is that when one is feeling the force of this word-processing program, and of the large corporation and the capitalist infrastructure with which it is linked, one may be getting an idea of how language imposes itself, from the outside, on our thoughts and feelings.

I was no longer a speechless infant, but a speaking boy . . .
launched deeper into the stormy intercourse of human
life

Both Abel and I dwell on the fact that Wittgenstein's excerpt from this chapter of the *Confessions* left out both of these phrases, and this notwithstanding the fact—or because?—these phrases give the theme of Augustine's brief chapter. I note here that, according to Roman/Latin custom, it was precisely through the acquisition of speech—or of the common spoken language—that an infant (*infans*) was transformed into a child (*puer*). Thus there is a certain absurdity in Wittgenstein raising the issue that a child might already have language; by Augustine's way of thinking/speaking, this is what makes him a child: he can speak, he has language. This is what made *him*, Augustine, a child and launched him into *vitae humanae procellosam societatem*: He had learned to speak!

Here we also have hit our heads on an aspect of the German language. Although Germans do make use of the English word "baby," and they have other, more particular terms like *Säugling* (suckling) and *Brustkind* (breast-child, unweened infant), the standard German word for infant is *kleines Kind* (or *Kleinkind*)—small child. Where in English we say that a woman is "going to have a baby," Germans say *ein Kind bekommen*—a child is coming. On a linguistic level, the distinction between child and infant is not marked in German as it is in English or Latin. And so, in section 32 when Wittgenstein uses the word *Kind* in association with Augustine's text, to what is he referring? *Infans . . . puer . . . Kind . . . kleines Kind . . . Brustkind . . .*? Is Wittgenstein saying that it is as if an infant had a language and could already think, or as if a child—a *puer*—did? Nicely, as shall soon be seen, Augustine would have answered "yes" in either case; an infant, before s/he can speak, can think *and* has a language—more than one.

For their parts, Abel and Marsalina assume that Augustine's *infans* must be a very young child, first learning to speak. This is certainly not a wild assumption, and I take it to have been Wittgenstein's assumption as well. And in Book I, Chapter 6 of the *Confessions*, Augustine (as translated by Pine-Coffin) says clearly: "as I came towards the end of infancy I tried to find signs to convey my feelings to others." However, a little farther along in the *Confessions* (I:14), Augustine writes that (in fact) he learned to speak not by studying and imitating his elders, but as a result of *blandimenta nutricum*—the oohing and aahing of nurses.

> As a baby, of course, I knew no Latin either, but I learned it without fear or fret, simply by keeping my ears open when my nurses fondled me and everyone laughed and played happily with me. I learned it without being forced by threats of punishment, because it was my own wish to be able to give expression to my thoughts.

It is always possible that Augustine is simply contradicting himself, contradicting his earlier statements, something we all do and rather frequently. But there is also the possibility that in the earlier chapter, the chapter Wittgenstein challenges—or only *seems* to challenge, we may decide— It is possible that in Book I, Chapter 8 of the *Confessions*, Augustine, in talking about how he learned to speak, did not mean what we in the United States have meant by this phrase: a baby learning his first words. Rather, it may well be that Augustine is referring to the phase of learning to speak that involves acquiring sufficient vocabulary as to give the impression that one can fully express in words one's will, one's desires and reactions, and so forth. Apparently, contemporary scientists believe that much of this vocabulary acquisition takes place between the ages of six and eight, and this would fit with the fact that Augustine identifies the transition from Chapter 7 (infancy) to Chapter 8 (boyhood) as also involving a transition from the period of his life that he cannot remember to the period of his life, the rest of his life, that he can remember.

> Even using our own (rather than Augustine's) conception of memory, it is not that difficult to accept that Augustine could remember how he built his vocabulary when he was a young boy. I can remember the smell of Cuisinaire rods in my second-grade classroom, if not what math I, as a result, learned (olifactorily?). I believe, however, that, in any case, we must share Marsalina's view that this is an unusual child, to be setting himself to vocabulary building in such an organized fashion at, say, 7 years old. And, if we embrace this reading, we may find ourselves thrown back on basic questions: How did Augustine, or how does any infant, learn language? And what was there in his nurses' caresses, and in the laughing and happy play, that could teach a boy Latin (or English or German)?

Learning for Augustine, from Augustine

So now we come to this promised, next "major distinction": Augustine was much less interested in language and language learning than Wittgenstein. Augustine, rather, was interested in how human beings learn more generally, and in particular in how some of us learn to embrace God and to live virtuously, and what role God plays in this process.* In fact, Augustine did not believe that human beings learned much of importance from one another; true learning comes from within and from the presence of God within, along with His interventions. Adapting the beautiful lines from the end of the *Confessions—quis angelus angelo? quis angelus homini?—*

> What man can teach another? What angel teach an angel? What angel teach a man? We must ask of you [God]. We must knock at your door. Only then will we learn, will the door be opened to us.†

Augustine was also very interested in the violence and suffering connected to his own learning process, and also connected, he believed, to transcendental, transformational learning in general. For example, in Book I, Chapter 14, we find, first, that Augustine says he learned Latin as an infant in happy play, "without being forced by threats of punishment,"

---

* Toom, 361:

> In the *Confessions*, Augustine's goal is to praise God and confess God's mercy. Because praising and confessing are linguistic activities, Augustine says first a few words about becoming articulate. Then, after becoming both articulate and literate, he is able to say, "And now, Lord, I make my confession to you in writing." ["*Et nunc, domine, confiteor tibi in litteris.*" *Confessions*, IX:12.]

† *Confessions* XIII: 38. Quoting more exactly, first from Augustine and then from Pine-Coffin's translation:

> *et hoc intellegere quis hominum dabit homini? quis angelus angelo? quis angelus homini? a te petatur, in te quaeratur, ad te pulsetur: sic, sic accipietur, sic invenietur, sic aperietur.* (What man can teach another to understand this truth [that God is Goodness itself and forever at rest]? What angel can teach it to an angel? What angel can teach it to a man? We must ask it of you, seek it in you; we must knock at your door. Only then shall we receive what we ask and find what we seek; only then will the door be opened to us.)

but rather

> because it was my own wish to be able to give expression to my thoughts. I could never have done this if I had not learnt a few words, not from schoolmasters [i.e., under threat of violence], but from people who spoke to me and <u>listened</u> when I delivered to their ears whatever thoughts I had conceived. This clearly shows that we learn better in a free spirit of curiosity than under fear and compulsion. [My underscoring.]

This sounds like a speech in favor of modern-day, Rousseauian progressive education, but then comes the second point, the Augustinian kicker, the last two sentences of the chapter:

> But your law, O God, permits the free flow of curiosity to be stemmed by force. From the schoolmaster's cane to the ordeals of martyrdom, your law prescribes bitter medicine to retrieve us from the noxious pleasures which cause us to desert you.

Was there, then, something wrong, even evil, in that happy nursery, for all this something contributed to Augustine's learning his first words? Must we, in order to come closer to God, in order to recognize and appreciate the presence of God within us—must we renounce Earthly pleasures, the caresses of women included? (A widowed scholar asks himself!) Must we embrace suffering, or at least the opportunity suffering may give us to transcend our trivial existences and our enslavement to *falsas divitias* (false wealth)?* Is this the only way we can find peace, an end to conflict—both between human beings and within our selves; relief from our social, psychological, philosophical, spiritual struggles? Or is life, in fact, struggle, and we feel most alive when we are struggling, and dead when the struggle ceases?†

---

* Latin is from *Confessions* I:9. Augustine is saying he was told as a boy to pay attention to his teachers "ut in hoc saeculo florerem, et excellerem linguosis artibus, ad honorem hominum et falsas divitias famulantibus." So he could succeed in his life, excel in the language arts, gain the respect of others and not be a slave to false riches.

† Retuning to the *Confessions* after many years away, I am fascinated to find that "the good" for Augustine is rest. See, for example, these sentences from the last two chapters (XIII: 37-38) of the book (with Pine-Coffin's translations):

Augustine's many languages

Goaded by Wittgenstein, let us now turn our attention to what Augustine did in fact write about language—observations that, again, *did not* reflect Augustine's primary interests and that *did* reflect conceptions of language prevalent during his lifetime. In De doctrina Christiana, Augustine distinguishes between "*signa naturalia*" and "*signa data*." The former—e.g., smoke from a fire—signify "*sine voluntate,*" without wishing to do so. As human beings we learn to interpret *signa naturalia* and *signa data*, and we also learn to produce *signa data* that can be interpreted by other human beings. In particular, we learn to use words: "the principal means used by human beings to signify the thoughts they have in their minds." *Signa data* are used by living things "to show, to the best of their ability, the movements of their minds, or anything they have felt or learnt."[111] (Again, it's inside out here.)

We may glimpse here how far our Wittgensteinian "life in language" extends—the several languages it involves—but the specific point is that for Augustine thinking came before speaking. According to the Epicureans and Pyrrhonists, human words were simply "habituated responses associated with observed situations."* But, as shall be discussed,

> *etiam tunc enim sic requiesces in nobis, quemadmodum nunc operaris in nobis, et ita erit illa requies tua per nos, quemadmodum sunt ista opera tua per nos.* (In that eternal Sabbath you [God] will rest in us, just as now you work in us. The rest we shall enjoy will be yours, just as the work that we now do is your work done through us.)

> *tu autem bonum nullo indigens bono semper quietus es, quoniam tua quies tu ipse es.* (You [God] are Goodness itself and need no good besides yourself. You are forever at rest, because you are your own repose.)

My sense is that what we have here is yet another example of how spoken and written ideals and wishes are used to balance quite different behaviors. Augustine was a very aggressive political leader. In his life he had not chosen or followed a peaceful, restful path. He had not allowed others, either his opponents or the people to whom he preached, to live in peace. Rather the opposite. And so peace was a great ideal for him.

---

* Toom, 364, himself quoting D. Glidden, "Parrots, Pyrrhonists and Native Speakers", in *Companions to Ancient Thought, 3: Language,* edited by Stephen Everson (Cambridge University Press, 1994), 138. Toom's article, "Augustine and

for Augustine, more attuned to the Stoics, thought intervenes, both preceding and—for the listener—coming after the spoken words, in order for there to be understanding. *Inter alia*, in this way human language is different from that of animals. (See segment on Lacan and the dance of the bees in Appendix C.) As speakers, humans seek to translate a thought into commonly recognized sounds, and as listeners we try to retranslate the sounds back into thoughts. Since we are able to do this, and extraordinarily quickly, we are able to understand one another and converse. (And Augustine assumed that we do understand one another quite well.) Thus, Toom states: for Augustine, language learning "is more than the mere learning of a conventional stimulus-response. It also involves comprehension."[112]

Thus, for Augustine:

(a) In the ordinary course of life, when we speak we are expressing thoughts we have already had, all be this only an instant before we begin expressing them;* and

(b) Before an infant begins speaking (as opposed to babbling), s/he has to already be able to think.

Moreover, as regards infant language-learning, Augustine shared a view, or intuition, of the Stoics: even for infant human beings, spoken language—or intentional language, *signa data*—was always the expression of something prior, a thought, which itself had its own language, *a language common to all human beings without their ever sharing it or learning it*.

We moderns and post-moderns believe, and indeed *feel*, that thinking and spoken language ("talking to oneself," e.g., in English or German) go hand in hand. Thus we have significantly reduced the possibility that, in *our, adult* conceptions, a 1-year-old—babbling toward words—might in fact be capable of thought. But Augustine's Stoical view was that there on the inside—in our literal or figurative hearts, it would seem—thoughts have their own language (e.g., *not* English, German or Latin), and this language is innate, and thus usable by an infant—for example, in order to learn a spoken language.

Ancient Theories of Language Acquisition" was inspired by what we might call "Wittgenstein's" passage in the *Confessions*.

* Recall the last line of Wittgenstein's §32: "And 'think' would here mean something like 'talk to itself'".

N.B.: This is not Chomsky's theory *avant la lettre*; this is not a proto-language or a capability to learn language that is built into the human infant's brain; this is a language—the language of thought—ready made. I have seen this referred to as an "inner language" and as "basic language," which, we might say, comes pre-loaded in our computers (brains). Unlike the language of gestures and expressions, it does not need to be learned.* Nor would it be susceptible to cultural influences; pre-loaded it would also be pre-conventional, and there would be a built-in agreement among all human beings who came fully equipped with this language. They could not presume that their pains were the same as other people's pains, but

---

* "Inner language": Bearsley, 234. "Basic language": Toom, 368, citing David E. Zoolalian, "Augustine and Wittgenstein: Some Remarks on the Necessity of a Private Language," *Augustine Studies* 9 (1978): 25-33.

Toom also notes that Sextus Empiricus pointed out long ago that if one accepted either the Stoic conception of a built-in basic language for internal speech, or the Epicurean stimulus-response model, the question of language learning becomes moot. How can you be said to learn if you already know or if you are able to act effectively without conscious thought, simply out of habit, repeating as others around you repeat?

This brings us back to Augustine's discussion of memory in Book X of the *Confessions* (see particularly X:12), and its forerunner: the discussion in Plato's *Meno* regarding how it is that we can know some things (or perhaps everything we do in fact know) internally, without having "learned"—i.e., from external inputs? If we take the Augustinian or Socratic or Cartesian view that the truth is to be found within, then how did it get there? If Meno's slave can solve a geometry problem without ever having been taught geometry, . . . ? Is geometry, then, a genetic endowment of human beings? Is Descartes' *cogito*—I think therefore I am—a genetic endowment, a truth any one of us would come to if we had the will and self-confidence to strip away all the misleading things we had been taught, if we had the courage to set aside all external "learning" in order to be able to know something: what we already know and have always known?

Regarding Sextus Empiricus, Toom cites *Math.* 1.37-8, 11.242-3 and *Pyrrh.* 3.266-9 in the Loeb Classical Library. In the *Meno* see 80D *ff.* and especially 85D-86A:

> Socrates: Either then he [Meno's slave] has at some time acquired the knowledge which he now has, or he has always possessed it. If he always possessed it, he must always have known; if on the other hand he acquired it at some previous time, it cannot have been in this life, unless somebody has taught him geometry. . . .
>
> [M]ay we say that his soul has been forever in a state of knowledge?

thoughts phrased in the basic-language equivalent of "I am in pain" could be presumed to be the same thought in the mind of each human who had such a thought.

This is part of what Wittgenstein is getting at, though seemingly without realizing that Augustine would not be surprised, let alone ashamed, to have such a conception attached to his name. In Augustine's model (translated into German), a *Kind* is like a stranger coming into a foreign country already having a language; the *Kind* has (among other languages, in fact) the language of thought and comes into the land of spoken language and uses his first language (i.e., of thought) to learn his second one.

Again, from Augustine's perspective there would be nothing shocking about this revelation, and one doubts that he would understand why Wittgenstein felt the need to be coy about it. Yes, this is what he, Aurelius Augustinus Hipponensis, and distinguished philosophers before him, believed: there is a language of thought which is one of our natural endowments and which we use, *inter alia*, to learn spoken language.

We might imagine for ourselves the reactions of a time-travelling Augustine, come to wonder at this Ludwig Wittgenstein and why he feels a need to make the point that the *Kind* (young Augustine), even were he a *Brustkind*, "*so als habe es bereits eine Sprache, nur nicht diese*"—seems to already have a language, though not this one. "There is no '*so als*' 'as if,' 'seems' about it," our Augustine might say. "A *Kind*/child/infant already has a language right from the get-go—or two, in fact." There is the language of thought and there is "*verbis naturalibus omnium gentium*": facial expressions, the play of the eyes, the movement of other parts of the body, tone of voice, crying. In Augustine's view, without these two innate languages, and the work of God, learning a spoken language would not be possible. And for Augustine there is also the third language or not-quite-language that Abel mentions: the flailing about, the language-like signs that do not quite signify as the flailer wishes they would. The Stoics apparently distinguished between voicing and saying.[113] Such flailing and voicing is likely a much larger part of our "life in language" than we realize—or a much larger part of our life (as adults) living on the border between language and flailing.

Inside out again

There is a yet more fundamental point here, however, and one on which the whole Wittgensteinian approach hinges (as does, inversely, the Augustinian idea of language and thought, for all this idea was less central to what Augustine was trying to say more generally). Contrary to Wittgenstein's conception, for Augustine spoken language—interhuman language—was not necessary either for willing and desiring, *nor* for knowing what we will and desire. So, quite contrary to what Abel, and his and my reading of Wittgenstein, propose in the main text, interhuman language and all the socially established conventions it embodies would not be intervening between some core "I," if such a thing indeed exists, and this I's understanding of its desires—or pains. The "I" has the desires and pains, knows what they are in "basic language." There is no internal problem or gap. If there is any gap or confusion it would all be on the outside. It would arise from imperfections in our ability to express ourselves in spoken language, or to understand the spoken language of others.

This Augustinian view is of course also the common view—the *gewöhnlich* (ordinary, normal, customary) view, as Wittgenstein frames it.* I will offer one example, however, to illustrate the difference between this view and Wittgenstein's. In English we "have" dreams, and indeed we treat them as if they were yet another of our possessions, another object, not unlike a painting, or a DVD with a short half-life. The Russian language, meanwhile, teaches Russians to "see" dreams—almost as if dreams were, like clouds, floating outside ourselves—or outside Russians?—and the question is whether and from what perspective an individual sees them, and before they continue on their way—perhaps to be seen by others? (And that same night or another?) From a Wittgensteinian perspective, anglophones' and russophones' lives in language result in their understanding dreams differently. And this, if you will, right up to the limit of the function, to the point where one would want to say that anglophones

---

* "But I cannot be content with the ordinary. I have to understand the underlying principles. I cannot go about as other people; I have to go in stiff boots!" This (from Kierkegaard) well captures both how philosophers end up heading into empty territories *and* Wittgenstein's own natural inclination (to not be content with the ordinary, to insist on going about in stiff boots). (Kierkegaard, *Repetition* (in *Repetition* and *Philosophical Crumbs*, 41).

and russophones, because of the differences in their languages, do not have the same experiences of dreams.* Even though bilingual dictionaries offer equivalents—"dreams"/"сoны"—these are not referring to, pointing to the same things. But from an Augustinian perspective—which, again, remains the more conventional, the *gewöhnlich*, commonly accepted one— the experience of the dream—for everyone, and for all that the images of dreams seem a kind of language to us, and seemed so long before Freud or Joseph came along— The Augustinian perspective is that our dreams are independent of inter-human language. It is only later that, in telling others about a dream or in trying by ourselves to understand one of our dreams, we recall the dream using the language we have learned, complete with its conventional ways of viewing and organizing experiences. The *content* of anglophones' and russophones' dreams may well be different, but not the *nature* of their dreams, not the *seltsames Gedächtnisphänomen*, the queer memory phenomenon, people are referring to when they use their words for dreams/сoны/*Träume* . . . .

Recapitulating

If we take a pan-millennial perspective—not rejecting Augustine's, Wittgenstein's or others' theories because they are ancient, iconoclastic or simply do not accord with what we have absorbed, with precious little questioning, from our parents, teachers, peers, media—Augustine's observations, his conception of our language faculties, raise several

---

* It may help if I here offer a description of the Platonic view which Wittgenstein, like a jousting knight, was doing battle. This adapted from Lindberg (38):

> When Plato assigned reality to the forms, he was, in fact, identifying reality with the properties that classes of things have in common. The bearer of true reality is not *this* dream that I had or saw last night, but the idealized form of a dream shared (imperfectly) by every individual dream—those characteristics by virtue of which we are able to classify a whole range of individual experiences as dreams.

To which, some Wittgenstein might answer:

> But look more closely at the experiences we refer to as dreams, or the activities we refer to as games. You will see—for example, if you compare English dreams and Russian сoны—that there are connections, similarities, "family resemblances," but no essence or idealized form.

questions, as do Wittgenstein's investigations taking off in part from his reading of Augustine, or of a fragment of Augustine. These questions include whether there is indeed some sort of innate natural or basic language, or languages, of all peoples, or whether, and to what extent, we *learn* this language and whether it is the product of conventions? For example, does a certain set of the lips and showing of the teeth indicate pleasure throughout all cultures throughout time? Do we learn this facial expression by observation and imitation, or are we born knowing how and when to make this sign, or set of signs? And if this sign signifies pleasure, does this mean we are necessarily feeling good when we deploy it? And is this "pleasure" the same feeling throughout all cultures throughout time?

In the *Confessions* I:6, Augustine writes: "By watching babies [throwing tantrums when they did not get what they wanted] I have learnt that this is how they behave, and they, quite unconsciously, have done more than those who brought me up and knew all about it to convince me that I behaved in just the same way myself."* Ergo and as previously discussed: For Augustine (as for all of us!) our memories of ourselves can include, among many other things, experiences we never had but only observed (or, say, read about). And thus Augustine in the first Book of the *Confessions* was making use of his adult observations of other infants. Among the ideas Augustine seems to have gotten from this observing of infants was that he himself first began to smile in his sleep, only later smiling when he was awake. If this is true, and not just of Augustine, but of all or most of us, should smiling be considered a sign at all, let alone some bit of natural language? Perhaps—and this fits with my remarks in the main text about how we are, as it were, colonized through language—perhaps smiling is just something we do, for our own private or neuromuscular reasons, whatever those may be. But, afterwards, in response to our smiling, an interpretation is imposed by others—larger, older, more powerful others—and we see no option, and have little desire, but to accept, embrace this interpretation of our smiling and of smiling more generally. This positioning of my lips and teeth must be a sign that I am happy and that I want others to know that I am happy, and so, when I do this positioning . . . Either I am happy or I do not know my own feelings? or I do not know what happiness is?

---

* Similarly, in Book I, Chapter 7 of the *Confessions*, Augustine writes that he has believed what other people have told him about his infancy, "and from watching other babies I can conclude that I also lived as they do."

At stake here, among other things, are basic theories of epistemology. Does language, or some subset of our language(s) express a basic, "natural" truth, or do we rather, as we begin to use language, get caught up in the assumed truths that are conveyed and given weight by our particular language? Allow me here to insert a central proposition of Willard Quine's, a proposition which well expresses the latter possibility, regarding assumed truths:

> The totality of our so-called knowledge or beliefs, from the most casual matters of geography and history to the profoundest laws of atomic physics or even of pure mathematics and logic, is a man-made fabric which impinges on experience only along the edges.*

A word not to pass over too quickly, this "impinges." Its strength lies in its counter-intuitiveness. One might well, an Augustinian might well, picture the inverse: experience impinging on language. With all this in mind, however, can we say of spoken language at least that it is vastly more conventional than natural: It is a human fabric that impinges on experience/is impinged on by experience only along the edges? As to *which* edges, . . . good luck.

---

* Quine, "Two Dogmas of Empiricism," part VI: Empiricism Without the Dogmas. Quine goes on to explicate:

> Or, to change the figure, total science is like a field of force whose boundary conditions are experience. A conflict with experience at the periphery occasions readjustments in the interior of the field. Truth values have to be redistributed over some of our statements. Re-evaluation of some statements entails re-evaluation of others, because of their logical interconnections—the logical laws being in turn simply certain further statements of the system, certain further elements of the field. Having re-evaluated one statement we must re-evaluate some others, whether they be statements logically connected with the first or whether they be the statements of logical connections themselves. But the total field is so underdetermined by its boundary conditions, experience, that there is much latitude of choice as to what statements to re-evaluate in the light of any single contrary experience. No particular experiences are linked with any particular statements in the interior of the field, except indirectly through considerations of equilibrium affecting the field as a whole.

Whisper in my heart

One last point about Augustine's conception, or about his heart. As previously mentioned, for Augustine the heart—and again, presumably not the organ so much as his very core—had its own language, for its thoughts and desires. "Even if no words are spoken, the man who is thinking is of course uttering in his heart" ("*in corde suo dicit utique qui cogitat*"). "*Sensa cordis mei*": the intentions of my heart. The further point here is that for Augustine the heart could also hear language: the words of God.

> Have pity on me and help me, O Lord my God. Tell me why you mean so much to me. *Whisper in my heart, I am here to save you.* Speak so that I may hear your words. My heart has ears ready to listen to you, Lord. Open them wide and *whisper in my heart, I am here to save you.**

Wittgenstein

We now come to a fundamental aspect of Wittgenstein's relationship to Augustine and to the other important people in his life. An exploration of this aspect may enhance our understanding of philosophical claims in the *Investigations*. It may also deepen our psychological understanding of Wittgenstein—which understanding, I keep arguing, must be part of our understanding of the circumstances to which his work responds, and thus, again, to our understanding of the work's claims.

Myles Burnyeat concludes his article on Wittgenstein and Augustine by proposing, *inter alia*, that we might read Wittgenstein *not* as exposing Augustine's thinking about language in all its nakedness, if you will, but as reviving Augustine's appreciation of how hard it is to learn or

---

* The extract comes from the *Confessions* I:5, and my understanding has been that the italicized portions are quotations from the Bible. The closest I have been able to come, however, is Psalm 35 ("A Prayer for Rescue from Enemies"), here in the King James version, 35:22 and 35:24: "O LORD: keep not silence: O Lord, be not far from me. . . . Judge me, O LORD my God, according to thy righteousness; and let them not rejoice over me." Psalm 71 has some similar lines.

The sentence quoted prior to this ("Even if no words...") comes from Augustine, *De Trinitate* 15.17; as quoted in Toom, 368. See also *De Trinitate* 15:10. "*Sensa cordis mei*" is a phrase in the passage from the *Confessions* I:8 that has been under discussion by, among others, Abel, Marsalina, Wittgenstein and me.

know anything, language included. Burnyeat proposes that Wittgenstein adds to Augustine's relatively simple conception "subtle arguments."[114]

Anachronism in cheek, Burnyeat proposes, for example, that Augustine in the *Confessions* agrees with Wittgenstein's analysis that the description provided of how the infant Augustine came to grasp his first words is wholly inadequate. From Augustine's perspective, as we have already noted, among other things "Divine help was needed, "the inner light of truth," the truths that inwardly God makes manifest to each of us.[115] For his part, Wittgenstein speaks much less often than Augustine of God and of faith, but in the *Investigations* there is, as also discussed earlier, a sense that our "life in language" depends not on the fact that individuals may happen to agree (or disagree) with one another in their most fundamental judgments, but rather on our *faith* that we do indeed agree. Wittgenstein rarely connects God to either this faith or this agreement, but there is, again, §234:

> Would it not be possible . . . to have a feeling of being guided by the rules as by a spell, feeling astonishment at the fact that we agreed? (We might give thanks to the Deity for our agreement.)*

The question for the moment is the extent to which Wittgenstein in the *Investigations* (and elsewhere) was trying to expose and explode

---

* We might wish to say that for Wittgenstein the miracle, the sign of God's presence, may be found right here, in this unmediated agreement between isolated individuals: between human beings. See also *Remarks on the Foundations of Mathematics*, Part V, §33, 184e:

> A language-game: to bring something *else*; to bring the *same*. Now, we can imagine how it is played.—But how can I explain it to anyone? I can give him this training.—But then how does he know what he is to bring the next time as "the same"—with what justice can I say that he has brought the right thing or the wrong? Of course I know very well that in certain cases people would turn on me with signs of opposition.
>
> And does this mean e.g. that the definition of "same" would be this: same is what all or most human beings with one voice take for the same?—Of course not.
>
> For of course I don't make use of the agreement of human beings to affirm identity. What criterion do you use, then? None at all.

Augustine's conceptions, and the extent to which he was endorsing Augustine's concerns, and at least an aspect of Augustine's faith? (And to what extent was Wittgenstein aware of what he was doing?)

In search of answers, we begin the threatened dive into psychobiography, in the course of which I will suggest, *inter alia*, that Wittgenstein's basic "game" involved admiration/attraction/repulsion/escape. And, along the way, we find an answer: Wittgenstein was doing his damndest to undermine Augustine's conception *because of* how it spoke to him. Wittgenstein's attraction to, sympathy with Augustine's views was made manifest in the extent and aggressiveness of his attacks. (*Cf.*, Wittgenstein's relationship with Bertrand Russell or his comment that his mentor G.E. Moore "shows you how far a man can get with absolutely no intelligence whatever".*) It may come to seem that here and elsewhere the word "game" is being used euphemistically. We may be getting quite close to THIS pain.

Many pages earlier, in discussing Wittgenstein's personality, I reprised an anti-Wittgensteinian comment from the distinguished American philosopher Richard Rorty: Wittgenstein took out his intense self-loathing on everyone he met. In working away on the present rendition of Abel and Marsalina's conversation, in reading further in biographical works—above all in Ray Monk's biography, *Ludwig Wittgenstein: The Duty of Genius*—I came to the impression, thanks in particular to pages 235 and 380, that "self-loathing" was not quite the way to put it.

I will begin on page 380, where one may find brought together Wittgenstein's feelings for and guilt about his relations with his sister Margarete (also spelled Marguerite in English texts, and nicknamed Gretl) and for his companion/lover Francis Skinner. Monk quotes from two diary entries Wittgenstein made (in German) in 1937:

> Think of my earlier love, or infatuation, for Marguerite and of my love for Francis. It is a bad sign for me that my feelings for M could go so completely cold. . . . May I be forgiven; i.e., may it be possible for me, to be sincere and loving. [January 12, 1937]

---

* As reported by F.R. Leavis, "Memories of Wittgenstein," 64. Please see the segment on Moore in Appendix 3, where I put forward my view on how important Moore's teaching was to Wittgenstein.

Masturbated last night. Pangs of conscience. But also the conviction that I am too weak to withstand the urge and the temptation if they and the images which accompany them offer themselves to me without my being able to take refuge in others. Yet only yesterday evening I was reflecting on the need to lead a pure life. (I was thinking of Marguerite and Francis.) [February 12, 1937]

Two notes of my own. First, masturbation is (the Bible tells us) a way of not connecting, of spilling one's seed rather than connecting with another in an ongoing, creative process. This is not to come out against masturbation—nor to draw conclusions about the state of human relations given the current enthusiasm for masturbation, sex toys, et al.—but rather to not forget that Wittgenstein as a rule preferred, to connecting, *not connecting* with the people to whom he was most attracted and whom he most admired. He preferred not connecting with the people with whom he most wanted to connect: e.g., in the present case, his sister Margarete and his companion/lover Francis.* I write all this not to wrap up Wittgenstein's psychodynamics in a neat package, but to bring to the fore how for him—and hardly just for him—there was, if you will, a connection between attraction/admiration/desire, on the one hand, and repulsion/rejection/undermining/destruction, on the other.†

---

* At least part of the reason Wittgenstein exiled himself from England to Norway was because he received a letter from Margarete saying that she and her husband, Jerome Stonborough, were coming to live in London. Wittgenstein told a friend that he could not stand to live in England if he were perpetually liable to visits from the Stonboroughs. (Monk, 89, apparently relying on David Pinsent's diaries. *N.B.*: "Stonborough" was a name that Jerome had adopted, himself running away from his New York home and his bankrupt father, Herman Steinberger, a former kid-glove importer. Waugh, 19.)

† *Cf.*, Freud, "Analysis Terminable and Interminable," 246:

> The two fundamental principles of Empedocles— φιλία [love] and νεῖχος [strife]—are, both in name and function, the same as our two primal instincts, *Eros* and *Destructiveness*, the first of which endeavours to combine what exists into ever greater unities, while the second endeavours to dissolve those combinations and to destroy the structures to which they have given rise. [*Fin-de-siècle* Jewish Vienna was a small town: In *Geschlecht und Charakter* (Gender and Character) Otto Weininger also quoted Empedocles on love and strife.]

Continuing in this vein, I note that, for all in one sense Wittgenstein removed himself from Austria to England and eventually set up a sort of a home base at the top of a tower at Cambridge University, still, apparently, he would (like a college student) go home to Vienna and his family every year at Christmas. There was, however, a lapse of a dozen years—the years between his father's death and his mother's. The first year after his father died, Ludwig did go home, but, Monk writes, this visit, in 1914, "filled him with such dread and produced in him such confusion". He did not return again until after his mother died. After his mother's death he looked forward to these "homecomings," if they can be called that, "with delight."[116] From a psychobiographical perspective, from an Oedipal perspective, I cannot help asking if we are not here getting rather close to that which really could not be spoken about, even internally, in coded notebooks or in what we might want to call private language, in Wittgenstein's thoughts: his attraction to, desire for his mother: the *ur* person to whom Ludwig was attracted and therefore kept his distance from, afraid of connecting all too well with her?* As he later

---

See also the concluding paragraph of Freud's *Civilization and Its Discontents*, which was first published in 1930:

> The fateful question for the human species seems to me to be whether and to what extent their cultural development will succeed in mastering the disturbance of their communal life by the human instinct of aggression and self-destruction. It may be that in this respect precisely the present time deserves a special interest. Men have gained control over the forces of nature to such an extent that with their help they would have no difficulty in exterminating one another to the last man.

* *Cf.*, the famous closing line of the 1922 *Tractatus*—"*Wovon man nicht sprechen kann, darüber muss man schweigen.*" What we cannot speak about we must past over in silence. The standard reading would most definitely *not* have this "what" include Wittgenstein's feelings for his mother or his sister (and certainly not for Francis Skinner, who Ludwig did not meet until the early 1930s). According to the standard reading, Wittgenstein is, rather, not speaking about various philosophical subjects, ethics in particular. That is, we cannot speak intelligently, meaningfully about what we should and should not do—e.g., about whether we should or should not try to speak about ethics?—and therefore we should leave these questions be. Perhaps as we might treat a radioactive substance, not denying its radioactivity, but understanding that we needed to keep our distance from the object because of its cancerous powers.

Again, the standard reading of the *Tractatus* does *not* connect any of this to emotions, let alone to Ludwig's feelings for his mother, his sister and any of his male

feared and ran away from his all too rich connections with Bertrand Russell and Francis Skinner?*

---

professors, friends or fellow students. Rather, the idea is generally traced back to a passage in Heinrich Hertz's *Principles of Mechanics* which I referred to in the First Interpolation. I reprise Monk's summary (26) here:

> In *Principles of Mechanics* Hertz addresses the problem of how to understand the mysterious concept of "force" as it is used in Newtonian physics. Hertz proposes that, instead of giving a direct answer to the question: "What is force?", the problem should be dealt with by restating Newtonian physics without using "force" as a basic concept. "When these painful contradictions are removed," he writes, "the question as to the nature of force will not have been answered; but our minds, no longer vexed, will cease to ask illegitimate questions." [My underscoring.]

What I would say is that in Wittgenstein's case—as in the case of most every, if not every, human being—it would be more accurate to say that the goal is ceasing to ask certain, quite *legitimate* questions. I am also sure that on one level our questions are all the same and have to do with the human predicament: with our mortality, with human consciousness and with the challenges of being a social animal. I will, for example, be discussing soon enough a "crisis of the self." Of course variety may be found in the specific terms in which our predicament manifests itself—in the particularities of our questions, the particular manifestations of our self crises and so forth.

Incest is a major taboo, and there was no need for incest to become taboo if, *inter alia*, many human beings did not have powerful incestuous urges. But this does not mean that incest is—e.g., rather than death—necessarily the big issue for every one of us, the source of the legitimate/illegitimate questions we most wish to cease to ask.

* From Wittgenstein's *Lectures and Conversations*; as quoted in McGuinness, "Freud and Wittgenstein," 33:

> It may then [e.g., after serious troubles, thoughts of suicide] be an immense relief if it can be shown that one's life has the pattern rather of a tragedy—the tragic working-out and repetition of a pattern which was determined by the primal scene.

From *The Maturational Process* (144), by the Freudian psychoanalyst Donald Winnicott:

> When a False Self becomes organized in an individual who has a high intellectual potential there is a very strong tendency for the mind to become the location of the False Self, and in this case there develops a dissociation between intellectual activi-

When Oedipus came home after his father was dead, neither he nor his mother could resist "the urge and the temptation." As Sophocles (via Robert Fagles) puts it, "the same wide harbor" came to serve the son much as it had served the father before him.

> Dark, horror of darkness,
>   *my* darkness, drowning, swirling around me,
>   crashing wave on wave—unspeakable, irresistible
>   headwind, fatal harbor!*

Thus my conclusion that, rather than using the compound "self-loathing," we might say with greater accuracy that Ludwig worked very hard—using scorn, logic, trains and boats—to keep his distance from the people he wanted to embrace, *to include* from the authors—e.g., Augustine—whose work he wanted to embrace, with whom he felt an intellectual and emotional kinship. In Appendix A I quote from Voltaire's "Poème sur le désastre de Lisbonne":

> *tandis qu'on raisonne*
> *Des foudres souterrains engloutissent Lisbonne,*
> *Et de trente cités dispersent les débris,*
> *Des bords sanglants du Tage à la mer de Cadix.*†

---

    ty and psychosomatic existence. (In the healthy individual, it must be assumed, the mind is not something for the individual to exploit in an escape from psychosomatic being. . . .) [But, doctor, we *all* use our minds for this purpose!]

    When there has taken place this double abnormality, (i) the False Self organized to hide the True Self, and the (ii) an attempt on the part of the individual to solve the personal problem by the use of a fine intellect, a clinical picture results which is peculiar in that it very easily deceives.

* Sophocles, "Oedipus the King", lines 1345 and 1450-53. The phrase "the urge and the temptation" is from the translation of Wittgenstein's diary quoted earlier. Somewhat as with Quine's "impinges," I find myself wondering about Sophocles's or Fagles's "headwind." It would seem that a tailwind would be more threatening in such a situation—driving you and your trireme against the treacherous shore. Or does this headwind, along with the crashing waves of darkness, refer to winds in Oedipus's head, in his psyche?

† Among the theorizers that Voltaire was deliberately challenging, excoriating in this poem was Augustine, in particular an idea Voltaire found in Augustine's long-running attack on, vilification of Julian of Eclanum: "*Sub Deo justo nemo mi-*

> while they prate,
> The hidden thunders, belched from underground,
> Fling wide the ruins of a hundred towns
> Across the smiling face of Portugal.*

ser meraatur." Under a just God no one is miserable who has not deserved misery. Thus, by implication, the people, including little children, killed by the Lisbon earthquake deserved their suffering and their fate. (The earthquake occurred on All Saints Day, November 1, 1755.)

"We have only begun to appreciate the extent of [Julian's] learning and originality," Brown writes in his biography of Augustine. It has been said that Julian's optimistic view of human nature fitted him for any century but his own. Beginning a bishop, he ended up, long in exile, teaching the Latin alphabet to a wealthy man's children. His heresy, or his part in the Pelagian heresy, involved arguing that a just God must be like a just human judge. He wrote at great length against Augustine's ideas of original sin, the corruption of infants, hell fires for the unbaptized. "'Tiny babies,' you say," he wrote, "are not weighed down by their own sin, but they are being burdened with the sin of another [i.e., Adam and Eve]." And, "Tell me who is this person who inflicts punishments on innocent creatures? . . . . You answer: God. . . . He Who commended His love to us. . . . He it is, you say, Who judges in this way."

The "you" here is Augustine, and Augustine's answer, in effect, was that it was an angry, vengeful and ineffable God who enforced a logic and law all his own, and who could not be compared to human beings, let alone judged according to human standards. "You must distinguish the justice of God from human ideas of justice." (See the quotations from *The City of God* given earlier in this appendix, and see Job.)

"The duel [with Julian] was a dingy, rushed affair," Brown writes (384), "and it lasted until Augustine's death, . . . Augustine was a hardened campaigner. His works against Julian have the cold competence of an old, tired man, who knew only too well how to set about the harsh business of ecclesiastical controversy."

The "*Sub Deo justo*" line is a quote from Voltaire's notes attached to the poem, not a direct quote of Augustine's text, or at least not of any versions I have searched. The quotations from Julian are from Brown, 391, citing *Opus impeifectum in Iulianum* (*Op. Imp.*) I, 48 sq. Augustine's reply is from Brown, 393, citing *Op. Imp.* III, 27. Most all I know about Julian and his conflict with Augustine comes from Brown's chapter "Julian of Eclanum," 381-97, with the lines from Brown and others about Julian's originality and optimism appearing on pages 387 and 391.

* The translation offered here is the one that pops up repeatedly after a quick Web search. My own translation was offered in the "Scaffolding" segment of Appendix A. Voltaire's "*foudres souterrains*" might well bedevil a translator. A first thought, or pre-thought—or non-thinking thought?—could be that Voltaire was, with poetic license, describing some kind of powerful underground lightning, as the usual

In the present context, and nodding in the direction of my footnote regarding how one might translate Voltaire's phrase, we may appreciate that human lives are threatened by *"foudres souterrains"* external and internal—by earthly, earthy wrath and by thunderbolts and reproaches within. And while many cities and people live out their lives without being demolished by such forces, this does not mean we are insensible to them—either to our deepest fault lines or to our molten rage.

My sense is that Ludwig thought that at its core, in his heart, his desire to embrace others was "sinful": i.e., incestuous (or incestuous: i.e., sinful). And he was also afraid that if he let himself go, he would indeed be letting himself go. He would be—fluid in a river—lost in a world truly without rules, because one of the most fundamental rules—the prohibition against incest—would have been dismissed.* And it is

---

English equivalent of "*la foudre*" is lightning accompanied by noise, and this sense of the word is traditionally rendered in poetic or flowery texts as "*le foudre*". But "*le foudre*" is also used to refer to Zeus's thunderbolts; and so *foudres souterrains*: Hades's thunderbolts? And *le foudre* can also refer to weapons that have a thunderbolt-like quality: artillery, cannons, mines. And *un foudre de guerre* used to be a great general, a sort of Hector or Sherman, who makes his enemies quake in their boots. Now the term has come to be used largely in the negative and deprecatingly: "Il n'est pas un foudre de guerre." A bit as in the United States we say, "He's not the brightest bulb in the universe." Don't expect much out of him.

But Voltaire's *foudres* are not only masculine, they are plural. Thus the "hidden thunders" of the translation plucked from the Web.

We have only just made our way into the vestibule of this large family of meanings, however. In the plural (though normally in the feminine as well) *les foudres*—*les foudres de l'Église, du Vatican*—refer to condemnation, reproach by the Church: i.e., by the Roman Catholic Church. "*Il a été frappé des foudres de l'Église*": He was excommunicated. ("The jaws of the earth condemn Lisbon"?)

And then, finally—or not finally; this is just where I, personally, have stopped—there are various uses of *la* and *le foudre* to refer to anger, rage, wrath, in particular the wrath of God, or divine vengeance. There is a figurative expression: "*s'attirer les foudres de quelqu'un*": to bring down on oneself someone's wrath. This seemed to me to be the sense in which Voltaire was using this word "*foudre*"; hence my earlier translation, "the wrath of the earth".

All thanks here to the *Dictionnaire de français "Littré"* on-line: http://littre.reverso.net/dictionnaire-francais/definition/foudre.

* During the Middle Ages, the mendicant orders were considered "regular clergy" because, as opposed to "secular clergy," these monks lived under a *regula* or rule (which included, for example, the vow of poverty). Making use of the conceptual

easy enough to realize that the incest taboo is simply a convention, a rule adopted at a certain point in human history, and not all that long ago, because human beings had come to feel that obedience to this rule served their interests, for all neither could our ancestors nor can we today quite put our fingers on what our interests are.

> Following a rule is analogous to obeying an order. We are trained to do so; we react to an order in a particular way. But what if one person reacts in one way and another in another to the order and the training? Which one is right?[117]

Start thinking this way and one can become afraid. One becomes afraid. I think it is fair to say that Ludwig was afraid, or became afraid as he explored his thoughts and feelings, and with his particular aggressiveness. It can seem that one might do anything, there are no limits to one's behavior, which is also to say there is nothing to do, nothing needs doing. One reads descriptions of Wittgenstein—often it is in the company of a young man—just sitting "quite still and silent" (as if waiting? waiting patiently or without hope, or in and with what for him was love?).*

> I said to my soul, be still, and wait without hope
> For hope would be hope for the wrong thing; wait
>   without love
> For love would be love of the wrong thing: there is yet
>   faith
> But faith and love and the hope are all in the waiting.
> Wait without thought, for you are not ready for thought
>   . . .†

Und nun können wir, glaube ich, sagen—and now, I think, we can say—looking, we can see—that, if language both allows us to communicate with other people and keeps us apart, this is not only language's doing.

---

apparatus of modern psychology, we could say that the Franciscans and Dominicans were "holding" order, discipline, rules and rule-following for an otherwise anarchic population.

* The phrase "quite still and silent" comes from a passage in Monk (443) in which a young male colleague of Wittgenstein's describes visiting Wittgenstein's room, his completely bare room, and sitting there reading while Ludwig sat still and silent nearby.

† T.S. Eliot, "East Coker," *Four Quartets,* III, 186.

There is nothing we would rather do—nothing I would rather do than give myself to another. Be he or she a lover, an intellectual companion, a guru or kindred spirit, soulmate, a writer—such as Augustine was for Wittgenstein—who seems to share my concerns. But of course I would not give myself if this giving should come, or should feel as if it were coming, at the price of my boundaries, my self, my integrity—yet more in a physical and psychological sense than in an ethical sense. If giving myself means giving up myself, if giving myself means being swallowed—be it by the vagina or the mothering of the mother, or by the ego or business career or golf fetish or philosophical writings of some man or woman . . . ? Then what would *I* have left to give?

And this is not just sophistry! Over the years how many young women, students, have come into my office with a tale, or with a struggle, that may be summarized as "I can't be myself when I am with him." "I want to be with him," or "I want to be there for him," "I want to be who he wants me to be" (who he needs someone to be for him? or so he thinks?)—"but it's making me miserable." From this perspective we see no self-loathing. We see what might be called a desperate clinging to selfhood. We see a crisis of the self, or what we might wish to call *the* crisis of the self. The desire for love—to understand and be understood by another—perhaps even to lose one's self, one's individuality, in this love, in this communion. And the recognition of the fragility of the boundaries that keep a self from just dissolving into the general mass, the ever-present *outer* space. The recognition of how close we are to meaning nothing, and even to wanting to mean nothing.

Appendix C

Decontextualizing . . . Hume . . . The Good . . . Marx . . . Moore . . . Freud

---

Once again, as noted earlier, genealogically speaking these segments have evolved from footnotes that got too long to remain at the bottoms of pages. May readers, as at a zoo, feel free to wander and to wander away, and to pause before one or another of these terrariums to examine the once-bottom-lying creatures brought to the surface here.

Decontextualizing

Following in the admirable footsteps of Stephen Toulmin, and with Wittgenstein studies in mind, I would propose that the decontextualizing of philosophical texts has helped get readers even more entangled in misleading analogies than they might otherwise have gotten. In a sense there is no need for me to propose this, as the whole of the present volume is an aggressive act of contextualizing Wittgenstein's work. The value of contextualizing is presumed, and the results of this presumption will, for some, expose its wrongheadedness, and for others point up its virtues.

Nonetheless, allow me to recall a piece the conceptual artist Hans Haacke did some decades ago: "Shapolsky et al. Manhattan Real Estate Holdings, A Real Time Social System, as of May 1, 1971." According to a Web entry for this piece:

> The work consists of 146 photographic views of New York apartment buildings, six pictures of transactions, an explanatory wall panel, and maps of Harlem and the Lower East Side. Each photograph is accompanied by a typed text that describes the location and the financial transactions involving the building in the picture. Haacke discloses the transactions of a real-estate firm between 1951 and 1971. Harry Shapolsky, the key figure, who is well protected by influential friends, is guilty of an assortment of fraudulent practices of which the judicial

system has been exceedingly forgiving. Haacke's one-artist show at the Guggenheim, of which this work was to be part, was canceled by the director of the museum six weeks before the opening, and artists occupied the premises in protest against this censorship.[118]

The museum director, Thomas Messer, apparently gave artistic impropriety as the grounds for the cancellation, and perhaps the vagueness of this explanation helped feed a rumor (apparently false) that the piece revealed business and personal connections of the museum's own trustees. As a result, the piece that I and others of my acquaintances were not able to see had for many decades this latter subject: the business and personal connections of a museum's trustees. And in my Augustinian "memory"—in my mind's overlapping of impressions and imaginings—these connections had something to do with the Nazis. And for decades this seemed to me to have been a most excellent, worthy, wonderful exhibit—about the business and political connections of a museum's trustees—for all neither I nor anyone else had ever gotten a chance to see it.*

So here, we might say, is a *Bild*, a picture, a sketchy picture, an odd sketchy picture, to illustrate the following argument, which I would propose is a Wittgensteinian argument. Again:

> What is to be done with the picture, how it is to be used, is still obscure. Quite clearly, however, it must be explored if we want to understand the sense of what we are saying. But the picture seems to spare us this work: it already points to a particular use. This is how it takes us in.†

Wittgenstein is here writing about *Bilder*, pictures, in a more general, conceptual sense, but his observation remains germane when it comes to pictures hung on museum walls. The sources of funds, business dealings, and social and political connections of a museum's trustees are not

---

* A source I have relied on to "supplement" (re-program) my memory is a 2004 *ART PAPERS* article, found on-line: Jerry Cullum, "Between Berlin and Benin: Hans Haacke and Meschac Gaba, Two Political Artists in the Age of Globalization." Cullum also reports that a subsequent Haacke piece did document "connections of Guggenheim trustees to a corporation engaged in exploitative behavior in Chile," and that Edward Fry, the curator for Haacke's aborted Guggenheim museum piece, "never again worked in the United States."

† *Investigations*, Part II, vii, 157e.

all one needs to know about the art on the walls, but this information—and notwithstanding that it is never provided—is essential should we wish not to be confused, or not *too* confused, by the work. (And if we wish to escape a certain dead feeling that one may have—that children in particular have?—in museums?)

Were such information to be provided, it would deepen viewers' engagement with the works. It would expand our understanding of why, or for whom, the art works were made, insofar as the tastes and desires of the people who buy and exhibit art works have a tremendous effect on the art that gets made, exhibited prominently and written about. (See, for one example among millions, the history of the painting of the ceiling of the Sistine Chapel and of its particular iconography.) Information about a museum's trustees (and about its management, annual attendance and sources of funds more generally) would also help us understand why particular art works are being shown, and others not, and why the curators highlight certain aspects of the works on display and not others. (Among many other things, museums serve a particular interest of their trustees and major donors: in seeing the value of their private art collections increase. So, simplifying what is a more complex process, should a major donor have a substantial collection of works by a certain artist, s/he will have an interest in that artist's work being featured prominently in museum exhibitions and in having articles written about the important place of that artist in the history of art.)

We may bring this line of thinking back closer to Wittgenstein's *Heimat* if we ask why Karl Wittgenstein became such a supporter of music and art in Vienna? Of course, from one perspective one might say, Well, Karl was a lover of music and a talented violinist and his wife seems to have been even more devoted to music and more musically talented than he. But, from a social perspective, one finds that the only way that was available to Viennese Jews to gain entry (however temporary!) into so-called polite Viennese society was through the arts.

I quote from Carl Schorske's *Fin-de-Siècle Vienna*:

The reason for the high place of art in the scale of bourgeois values was obscure even to its devotees. Art was closely bound up with social status, especially in Austria, where the representational arts—music, theater, and architecture—were central to the tradition of a

Catholic aristocracy. If entry into the aristocracy of the genealogical table was barred to most, the aristocracy of the spirit was open to the eager, the able, and the willing. Museums and theaters could bring to all the culture that would redeem the *novi homines* from their lowly origins.

[Ambitious to be "noble," the Viennese Theodor] Herzl's social position and his mother's values both led him to espouse a romantic aristocracy of the spirit as a surrogate for aristocracy of pedigree or patent. In common with many young bourgeois intellectuals, Herzl acquired aesthetic culture as a substitute for rank. The ladder of the spirit was a social ladder too. . . . [119]

Similar comments have been made regarding how Jews came to play such a leading role in music, literature, theater and the visual arts in New York, but coming back (as to a touchstone) to Ludwig Wittgenstein, I note that in the introduction to the present work I quoted Wittgenstein's remark that his "originality (if that is the right word) is an originality that belongs to the soil, not the seed." There I also recalled that Karl Kraus, the grand mentor of socially ambitious, artistically inclined Viennese youth of Wittgenstein's time, vaunted integrity above all. Schorske discusses how the work and attitude of an artist contrasted, or at least seemed to the artist to contrast, "with the crass dishonesties of a materialistic world" and to share some of "the nobiliar spirit of chivalry and honor."[120] So much of Ludwig Wittgenstein's work and attitudes are described right here, in this picture of a Viennese Jew who is caught between, on the one hand, the values and crass dishonesties of his father and, on the other hand, his family's ambition to attain a higher status and adopt a more genteel approach to *vitae humanae procellosam societatem*, a status and approach that seem (quite misleadingly) to involve higher levels of honor, integrity and equanimity.

So where are we as regards decontextualizing? The overarching Wittgensteinian point is that the meaning of an art work or philosophical work lies in the ways in which it is used. And in the absence of reflection on these uses—on the range of uses, aesthetic appreciation and diversion certainly included—we cannot understand these works any better than we might understand the word "game" by just watching a tennis match.

Oddly enough, in grounding his criticisms of the emptiness of philosophers' and others' ways of speaking in discussions of language, Wittgenstein seems somehow to have given a whole troop of his successors yet another means of ignoring the larger, social and psychological uses of *their* writing and teaching—of *their* words. As if works of philosophy were elegantly framed, discretely hung museum pieces, or games of tennis.

Which brings this comment full circle: back to Toulmin, and his book of intellectual history, *Cosmopolis: The Hidden Agenda of Modernity*:

> If Wittgenstein is right, the philosopher's task is precisely to show why we are tempted into these intellectual "dead ends." If that task takes research into social and intellectual history, so be it. The claim that all truly philosophical problems must be stated in terms independent of any historical situation, and solved by methods equally free of all contextual references, is one of the rationalist claims typical of modern philosophy from 1640 to 1950, rather than of philosophy in either its medieval or its post-Wittgenstein form.[121]

Thus, for example, when I ask my students to read Plato, I also ask them to read about how teachers attracted business and made their livings in Socrates's day, and about how Plato was a member of the aristocratic class at a time when this class had been driven from power in failure and disgrace. When we read Kant, I ask them to think about how he was the son of a guild master, and about how Kant's writing—to include its abstruseness—may be seen as a key moment in the effort of German academics and of academics more generally to win a sort of guild status for their profession and their students. Working on the present book has gotten me interested in thinking about the theological battle between Augustine and Julian of Eclanum as class conflict. And so forth and so on.

Hume

In a work that keeps touching on the difficulty of establishing ethical principles or rules, it seems necessary to at least nod in the direction of David Hume, or of Mencius or Bishop Butler, or another who argued that our moral sense is preprogrammed, based on innate abilities. If this is indeed the case, it is argued, than we can put to rest many concerns, be they raised by followers of Socrates, Wittgenstein or others, about the lack of foundations for ethical thinking. We need not worry ourselves o'er much about what the rules are and whether they are correct. They are inside us (or constructions of our insides), guiding us inexorably, in theory for our good, but even if not—how could we object? What could it mean to object? As if a computer were to object to binary code, or a snake to its lack of legs.

Since Abel quoted Mencius, and history puts him first, I will begin with Mencius's "Four Sprouts" (or Beginnings)—*ren* (benevolence, humaneness), *li* (observance of rites), *yi* (propriety) and *zhi* (wisdom)— and with his idea that our ethical sense and behavior should grow from these predispositions the way a plant grows from a sprout.

> The feeling of commiseration is the beginning of humanity; the feeling of shame and dislike is the beginning of righteousness; the feeling of deference and compliance is the beginning of propriety; and the feeling of right or wrong is the beginning of wisdom. Men have these Four Beginnings just as they have their four limbs.[122]

Bishop Butler, one of Wittgenstein's intellectual anchors and a contemporary of Hume's, proposed that God instills in us a "principle of reflection or conscience" which causes us to disapprove of various behaviors, such as fraud and injustice. That is, Butler's conscience is something more sophisticated than Mencius's Sprouts or than Hume's moral sentiments, which we will get to soon enough, but like these concepts, this conscience is not a product of teaching, preaching and other social pressures; it is what we can call hard-wired (by God), if not innate (or what we might call genetic). The key passage from Butler's sermon "Upon the Natural Supremacy of Conscience":

> [T]here is a superior principle of reflection or conscience in every man which distinguishes between the internal principles of his heart, as well as his external actions; which passes judgment upon himself and them; pronounces determinately some actions to be in themselves just, right, good; others to be in themselves evil, wrong, unjust: which, without being consulted, without being advised with, magisterially exerts itself, and approves or condemns him, the doer of them, accordingly; and which, if not forcibly stopped, naturally and always of

course goes on to anticipate a higher and more effectual sentence, which shall hereafter second and affirm its own. But this part of the office of conscience is beyond my present design explicitly to consider. <u>It is by this faculty, natural to man, that he is a moral agent</u>, that he is a law to himself. (My underscoring.)*

For his part, Hume, in *A Treatise of Human Nature*, proposes that "morality is not an object of reason," that "vice and virtue . . . may be compar'd to sounds, colours, heat and cold."[123] That is, as with pleasure and pain—and through "sentiments," through our feelings of pleasure and "uneasiness"—we feel and thus perceive that behaviors are virtuous or vicious, somewhat as we perceive the sky to be blue or gray. (Though our sense of colors would seem to be more direct, not mediated by other feelings such as of pleasure and uneasiness.) No matter how vigorously and ingeniously someone may argue that I am wrong, and that this morning the sky is red, if I see the sky as blue, it's blue. And similarly it does not make any more sense to argue about the foundations for my ethical judgments than it would to argue about the foundations for my color perceptions. They are wired in my brain and are not susceptible to rational argument.

So then, given Hume's emphasis in other contexts on the importance of custom and habit, and given Wittgenstein's emphasis on the importance of convention (e.g., linguistic convention), it is worth asking whether the mechanisms of our ethical perceptions (or for our Sprouts or conscience) are indeed hard-wired in our brains? And thus are these perceptions the same for all "normal" human beings, or, say, for all normal male adults and, separately, for all normal female children, and so forth? Or, alternatively, is the wiring "softer," more in line with the use the sociologist Pierre Bourdieu has made of the concept of "habitus"—by which our value

---

* The Biblical text for Butler's sermon was Romans 2:14. This verse and 2:15 appears below in a "New International Version" of the Bible found on-line. In 2011 this translation is easier to read than the King James version of this passage.

> . . . when Gentiles, who do not have the law, do by nature things required by the law, they are a law for themselves, even though they do not have the law.

They show that <u>the requirements of the law are written on their hearts</u>, their consciences also bearing witness, and their thoughts sometimes accusing them and at other times even defending them. [My underscoring.]

judgments (be they of music, food, fashions, or of virtue and vice) are indeed products of something like wiring in our brains, but this wiring owes a great deal to the environments (geographical, political, cultural, economic) in which we were raised and the education we have been given?* If the former is the case—if our ethical perceptions are the products of the human brain independently of circumstances and education—then ethics is not a subject for philosophy or sociology, but rather for neurology and psychology.

Hume focuses a great deal on the psychological dimension of our ethical judgments, and in one particular discussion he refers to "the practice and sentiments of all nations and ages," and in another argues, against Hobbes and Mandeville, that the "selfish hypothesis" is "contrary both to common feeling and to our most unprejudiced notions". The language of morals

> implies some sentiment <u>common to all mankind</u>, which recommends that same object to general approbation, and makes every man, or most men, agree in the same opinion or decision concerning it. It also implies some sentiment, so universal and comprehensive as to extend to all mankind, and render the actions and conduct, even of the persons most remote, an object of applause or censure, according as they agree or disagree with the rule of right which is established. (My underscoring.)

Here, it would seem, is a good deal of hard wiring, which produces this underlying universal sentiment—of benevolence or sympathy—which provides "the foundation of morals."†

But our customs and habits owe a great deal to our circumstances and education, and if these customs and habits are playing large roles in how we behave and/or in how we judge the vice or virtue of behaviors

---

* A footnote in the "Third Interpolation" offers a definition of "habitus," as Bourdieu has used the term.

† Hume, *Treatise*, 624; *Enquiry concerning the Principles of Morals*, 298 and 272.

I note that we are a long ways here from Augustinian ideas of original sin and that without God's grace we cannot know the good. In the Augustinian model, feelings and sentiments are hardly to be trusted; the truth is what God whispers in our hearts. If we are lucky, to include in being able to listen very closely.

(of premarital sex and homosexuality, of lending or borrowing money, of killing female newborns or boys and girls born with physical handicaps, just to pick a few examples), . . . Now we would want to make more room for the questions about which behaviors "feel" right to us, and how we might like to shift our customs and habits, our circumstances and education, to promote right behaving and discourage wrong behaving. For example, we could criminalize or decriminalize homosexual acts; we could enact laws to promote home buying on the grounds that people who own their own homes (or who have to pay mortgages) are more cautious and involved in civic affairs than those less tied into the financial system. But now we are right back to Wittgenstein, e.g., §186: "How is it to be decided what is the right step to take at any particular stage?" How is it to be decided if homosexuality or home buying is something to be embraced, accepted or rejected? (Mencius championed obedience to older brothers, among other things. This felt right to him)

At this point, let us say, Hume, in his *Treatise*, brings in the not-un-Wittgensteinian concept of use, or usefulness—suggesting that the answer, the means of deciding, lies in the usefulness or lack of usefulness of a given action, way of action or policy. E.g., we approve of benevolence, rather than selfishness, because benevolence is useful, advancing social interests and leading people to behave more justly. This is not to say that our rational faculties use usefulness as a criterion for making a decision, but that somehow this quality of usefulness affects the wiring of our brains, of our sentiments and perceptions, so that useful actions inspire feelings of pleasure and useless actions inspire feelings of uneasiness. To give an example, and to underscore the point about "habitus"—about the effects of circumstances and education—I will quote one of Hume's observations that seems to reflect to a great degree the particular culture in which he was raised: "Most of the works of art are esteem'd beautiful, in proportion to their fitness for the use of man, and even many of the productions of nature derive their beauty from that source."[124] Similarly, he writes that the qualities that are praised in great men "may be divided into two kinds, *viz.* such as make them perform their part in society; and such as render them serviceable to themselves, and enable them to promote their own interest."[125] As opposed, Hume proposes, to the great fault of indolence, or to faults such as poor judgment, irresolution or "want of address" which incapacitate men for business. (With those insufficiently capacitated including David Hume, Ludwig Wittgenstein and myself!)

But now it looks like the way the word "use" is being used is simply as a substitute for "good," and thus we may expect to have the same problems perceiving or determining the essence of usefulness as we have had with "good" (see the next segment), or with "game" for that matter. What we are going to be able to do instead is, per Wittgenstein, not think, but look: to look at how the words "use," "useful" and so forth are used in a particular language, e.g., in the language of a particular culture, such as eighteenth century Scotland or Zhou dynasty China.

Reinforcing this latter point, I would call attention to some words from the conclusion of Hume's *Treatise*:

> Thus upon the whole I am hopeful, that nothing is wanting to an accurate proof of this system of ethics. We are certain, that sympathy [feelings; pleasure and uneasiness] is a very powerful principle in human nature. We are also certain, that it has a great influence on our sense of beauty, when we regard external objects, as well as when we judge of morals. We find, that it has force to give us the strongest sentiments of approbation, when it operates alone, without the concurrence of any other principles; as in the cases of justice, allegiance, chastity, and good-manners. We may observe, that all the circumstances requisite for its operation are found in most of the virtues; which have, for the most part, a tendency to the good of society, or to that of the person possess'd of them.[126]

Here instead of "use" we are back to our good ol' "good" and left with variations on the usual questions: e.g., Is "chastity" good? Which manners should we call "good" and which "bad"? And now again Wittgenstein's *Investigations* §198, paraphrasing: How can a rule show me what to do at *this* point? Should I do just what my particular culture—be it the culture of Nazi Germany or the culture of the United States in the early twenty-first century or of China in the third century B.C.E.—has led me to *feel* is good? And if it *feels* good . . . ? Please see Augustine, *Confessions* I:16: "We are carried away by custom to our own undoing and it is hard to struggle against the stream."*

---

* *N.B.*: This should not lead people to think that Augustine himself was a great

While I would not claim to have mastered the various other approaches to ethics and to the challenge of the lack of foundations for ethical thinking, my sense is that in reviewing any one of these approaches one would soon enough find that there was a parochial idea of "the good," or of "a good," couched within them. If this idea happens to resonate with a given reader, stimulating more satisfying feelings than uneasy ones, . . . Such a reader may well feel little desire to ask any more questions. Other readers, readers who find themselves inclined to ask why the particular idea or ideas of the good on which the approach rests should be preferred over another, . . ? They are not likely to find good answers.

For many millennia human beings have heard the word of God, and, somewhat more recently, we have been able to read words of God that some of the hearers have written down. This, the hearing, the receiving of messages—or the having of seemingly innate sensations that seem to tell us what is wrong and right—all this, we might say, is not the problem. The problem lies in interpretation or translation, in trying to decide what these various messages mean, what they mean we are supposed to do or think or feel at this point? About this we have not been able to decide, nor have we—as a cover for our inability and as a substitute for deciding—been able to stop talking.

The Good

As the segment above on Hume suggests, the good has gone and goes by many names. In Plato's *Republic* in particular, but also in other dialogues, the word is *agathon*, and the good is what every soul pursues, and does everything for the sake of.[127] This does not mean, however, that we, or any one of us, knows, or can state, what this thing, this goal, is. It might seem that we are back to Wittgenstein's fork—pursuing the good without considering that it is the good, as we move our mouths when we eat, without aiming at moving them. This does not seem, however, to be how Plato saw the matter, and it is certainly not how his Socrates framed it in the famous lines of *The Republic* that state the problem most directly.

---

struggler against the stream. He was in many respects a politician, in his actions, his reasoning, his writings.

[W]e have no proper knowledge of the Form of the good. And if we don't know it, though we should have the fullest possible knowledge of all else, you know that that would be of no use to us, any more than is the possession of anything without the good.*

In later dialogues, the *Philebus*, the *Timaeus* and *The Statesman*, Plato explores another path, or paths. In the *Philebus* and the *Timaeus*, the good—or what we have come to call "the good life"—appears to be or to stem from a "mixed life," a combination of pleasure and wisdom.[128] In *The Statesman*, the good is not this or any particular mix, but rather, if you will, mix itself: the true mean, compared to which actions, works of art and so forth may come up short or go too far.† Without knowledge of this mean, all is simply relative, in this way or that more or less than other things, themselves more or less than other other things. But with knowledge of the true mean, we can know the true value of things, of actions, ideas and so forth.‡

Subsequently, Aristotle, Plotinus and many following in their wake altered the terminology and the discussion, and we came to speak of the *telos* or *summum bonum* (the ultimate goal, "that at which all things aim," or, again, the highest good). Amid all this, however, the problem of

---

* From 505 (Socrates speaking), as translated by A.D. Lindsay. Divergent translations of these famous lines have promoted rather different interpretations. Of the many translations I have seen, my favorite is Lindsay's, first published in 1906. I note that Plotinus and the neo-Platonists founded a good deal of their philosophy on their reading of and reflections on this segment of *The Republic*.

† We are, or Plato is, getting back close to the sixth century BCE and one the famous apothegms over the entrance to the temple of Apollo at Delphi. *Mêden agan*. Nothing in excess; or, Moderation in all things. The other famous apothegm from Delphi has been, we might say, one of the core subjects of the present book since its opening pages: *Gnothi sauton*—Know thyself. In Socrates's and Plato's interpretation or refashioning, this latter saying has come to us as the line from *The Apology* (37E-38A): "the life unexamined is not worth living."

See Wilkins, 7-8, which cites in turn W.H. Roscher. The relevant Roscher articles, on *"die Bedeutung des E zu Delphi"* appeared in *Philologus*, volumes 59 and 60, in 1900 and 1901.

‡ Plato, *Statesman*, 284A-284E. See Bréhier's reading of this passage, 137-38. Nietzsche comes quickly to mind as a philosopher who found no positive value in this metaphysical assumption: that the mean is good, or good enough.

knowing this goal or good has remained, as has the problem of a conceiving of an ethics—or of figuring out what to do, deciding whether to turn right or left—in the absence of such knowledge.*

It should be noted that here we may be touching on the philosophical problem Wittgenstein most wished to dissolve—make go away—by his new, anti-Platonist, "therapeutic" approach to philosophy. To say that we do not know what "the good" is—or could be—is to say that we do not understand what language is, that we do not "know"—or accept—that a meaning of a word is its use. Don't say what "the good" must mean (and thereby become entangled in pointless discussions that lead one to believe that human beings cannot know what "the good" must mean). Look and see how human beings, how human beings in our culture and of our times, use the word "good." Look at the various behaviors we call good. And do not imagine that your survey will lead to a single conclusion or dictionary definition: e.g., the good is that at which all things aim. Your survey will produce a collection of examples, and one may well be able to find family resemblances among these examples, though there may also be what we now call outliers, examples that do not seem to be members of the "family," and there will also be times we are confused. *Manchmal richtig, manchmal falsch raten*—sometimes we will guess right and sometimes wrong.

But of course there may also be a good deal of disappointment, of disillusioning in this process. Because this is not what we have wanted, and for so many millennia. We have wanted to know how we *should* go on, what rules we *should* follow. And now it appears that, like a boy knee-deep in a tidal pool, all we can do is notice our reflection in the water as we go about our specimen collecting. We can observe how we or other living things are going on and what our elders have been calling rules and how we are or are not following them. And this with our memories of yesterdays whispering in our ear that tomorrow there may well be something new to find—some new crab or plant or bit of ship's garbage, something different in our face or in the light; some new way of behaving, some new rule.

---

* For a scholarly review of the terminology, see Peters, 4-5 and 191-92. The "that at which . . ." is a standard translation of a phrase in the opening sentence of Aristotle's *Nicomachean Ethics*: "Every art and every inquiry, and similarly every action and pursuit, is thought to aim at some good; and for this reason the good has rightly been declared to be that at which all things aim."

And we will be led to think that our idea of the sea and of our selves, our ideas of our families and of this family of words and behaviors in which we find ourselves, is not quite as we had imagined it, and will change again tomorrow.

"But how can a rule show me what I have to do at *this* point? ... [C]an whatever I do be brought into accord with the rule?" (§198). If the meaning of a word is its use, then whatever my—or Albert Eichmann's or Albert Einstein's—approach to rule-following turns out to be will contribute its small or large weight to future understandings of rule-following, and thus, perhaps, to future behavior as well.

Moore

In the present, Gothic text, complete with gargoyles, flying buttresses and patron saints, one of the arguments has been that philosophy is a response—e.g., to one's times, one's family, the human predicament. But there is of course another sense in which philosophical texts are responses, and I would not ignore this sense, for all philosophers and intellectual historians are not in the habit of ignoring it either. I am referring to the sense in which a philosopher responds to, or follows on from, philosophers who have preceded him.

With this in mind, I would like to come back to and quote at greater length a passage in Keynes's "My Early Beliefs," the passage in which he describes the method of the Cambridge professor G.E. Moore, who was the most celebrated, most widely read contemporary philosopher in England when Wittgenstein arrived there. According to Moore, Keynes writes,

> you could hope to make essentially vague notions clear by using precise language about them and asking exact questions. It was a method of discovery by the instrument of impeccable grammar and an unambiguous dictionary. "What *exactly* do you mean?" was the phrase most frequently on our lips. If it appeared under cross-examination that you did not mean *exactly* anything, you lay under a strong suspicion of meaning nothing whatever. It was a stringent education in dialectic; but in practice it was a kind of combat in which strength of character was

really much more valuable than subtlety of mind. In the preface to his great work [*Principia Ethica*], . . . Moore begins by saying that error is chiefly "the attempt to answer questions, without first discovering precisely *what* question it is to which you desire to answer. . . . Once we recognize the exact meaning of the two questions, I think it also becomes plain exactly what kind of reasons are relevant as arguments for or against any particular answer to them." So we spent our time trying to discover *precisely what* questions we were asking, confident that, if only we could ask precise questions, everyone would know the answer. Indeed Moore expressly claimed as much. In his famous chapter on "The Ideal" he wrote: "Indeed, once the meaning of the question is clearly understood, the answer to it, in its main outlines, appears to be so obvious, that it runs the risk of seeming to be a platitude."[129]

Someone else someday will write the book showing how Wittgenstein's work can be seen in very large part as a response to G.E. Moore and a moving on from Moore's work. In a book about Moore, *Bloomsbury's Prophet*, Tom Regan has laid some of the groundwork.* The larger point to be made is that Wittgenstein was not the isolated genius he often appears to be, and that he perhaps imagined himself to be; rather, he was a leading figure in a community of philosophers at Cambridge University, or of several generations of philosophers, who were working on similar problems.† That Wittgenstein himself and some of his followers

---

* See, for example, the comparison of Moore's theory of meaning with that of the *Tractatus* (Regan, 215, and also 104-05), or Leonard Wolff's description of Moore which Regan quotes on 283.

† Edmonds and Eidinow propose that Wittgenstein's famous analogy of steam boiling in a pot (§297, quoted in the segment on "the gaps within" in Appendix A) came originally from a paper Wittgenstein's colleague John Wisdom gave to a Joint Session of the Mind Association and the Aristotelian Society at Cambridge. Wisdom, they write (69)

> raised the question of how we know when a person is angry. Is it exactly like knowing that a kettle is boiling—which we deduce by its physical symptoms? Can anger too—a mental phenomenon, a feeling—be deduced only from its outward manifestations?

scorned such a possibility—of the lesser Moore setting the stage for the greater Wittgenstein—has come to seem to me like an attempt to hide an all-too-obvious truth: Wittgenstein, like many other Cambridge students of his time, fell under the spell of Moore's method.

From one perspective, I propose, the spell was never broken, and we have this to thank for the rich interior dialogue of the *Investigations*. From another perspective, however, in using the method, Wittgenstein discovered something quite wrong with his mentor's approach. In fact, precise questions, if pursued diligently, lead not to precise answers, but to a deeper appreciation of the imprecision of our life in language, of human understanding. At the end of the rainbow of precise questions lies "family resemblances," the ever-evolving collection of (mis)uses of words and (mis) steps of human behavior—and also the particular madness latent in the quest for certainty.

Reckless professor of humanities that I am, I am willing to step further out on a limb and suggest that one way of reading the *Investigations* is as a refining of a comment Moore wrote in an early work, "The Elements of Ethics":

> It is something important to recognise that the best of reasons can be given for *anything* whatever, if only we are clever enough: sophistry is easy, wisdom is impossible; the best that we can do is trust to COMMON SENSE.[130]

In Wittgenstein's book, common sense has been replaced by the more sophisticated idea of what Wittgensteinians have come call our "life in language." And, we might say, the trust is persistently called into question. As if to say, "The best that we can do is trust to our life in language, as untrustworthy as it is."

Lacan

I am beginning to feel like I am beating a dead horse—or is it that I think there are points here, about our life in language, that will only sink in if they are made over and over again? Somewhat as I keep reading in Thoreau's Journal, hoping—will it be some very hot day, like Kuhn with Aristotle? or, say, wandering past the perfume-sprayers and make-up-appliers on the first floor of Macy's? or sailing through an "easy pass" lane on my way to LaGuardia?—that I will learn to see in my environment, my twenty-first century environment, variations on the objects and phenomena Thoreau saw in and around nineteenth century Concord. In the meantime, here, I am going to go running after bees—and only to get stung, once again, by language. "The youth gets together his materials to build a bridge to the moon, or perchance a palace or temple on the earth, and at length the middle-aged man concludes to build a wood-shed with them."*

Bishop Butler noted that "language is, in its very nature, inadequate, ambiguous, liable to infinite abuse, even from negligence; and so liable to it from design, that every man can deceive and betray by it."[131] We might say, somewhat misleadingly, several hundred years later, in a lecture on language and psychoanalysis, Jacques Lacan came back to this point, in a famous distinguishing of human language from the so-called language of bees—i.e., from the sort of dance by which a bee apparently gives other bees directions for getting to nectar, often at quite some distance away. "We can say," Lacan says (or said otherwise, in French), that this dance "is distinguished from language precisely by the fixed correlation of its signs to the reality that they signify."[132] The bees' dance, like an engineering drawing, is certainly a means of communication, but it lacks the flexibility, the dialogic character and influence of context which are fundamental to language (and also to people understanding engineering drawings).

Lacan's proposal is that the bees' dance (or, we might say, the human beings' (mis)understanding of the bees' dance) is not language because it cannot be misunderstood. What the dancing bee wishes to communicate and what the bee spectators learn from the communication are exactly the same. Or the connection may be yet tighter: It is stimulus-response (and innate, not learned stimulus-response). The dance stimulates the response of going to the nectar via the prescribed route. (But do any bees ever misunderstand and not make it to the nectar? I suppose—I would like to think—some do. Overly reflective bees? Bees who think there must be meaning in the geometry and sweetness of the honeycomb? Bees who stop to smell the flowers?)

By contrast, we might compare human language to a Heraclitean river (ever changing) in which our sounds, our words find their meanings as twigs or molecules of water make their way in dialogue with other sounds, twigs, words, molecules flowing around them, and in dialogue

---

* Thoreau, 157 (July 14, 1852).

with the objects and events that in years or eons past carved the river bed and defined its banks. It is the relational quality of speech and its flexibility, its responsiveness, that makes language language. And this also means that meanings and understandings cannot be pinned down; they are fluid.

This is, more or less, Lacan's view. But there is again that voice in the *Investigations* to whom it makes no sense to say at the sight of a knife and fork "Now I am seeing this as a knife and fork, . . ."[133] The voice, or appetite, that is not distracted by the fact that the fork it is using is a fork. The appetite, or creature of habit, that simply picks the fork up and uses it to pick up its tongue . . .

This would seem to be a bee's eye view of language, an elaboration of stimulus-response behavior. The bee knows what to do in response to the dance and has no need to interpret it, and so we know what to do with cutlery at a meal and do need to *try* to move our mouths in order to eat; our mouths just move and as necessary (most of the time).

Or, rather, what Wittgenstein says is that we do not *für gewöhnlich* (usually, ordinarily) try to move our mouths as we eat.[134] And what I wish to stress again here is that with words like "ordinarily" Wittgenstein opens a very large barn door, revealing both the larger world of his *Investigations* and the larger world of human language, communication, life.

In particular here I would call attention to the extent to which many of the "*Sprachspiele*" (language games) that Wittgenstein invented and ruminated upon come awfully close to stimulus-response. That is, they are like the non-language—or language, if you prefer—of the bees' dances. On the other side of this coin—the non-ordinary side, we *could* call it, while noting that a coin may come up non-ordinary as often as it does ordinary— On this other side may be found most everything that seems most intriguing, most particularly human about human language. (And perhaps about the languages of some—or even all?—animals? living things?) Yes, ordinarily, when we eat we may use a fork and not even think that it is a fork and not experience any confusion about what we are doing and what we are doing it with. But this is hardly the case in richer contexts—e.g., when we say "I love you." Nor, for example, when Abel takes his fork and plunges it into his coffee cup: that is, when people behave in unexpected ways.

Summarizing, schematizing and perhaps not revealing precisely how little I have studied ancient theories of language, I will propose that for the Epicureans and Pyrrhonists, human language consists of subconsciously learned responses to stimuli. For the Stoics and Augustine after them, spoken language is an outcome of reflection; things intervene between the stimulus and the response and between the response and the interpretation/understanding of the response. In some cases these "things"—thoughts—may themselves provide the stimulus. For Lacan, stimulus-response is not language; the essence of language lies in the gaps, or gulfs, between any stimuli, their conversion into sounds or words, and the ineluctable misinterpretations/misunderstandings of these, themselves inexact, conversions.* And Wittgenstein—we return yet again, if but briefly, to the forking—for his part Wittgenstein was interested in both the stimulus-response aspect of human language *and* in the gaps. He was interested in both the forks we just, unthinkingly pick up *and* in the fact that even as we just pick up a fork, or glance at our watch, and experience not the least confusion, our actions are shadowed by the fact (if can we call this a fact?) that we do not know what time is, and nor is there any fixed, Platonic essence of forkness. There is the fork we are using and a fork in the road and pitch forks and tuning forks and the lower part of the human body, and other ways of using this set of letters or sounds that have passed beyond our ken or that we have yet to encounter.

Marx

"Capitalism," I wrote in one of the little "personal essays" with which I amuse myself, "capitalism is a train carrying us—passengers, staff, executives and stockholders—faster and faster until that Judgment Day when the wheels come off, the sides blow apart and we—passengers, staff, executives and stockholders—fall like soft rain on the surface of the sea."

---

* Again, Philip Roth has explored this perspective—the extent to which human language is about getting it wrong—in *American Pastoral*. See, 35:

> You get them [people] wrong before you meet them, while you're anticipating meeting them; you get them wrong while you're with them; and then you go home to tell somebody else about the meeting and you get them all wrong again. Since the same generally goes for them with you, the whole thing is really a dazzling illusion empty of all perception, an astonishing farce of misperception. . . . The fact remains that getting people right is not what living is all about anyway. It's getting them wrong and then, on careful reconsideration, getting them wrong again. That's how we know we're alive: we're wrong.

Around the same time, a copywriter for one of Chase Bank's advertising agencies was making rather more than the $40 I have made from my essay by writing a koan for the bank: "Chase what matters." It might be said that I have been led not to drink, but to Wittgenstein by this slogan, and by the madness of a civilization—or is it now a whole species?—that is therein encapsulated, in just three little words.

Koans aside, it may well be that the significance of this aspect of contemporary human existence—the significance for the human race and for many other species of the particular and powerful force that is capitalism— The impact and consequences may be so great that a writer does best to simply call attention to this subject over and over again. And this not least because ignoring this aspect of our existence involves us in all sorts of futile or absurd policies and lines of thought. (Or, alternatively, because we are so anxious to ignore this aspect of our existence we opt for all sorts of policies and philosophies and ways of writing history and of having sex, and for new cars and furniture, breasts, hair, kids . . . that above all help us to deny our situation.)

"But"—a reader says—"why then all these pages—all these pages about Wittgenstein that I have now given so much of my one life to read, instead of, say, reading your friend Karl Marx?"

Can I, by way of an answer, paraphrase yet another writer, La Rochefoucauld: Because the truth, like the sun, cannot be looked at directly, or for very long?* "Don't think, but look!" Wittgenstein writes. "Look above you; look below you!" Augustine writes. But we can't, or *pas fixement*, not for very long. It is less frightening dwelling on our "life in language," rather than on how we are trapped and being ground up by, and hurtling out of control in a machine of our own making.

"It is not the consciousness of men that determines their being, but, on the contrary, their social being determines their consciousness."†

---

* La Rochefoucauld (*maxime* #26, p. 48): "*Le soleil ni la mort ne se peuvent regarder fixement.*" We cannot long look at either the sun or death.

† Marx, Preface to the *Critique of Political Economy*, in *Selected Writings in Sociology and Social Philosophy*, 51. See also a letter from Engels to Heinz Starkenberg, January 25, 1894 (a dozen years after Marx had died):

> Political, juridical, philosophical, religious, literary, artistic, etc., development is based on economic development. But all

Is it simply that a culture dominated by capital does not encourage the writing or the reading of trenchant critiques of capitalism? This is not to say that the culture or capital necessarily, or on a day-to-day basis, wastes a lot of time or resources prohibiting such behavior; it knows that it is enough not to pay for the critique, let the critiquers find work in one bureaucracy or another. (Or is it that in a culture dominated by capital, writing and reading about what is really going down is simply too frightening?)

And of course there are also Americans and others around the globe who would be afraid to be caught reading Marx. And there the many others who were told in college that, for all Marx was a brilliant thinker, his analysis and his solution—communism—have turned out to be wrong, and, in any case, none of this really applies in our post-industrial world.

I FEEL YOUNG AGAIN! Side by side with Caroline—my Marxist, dish-throwing girlfriend, since become one of the leading directors of TV crime dramas; beach house in Malibu, beach house on Gay Head)—leafleting immigrants from the Azores working in the not-so-high-tech factories on the back side of MIT. "*O povo, unido, jamais será vencido!*" Or have I become like the young Wittgenstein, telling an editor that it was the half of his book that he had not written which was the important half? Am I now going to tell you, dear readers, that now that you and I have almost reached the end, I realize it was all a mistake? I should not have let

---

these react upon one another and also upon the economic base. It is not that the economic position is the *cause and alone active*, while everything else only has a passive effect. There is, rather, interaction on the basis of the economic necessity, which ultimately always asserts itself.

Engels would seem to be foreshadowing Carl Schmitt (as quoted earlier): "What always matters is the possibility of the extreme case taking place, the real war." Except Engels recognizes that economic necessity is the realer war, and that, even if we do not think about it every day, it is nonetheless there, affecting our daily thinking and feeling and acting. As per Kierkegaard (quoted earlier), the universal, our day-to-day existence in this case, is explained by the exception—i.e., per Engels, by economic necessity, which could be a human being's need to feed his or her family, or capital's need to seek ever greater rates of return.

Engels—from Marx, *Selected Works* (Moscow: Foreign Language Publishing House)—as quoted in Merton, "Paradigm for the Sociology of Knowledge," excerpted in Curtis and Petras, 350.

myself, that one spring afternoon in a Barnes & Noble, get so distracted by a conversation about Wittgenstein? "Get back to work Dick, back to the source" (am I telling myself?). "Next book: Marx, Dick. Stop putting it off: Write something about Marx."

"The reform of consciousness consists *only* in making the world aware of its own consciousness, in awakening it out of its dream about itself, in *explaining* to it the meaning of its own actions" (Marx to Arnold Ruge, 1843.) Wittgenstein may not have read Marx or, if he did, he may not have been able to learn anything from Marx, but Wittgenstein certainly shared Marx's ambition of awakening us from dreams. And as regards Wittgenstein's concern with the sources of our rules and of our behavior, our understandings and misunderstandings, here, too, Marx has a great deal to tell us. If only we would listen. If we had the strength—the economic structures to encourage us—to listen.*

ALL THIS MUST BE the subject of another work—and of other writers' works, of the works of great writers such as Marx and Engels, and Max Weber and David Harvey. I am, however, using these few pages here to at least bring into the consciousness of the present book and of its readers and writer the possibility that there is another half, or more than half, remaining to be written. To conclude this effort, I will offer one quite un-Wittgensteinian example, from what, borrowing Carl Schmitt's term, we might call the "real war."

The example comes from a 2006 article by the *New York Times'* long-time labor reporter Louis Uchitelle. Apparently, for many years leading up to this date—and either despite or because of the relatively high wages and benefits received by its unionized workers—the factories of the Caterpillar (tractor-making) corporation were among the most productive

---

* For what it's worth, I, too, don't put a lot of stock or hope in Marx's chosen solution (communism, the workers of the world uniting), just as I do not, say, put a lot of stock in Rousseau's proposed solutions. It is their analyses I treasure!

Another way I would put this is to propose as regards Marx, Rousseau and Wittgenstein, just as much as in the cases of Augustine and Butler: If there is indeed any line between philosophizing and preaching, it is hardly as sharp as is commonly imagined. And we might take this the next step: God cannot die. Our ways of speaking, and writing, and making images, keep Him/Her alive—notwithstanding how tired S/He may have become. (But this would seem to be another book!)

in the world and the company had long thrived. Revenues were up more than 50 percent from 2003 to 2005, and net income had tripled over the same period. In attempting to justify the major reductions in employee compensation that were made during this period, Caterpillar's Director of Corporate Labor Relations told Uchitelle: "You could say that in good times you could afford a different kind of [compensation] package and in bad times you couldn't. The real question is: What's competitive? And our target is competitiveness."*

It seems to me that we have here returned to the Wittgensteinian question "How does it come about that this arrow points to the right and not to the left?" What is striking about the Caterpillar executive's comment is that while it accurately reproduces the rhetoric of the system, it flies in the face of the empirical evidence—the company *was* enjoying good times, it *was* extremely competitive. What was the need—or whose need was it—to reduce compensation?*

Given that senior management's aggressive efforts increased the level of labor-management conflict at Caterpillar, one might wonder if the logic of capitalism, of the exploitation of human labor, led the senior managers to take actions that went against their own interests. In fact, though, it was not in their (economic) interest to fail to take advantage of opportunities to increase their company's short-term return on capital. (We are back to Augustine's *falsas divitias famulantibus*.) Otherwise, the company would be vulnerable to the relentless rapaciousness of capital—

---

* *Cf.*, Marx, *Economic and Philosophical Manuscripts* of 1844, in *Early Writings*, 171-72:

> The less you eat, drink, buy books, go to the theater or to balls, or to the public house, and the less you think, love, theorize, sing, paint, fence, etc., the more you will be able to save and the *greater* will become your treasure which neither moth nor dust will corrupt—your *capital*. The less you *are* . . . the more you *have*. . . . Everything which the economist takes from you in the way of life and humanity, he restores to you in the form of *money* and *wealth*. And everything which you are unable to do, your money can do for you; it can eat, drink, go to the ball and the theater. It can acquire art, learning, historical treasures, political power, and it can travel. It *can* appropriate all these things for you . . . but although it can do all this, <u>it only *desires* to create itself, and to buy itself</u>. (My underscoring.)

here in the form of corporate raiders and investment bankers looking for "profit opportunities." Profit opportunities that—in addition to union busting, wage lowering and pension-fund raiding—could easily include dispensing with senior managers drawing high salaries while working a mere thirty-five or forty hours a week, and not even taking their Blackberries to the golf course!*

> The capitalist "shares with the miser the passion for wealth as wealth. But that which in the miser is mere idiosyncrasy, is, in the capitalist, the effect of the social mechanism, of which he is but one of the wheels. . . . [C]ompetition makes the immanent laws of capitalist production to be felt by each individual capitalist, as external coercive laws. It compels him to keep constantly extending his capital, in order to preserve it, . . . †

Returning to Wittgenstein and to the present work's focus on rules and rule following, we can observe that in the workplace context of this Caterpillar anecdote, the members of the largest of the classes, the workers, were only able to contribute to the rule-making (to enjoy a little agency) through large-scale social combination and collective action. ("Unions: The Folks That Brought You The Weekend," as one of the bumperstickers

---

* During one of the times Mitt Romney was running for President, two *Boston Globe* reporters did a story on one of the series of deals through which Romney and his company, Bain Capital, had made their money. According to the *Globe*, in 1992 Bain acquired American Pad & Paper, or Ampad, for $5 million. It then had Ampad borrow money to make further acquisitions in the office products industry, while charging Ampad $2 million a year in management fees, plus additional fees for each Ampad acquisition. Along the way, and for an additional $2 million, it took the company public, with Bain earning another $45-50 million by selling some of its own stock in Ampad. Meanwhile, by 1999, under Bain Capital's leadership, Ampad's debt had reached nearly $400 million, up from $11 million in 1993, and hundreds of workers had been laid off. Instead of paying workers to produce products, the new Ampad was paying banks for money. This led soon enough to workers losing their health-care coverage and their pensions, and to bankruptcy. Reporters Robert Gavin and Sacha Pfeiffer write, "Bain Capital and its investors ultimately made more than $100 million on the deal."

(I was led to the *Globe* story and picked up some background information from a Frank Rich article, "Obama's Original Sin.")

† Marx, *Capital*, volume 1, 592.

on my office door notes.) The managers and capitalists, for their part, could, as individuals or small groups, enjoy a *feeling* of power over others, a feeling of getting to establish the rules, and perhaps of getting to pick and choose among the rules that they themselves, the masters, were going to follow or ignore. Nonetheless, in the end these people's choices—to include their languages—were as determined as the choices, language included, of the workers.* And insofar as the managers and capitalists also enjoyed weekends off, this was also thanks to many, many hard years of labor organizing, to workers—and managers and capitalists, too—giving their lives in the struggle.

Now we are back to one of the basic questions that Wittgenstein was hoping to make go away by his therapeutic approach to philosophy: What is the good? (Or is it: *Where* is the good?) It would seem, looking at our present situation, that we have become drivers on a highway that—since we have been press-ganged or seduced into building and paying for it—we have decided is good. If have spent and keep on spending all this time and money constructing highways (or making and consuming consumer products), highways (or consumer products) *must* be good. And so must all the time we spend shopping and driving between stores and storage.

Of course along the way we are able at various times to change lanes or speed up or slow down, and even at times to pull over at a rest stop, but escaping our highway seems no longer an option, and this notwithstanding that from time to time some or all of us we may have intimations that the end is disaster or nothingness or Marsalina's futility.

> Daß das beste, was ich schreiben konnte, immer nur philosophische Bemerkungen bleiben würden; daß meine Gedanken bald erlahmten, wenn ich versuchte,

---

* *Cf.*, Weber's various comments regarding: how "the personal conduct of those who participate, on either the side of the rulers or the ruled . . . is essentially prescribed by objective situations"; about the "masterless slavery in which capitalism enmeshes the worker or the debtor"; about the individual bureaucrat who "cannot squirm out of the apparatus in which he is harnessed . . . he is only a single cog in an ever-moving mechanism which prescribes to him an essentially fixed route of march." *From Max Weber*, 58 (quoting *Wirtschaft und Gesellschaft*, vol. 1, page 800) and 228 (quoting *Wirtschaft und Gesellschaft*, Part 3, Chapter 6).

sie, gegen ihre natürliche Neigung, in einer *Richtung weiterzuzwingen*. (The best that I could write would never be more than philosophical remarks; my thoughts were soon crippled if I tried to force them on in any *single direction* against their natural inclination.)

So Wittgenstein wrote in his prefatory remarks to his *Philosophical Investigations*. This is to take Marxist determinism to the next level, to say that—be we more product of seed or soil, of genes, human nature, religion, nationality, historical period, economic relations, . . . We write and say what it is given to us to write and say, and can do nothing more and nothing else.

Freud

In one of the very first footnotes of this work, I noted that Wittgenstein was very taken with Freud's writings and ideas, at one point describing himself as a "disciple" or "follower" of Freud. The psychobiographer in me notes that Gretl (Margarete)—the sister for whom Ludwig had erotic feelings, and with whom he had perhaps first explored sex, in whatever youthful way—Gretl not only became a friend of Freud's and helped him escape Austria after the *Anschluss*, for two years she was analyzed by Freud. And so Freud may have seemed to be the possessor of one of Ludwig's darkest secrets (from Ludwig's perspective): the secret of whatever had happened between him and Gretl. Freud was the doctor who knew Ludwig's real disease or sin, or the depth of his disease, his sinfulness.*

More prosaically, I note that Wittgenstein was a fervent admirer of Freud's writings, and, as Abel and I have already indicated, Wittgenstein wrestled intellectually with Freud's ideas of the unconscious. What could this mean, to speak of a region without language, without signs? If one were to succeed in making the unconscious conscious—say, through analyzing dreams or via the technique of free association—then, magically,

---

* Allow me to note the rather different approach taken by Wittgenstein's contemporary Egon Schiele, another man who, as a boy, had found a sister with whom to explore erotic questions. Rather than getting knotted up with shame and suppressed desire, Schiele began paying pubescent working-class girls to take off their clothes and spread their legs so that he, from atop a ladder, could portray their vulvas in shocking detail and color—*Bilder* for which Schiele found eager, well-heeled clients.

it was no longer unconscious. As if the closer one approached to a reservoir the dryer it became, to the point where, if one were actually to make it to the shore, one would find the reservoir gone. As if one could only drink if one did not realize one was thirsty?

I have not been quoting or paraphrasing Wittgenstein, but trying to bring out some of the intellectual thoughts that might come to a Wittgensteinian in this context. This is to set the stage for noting the other side of Wittgenstein's obsession with Freud: Wittgenstein's unflagging opposition to psychotherapy; his opposition to friends going to psychotherapists, and his own not going. One might think that such a resolute seeker of the truth and of self-knowledge—to say nothing of a person so taken with himself and the workings of his mind—would at least try a visit or two, as Abel, for example, tried Gestalt psychotherapy. But no. To this, Ludwig was absolutely opposed. And this notwithstanding the fact that he came to refer to his philosophical method as "therapy" and had fantasies of himself becoming a psychiatrist.[135]

A bit from a letter Wittgenstein wrote to Norman Malcolm in 1945: "I, too, was greatly impressed when I first read Freud. He's extraordinary.—Of course he is full of fishy thinking & his charm & the charm of the subject is so great that you may be easily fooled."[136] A bit from 1947, from the last page of *Culture and Value*—interestingly, this may have been the last note Wittgenstein ever made:

> *Freud schreibt ausgezeichnet, und es ist ein Vergnügen, ihn zu lesen, aber es ist nie* groß *in seinem Schreiben.* (Freud writes excellently and it is a pleasure to read him, but his writing is never *great*.)

As suggested in the "Wittgenstein" segment, with Wittgenstein the attraction-repulsion game only ended with his death. Nor are we ready to stop finding in Wittgenstein, and through him, breathtaking clarity and not quite fathomable depths.

Acknowledgments

And now, finally, we can say, I can say! And there is so much I would say here, so many people (and a few institutions) I want to thank.

It is a pleasure to be able to acknowledge and thank Steven Affeldt, who allowed me to sit in on the class on Wittgenstein that he taught as a visiting professor at the New School in the spring of 2004. This course was my introduction to Wittgenstein, and it was such an inspiring introduction, it resonated so with things inside me, . . . The result is the present book. (Which is not to saddle Steven or his mentor, the late Stanley Cavell, with the various ideas regarding Wittgenstein that I have developed in the aftermath of Steven's course.)

Steven assigned the students in his class to explicate one section of the *Investigations*. Even though I was just auditing the class, I felt that, in order to learn what Steven had to teach, I should do the assignment. As I recall, the papers were to be five to seven pages long. And, like Abel, I chose section 32, thinking it would be relatively easy to explicate. But before I was done I had forty pages—the first draft of what became Abel and Marsalina's conversation.

Steven's generosity is, however, only one of the many acts of generosity that have been committed by New School philosophy professors on my behalf. Agnes Heller, James Miller and Dmitri Nikulin also allowed me to sit in on their excellent courses. In Dmitri's case, there were a few years there when you couldn't keep me *out* of his classes.

This is also a good place to note the New School's history of generosity, in particular the extent to which the New School opened its doors to refugee European intellectuals around the time of the Second World War. The wonderful thing about this openness is that—while other American universities have been poisoned by other approaches, e.g., by firing Leftist professors or by making deals with corporate sponsors—the New School's approach has nurtured so many, ongoing, generous and courageous discussions. And this university has been where not just I, but many Rogue Scholars with unconventional ideas, have felt most welcome.

While I am thanking people and institutions who have allowed me to sit in on their classes, I would also thank the Yale political scientist

Robert Lane who, in the late 1970s, allowed me to come weekly in my dusty work clothes (I was then earning a living as a handyman for a mental hospital) to an ambitious graduate seminar which combined psychology, sociology and political science, and which introduced me to many basic concepts that have stayed with me over the ensuing three decades. Not too long after this, at l'Université de Paris VIII, Jean-François Lyotard and Gilles Deleuze opened my eyes to a European approach to philosophy, and Professor Lyotard in particular impressed upon this American Baby Boomer the extent to which the world wars and the Holocaust (and, I will add, *Silent Spring*) had called the Enlightenment into question. Echoes of this aspect of Professor Lyotard's teaching may be found in Abel's and Professor Thorn's words and in the quoting of Stefan Zweig, as the representative of this point of view. Professor Lyotard also introduced me to Lucretius, and Professor Deleuze was a most generous supporter of the novel I wrote at that time (*Knute, and Knute Again*).

Have faith, dear readers, I have more than "just" professors to thank. There are "friends and family," as advertising has taught us to refer to them. And there are translators! Specifically, I thank Anne Fassotte, Susan Bernofsky and Verena Kneip-Kobylarz for their invaluable help with French, German and Latin translations. And I thank Isabel Bortagaray for her beautiful cover design!

Before arriving at my son Jonah, allow me to thank a few more professors. At Vassar College Mitchell Miller got me started studying philosophy on a very good footing. Professor Miller went on to make his reputation as a Plato scholar, but when I knew him (in his first year of teaching, I believe it was), he was interested in Hegel and in Marx's early manuscripts. Everyone was reading Marx's early manuscripts in those days, but Professor Miller's approach gave me a Marx who has lasted through thick and thin, who informs every day of my life. And the richness of this experience led me many years later to take David Harvey's course on *Capital* at the City University of New York, another of the rich educational experiences of my life.

And I would thank Stephen Koch with whom—in another lifetime for both of us—I studied fiction writing, and City University and Hunter College's Gerald Press, with whom I continued my study of Plato (begun at The New School with Dmitri Nikulin). Stephen, above all, validated my innate Modernist tendencies. In particular, as I was working on the present text, I often recalled a comment he made regarding plot, or regarding the confusion of writers who imagined that plot was central to novel writing. At the time he and I were both living near Astor Place and teaching/studying at Columbia. A perfectly legitimate "plot" for a novel, Stephen proposed, would have a protagonist, page 1, getting on the subway at Broadway and Eighth Street and, at the end, getting off at Broadway and 116th. For the present work, you might say, I pared down Stephen's idea. As the "novel" (work of fiction?) gets under way the main characters are seated in a bookstore cafe near Broadway and 16th. Several hundred pages later they all get up. Breathtaking! Heart-rending!

Long after Stephen and I had gone our separate ways—he to the Upper East Side and books full of political conspiracy, and me to philosophy and Stuyvesant Town—I had the good fortune of being accepted into a graduate seminar on Plato taught by Professor Press. Gerald has been one of the leaders of a sophisticated, enlightening approach to reading Plato (the roots of which may be traced to the Columbia professor Frederick Woodbridge, among others). This reading helped me focus on aspects of Plato's objectives and techniques that proved of great help when I returned to my Wittgenstein draft and began recasting and rewriting. (Among other things, adding Professor Thorn.)

AND HERE IS THE PLACE to thank, and not thank, a few restaurants and their staffs. It is ironic that at the end of his text Professor Thorn ends up going to the Knickerbocker—and I fought as hard as I could against this choice, casting about, drafting language for other choices. The problem is, or was, that, one day when I was at work on this book, I myself, and in Professor Thorn's honor, went to the Knickerbocker for lunch, and I lingered, entering corrections to my text in my laptop. Though the restaurant was almost empty, the manager tried the usual restaurant-manager tactic for getting rid of customers who are reading or writing: turning down the lights. When that did not work he came over and told me I had to leave, he needed my table. I said it was odd for him to need my table when the place was almost empty, and odd, too, for a restaurant that was two blocks from a university to be anti-intellectual. He didn't care. He was afraid it was going to look like studious people frequented his restaurant, and—worse—studious people who, like me, did not drink alcohol while they worked. What sort of message might this send to the right kind of people—the people who buy drinks and, getting drunk, buy more drinks and more food—with nary a studious thought in their heads? (In fact, the Greek-American novelist Irini Spanidou was sitting right next to me, and spending less money than I. And we had a very pleasant conversation. But she was not committing the sin of mixing dining and working.)

Which is also to say that it is my pleasure to thank the managements and staffs of four other New York restaurants: Bukhara Grill, Japonica, La Petite Abeille and the Nations Cafe. At least two of these went out of business well before the pandemic, but in good ol' days, the vast majority of work on this book was done in these four places, aided by the food that was brought me, the physical and psychological space that was accorded me, and by welcoming smiles and handshakes and brief conversations with the staff and owners. As I was finishing this book, my son went off to sleepaway camp for the first time, and I had some worries that, more isolated, my mind would begin to consume itself. I would lose the ability to focus. These worries proved well warranted, but I was helped along by my restaurant connections. Not only were the staffs and I happy to see one another and to exchange a little conversation, but customers I knew would stop by my back table to say hello, or I would come forward to say hello to them.

Toward the end of the dialogue Marsalina talked about how what matters may be "what lies in between, in the cracks." I would nominate for this category the sort of cafe society I have just described. Unfortunately, however, even before the arrival of COVID-19, such kinds of human interaction and the cafes and restaurants that supported them had more or less disappeared from Manhattan and likely from many other parts of the world as well.

When, if ever, will we wake up and realize—realize fully—how destructive our electronic gadgets and apps, and their purveyors are? Marx: "alles Heilige wird entweiht" (all that is holy is profaned). Wittgenstein: "*Man könnte sagen: Die Betrachtung muß gedreht werden, aber um unser eigentliches Bedürfnis als Angelpunkt.* " (One might say: the axis of our examination must be rotated, but about the fixed point of our real need.) Conversation. Plato's Socrates understood this. Not sociability. Conversation. Intimate, courageous, far-reaching.

WE COME TO JONAH, my son. For ten or fifteen years—making a home together, playing sports, listening to comedy CDs, snuggling, playing cards, walking and talking, and reading books side by side—Jonah was the great companion of my life. I recall the dilemma Wittgenstein faced in writing to the wife of one of his professors: should he try to express himself fully, knowing that she would have trouble understanding, or should he write "something that sounds halfway plausible but that can in no circumstances be understood, because it is not true."* This, inversely, well describes the luxury of my life with Jonah (and of his with me, I believe). Of course Jonah has not been interested in every subject that interests me, nor vice-versa, but he is the person who understands most quickly—without thinking—where my mind is headed or where it's coming from. (I take this to be not only because Jonah has a rare intelligence or because of how much time we have spent together, but also because of what might be called the childishness of my mind. Jonah's youthful ability to follow my thinking was matched by my ability to be on the same wave length as other children I ran into.) When in writing the present book I needed a little something—such as the right lottery ad for Abel to quote—Jonah had the perfect answer ("Hey, you never know") almost before the question had crossed my lips.

My book *Surviving the Twenty-First Century* includes many stories of my life with Jonah, so I won't go back over this territory here. Let me just repeat what I said in the opening of that book: No kind words can equal the warmth, companionship and intelligence Jonah has brought to my life.

LAST, BUT HARDLY LEAST, I would like to thank Sven Birkerts, Garry Hagberg and Kelly Jolley, who have not only made generous comments about the present work, but have been able to understand it! It is ironic and appropriate that I spent several years of my life creating the fictional conversation of the present book, since these were also years when non-fictional conversations anything like Abel and Marsalina's were few and far between. This latter fact is certainly regrettable—and it is regrettable, too, that this has been the fate of many American intellectuals and artists these past several hundred years. (To say nothing of Ludwig Wittgenstein!) But this fact certainly also makes all the sweeter those moments when one

---
* Wittgenstein's dilemma is mentioned and the letter quoted at greater length by Professor Thorn is his Introduction to the present volume.

feels there are a few people with whom you can talk (or dialogue with via e-mail), people who are willing to explore feelings and ideas, setting aside the usual blinders, conventions and fears. People who, despite the inevitable deformations of language, might try to understand you, and you them.

With thanks again, and to all,

William Eaton
Stuyvesant Town, New York July 2020

Endnotes

1 Gottlieb, "A Nervous Splendor."
2 Janik and Toulmin, 171.
3 McGuinness, *Wittgenstein: A Life*, 38.
4 Waugh, 17-18, 14-15 and 18.
5 Monk, xvii-xviii.
6 *Culture and Value*, 36e. He goes on to say that he believes Freud's originality was the same: of the soil.
7 Monk, 44.
8 As quoted in McGuinness, *Wittgenstein: A Life*, 58-59.
9 *Repetition* (in *Repetition and Philosophical Crumbs*, 6.
10 Wittgenstein to Ogden, May 5, 1922; as quoted in Monk, 207.
11 *Investigations*, §28.
12 *Investigations*, Part II, xi, 190e.
13 Edmonds and Eidinow, *Wittgenstein's Poker*, 100.
14 *Investigations*, §123.
15 Waugh, 21-22.
16 Edmonds and Eidinow, 138. See also Monk, 399-400.
17 Wikipedia articles on "Austria-Hungary" and the "Brusilov Offensive," accessed in February and March 2011. Waugh, 108, puts the loss at 1.5 million Austro-Hungarian troops.
18 Waugh, 46.
19 While Trakl's suicide is well documented, the story of his asking Wittgenstein to come visit him and so forth may be apocryphal. I found it on the Web, at praxisblog.wordpress.com/2008/02/25/wittgenstein-at-war, accessed June 2011.
20 Quoted in Edmonds and Eidinow, 98. Monk, 9, renders this: the "research laboratory for world destruction."
21 The description of Karl—he carried "the germ of disgust for life within himself"—was his sister Hermine's; as quoted in Waugh, 123.
22 Letter to Morrell, September 4, 1912; as quoted in Monk, 57.
23 From Wittgenstein's *Notebooks*, January 10, 1917, as quoted in McGuinness, *Wittgenstein: A Life*, 157.
24 Monk, 232-33.
25 Monk, 234.
26 Monk, 370-71.
27 Letter to Morrell, May 2, 1912; in McGuinness, *Wittgenstein: A Life*, 106.
28 *On Certainty*, §94.

29 *Remarks on the Foundations of Mathematics*, Part I, §5, 47e; *Investigations*, §381.
30 Sextus Empiricus, *Outlines of Scepticism*, 4.
31 Plato, *Phaedo*, 117-118, as translated by Benjamin Jowett. (Here and elsewhere, pages given for quotations from Plato are the Stephanus pages.)
32 Edmonds and Eidinow, 13, from an interview with Peter Musz. Note that this is not a direct fromy quote from Munz.
33 Carnap, 34.
34 Monk, 107, quoting Ludwig von Ficker, the writer and editor to whom Wittgenstein gave money to distribute to Austrian artists without means. (As mentioned earlier in the text.)
35 A personal communication to Eidinow and Edmonds, as quoted in their book, 14 ("incandescent . . .") and 190.
36 *On Certainty*, §10.
37 Monk, chapter 21, "War Work," and especially, 453.
38 Monk, 244, quoting from Carnap's "Autobiography," *op. cit.*
39 Monk, 53.
40 Report of Wittgenstein's Russian teacher, Fania Pascal, "Memories of Wittgenstein," 17.
41 Monk, 46; quoting Russell's *Autobiography*.
42 Monk, 47; quoting Russell, letter to Morrell, April 24, 1912.
43 Malcolm, *Memoir*, 27 and 32.
44 Malcolm, *Memoir*, 61.
45 Malcolm, 81.
46 A medley combining elements of §422, §587 and from Part II, i, 148e and Part II, x,162e.
47 In April 2011, I found what was perhaps the ur version of Abel's statements on a Spark Notes website on Wittgenstein.
48 From *Investigations*, §234. A fuller quotation, without the ellipses, appears in a footnote in the "Second Interpolation," as well as in the segment titled "Wittgenstein" in Appendix B.
49 *Investigations*, §106.
50 Augustine, *Confessions* I: 8; as quoted in *Investigations*, §1.
51 Quine, *Word and Object*, 60-62.
52 *Investigations*, §1.
53 Cavell, "Notes and Afterthoughts," 129.
54 Augustine, *Confessions*, Pine-Coffin translation, I:6.
55 Galileo, *Il Saggiatore (The Assayer)*.
56 The only version of this I was able to track down appeared in a 2011 magazine article about Krugman by one Benjamin Wallace-Wells (page 86).

57 Marx, *Theses on Feuerbach*, XI.
58 Comment reported by Malcolm, 27-28.
59 *Investigations*, §342.
60 Emerson, "Montaigne; or the Sceptic," 377.
61 Lucretius, *De natura rerum* (On the Nature of the Universe), Book II: Movements and Shapes of Atoms, 66. Lucretius's term for "the swerve"—i.e., clinamen—is often used in non-Latin texts.
62 Bouwsma, "The Blue Book,"178.
63 Wittgenstein, *Preliminary Studies*, 29.
64 *Discours*, Seconde partie, 89.
65 Moore, *Commonplace Book*, 1919-57, edited by Casimir Levy (George Allen and Unwin, 1962), 193; as quoted in Regan, 91.
66 *Tractatus*, §6.42.
67 Wittgenstein, "Lecture on Ethics."
68 Perlstein, 27. Apparently on April 22, 1973, President Nixon called his chief of staff H. R. Haldeman, who was resigning in the midst of the Watergate scandal. Nixon said to Haldeman: "You're doing the right thing. That's what I used to think when I killed some innocent children in Hanoi." Perlstein's source may have been Richard Reeves, *Nixon: Alone in the White House* (Simon & Schuster, 2002).
69 *Investigations*, Part II, xi, 192e.
70 The first lines of *Investigations*, §75.
71 *Investigations*, §66. More complete text of this section quoted in an earlier footnote.
72 *Investigations*, §414.
73 Wittgenstein, *On Certainty*, §55.
74 Zweig, *The World of Yesterday*, 3-4.
75 Monk, 17-18.
76 Letter from December 1913; as quoted in McGuinness, *Wittgenstein: A Life*, 192. For the concluding phrase I have used the alternative translation McGuinness proposes in footnote 20 on page 192. McGuinness's first translation is "to settle accounts with myself." In both cases the sense is metaphorical not literal.
77 Diary entry, May 27, 1942; as quoted, as translated, in Monk, 443.
78 Augustine's *Enchiridion* 7.22, as quoted in Toom, 367, fn 64: "*Et utique verba propterea sunt instituta non per quae se homines invicem fallant sed per quae in alterius quisque notitiam cogitationes suas perferat.*"
79 Kenny, 4.
80 Cavell, "The Availability of Wittgenstein's Later Philosophy," 72.
81 *Confessions*, IV:14 and X:5; as quoted in Brown, 172 and 178.

82 Monk, 75.
83 Richards, 256.
84 Edmonds and Eidinow, 187.
85 Malcolm, *Memoir*, 32.
86 Shakespeare, "Macbeth," Act I, Scene vii.
87 Cratylus, 384B, Socrates speaking.
88 *Investigations*, Part II, xi, 172e.
89 Edmonds and Eidinow, 158-59.
90 Bryan and Dodge, "Bert and I."
91 *Investigations*, §366.
92 *Investigations*, footnote below §30, p. 12e.
93 *Investigations*, §217.
94 Dickinson, poem 164 or 419.
95 Schmitt *Political Theology*, 12, and *The Concept of the Political*, 35.
96 Schmitt, *Political Theology*, 15.
97 *Investigations*, Part II, xi, 188e.
98 Winnicott, "Fear of Breakdown."
99 Kenny, 4.
100 *Investigations*, §257.
101 Yeats, "Easter 1916."
102 *Investigations*, §293.
103 *Investigations*, §297.
104 *Investigations*, §304.
105 Bréhier, 25. My translation.
106 Plotinus, §9 of the sixth *Ennead*, on "The Good or The One."
107 Monk, 451.
108 *Confessions* X:8 and X:10, Pine-Coffin translation.
109 Burnyeat, 1.
110 Burnyeat, 2.
111 Augustine, *De doctrina Christiana* 2.1.2, 2.3.4 and 2.23; as quoted in Toom, 365-66. Toom also references *De Civitate Dei* (The City of God), 7.14. Toom worked from the translation of R.P.H. Green, Augustine: *De doctrina Christiana* (Clarendon Press, 1995).
112 Toom, 366.
113 Toom, 365.
114 Burnyeat, 23.
115 "Divine help": Burnyeat, 24. "Inner light": Augustine, *De Magistro* XII: 39-40.
116 Monk, 235.
117 *Investigations*, §206.

118 Medien Kunst Netz (Media Art Net): http://www.medienkunstnetz.de/works/shapolsky, consulted July 2011.
119 Schorske, 296 and 148.
120 Schorske, 149.
121 Toulmin, *Cosmopolis*, 26.
122 Mencius 2A6; as quoted in Chen, 65.
123 Hume, *Treatise*, 520-21.
124 *Treatise*, 627-28.
125 *Treatise*, 637-38.
126 *Treatise*, 667-668.
127 Plato, *The Republic*, 505D-E. The discussion of the good runs from 504E to 509E.
128 See Plato, *Philebus*, 20A-B and 59C-61C.
129 Keynes, 88-89.
130 Moore, "The Elements of Ethics", as quoted in Regan, 136. Caps in the original.
131 Butler, *Analogy of Religion*, Part II, Chapter III, 225.
132 Lacan, "Fonction et champ", section III.
133 *Investigations*, Part II, xi, 166e.
134 *Investigations*, Part II, xi, 166e.
135 In Monk, see 16, 356-57, 438.
136 Malcolm, 44.

Works Cited

(*Plus a few sources that, while not cited, have provided essential help.*)

Here at the outset let me thank Wikipedia and its many authors and editors. Wikipedia sources are not easy to cite given how the contents may change and the authors remain unknown; however, for me, as for many, a Wikipedia article is often the first step in a research process. And let me here tip my hat to many other Web sources, from OneLook Dictionary through thesaurus. com, yiddishdictionaryonline.com, Wiktionary, the Reverso German-English dictionary, the Compact Oxford Dictionary *consulted via the Web,* le Dictionnaire de français "Littré," *also consulted on-line via Reverso.net.*

  I would also like to thank the staff of the libraries of the City University of New York and of the New York Public Library for their assistance. In particular, the research librarian Maurice Klapwald was able to track down the petition of German businessmen to President Hindenburg, as well as useful background information in this regard.

  Translated works are translated into English except where otherwise noted.

Henry Adams. *The Education of Henry Adams*. Vintage Books/The Library of America, 1990. Originally published in 1907.

Theodor Adorno. *Prisms*. Translated by Samuel and Shierry Weber. MIT Press, 1967.

Steven G. Affeldt. "Captivating Pictures and Liberating Language: Freedom as the Achievement of Speech in Wittgenstein's *Philosophical Investigations*." *Philosophical Topics* 27, No. 2 (Fall 1999).

——. "On the Difficulty of Seeing Aspects and the 'Therapeutic' Reading of Wittgenstein." In *Seeing Wittgenstein Anew*. Edited by William Day and Victor J. Krebs. Cambridge University Press, 2010: 268-88.

——. "The Difficulty of Philosophy, Dead Signs, and *Investigations* 185." Paper delivered as part of the conference Una Nueva Forma de Ver: Wittgenstein y el pensamiento del siglo XXI, at the Pontifica dad Catolica del Perú, in Lima, Peru, December 4, 2010.

Giorgio Agamben. *State of Exception*. Translated by Kevin Attell. University of Chicago Press, 2005.

Aristotle. *Nicomachean Ethics*. Translated by J.L. Ackrill. Humanities Press, 1973.

Matthew Arnold. "The Buried Life." Accessed via http://www.victorianweb.org, June 2011.

Harold Arlen and Johnny Mercer. "Ac-cent-tchu-ate the Positive." MPL Communications, 1944.

Robert L. Arrington and Hans-Johann Glock. "Editors' Introduction" to *Wittgenstein and Quine*. Routledge, 1996. (Accessed via Kindle electronic edition, 2010.)

Robert Audi, general editor. *The Cambridge Dictionary of Philosophy*, second edition. Cambridge University Press, 1995.

Augustine (Aurelius Augustinus Hipponensis). *City of God*. Translated by Marcus Dods. Accessed via Saint Wiki ("a free repository of Catholic resources"), June 2011.

———. *Confessiones* (Liber 1, Caput 8). Edited by J.J. O'Donnell. Text retrieved March 2004 from http://www.stoa.org/hippo/text1.html. Presented with an English title: *The Confessions of Saint Augustine*.

———. *Confessions*. Translated by R.S. Pine-Coffin. Penguin Books, 1961.

———. *Confessions* I:8. Translated by E.B. Pusey. Text retrieved March 2004 from http://ccat.sas.upenn.edu/jod/augustine/Pusey/book01.

———. *Confessions* (I:8, and III:1). Translated by Albert C. Outler. Text retrieved April 2011 from http://wadsworth.com.

———. *The Essential Augustine*, second edition. Edited by Vernon J. Bourke. Hackett, 1974.

Jonathan Barnes. *Early Greek Philosophy*. Penguin Books, 1987. Barnes's source for the fragments of early Greek philosophy is the standard: H. Diels and W. Kranz, *Die Fragmente der Vosokratiker* (Berlin, 1952, 10th edition).

Bela Bartok and Béla Balázs. "*A kékszakállú herceg vára*" (Duke Bluebeard's Castle). Composed in 1911, with modifications made in 1912 and a new ending added in 1917. First performed on May 24, 1918 in Budapest.

Charles Baudelaire. "Correspondances." One of the selections from *Les Fleurs du mal* published in *Les plus belles pages de la poésie française*. Sélection du Reader's Digest, 1985.

Patrick Bearsley. "Augustine and Wittgenstein on Language." *Philosophy* 58, No. 224 (April 1983): 229-36.

Samuel Beckett. *L'Innomable*. Les Éditions de Minuit, 1953. (Beckett ends text with the date 1949.) *The Unnamable*, the English version produced by the author, was first published by Grove Press, 1958.

———. "Waiting for Godot." Accessed via http://www.samuel-beckett.net, July 2011.

Jessica Benjamin. *The Bonds of Love: Psychoanalysis, Feminism, and the Problem of Domination*. Pantheon, 1988.

David Bloor. *Wittgenstein: A Social Theory of Knowledge*. Columbia University Press, 1983.

H. Lawrence Bond. Introduction to *Nicholas of Cusa: Selected Spiritual Writings*. Translated by H. Lawrence Bond. Paulist Press, 1997.

Pierre Bourdieu. *La Distinction*. Les Éditions de Minuit, 1979. English translation: *Distinction: A Social Critique of the Judgment of Taste*. Translated by Richard Nice. Harvard University Press, 1984.

O.K. Bouwsma. "The Blue Book." In *Philosophical Essays*. University of Nebraska Press, 1965. Text first appeared in *The Journal of Philosophy* 58, No. 6 (1961), and is also reprinted in *Ludwig Wittgenstein: The Man and his Philosophy*. Edited by K.T. Fann. Humanities Press and Harvester Press, 1978, 49-55.

Émile Bréhier. *La philosophie de Plotin*. Bovin & Cie, 1928.

Luc Brisson and Jean-François Pradeau. *Le vocabulaire de Platon*. Ellipses, 1998.

David Brooks and Gail Collins. "In Praise of Progress." Dialogue appearing in the "Opinionator" blog, *New York Times* on-line, July 28, 2010.

Peter Brown. *Augustine of Hippo: A Biography*. University of California Press, 1970.

Robert Bryan and Marshall Dodge. "Bert and I . . . And Other Stories from Down East." Comedy album originally recorded 1958. Subsequently available from Islandport Press.

M. F. Burnyeat. "The Inaugural Address: Wittgenstein and Augustine *De Magistro*." *Proceedings of the Aristotelian Society, Supplementary Volumes* 61 (1987): 1-24.

Joseph Butler. *The Analogy of Religion, Natural and Revealed, to the Constitution and Course of Nature; to which are added two brief dissertations: on personal identity and on the nature of virtue; and fifteen sermons.* Henry G. Bohn, 1852.

———. *Five Sermons, preached at the Rolls Chapel, and "A Dissertation upon the Nature of Virtue."* Edited by Stephen L. Darwall. Hackett, 1983.

———. "Upon the Natural Supremacy of Conscience." Sermon II in *Fifteen Sermons Preached at the Rolls Chapel.* Hilliard and Brown, 1827. As transcribed by LeRoy Dagg, 2002, and reproduced with permission of the Bishop Payne Library, Virginia Theological Seminary, 2005, at http://anglicanhistory.org/butler.

Italo Calvino. *Invisible Cities.* Translated by William Weaver. Harcourt Brace Jovanovich, 1974. First published in Italy (*Le città invisibili*) in 1972.

Rudolf Carnap. "From his 'Autobiography'." In K.T. Fann. *Ludwig Wittgenstein: The Man and His Philosophy* (Dell, 1967): 33-39. Text originally appeared in *The Philosophy of Rudolf Carnap*, edited by Paul Schlipp, a book which has been published by, *inter alia*, Open Court Publishing, 1964.

Stanley Cavell. "Declining Decline: Wittgenstein as a Philosopher of Culture." In *This New Yet Unapproachable America* (see below). Also chapter 16 of *The Cavell Reader* (see below).

———. *Disowning Knowledge in Six Plays of Shakespeare.* Cambridge University Press, 1987.

———. "Excursus on Wittgenstein's Vision of Language." Chapter 7 of *The Claim of Reason.* Oxford University Press, 1979.

———. "Notes and Afterthoughts on the Opening of Wittgenstein's *Investigations*." In *Philosophical Passages: Wittgenstein, Emerson, Austin, Derrida.* Blackwell, 1995. Also chapter 8 of *The Cavell Reader.* Edited by Stephen Mulhall. Blackwell, 1996.

———. "The Availability of Wittgenstein's Later Philosophy." Chapter II of Cavell, *Must We Mean What We Say? A Book of Essays.* Charles

Scribner's Sons, 1969.

———. *The Claim of Reason: Wittgenstein, Skepticism, Morality, and Tragedy.* Oxford University Press, 1979.

———. *This New Yet Unapproachable America: Lectures after Emerson after Wittgenstein.* Living Batch Press and University of Chicago Press, 1989. Published version of the 1987 Frederick Ives Carpenter Lectures.

Javier Cercas. *The Anatomy of a Moment: Thirty-Five Minutes in History and Imagination.* Translated by Anne McLean. Bloomsbury, 2009.

Wing-Tsit Chan. *A Source Book in Chinese Philosophy.* Translated and compiled by Wing-Tsit Chan. Princeton University Press, 1963.

Noam Chomsky. "Review of Skinner's *Verbal Behavior.*" *Language* 35 (1959): 26-58.

Gillian Clark, editor (and commentator). *Augustine Confessions Books I-IV.* Cambridge University Press, 1995.

Peter Cook, Dudley Moore, Alan Bennett and Jonathan Miller. "Beyond the Fringe." Acorn Media, 2005. Recording of a later production of a revue which premiered August 22, 1960 at the Royal Lyceum Theatre, Edinburgh.

Pierre Courcelle. *Late Latin Writers and their Greek Sources.* Translated by Harry E. Weddeck. Harvard University Press, 1969.

Ian Craib. *The Importance of Disappointment.* Routledge, 1994.

Alice Crary. Introduction to *The New Wittgenstein.* Edited by Crary and Rupert Read. Routledge, 2000.

William Cronon. *Changes in the Land: Indians, Colonists, and the Ecology of New England.* Hill and Wang, 1983.

Jerry Cullum. "Between Berlin and Benin: Hans Haacke and Meschac Gaba, Two Political Artists in the Age of Globalization." *ART PAPERS.* September/October 2004. Accessed via http://www.artpapers.org, June 2011.

James E. Curtis and John W. Petras, eds. *The Sociology of Knowledge: A Reader.* Praeger, 1970.

Jacques Derrida. "Cogito et l'histoire de la folie." Lecture delivered March 4, 1963 at the Collège philosophique; first published in *Revue de métaphysique et de morale,* 1964, nos. 3 and 4; later collected in

L'écriture et la différence (Seuil, 1967), 51-97. Alan Bass's translation of this lecture appears in Derrida, *Writing and Difference* (The University of Chicago Press, 1978).

René Descartes. *Discours de la méthode*. Livre de poche, 2000. First published in 1637.

———. *Méditations métaphysiques*. Flammarion, 1979. Bilingual edition: Original Latin text (1641 and 1642) plus the 1647 French translation by Charles d'Albert, le duc de Luynes (reviewed and authorized by Descartes), as well as the "Objections et Réponses" as translated by Claude Clerselier.

Emily Dickinson. *Final Harvest: Emily Dickinson's Poems*. Little, Brown, 1961. *Note:* In this case the numbers given in the footnote are not page numbers but rather the two numbers with which the poems have been classified under two different classification systems.

Chitra Banerjee Divakaruni. *The Conch Bearer*. Roaring Book Press, 2003.

Document 3901-PS: "Petition to Hindenburg, signed by Schacht and a number of leading economists, November 1932: Request that the chairmanship of the presidential cabinet should be entrusted to the Führer of the National Socialist Party (found on the premises of the banking firm Stein in Cologne)" (Exhibit USA-837). In *Trial of the Major War Criminals before the International Military Tribunal*, Nuremberg, 14 November 1945-1 October 1946; Vol. XXXIII, Offical Text, English Edition, Documents and Other Material in Evidence, Numbers 3729-PS to 3993-PS. International Military Tribunal, 1949. *N.B.:* Text of petition is in German, without a translation; however, the German text has no title, and the English title might be considered a rough draft (e.g., "economists" rather than "businessmen"). At the bottom of the petition there are the surnames of approximately 70 people, but it is not believed that all these people in fact signed the petition. The entry below for Ferguson and Voth, "Betting on Hitler" describes how to access their list which identifies, *inter alia*, the signatories.

Alain Duchesne and Thierry Leguay. *Dictionnaire des subtilités du français : La nuance*. Larousse, 2002.

Dudenredaktion and the German Section of the Oxford University Press Dictionary Department. *The Oxford-Duden German Dictionary*,

German-English/English-German. W. Scholze-Stubenrecht and J.B. Sykes, chief editors; second edition edited by M. Clark and O. Thyen. Oxford University Press, 1999.

Bruce Duffy. *The World As I Found It*. New York Review Books, 2010. Originally published in 1987.

———. "The do-it-yourself life of Ludwig Wittgenstein." *New York Times*, November 13, 1988.

Eknath Easwaran. *The Upanishads*. Nilgiri Press, 1987.

David Edmonds and John Eidinow. *Wittgenstein's Poker: The Story of a Ten-Minute Argument Between Two Great Philosophers*. Faber and Faber and HarperCollins, 2001. *While this is a very well written and engaging book, and while it has an extensive bibliography, there are no footnotes—frustrating any attempt to confirm or even evaluate any number of the authors' contentions.*

Albert Einstein. Message to the World Disarmament Conference of Geneva in 1932. Accessed via http://being.publicradio.org/programs/einsteinethics, June 2011.

T.S. Eliot. *Collected Poems, 1909-1962*. Harcourt Brace Jovanovich, 1963.

Ralph Waldo Emerson. "Goethe; or, the Writer." In *Representative Men* (1850). Accessed via http://www.emersoncentral.com, April 2011.

———. "Montaigne; or the Sceptic." In *The Complete Essays and Other Writings of Ralph Waldo Emerson*. Edited by Brooks Atkinson. Modern Library, 1940.

———. "Self-Reliance." In *The Complete Essays and Other Writings of Ralph Waldo Emerson*. Edited by Brooks Atkinson. Modern Library, 1940.

James Ferguson. *The Dominican Republic: Beyond the Lighthouse*. Latin America Bureau, 1992.

Thomas Ferguson and Hans-Joachim Voth. "Betting on Hitler—The Value of Political Connections in Nazi Germany." *The Quarterly Journal of Economics* (February 2008): 101-37. "Appendix I: Defining Connected Firms" gives a list of German businessmen who contributed financially to Hitler or Göring and/or provided political support for the Nazis at crucial moments. Included in the list are the financiers and industrialists who attended the February 20, 1933 meeting at Göring's residence in Berlin, as well as the businessmen who signed the November 1932 petition to President Hindenburg, urging him to appoint Hitler as chancellor of Germany. The appendix has been available on the Web via http://www.econ.upf.edu/~voth/hitler_appendices.pdf.

Wolfgang Georg Fischer. *Egon Schiele 1890-1918: Desire and Decay.* Taschen, 2007.

F. Scott Fitzgerald. "The Crack-Up." In *The Crack-Up*, a collection edited by Edmund Wilson. New Directions, 1945. The title piece was written in 1936.

Peter Fonagy, György Gergely, Elliot Jurist and Mary Target. *Affect Regulation, Mentalization, and the Development of the Self.* Other Press, 2004. First published in 2002.

Sigmund Freud. "Analysis Terminable and Interminable." In *The Standard Edition of the Complete Psychological Works of Sigmund Freud*, volume 23. Translated by James Strachey. Hogarth Press, 1968: 209-53.

———. *Civilization and Its Discontents.* Translated by James Strachey. W.W. Norton, 1961.

———. "Leonardo da Vinci and a Memory of his Childhood." In *The Uncanny*. Translated by David McClintock. Penguin, 2003. German text first published in 1910.

Galileo Galilei. *Il Saggiatore.* Biblioteca Italiana Zanichelli. Amazon Kindle edition, accessed 2010. Has also been available at http://www.liberliber.it/biblioteca/g/galilei.

D.A.T. Gasking and A.C. Jackson. "Wittgenstein as a Teacher." In *Ludwig Wittgenstein: The Man and his Philosophy*. Edited by K.T. Fann. Humanities Press and Harvester Press, 1978, 49-55.

Robert Gavin and Sacha Pfeiffer. "The Making of Mitt Romney." *Boston Globe.* June 26, 2007.

Emmanuel Ghent. "Paradox and Process." *Psychoanalytic Dialogues* 2 (1992): 135-59.

Anthony Giddens. *The Constitution of Society: Outline of the Theory of Structuration.* Polity Press, 1984.

Johann Wolfgang von Goethe. *Selected Poems.* Edited by Christopher Middleton. Suhrkamp/Insel, 1983.

Jack Goody and Ian Watt. "The Consequences of Literacy." *Comparative Studies in Society and History* 5 (1962-63): 304-45.

Anthony Gottlieb. "A Nervous Splendor." *The New Yorker*, April 9, 2009. A review of Waugh, *House of Wittgenstein*.

Ulysses S. Grant. *Memoirs*. Edited with notes by E.B. Long. De Capo Press, 1982.

Winston Groom. *A Storm in Flanders: The Ypres Salient, 1914-18: Triumph and Tragedy on the Western Front*. Cassell, 2002.

Douglas Hand. *Gone Whaling: A Search for Orcas in Northwest Waters*. Sasquatch Books, 1996.

David Harvey. *A Brief History of Neoliberalism*. Oxford University Press, 2005.

———. Introduction to *The Communist Manifesto*. Pluto Press, 2008, 1-30.

———. *Spaces of Capital: Towards a Critical Geography*. Routledge, 2001.

———. *The New Imperialism*. Oxford University Press, 2003.

Hugh Haughton. "Introduction" to Sigmund Freud, *The Uncanny*. Penguin, 2003.

The Holy Bible. King James Version. World Publishing Company.

David Hume. *A Treatise of Human Nature*. Penguin, 1969. First published in 1739 and 1740.

———. *Enquiry concerning the Principles of Morals*. Edited by L. A. Selby-Bigge, 3rd edition revised by P. H. Nidditch. Clarendon Press, 1975.

Werner Jaeger. *Paideia: the Ideals of Greek Culture*, vol. 2: *In Search of the Divine Center*. Translated by Gilbert Highet. Oxford University Press, 1943.

Allan Janik and Stephen Toulmin. *Wittgenstein's Vienna*. Simon and Schuster, 1973.

Jerome. Letter 141 (to Augustine). Original Latin accessed via http://www.augustinus.it/, April 2011. English translation from http://www.newadvent.org/fathers/1102195.htm. *Also classified as Augustine letter 195*.

Anthony Kenny. "The Ghost of the *Tractatus*." In *Royal Institute of Philosophy Lectures* 7, 1972/73. Edited by Godfrey Vesey. Macmillan,

1974.

John Maynard Keynes. "My Early Beliefs." In *Two Memoirs*. Rupert Hart-Davis and Augustus M. Kelley, 1949. Text dated 9 September 1938.

Soren Kierkegaard. *Fear and Trembling and Repetition* (Kierkegaard's Writings, VI). Edited and translated by Howard V. Hong and Edna H. Hong. Princeton University Press, 1983.

———. *Repetition* and *Philosophical Crumbs*. Translated by M.G. Piety, with an introduction by Edward F. Mooney. Oxford University Press, 2009.

Jacob Klein. "About Plato's *Philebus*." *Interpretation: A Journal of Political Philosophy* 2/3. Spring 1972: 157-82.

Saul Kripke, *Wittgenstein on Rules and Private Language*. Harvard University Press, 1982.

Thomas S. Kuhn. *The Essential Tension: Selected Studies in Scientific Tradition and Change*. The University of Chicago Press, 1977.

Jacques Lacan. "Fonction et champ de la parole et du langage en psychanalyse" (Rapport du Congrès du Rome tenu à l'Instituto di Psicologia della Universitá di Roma, les 26 et 27 septembre, 1953). This is the first version of the text, as it appeared under the title "Sur la parole et le langage" in *La psychanalyse* 1 (1956): 81-166.

La Rochefoucauld. *Réflexions ou Sentences et Maximes morales suivi de Réflexions diverses et des Maximes de Madame de Sablé*. Gallimard: 1976. First published in 1664.

F.R. Leavis. "Memories of Wittgenstein." In *Ludwig Wittgenstein: Personal Recollections*. Edited by Rush Rhees. Rowman and Littlefield, 1981.

David C. Lindberg. *The Beginnings of Western Science: The European Scientific Tradition in Philosophical, Religious, and Institutional Context, Prehistory to A.D. 1450*, second edition. The University of Chicago Press, 2007.

Adolf Loos. "Ornament and Crime." In *Ornament and Crime: Selected Essays*. Translated by Michael Mitchell. Ariadne Press, 1998. Essay first published in 1908; here as subsequently published in 1929.

Lucretius. *De natura rerum* (*On the Nature of the Universe*). Translated by R.E. Latham. Penguin Books, 1951.

Norman Malcolm. *Ludwig Wittgenstein: A Memoir*, with a Biographical

Sketch by Georg Henrik von Wright. Oxford University Press, 1958.

Charles C. Mann. *1491: New Revelations of the Americas Before Columbus.* Alfred A. Knopf, 2005.

Karl Marx. *Capital: A Critique of Political Economy.* Volume 1. Translated by Ben Fowkes. Penguin in association with the *New Left Review.* 1976.

———. *Early Writings.* Edited and translated by T.B. Bottomore. Watts, 1963; McGraw-Hill, 1964).

———. *The Marx-Engels Reader*, second edition. Edited by Robert C. Tucker. Norton, 1978. Includes, *inter alia*, "Theses on Feuerbach" (quoted by Abel).

———. *Selected Writings in Sociology and Social Philosophy.* Translated by T.B. Bottomore. McGraw-Hill, 1964.

Karl Marx and Friedrich Engels. *The Communist Manifesto.* Pluto Press, 2008.

Brian McGuinness. *Wittgenstein: A Life; Young Ludwig 1889-1921.* The University of California Press, 1988.

———, editor. *Wittgenstein and his Times.* The University of Chicago Press, 1982. Includes McGuinness's own article "Freud and Wittgenstein."

Dennis McManus. "The Mysterious Appeal of 'Wittgenstein's Conservatism'." *Wittgenstein Studies* 2, No. 95 (February 16, 1995). Accessed via http://sammelpunkt.philo [Sammelpunkt. Elektronisch archivierte Theorie], February 2011.

Perry Meisel. "Young Wittgenstein." *New York Times*, October 11, 1987. A review of Bruce Duffy's *The World as I Found It.*

Robert K. Merton. "Paradigm for the Sociology of Knowledge." In *Social Theory and Social Structure.* The Free Press, 1968. First published in 1949.

Thomas A. Meyer. "A Gesture of Understanding: Wittgenstein, Moore, and 'Therapy'." Accessed via http://sammelpunkt.philo [Sammelpunkt. Elektronisch archivierte Theorie], February 2011.

Jeffrey Meyers. *Joseph Conrad: A Biography.* John Murray, 1991.

James Miller. *Examined Lives: from Socrates to Nietzsche.* Farrar, Straus and Giroux, 2011.

Sonia Misak. "The Jewish Community of Vienna: Existing against all the Odds." Jerusalem Center for Public Affairs, *Jerusalem Letters* No. 356, 8 Nisan 5757 / 15 April 1997. Accessed via http://www.jcpa.org/cjc/jl-356-misak.htm, February 2011.

Lorena Mongelli. "Lower E. Side scaffold shock." *New York Post*, June 3, 2011: 6.

Ray Monk. *Ludwig Wittgenstein: The Duty of Genius*. The Free Press, 1990.

Michel de Montaigne. "Apologie de Raimond Sebond." Chapitre XII in n *Essais*, Livre second. Gallimard, 1965.

——. "Du dementir." Chapitre XVIII in *Essais*, Livre second. Gallimard, 1965.

George Edward Moore. "The Elements of Ethics, with a View to an Appreciation of Kant's Moral Philosophy." The Moore Papers, Cambridge University Library.

——. "Proof of an External World." In *Philosophical Papers*. George Allen & Unwin, 1959.

——. "Wittgenstein's Lectures in 1930-33." In Moore, *Philosophical Papers*, op. cit.

Martin Mueller. "Children of Oedipus." In *Children of Oedipus and other essays on the imitation of Greek tragedy 1550-1800*. University of Toronto Press, 1980, 105-52.

Iris Murdoch, "The Idea of Perfection." In *The Sovereignty of Good*. Schocken Books, 1971. Originally published in the *Yale Review*, 1964.

Vladimir Nabokov. *Lolita*. Berkley, 1977. Originally published in 1955.

Friedrich Nietzsche. *The Birth of Tragedy and The Genealogy of Morals*. Translated by Francis Golffing. Anchor Books, 1956.

Blaise Pascal. *Pensées*. Folio classique edition. Edited by Michel Le Guern. Gallimard, 1977.

Fania Pascal. "Memories of Wittgenstein." In *Recollections of Wittgenstein*, revised edition, edited by Rush Rhees. Oxford University Press, 1984.

Marjorie Perloff. *Wittgenstein's Ladder: Poetic Language and the Strangeness of the Ordinary*. University of Chicago Press, 1966. As excerpted at http://www.press.uchicago.edu.

Rick Perlstein. "Fact-Free Nation: From Nixon's Dirty Tricksters to James

O'Keefe's Video Smears: How Political Lying Became the New Normal." *Mother Jones*, May/June, 2011.

F.E. Peters. *Greek Philosophical Terms: A Historical Lexicon*. New York University Press, 1967.

Adam Phillips. *Houdini's Box: The Art of Escape*. Pantheon, 2001.

———. "On Love." In *On Flirtation*. Harvard University Press, 1994.

———. "Self-Made Aristocrats." *London Review of Books*, December 4, 2008. Accessed via http://www.lrb.co.uk.

Plato (Platon). *L'Alcibiade majeur*. Translated into French by Pierre-José About. Hachette, 1980. In "Looking for Clues" (32, n. 35), Holger Thesleff proposes that this dialogue was not written by Plato himself but by a friend or pupil.

———. *Apologie*. In *Apologie de Socrate / Criton*. Translated into French by Luc Brisson. Flammarion, 1997.

———. *Apology*. Translated by Benjamin Jowett. Http://classics.mit.edu/Plato/apology.html, accessed May 2008.

———. *Cratylus*. Translated by Harold N. Fowler. In *Plato in Twelve Volumes*, Vol. 12. Harvard University Press, 1921. As accessed via http://www.perseus.tufts.edu, May 2011.

———. *Meno*. In *Protagoras and Meno*. Translated by W.K.C. Guthrie. Penguin Books, 1956, 115-57.

———. *Phaedo*. Translated by Benjamin Jowett. Accessed at http://www.pinkmonkey.com, February 2011.

———. *Phaedo*. Translated by David Gallop. Oxford University Press, 1993.

———. *Phaedrus and the Seventh and Eighth Letters*. Translated by Walter Hamilton. Penguin Books, 1973.

———. *Philebus*. In *The Dialogues of Plato translated into English with Analyses and Introductions by B. Jowett, M.A. in Five Volumes*. Third edition revised and corrected Oxford University Press, 1892. Accessed on-line via The Online Library of Liberty, July 2011.

———. *Statesman*. Translated by Harold N. Fowler. In *Plato in Twelve Volumes*, Vol. 12. Harvard University Press, 1921. As accessed via http://www.perseus.tufts.edu, May 2011.

———. *The Republic*. Translated by A.D. Lindsay. Everyman's Library, J. M.

Dent and E. P. Dutton, 1935. Reprint of translation first published in 1906.

Plotinus. *The Essential Plotinus: Representative Treatises from the Enneads.* Translated by Elmer O'Brien. Hackett, 1964.

Frank Moya Pons. *The Dominican Republic: A National History.* Markus Wiener, 1998.

Gerald A. Press. *Plato: A Guide for the Perplexed.* Continuum, 2007.

———, ed. *Plato's Dialogues: New Studies and Interpretations.* Rowman & Littlefield, 1993.

Willard Van Orman Quine. "On What There Is." *Review of Metaphysics*, 1948. Reprinted in *From a Logical Point of View.* Harvard University Press, 1953.

———. "Two Dogmas of Empiricism." Accessed via http://www.ditext.com/quine, June 2011.

———. *Word and Object.* MIT Press, 1960.

Tom Regan. *Bloomsbury's Prophet: G.E. Moore and the Development of His Moral Philosophy.* Temple University Press, 1986.

Frank Rich. "Obama's Original Sin." *New York* magazine. July 3, 2011.

I.A. Richards. "An Interview Conducted by B.A. Boucher and J.P. Russo." In *Complimentarities: Uncollected Essays.* Edited by John Paul Russo. Harvard University Press, 1976.

Lisa Robinson. "Lady Gaga's Cultural Revolution." *Vanity Fair.* September 2009. Accessed via http://www.vanityfair.com, July 2011.

Elisabeth Roudinesco. *Lacan, envers et contre tout.* Seuil, 2011.

Richard Rorty. "The Education of John Dewey: The Invisible Philosopher." *New York Times*, March 9, 2003.

Alex Ross. *The Rest is Noise: Listening to the Twentieth Century.* Picador; Farrar, Straus and Giroux, 2007.

Philip Roth. *American Pastoral.* Vintage, 1997.

Joseph Sandler, Robert Michels and Peter Fonagy. *Changing Ideas in a Changing World: The Revolution in Psychoanalysis; Essays in Honour of Arnold Cooper.* Karnac, 2000.

Jean-Paul Sartre. *L'être et le néant: Essai d'ontologie phénoménologique.*

Gallimard, 1943. *La mauvaise foi* is the subject of *la Première partie, chapitre II.*

Carl Schmitt. *Political Theology: Four Chapters on the Concept of Sovereignty.* Translated by George Schwab. MIT Press, 1985. Translation of the 1922 *Politische Theologie: Vier Kapitel zur Lefhre von der Souveränität.*

———. *The Concept of the Political.* Translated by George Schwab. University of Chicago Press, 1996. Translation of 1932 *Der Begriff des Politischen.*

Carl E. Schorske. *Fin-de-Siècle Vienna: Politics and Culture.* Vintage Books, 1981.

Michel Serres. *La naissance de la physique dans le texte de Lucrèce: Fleuves et turbulences.* Les Éditions de Minuit, 1977.

Dr. Seuss (Theodor Geisel). *And to Think That I Saw It on Mulberry Street.* Random House, 1937.

Sextus Empiricus. *Outlines of Scepticism.* Translated by Julia Annas and Jonathan Barnes, Cambridge University Press, 1994.

William Shakespeare. *The Complete Plays and Poems of William Shakespeare.* Edited by William Allan Neilson and Charles Jarvis Hill. Houghton Mifflin, 1942.

Richard Sherman. "Pain after amputation—a lifelong problem?" Abstracted from book by Sherman and associates: *Phantom Pain.* Plenum Press, 1997. Accessed via http://www.behavmedfoundation.org, February 2010.

Georg Simmel. "Sociability: An Example of Pure, or Formal, Sociology." Part I, Chapter 3 of *The Sociology of Georg Simmel.* Translated by Kurt H. Wolff. The Free Press, 1950.

John Sinclair, Editor in Chief. *Collins Cobuild English Language Dictionary.* HarperCollins, 1987.

Adam Smith. *The Wealth of Nations.* Accessed via http://www.econlib.org, August 2011.

Stevie Smith. *Collected Poems.* New Directions, 1983.

Timothy Snyder. *Bloodlands: Europe between Hitler and Stalin.* Basic Books, 2010.

Sophocles. *The Three Theban Plays: Antigone, Oedipus the King, Oedipus at Colonus.* Translated by Robert Fagles. Penguin Books, 1982.

Isabelle Sorente. *Addiction générale (Comptez vite, comptez encore, surtout n'arrêtez pas)*. Jean-Claude Lattès, 2011.

Keith Stimely. "Uproar in Clio's Library: The Case Of Dr. David Abraham And 'The Collapse Of The Weimar Republic'." Institute for Historical Review. Accessed via http://www.ihr.org, May 2011.

Barry Stroud. "Wittgenstein and Logical Necessity." *The Philosophical Review* 74, No. 4 (October 1965): 504-18.

The Sutra of 42 Sections. Translated from Chinese by Upasaka Chu Chan (John Blofeld). Accessed via http://www4.bayarea.net/~mtlee/42.txt, August 2010. The Chinese text is thought to be itself a translation from Sanskrit, made by two monks, Kasyapa-Matanga and Dharmaraksha (also called Gobharana), in 67 CE.

Holger Thesleff. "Looking for Clues: An Interpretation of Some Literary Aspects of Plato's 'Two-Level Model'." In Press, *Plato's Dialogues, op cit.*

Henry David Thoreau. *The Journal 1837-1861*. Edited by Damion Searls. New York Review Books, 2009.

Krista Tippett. "Reviving Sister Aimee." Broadcast of "On Being" program, National Public Radio, June 9, 2011. Transcript available via http://being.publicradio.org.

Tarmo Toom. "'I Was a Boy with Power to Talk' (*Conf.* 1.8.13): Augustine and Ancient Theories of Language Acquisition." *Journal of Late Antiquity* 2, No. 2 (Fall 2009): 357–73.

Stephen Toulmin. *Cosmopolis: The Hidden Agenda of Modernity*. The University of Chicago Press, 1992.

Georg Trakl. *The Poems of Georg Trakl*. Translated by Margitt Lehbert. Anvil Press, 2007. The German originals of "Rondel" and other Trakl poems have been available on-line at http://membres.multimania.fr/crcrosnier/mur/palp/trakl.htm.

Lionel Trilling. *Sincerity and Authenticity*. Harcourt Brace Jovanovich, 1980.

Henry Ashby Turner, Jr. "Big Business and the Rise of Hitler." *The American Historical Review* 75, No. 1 (October, 1969): 56-70.

Louis Uchitelle. "Two Tiers, Slipping Into One." *New York Times*, February 26, 2006.

Voltaire (François-Marie Arouet). "Poème sur le désastre de Lisbonne." In

Mélanges de Voltaire. Gallimard, Bibliothèque de la Pléiade, 1961.

———. "Sur M. Locke." *Treizième lettre. Lettres philosophiques*. In Voltaire, op. cit.

Loïc Wacquant. "The Structure and Logic of Bourdieu's Sociology." Section 1 in *An Invitation to Reflexive Sociology*, by Pierre Bourdieu and Loïc J.D. Wacquant. University of Chicago Press, 1992.

Benjamin Wallace-Wells. "What's Left of the Left: Paul Krugman's lonely crusade." *New York*, May 2, 2011.

Alexander Waugh, *The House of Wittgenstein: A Family at War*. Doubleday, 2008.

Max Weber. *From Max Weber: Essays in Sociology*. Edited by H. H. Gerth and C. Wright Mills. Routledge & Kegan Paul, 1948.

Lawrence Weschler. *Seeing is Forgetting the Name of the Thing One Sees: A Life of the Contemporary Artist Robert Irwin*. University of California Press, 1982.

Walt Whitman. *Leaves of Grass*. In *The Portable Walt Whitman*. Penguin, 1977.

Eliza Gregory Wilkins, *"Know Thyself" in Greek and Latin Literature*. Private edition distributed by The University of Chicago Libraries, 1917. This is a Ph.D. dissertation, Department of Greek, The University of Chicago.

Michael Williams. "Wittgenstein's Refutation of Idealism." Accessed via http://www.nyu.edu/gsas/dept/philo. Anthologized in *Wittgenstein and Scepticism*, edited by Denis McManus (Routledge, 2004).

D.W. Winnicott. "Fear of Breakdown." *International Review of Psycho-Analysis* 1 (1974): 103-07. Article was put together after Winnicott's death.

———. *The Maturational Process and the Facilitating Environment: Studies in the Theory of Emotional Development*. International Universities Press, 1965.

Ludwig Wittgenstein. "Conversations on Freud." Excerpt from 1932-3 lectures, in *Philosophical essays on Freud*. Edited by Richard Wolheim and James Hopkins. Cambridge University Press, 1982. Reprinted from Ludwig Wittgenstein. *Wittgenstein, Lectures and Conversations*. Edited by Cyril Barrett. Basil Blackwell & Mott and University of California Press, 1966, 42-52.

———. *Culture and Value*. Edited by G. H. von Wright in collaboration with Heikki Nyman. Translated by Peter Winch. The University of Chicago Press, 1980. Bilingual edition: original German (*Vermischte Bemerkungen*) with English translation.

———. "Lecture on Ethics." 1929. Published in the *Journal of Philosophy* 74, No. 1 (January 1965). Accessed via http://galilean-library.org, October 2008.

———. "Lectures on Aesthetics." In *Philosophy of Art and Aesthetics: From Plato to Wittgenstein*. Edited by Frank A. Tillman and Steven M. Cahn. Harper & Row, 1969. Reprinted from *Wittgenstein: Lectures and Conversations on Aesthetics, Psychology and Religious Beliefs*. Edited by Cyril Barrett. University of California Press and Basil Blackwell, 1966.

———. *Lectures on the Foundations of Mathematics*. Edited by C. Diamond. Harvester Press, 1976.

———. *On Certainty*. Translated by Denis Paul and G.E.M. Anscombe. Harper & Row, 1972. Bilingual edition: original German (*Über Gewissheit*) with English translation.

———. *Philosophische Untersuchungen / Philosophical Investigations*. German text with a revised English translation, 3d ed. Translated by G. E. M. Anscombe. Blackwell, 2001.

———. *Preliminary Studies for the "Philosophical Investigations", generally known as The Blue and Brown Books*. Harper & Row, 1960.

———. *Remarks on the Foundations of Mathematics*. Edited by G.H. von Wright, R. Rhees and G. Anscombe. Translated by G.E.M. Anscombe. Macmillan, 1956. Bilingual edition: original German (*Bemerkungen über die Grundlagen der Mathematik*) with English translation.

———. *Tractatus Logico-Philosophicus*. Translated by C.K. Ogden. Barnes & Noble Books, 2003. First published in German in *Annalen der Naturphilosophie*, 1922. Monk (205) gives the strong impression that Frank Ramsey, then an 18-year-old undergraduate at Cambridge, did a good deal of the work.

———. *Tractatus Logico-Philosophicus*. Translated by D.F. Pears and B.F. McGuinness. Routledge, 2001.

———. Über *Gewissheit* (*On Certainty*). Edited by G.E.M. Anscombe and G.H. von Wright. Translated by Denis Paul and G.E.M. Anscombe.

Harper & Row, 1972.

Frederick J.E. Woodbridge. *The Son of Apollo: Themes of Plato*. Ox Bow Press, 1989. Reprint of book originally published by Hogshead Mindedness in 1929.

Georg Henrik von Wright. "Biographical Sketch." In Norman Malcolm, *Ludwig Wittgenstein: A Memoir*, with a Biographical Sketch by Georg Henrik von Wright. Oxford University Press, 1958.

William Butler Yeats. "Aedh wishes for the Cloths of Heaven." In *The Wind Among the Reeds*. J. Lane, The Bodley Head, 1899.

———. "Easter 1916." *The Dial* 69, No. 25 (November 1920).

Stefan Zweig. *Montaigne*. Translation from German into French by Jean-Jacques Lafaye et François Brugier. Quadrige / Presses Universitaires de France, 1982. French volume developed from a larger German text, *Europäisches Erbe*.

———. *The World of Yesterday: An Autobiography*. Translated by Benjamin W. Huebsch and Helmut Ripperger. Viking Press, 1943. German title *Die Welt von Gestern: Erinnerungen eines Europäers*.

Texts of Confessions I:8 and Investigations §32

Augustini *Confessiones*, Liber 1, Caput 8, original Latin text:

nonne ab infantia huc pergens veni in pueritiam? vel potius ipsa in me venit et successit infantiae? nec discessit illa: quo enim abiit? et tamen iam non erat. non enim eram infans qui non farer, sed iam puer loquens eram. et memini hoc, et unde loqui didiceram post adverti. non enim docebant me maiores homines, praebentes mihi verba certo aliquo ordine doctrinae sicut paulo post litteras, sed ego ipse mente quam dedisti mihi, deus meus, cum gemitibus et vocibus variis et variis membrorum motibus edere vellem sensa cordis mei, ut voluntati pareretur, nec valerem quae volebam omnia nec quibus volebam omnibus, prensabam memoria. cum ipsi appellabant rem aliquam et cum secundum eam vocem corpus ad aliquid movebant, videbam et tenebam hoc ab eis vocari rem illam quod sonabant cum eam vellent ostendere. hoc autem eos velle ex motu corporis aperiebatur tamquam verbis naturalibus omnium gentium, quae fiunt vultu et nutu oculorum ceterorumque membrorum actu et sonitu vocis indicante affectionem animi in petendis, habendis, reiciendis fugiendisve rebus. ita verba in variis sententiis locis suis posita et crebro audita quarum rerum signa essent paulatim conligebam measque iam voluntates edomito in eis signis ore per haec enuntiabam. sic cum his inter quos eram voluntatum enuntiandarum signa communicavi, et vitae humanae procellosam societatem altius ingressus sum, pendens ex parentum auctoritate nutuque maiorum hominum.

Nineteenth century translation by E.B. Pusey

Passing hence from infancy, I came to boyhood, or rather it came to me, displacing infancy. Nor did that depart (for whither went it?), and yet it was no more. For I was no longer a speechless infant, but a speaking boy. This I remember; and have since observed how I learned to speak. It was not that my elders taught me words (as, soon after, other learning) in any set method; but I, longing by cries and broken accents and various motions of my limbs to express my thoughts, that so I might have my will, and yet unable to express all I willed, or to whom I willed, did myself, by the understanding which Thou, my God, gavest me, practise the sounds in my memory. When they named any thing, and as they spoke turned towards it, I saw and remembered that they called what they would point out by the name they uttered. And that they meant this thing and no other was plain from the motion of their body, the natural language, as it were, of all nations, expressed by the countenance, glances of the eye, gestures of the limbs, and tones of the voice, indicating the affections of the mind, as it pursues, possesses, rejects, or shuns. And thus by constantly hearing words, as they occurred in various sentences, I collected gradually for what they stood; and having broken in my mouth to these signs, I thereby gave utterance to my will. Thus I exchanged with those about me these current signs of our wills, and so launched deeper into the stormy intercourse of human life, yet depending on parental authority and the beck of elders.

Twentieth century translation by R.S. Pine-Coffin

The next stage in my life, as I grew up, was boyhood. Or would it be truer to say that boyhood overtook me and followed upon my infancy--not that my infancy left me, for, if it did, where did it go? All the same, it was no longer there, because I ceased to be a baby unable to talk, and was now a boy with the power of speech. I can remember that time, and later on I realized how I had learnt to speak. It was not my elders who showed me the words by some set system of instruction, in the way they taught me to read not long afterwards; but, instead, I taught myself by using the intelligence which you, God, gave to me. For when I tried to express my meaning by crying out and making various sounds and movements, so that my wishes should be obeyed, I found that I could not convey all that I meant or make myself understood by everyone whom I wished to understand me. So my memory prompted me. I noticed that people would name some object and then turn towards whatever it was that they had named. I watched them and understood that the sound that they made when they wanted to indicate that particular thing was the name which they gave to it, and their actions clearly showed what they meant, for there is a kind of universal language, consisting of expressions of the face and eyes, gestures and tones of voice, which can show whether a person means to ask for something and get it, or refuse it and have nothing to do with it. So, by hearing words arranged in various phrases and constantly repeated, I gradually pieced together what they stood for, and when my tongue had mastered the pronunciation, I began to express my wishes by means of them. In this way I made my wants known to my family and they made theirs known to me, and I took a further step into the stormy life of human society, although I was still subject to the authority of my parents and the will of my elders.

Ludwig Wittgenstein's Philosophical Investigations, Section 32

Wer in ein fremdes Land kommt, wird manchmal die Sprache der Einheimischen durch hinweisende Erklärungen lernen, die sie ihm geben; und er wird die Deutung dieser Erklärungen oft raten müssen und manchmal richtig, manchmal falsch raten.

Und nun können wir, glaube ich, sagen: Augustinus beschreibe das Lernen der menschlichen Sprache so, als käme das Kind in ein fremdes Land und verstehe die Sprache des Landes nicht; das heißt: so als habe es bereits eine Sprache, nur nicht diese. Oder auch: als könne das Kind schon *denken*, nur noch nicht sprechen. Und "denken" heiße hier etwas, wie: zu sich selber reden.

Standard English translation, by Elizabeth Anscombe:

Someone coming into a strange country will sometimes learn the language of the inhabitants from ostensive definitions that they give him; and he will often have to *guess* the meaning of these definitions; and will guess sometimes right, sometimes wrong.

And now, I think, we can say: Augustine describes the learning of human language as if the child came into a strange country and did not understand the language of the country; that is, as if it already had a language, only not this one. Or again: as if the child could already *think*, only not yet speak. And "think" would here mean something like "talk to itself".

About the Author

WilliamEaton

Award-winning journalist, essayist, novelist, artist and writer of intellectual dialogues. William Eaton's "The Professor of Ignorance Condemns the Airplane" was staged in New York in 2014. Serving House published his *Surviving the Twenty-First Century* (personal essays) and *Art, Sex, Politics* (intellectual essays). His trilingual Montaigbakhtinian blog is followed by 5,000 readers worldwide.

www.ingramcontent.com/pod-product-compliance
Lightning Source LLC
LaVergne TN
LVHW041247080426
835510LV00009B/624